WITHDRAWN

MIND MATTERS
A Tribute to Allen Newell

Carnegie Mellon Symposia on Cognition

David Klahr, Series Editor

MIND MATTERS
A Tribute to Allen Newell

Edited by

David Steier
Price Waterhouse Technology Centre,
Menlo Park, CA

Tom M. Mitchell
Carnegie Mellon University,
Pittsburgh, PA

LEA LAWRENCE ERLBAUM ASSOCIATES, PUBLISHERS
1996 Mahwah, New Jersey

Lawrence Erlbaum Associates, Inc., Publishers
10 Industrial Avenue
Mahwah, New Jersey 07430

Library of Congress Cataloging-in-Publication Data

Mind matters : a tribute to Allen Newell / David Steier, Tom M.
  Mitchell, editors.
     p.   cm.
  Papers originally presented at a symposium sponsored by the School
of Computer Science at Carnegie Mellon University.
  Includes bibliographical references and index.
  ISBN 0-8058-1363-2 (alk. paper). — ISBN 0-8058-1364-0
  1. Cognition—Congresses. 2. Cognitive psychology—Philosophy—
Congresses. 3. Cognitive science—Philosophy—Congresses.
I. Newell, Allen. II. Steier, David. III. Mitchell, Tom M. (Tom
Michael), 1951–   .
BF311.M5534 1996
153—dc20   95-34683
                                            CIP

Books published by Lawrence Erlbaum Associates are printed on acid-free paper,
and their bindings are chosen for strength and durability.

Printed in the United States of America
10 9 8 7 6 5 4 3 2 1

In tribute to
Allen Newell

Contents

Preface

Allen Newell is most often described as one of the founders of artificial intelligence, but he could be equally well described as a founder of cognitive science, the field of human–computer interaction, or the systematic study of computational architectures. When the School of Computer Science at Carnegie Mellon University decided to hold a symposium in Allen's honor, finding a structure that would honor all these facets of his career was a true challenge. Allen would have described the process we went through as he would have described any other problem-solving episode: as a search through many alternatives, subject to myriad constraints on the acceptable solution. One significant constraint on the solution came from Allen himself: that any scientific tribute to him would lean far more heavily on science than on tribute. A second constraint arose from the amazing diversity of Allen's research contributions. Although Allen's career was devoted to understanding how computers could be used to understand the nature of mind, no single one of the traditional scientific disciplines could lay a dominant claim on Allen's interests. Indeed, he seemed to win the highest honor in virtually every field in which he became involved. These included the Harry Goode Award of the American Federation of Information Processing Societies (1971); the A. M. Turing Award of the Association for Computing Machinery, joint with Herbert Simon (1975); the Alexander C. Williams, Jr., Award of the Human Factors Society (1979); the Distinguished Research Contribution Award of the American Psychological Association (1985); the Research Excellence Award of the International Joint Conference on Artificial Intelligence (1989); the Emanuel R. Piore Award of the Institute for Electrical and Electronic Engineers (1990); and the Franklin Institute's Louis E. Levy medal (1992). He also was awarded honorary doctoral degrees from the Unia and Groningen University in the Netherlands, and served as the president of the American Association for Artificial Intelligence (AAAI) and the Cognitive Science Society. Finally, in June 1992, U.S. President George Bush awarded Allen Newell the National Medal of Science. How could a single symposium lasting only a few days do justice to this outstanding record of achievement?

The final structure of the symposium resulted from the committee's decision to honor the scientific breadth of Allen's career with scientific depth from the research communities he inspired. From each of these research communities we invited top scientists who had made fundamental contributions of their own and whose work had been deeply influenced by Allen along the way. Speakers were invited to use the occasion of the symposium to advance the science (which is what Allen wanted in any event) in the styles they knew best. Because the theme of understanding the nature of mind dominated Allen's scientific concerns, most of the speakers chose to discuss topics from cognitive science. But Allen also believed in *diversions* when necessary to develop the experimental apparatus needed to make progress along the main research theme (he called these *diversions* even though some of them lasted for many years). Therefore, we included chapters on hardware and software architectures, fields in which Allen also made significant contributions. The resulting array of ideas presented at the symposium, and in the chapters of this volume, reflect the surprising range of Allen's impact on science.

Over the past decade, much of Allen's work had been spent developing a computational architecture called Soar, which he sought to develop as a unified theory of cognition. It was clear that Soar, and the community of researchers who worked with Allen on this effort, should have a special role in the symposium. Therefore, it was decided that each invited paper would be followed by a presentation from a member of the Soar research community. The responsibility of this discussant was to draw out the connections between the work of the speaker and the implications for Soar. The symposium thus presented an opportunity for several Soar researchers to present their latest work in explicit comparison to other major research styles in cognitive and computer science, a healthy trend that persists to this day.

In the first chapter, John Laird, who, together with Paul Rosenbloom, developed the Soar architecture under Allen Newell's guidance, reviews the basic principles of Soar and traces its historical evolution in its first decade of existence. Since the first version of Soar in 1982, a few changes, such as adoption of the single-state principle, had significant implications for the structure of Soar systems. But for the most part, the core of the architecture, including problem spaces, impasse-driven subgoaling, and chunking as a mechanism for learning from experience, have remained constant and have been tested over a wide variety of task environments and psychological models. If any major changes are to be expected, they will probably arise from requirements for interaction with the external world.

The second chapter, by Zenon Pylyshyn, discusses methodological issues in the study of cognitive architectures. He notes that, in contrast to what he characterizes as Allen's "high-road" approach to the creation of a single unified theory of cognition in the context of a complete cognitive architecture, most cognitive psychologists continue to take the "low road" of developing minimodels of individual psychological phenomena. Through several examples, Pylyshyn identifies ways in which the low-road strategy might fail, and then describes an alternative strategy inspired by the high-road, based on a principle of least commitment in designing a cognitive architecture. This "minimal mechanism" strategy is a computational Occam's Razor that Pylyshyn has applied in the development of the FINST Index theory of early vision. Rick Lewis' commentary on this chapter is an instance of application of this strategy to understanding modularity in natural language comprehension.

Tom Mitchell and Sebastian Thrun's contribution in the third chapter deals with the integration of two threads of machine learning research that have previously proceeded independently of each other. Explanation-based learning has been shown to be a powerful method of learning when the learner has prior knowledge of the domain rich enough to explain its new experiences. In contrast, inductive learning methods such as neural network backpropagation have been shown to be useful in applications where such prior knowledge is not available, provided sufficient training data is available in its place. Mitchell and Thrun present a hybrid method, called explanation-based neural network (EBNN) learning, that blends the strengths of both methods. In this chapter they present experimental results applying EBNN to robot learning problems, and suggest that Soar might benefit by augmenting its current learning mechanism, chunking, with a second, explicitly inductive learning mechanism. But Paul Rosenbloom's commentary argues that it may be possible for a system like Soar that is built on just the chunking learning mechanism to also exploit the sources of knowledge utilized by EBNN, without the addition of new mechanisms.

George Miller's chapter begins by identifying sense resolution, choosing the right interpretation of a word for a given context, as a central problem for natural language understanding. In comparing several approaches to solve this problem based on statistics of word co-occurrence, he notes that they achieve reasonable results, but none do as well as humans, and more importantly, all display performance characteristics, such as decreased accuracy on polysemous words, that are not exhibited in human performance.

Miller proposes an alternative approach to sense resolution involving contextual templates with variables, using the WordNet system as a source of alternative bindings for those variables. He relates the content of his chapter to Soar by asking if there is a way that Soar can help with his approach to sense resolution. Jill Fain Lehman provides several possible answers to this question, including the suggestion that the combined flexibility of subgoals and transition to recognition-driven behavior provided by chunking may yield more human-like behavior in sense resolution than the statistical approaches.

The chapter by Marcel Just, Patricia Carpenter, and Darold Hemphill gathers an array of evidence that capacity constraints on working memory can account for a variety of observed human behavior. This evidence comes from a degradation in subject performance on Towers of Hanoi and Raven Progressive Matrices tasks, and a corresponding increase in subject pupil dilation in situations that seem to place a high load on working memory. Furthermore, such working memory effects are closely correlated across domains, and age-dependent performance effects are also tied to working memory demands. The authors explain these effects with the aid of an architectural simulation implemented in an activation-based scheme called 3CAPS, in which there is an explicit resource cap on the maximum allowable activation. Richard Young's response suggests that in some cases alternative accounts of these phenomena may be obtained by appealing to functional explanations, in which behavior arises from general agent capabilities and the knowledge possessed by the agent.

To remind us of Allen Newell's seminal contributions in studying computers as well as the nature of mind, Gordon Bell's chapter traces the evolution of some of the "big ideas" in computer architecture. Bell claims that rapid progress in processor speed and memory density comes from exploiting spatial and temporal locality in conjunction with three general design principles: replication of components, use of economics to force compatibility and balanced designs, and the search for general-purpose mechanisms. He concludes by instantiating some of these ideas in his description of the KSR-1 scalable multiprocessor. The potential role of multi-processing and parallel computation in producing large, fast production systems is explored in Milind Tambe's commentary after the chapter.

Mary Shaw's chapter complements Bell's thoughts on hardware architecture evolution by identifying patterns in the evolution of software systems. Shaw focuses on shared information systems, tracing patterns in three areas: data processing, software development environments, and software for building design. The common thread is a progression from non-interacting software components, to a minimal interaction in which a batch process executes components in sequence, to the creation of a centralized data repository, and finally to layered, hierarchically organized software systems. Innovations in software architecture can often be characterized as variations on these stages of evolution, for example, a blackboard as a type of repository that facilitates opportunistic control. Shaw mentions as a likely next stage of software architecture evolution the use of intelligent agents for software control, a prospect explored in more detail in David Steier's commentary.

Stuart Card provides a historical perspective on the study of human–computer interaction to argue that interfaces should be created with the assistance of models that reflect the context in which the interface will be used. These models include the user performance model, the user conceptual model, the user interface illusion model, and the task model. In many cases, such as the design of a pointing device where Fitts' law applies, we are in a position to apply engineering-style laws to derive predictions of the effectiveness of an interface. In some cases the results of evaluation will identify interaction bottlenecks and suggest possible alternative designs. The chapter concludes with an extensive inventory of teachable results in human–computer interaction. Bonnie John's commentary shows how Soar has been applied in several cases to the detailed evaluation of human–computer interfaces.

David Klahr has studied the psychology of scientific discovery, characterizing the process as one of search of a hypothesis space, search of the experiment space, and evaluation of the evidence from the experiments. In recounting the results of experiments on discovery in children and adults, he found that children were able to function effectively as "scientists" in domains where the search spaces were small and feedback directly relevant. Klahr's chapter concludes with a number of observations about machine discovery systems, and issues for further research in the area. The commentary by Tony Simon considers how scientific discovery and other cognitive abilities might develop over the life span of an intelligent agent, a theme raised repeatedly in other presentations and characterized by Simon as the need to understand how Soar can acquire domain-general knowledge.

Philip Johnson-Laird's chapter on deduction discusses several theories of how humans perform deductive reasoning while solving syllogisms. His contribution points out several difficulties for any theory that claims that people use a formal system of inference rules to solve syllogisms, and presents an alternative in which conclusions are created by semantic reasoning with mental models. His use of mental models has been shown to account for a variety of regularities noted in the psychological literature on syllogisms, such as figural bias. Recent work by Thad Polk and Allen Newell, described in Thad's commentary, presents another theory based on mental models that casts the reasoning processes for untrained subjects as linguistic processes of comprehension and description.

The final chapter in the book is by Herb Simon, who revisits the status of the physical symbol system that he and Newell set forth in their Turing award lecture of 1976. He reviews the concepts of patterns and symbols, and posits that symbols may function as names (pointers) or as direct encodings of information. A taxonomy of symbols show that there are corresponding categories for symbols in humans and in computers. These equivalences, and indeed the ubiquity of symbol systems in general, are independent of whether the implementation of a symbol system is classified as connectionist/parallel or classical/serial, how the symbols are acquired, and whether the symbols are classified as linguistic or visual.

It is a pleasure to be able to honor Allen Newell with this collection contributed by his friends and colleagues. We thank the many people who contributed to the symposium and to this book, especially the authors and the other members of the organizing committee: Catherine Copetas, Nico Habermann, Jill Fain Lehman, and John McDermott. Catherine's monumental efforts organizing the symposium were a major factor in its success. Betsy Herk served as the central person for collecting and reformatting the authors' contributions, and generally guiding the book through to completion. Allen's wife, Noel Newell, provided advice as we organized this tribute to Allen. We are also grateful to the National Science Foundation and the Office of Naval Research for financial support for the symposium, and to Maya Design for making available the design talents of Hugo Cheng.

—*David Steier*
—*Tom M. Mitchell*

Chapter 1

The Evolution of the
Soar Cognitive Architecture

John E. Laird
University of Michigan

Paul S. Rosenbloom
Information Sciences Institute and University of Southern California

In the spring of 1976, while trying to decide on which computer science graduate school to attend, we (John Laird and Paul Rosenbloom) independently visited the Computer Science Department of Carnegie Mellon University (CMU) in Pittsburgh. We were both interested in AI as our field of study, so we naturally met with Allen Newell. Newell was fully immersed in production systems at the time, and was in the process of starting the Instructable Production System project. His boundless enthusiasm was infectious, and we decided independently—we did not meet each other until the first day of graduate school—to attend CMU and work with Newell. That was undoubtably the best decision of our professional careers.

In deciding to work with Newell, we had been captivated by the concept of creating architectures in which AI systems could be built. Not necessarily hardware, but *cognitive architecture* in the sense of the fixed structures underlying intelligence (Newell, Rosenbloom, & Laird, 1989; Rosenbloom & Newell, 1993). We saw this as a way of studying the properties of intelligence in general, not just specific algorithms for specific problems, but architectures that could support the variety of behaviors so characteristic of humans.

Over the next 6 years, there were many stops and starts in our research. For example, during our first year, Newell was on sabbatical and both of us worked on other research projects. Also, both of us left Pittsburgh at different times in the middle of graduate school to take a year off. However, by 1982, the first version of Soar was up and running. During the next 12

1

years, Soar evolved through six different major versions, and by 1994, over 100 researchers were using Soar worldwide.

This chapter is the story of the evolution of the Soar architecture, structured according to its major versions, 1–6. Roughly, the major contributions of these six versions can be characterized as follows:

1. Combining flexible search and knowledge, via problems spaces and productions.
2. Universal automatic subgoaling and reflection, via impasse detection and subgoal generation.
3. Learning, via chunking.
4. Public distribution, via robustification and documentation.
5. External interaction, via destructive state modification.
6. Speed, portability, and maintainability, via formal specification and reimplementation in C.

To improve the conceptual coherence of the presentation, we occasionally "rationalize" history by moving the discussion of some capabilities forward and/or backward in time (i.e., to an earlier or later version). For example, chunking was first developed in Soar 2, was the major focus of Soar 3, and was a continued locus of development in Soar 4 and (to a lesser extent) in subsequent versions. For conceptual coherence, we focus on chunking during the discussion of Soar 3.

Within each major version of Soar, the presentation is organized around four levels of description: the knowledge level, the problem space level, the symbolic architecture level, and the implementation level. The notion of levels of description first shows up in computer science in Newell's work with Gordon Bell on computer structure (Bell & Newell, 1971). The levels for computer structure start with electronic devices and move up through electrical circuits, logic circuits, register transfer systems, and ultimately provide program-level systems. Our analysis of Soar has the symbolic architecture level that corresponds to the programming level, but the implementation level covers important details below the symbol level that cannot be directly mapped on to the register transfer level.

The knowledge level and problem space level are higher levels of description, both of which were articulated recently by Newell (1982). The knowledge level is the most abstract level used to characterize the behavior of an intelligent agent. It was originally proposed by Newell (1982) as an analysis tool. At the knowledge level, an intelligent agent is described only in terms of its knowledge, goals, and body (perceptions and actions). The agent is considered to be a knowledge-level system if it behaves according to the *principle of rationality*: the actions it intends are those that its knowledge indicates will achieve its goals. One of the central goals of the Soar project is to create agents that provide a good approximation to the knowledge-level ideal of rational behavior across a wide range of knowledge and goals (Rosenbloom, Newell, & Laird, 1991); however, the limitations on space and time imposed by the real world imply that this ideal can never be completely achieved for sufficiently broad and complex combinations of knowledge and goals. Here we trace the expansion of types of goals and knowledge accessible to Soar through the sequence of versions. For the reader who just wishes to get a flavor of "what Soar can do," this is the level on which to concentrate; however, the emphasis of this chapter is on the evolution of the other levels.

The problem-space level characterizes the structure of problem solving and reasoning in an intelligent agent. It is intended to provide a physically realizable approximation of the knowledge level. In general, it is concerned with the characterization of operators, states, and problem spaces, plus the relationships between goals and subgoals. It sits between the knowledge level, which abstracts away from all internal processing considerations, and the symbolic architecture level, which includes details of control flow and memories. One hypothesis underlying the research on Soar is that the problem-space level is a real computational level with its own types of processing and media (Newell, Yost, Laird, Rosenbloom, & Altmann, 1991). In Soar, the problem space level determines how tasks are formulated. In many ways it is the level at which Soar is most firmly entrenched and where it is the most unique (sic). Major changes could be—and are—made to the lower levels, and as long as they continued to support the problem-space level, Soar would still be Soar. Of course, evolution does also occur at this level as our understanding of problem spaces increases, particularly as driven by a continuous expansion of the range of tasks that we attempt to formulate in problem spaces.

The symbolic architecture level provides the basic control structure, memory organization, and processing structure to support the problem-space level. Just as the task of the problem-space level is to support the knowledge level, a major task throughout the development of the Soar architecture has been to derive a symbolic architecture level that can support the required flexibility of the problem space level.

The implementation level is the underlying technology that provides the symbolic architecture level. For the most part, the details of the implementation are irrelevant to the Soar architecture. The implementation does show through though in terms of the efficiency, boundedness, and correctness of executing the various processes of the symbolic architecture level. For example, at the symbolic architecture level, Soar assumes that productions can be matched with a time complexity independent of the number of productions. Does there exist an implementation that supports this assumption? Thus, this level is an important level both practically and theoretically.

PRE-SOAR

Although Soar has evolved significantly over the last 12 years, its central intellectual core still can be traced to a range of research done earlier by Allen Newell and Herbert Simon. In this section we review the key developments that set the stage for Soar before launching into the evolution of Soar.

LT

In 1954, Newell, Shaw, and Simon considered the possibility of creating a program that could solve problems that required complex thought processes. Newell initially worked on a chess machine (Newell, 1955) and then, after considering geometry as a domain, settled with Shaw and Simon on trying to construct a program that could prove some of the theorems in Whitehead and Russell's *Principia Mathematica.* On August 9, 1956, the Logic Theorist (LT) created the first mechanical proof of a theorem (Newell, Shaw, & Simon, 1957; Newell & Simon, 1956).

LT contained two innovations that would later show up in Soar.

1. *Symbolic representations:* All of the knowledge in LT was represented by symbol structures, and all of the cognitive processing occurred by symbol manipulation. This was in sharp contrast to the numeric processing that was (and often still is) standard in computer programming.

2. *Heuristic search:* To build the proofs, LT created an initial data structure containing the initial axioms and theorem to be proved. It then had discrete transformations that it could apply to data structures to create new theorems by combining, modifying, or decomposing existing axioms and theorems. The data structure was called the *state* and the transformations were called *operators.* A problem was solved by selecting the appropriate operators to apply to a state to transform it step by step until a proof was constructed. Although the term *problem space* would emerge years later, this was the first program to formulate a task in terms of a problem space. The selection of operators was guided by *heuristics,* and the complete process was called heuristic search. Heuristic search introduces a framework for problem solving (operators applied to states to achieve a goal) controlled by knowledge.

GPS

Following the success of LT and some related work on chess (Newell, Shaw, & Simon, 1958), Newell, Shaw, and Simon attempted to generalize the concepts of heuristic search and symbol systems so that they could construct a single program that could solve many different problems. They were guided in their work by comparisons between LT's behavior and the protocols of humans attempting to solve similar problems. The humans used a more goal-directed approach, where operators were selected based on how well they reduced the difference between the current state and the goal. This method, called *means-ends analysis*, was ubiquitous in the human protocols. Another observation was that humans created their own goals to help them break the problem up into simpler problems. They did not restrict themselves to just the goals of the task, but instead would create goals to achieve situations in which they could apply operators that could not apply in the current situation, a method called *operator subgoaling*. The system based on this insight was called the General Problem Solver (GPS), because it was not limited to working in just a single domain (Newell & Simon, 1961).

As with LT, GPS also contained two key innovations that would later show up in Soar.

1. *Symbolic architecture:* Although means-ends analysis and operator subgoaling are powerful methods for problem solving—and are used in Soar applications—the most important lesson to be taken from GPS is the separation of the fixed underlying control structure of the program from the operator and control knowledge about the task: that is, the separation of architecture from knowledge. Thus, GPS was the first real symbolic architecture.

2. *Automatic subgoaling:* Operator subgoaling was the first example of a general class of automatic subgoaling techniques, in which an architecture automatically generates subgoals based on an inability to make progress. All versions of Soar, except for the very first, depend heavily on automatic subgoaling.

Problem Spaces and Weak Methods

In both LT and GPS, a problem was represented as an initial state and a set of desired states to be achieved by applying operators. Newell and Simon recognized this and proposed that a general way to formulate tasks was in terms of a problem space. The problem space is the set of states and the set of operators in which a problem can be attempted. The complete set of states can either be pre-enumerated, or can be generated by applying operators to existing states. Problem spaces provide a framework for organizing knowledge in terms of operators, states, and control knowledge.

A given problem space can be used for many different problems. For each problem there would be a different initial state and desired states. Likewise, a given problem can be attempted in different problem spaces, where different operators are possible and different states could be generated. The difficulty of a problem, as formulated in a particular problem space, is determined by the difficulty of transforming the initial state into one of the desired states, which in turn is determined by factors such as the number of operators available at each point of the search (the branching factor), the number of operators that must be applied to achieve a desired state (the depth), and the knowledge available to control the problem solving.

As work in AI progressed during the 1960s, Newell was struck by the fact that many systems—and not just LT and GPS—were based on search in problem spaces. This observation led to the problem space hypothesis, that all symbolic goal-oriented behavior takes place in problem spaces (Newell, 1980). This hypothesis promised to provide a uniform structure for casting all problem solving. The observation also led to an attempt to characterize the types of methods being used to control search in problem spaces. In analyzing various AI systems of the era, Newell noticed that many of them shared the same methods, such as means-ends analysis, generate and test, hypothesize and match, and hill climbing. He hypothesized that these types of methods, which were used when there was little task-specific knowledge available, were not just a random collection, but instead a family, which he termed *weak methods* (Newell, 1969). (From here on in we refer to this as the *weak methods hypothesis*, although Newell did not explicitly so name it.) The weak methods were weak, not because they failed to tightly constrain the search, but because they made weak demands on the knowledge about the task required to apply the method. Many different tasks could use hill climbing. All that is required is the ability to compare neighboring states and select the best. Thus, the weak methods are exactly those methods that get used when there is not "strong" knowledge available to solve a problem directly. They are the methods of last resort, but they are also the methods that provide robustness in the face of novelty. Thus, an understanding of the weak methods may provide an understanding of important classes of control.

Both the problem space and weak methods hypotheses were foundational in the development of Soar.

Production Systems

In the late 1960s, Newell and Simon began to recognize that the control structure for GPS was too inflexible to capture of all of the variety of human behavior. Specifically, the table of connections underlying means-ends analysis was only a part of the knowledge that the subjects were using. They would also use knowledge that seemed specific to the situation, and not necessarily goal directed. This led Newell and Simon to consider production systems as the underlying representation of knowledge for intelligent systems. Newell experimented with a variety of production system languages (Newell, 1972, 1973; Newell & Simon, 1972) in the late 1960s and early 1970s. In 1975, he formed a group to investigate building large production systems, which evolved into the Instructable Production System (IPS) project (Rychener & Newell, 1977). During the lifetime of this project, the OPS family of languages was developed—with OPS5 eventually becoming a de facto standard for much of the expert systems community (Forgy, 1981)— along with the RETE match algorithm (Forgy, 1982). Although IPS led to the creation of the OPS languages, the RETE match algorithm, and indirectly the creation of R1 (McDermott, 1982), it failed at its main mission, which was to create large, instructable production systems. One diagnosis of its failure was that there was no overall framework for organizing tasks or control knowledge.

The concept of a production system as a model of memory was carried over verbatim to Soar, as was the RETE match algorithm. However, their direct use as a control structure was not.

Review

Newell and Simon's work prior to Soar provided strong direction at all four levels of descriptions, but still left much remaining to be done:

1. *Knowledge level:* The idea of the knowledge level was proposed, but it was not yet clear how to apply it constructively to the development and analysis of intelligent systems.

2. *Problem space level:* The basic concept of the problem space developed from LT, through GPS, and on to the problem space and weak methods hypotheses. So it was well defined prior to the development of Soar. However, there was little agreement as to the details of the structure of the objects involved (goals, problem spaces, states, operators), the control mechanisms for them (the weak methods), or the representation of knowledge. Also, most systems that were created using the problem space paradigm were one of a kind, with only a single problem space, and only limited types of goals and subgoals.

3. *Symbolic architecture level:* Symbolic representations and architectures, as developed in LT and GPS, are foundational concepts in Soar. In addition, automatic subgoaling (as existed in a limited manner in GPS) and the OPS production system languages (Forgy & McDermott, 1977) provided initial models of subgoaling and memory for Soar. However, the former doesn't specify how all of the other types of subgoals needed by

an intelligent system are to be created, whereas the latter requires significant adaptation for it to support the problem space computational level.

4. *Implementation level:* The RETE match algorithm provided an efficient algorithm for pattern matching in production systems, but still had a variety of scaling and efficiency problems, particularly when rules were being learned automatically.

SOAR 1 (1982)

Soar 1 arose out of two intertwined goals. The first was to create an architecture that supported problem spaces where production systems were used as the underlying representation of knowledge. The second was to create an architecture that could support many different weak methods. Both goals had existed in some form since the early 1970s when the importance of weak methods, problem spaces, and production systems was identified. However, their integration was to wait for at least a decade and the development of Soar 1. Soar 1 is described in Laird and Newell (1983a) and summarized in Laird and Newell (1983b).

Knowledge Level

An analysis of architecture at the knowledge levels starts with considering the goals, physical body (for actions and perception), and knowledge that are supported by the architecture. As mentioned earlier, a knowledge-level agent will act in a way that is consistent with its goals and knowledge. This abstracts away from the internal structures and processes of the agent, which are exactly what must be determined in constructing Soar 1 as a production system. However, by viewing the system at the knowledge level, we can confront issues concerning the generality and acquisition of the system's knowledge, independent of the underlying structure.

Soar 1 was based on the observation that humans—our best example of knowledge-level agents—can use many different methods for solving problems. The key question was whether getting an agent to use such a range of methods required adding explicit knowledge about the methods—as, for example, a library of methods—or whether just adding task knowledge by itself can be sufficient to result in behavior that follows these methods. If task knowledge alone is sufficient, the agent approaches a knowledge-level agent.

Our approach to this problem was to identify the following capabilities we wanted our agent to support.

1. Different methods are used for different tasks.
2. Different methods are used on the same task.

3. The methods arise from whatever knowledge is available at the time, without explicit programming.

In sum, the idea was that the agent would behave as if it had every weak method, and as if the method that was most appropriate to the current task would be applied automatically. With little or no knowledge about the task, the method would resemble the weakest of the weak methods, exhaustive search. As more knowledge was added, the behavior of the agent would change, and the method would evolve to more powerful methods. This required an architecture in which knowledge can be added incrementally, and there is no precompiled set of methods, but instead the methods emerge from the available knowledge. An agent that behaved in this way was said to have a *universal weak method* (UWM).

Problem Space Level

Given a desire to support the knowledge level and a universal weak method, it was critical that our formulation had a flexible control scheme that allowed many different methods to be specified, as well as allowing a variety of knowledge to be used in controlling the problem solving. Based on our experience with the IPS project, we realized that trying to achieve a knowledge-level agent without an intermediate organizational framework would be futile. This led Newell to consider problem spaces as a possible intermediate level of computation (Newell, 1980) and, in turn, led us to use problem spaces as a separate computational level within Soar 1.

Many previous AI systems solved problems by casting them as search within a problem space. LT, GPS, and STRIPS (Fikes & Nilsson, 1971) are canonical examples. However, they all had two basic weaknesses. Their first weakness was that they all used a single method to control all problem solving, independent of the task. (In fact, one of the contributions of GPS and STRIPS was that they demonstrated the usefulness of means-ends analysis.) This restricted the types of knowledge they could encode. For example, it was not possible to encode goal-independent operator selection heuristics or state evaluation knowledge in GPS or STRIPS. Their second weakness was that they could support only a single problem space. Thus, they could not use different problem spaces, that is, different sets of operators and different representations, for different problems. GPS could be "programmed" with different tasks, but it could encode only a single problem space at a time. Similarly, these systems could not switch problem spaces, nor could they use specialized problem spaces for subproblems.

If problem spaces are to be a distinct computational level, it is necessary to precisely define the processing that occurs within problem spaces and the types of objects that are manipulated. The objects include goals, problem spaces, states, and operators. The exact structure of these objects is unspecified at the problem space level, and their semantics are defined in terms of the functions that apply to them. During the construction of the first Soar implementation, it was unclear what functions were required at the problem space level. We were driven by a combination of concerns, some arising from behavior we wished the agent to exhibit (the UWM) and some from what had been learned about search and problem spaces in AI. The original set of functions proposed by Newell (1980) included:

1. Decide on success (the state is a desired state).
2. Decide on failure or suspension (the goal will not be achieved on this attempt).
3. Select a state from those directly available (if the current state is to be abandoned).
4. Select an operator to apply to the state.
5. Decide to save the new state for future use.

One of the breakthroughs in Soar 1 was to move to a more uniform list that arises from the acts of generation and selection. Some of the original functions are subsumed by more general functions (goal success and failure become selection of new goals), whereas others were eliminated and assumed to happen automatically (saving a new state for future use). The Soar 1 scheme assumes that there are two basic functions of generation and selection that can be applied to any problem space object (goal, problem space, state, and operator), plus there is operator application.

1. *Goal generation and selection:* The agent can generate new goals for itself, and can also use knowledge to select the goal that is most appropriate for the current situation. This includes detecting success or failure for the current goal.

2. *Problem space generation and selection:* The agent can generate problem spaces that are appropriate for a given goal, and select the one most appropriate. It should also be possible to change problem spaces during work on a goal if, for example, the current problem space is exhausted without achieving the goal.

3. *State generation and selection:* The agent can generate the initial state of the problem, thereby partially instantiating the goal within the current problem space (the description of the desired state is often left on the goal itself). It should also be possible to freely select from previously generated states during the search, so that the agent can use methods that require selections of prior states, such as best-first search or depth-first search.

4. *Operator generation and selection:* The agent can generate the operators of the problem spaces that are appropriate for the current state (or all of the operators in the space) and use knowledge to select the one most appropriate for achieving the goal.

5. *Operator application:* The agent creates new states through operator application. These new states then become candidates for state selection. Although this function is a state generation function, we distinguish it from state generation, because it is based on the current state and operator. Under this approach, the operators create completely new states. Progress is made in the problem space by jumping from one state to the next, possibly backing up to a state generated earlier, that is, one that is available from the stock of previously generated states.

Our formulation assumed that the agent is serial at the problem space level, in that there is only a single current goal, problem space, state, and operator at any time. For Soar 1, there was also an unlimited stock of states that could be generated during problem solving and the current state was selected from that stock.

This formulation of problem spaces is extremely flexible, allowing knowledge to be used to generate and select any problem space objects. It is possible to encode the operator selection methods of GPS and STRIPS, as well as state selection methods, such as depth-first search, best-first search, or even alpha-beta and A*. However, this flexibility comes at the cost of requiring that knowledge be available for all of these functions for every problem the system attempts. This requirement was partially ameliorated by providing default knowledge to control for those decisions in which no domain-specific knowledge was available.

Symbolic Architecture Level

Given the prior formulation of the problem space level, how is it realized in a symbolic architecture? Our initial inclinations for building a problem space architecture were to avoid production systems, thinking that they would only complicate the project, and thus we developed a Lisp-based system called the Task Experimenter (TEX). TEX provided us with immense experience in problem spaces and methods, but it was obvious that Lisp did not provide the appropriate control structure for incrementally adding more control knowledge. To achieve the desired flexibility we would need to build a second representation of knowledge on top of Lisp, possibly similar to production systems.

After abandoning Lisp, we needed to identify the appropriate role for productions within a problem space. The standard view at the time, and one that seems to still be ubiquitous in AI and cognitive science, is that productions are to be mapped onto operators in problem spaces. Thus, the selection and firing of a production is equivalent to taking a step in problem solving. Under this view, the problem state is the complete working memory, the operators are productions stored in long-term memory, and the control of the problem solving corresponds to *conflict resolution*: finding the right production to fire for the current situation.

Unfortunately, this integration of problem spaces and production systems greatly restricts the types of methods that could be used for problem solving. In most approaches, such as OPS5, the selection of the next production/operator is fixed by the syntax of the productions and the recency of the working memory elements it matches. This provides a depth-first style to problem solving and it cannot be influenced by additional knowledge. Other approaches include using activation schemes as in ACT* (Anderson, 1983) or meta-rules—additional rule bases that match against the competing rules and pick the best one (Davis, 1980; Genesereth, 1983). However, all of these schemes identify the state of the problem solving as the complete working memory, and thus do not support multiple goals, multiple problem spaces, or the various search methods that require multiple states.

The list of problem space functions suggests another approach to integration. In our earlier list, there are two basic functions: generation and selection. These two functions are applied uniformly to the four types of problem space objects: goals, problem spaces, states, and operators. The generation function is a recall from long-term memory of candidate objects. Selection then uses additional knowledge to decide on the current goal, problem space, state, or operator. Thus, the agent must be able to represent candidates, as well as the current selections. There is one additional function, which is that of applying operators to states to generate new states.

In Soar 1, we took what now seems to be the obvious approach of supporting generation and selection by having a special data structure in working memory called the *current context* that has slots to hold symbols representing the current selections for the goal, problem space, state, and operator. Thus, these object became "first-class" objects that would be explicitly generated and selected. In addition, there was a stock of generated candidate operators, states, problem spaces, and goals. Table 1.1 shows an example of the stock and current context for Soar 1. Each object in working memory could have additional attributes and values, which could also have attributes and values, providing a semantic network representation for objects and their substructures.

These working memory structures support the problem space functions of generation, selection, and application by explicitly representing the generated candidates and the current selections. But how are the problem space functions performed? In Soar 1 we supported the different functions by functionally distinct types of productions.

TABLE 1.1
Context and Stock of Soar 1

Goal	Problem Space	State	Operator
Current context			
$goal_{10}$	problem space$_3$	state$_{107}$	operator$_6$
Stock			
$goal_{102}$	problem space$_{14}$	state$_{34}$	operator$_{74}$
$goal_{30}$	problem space$_{23}$	state$_{702}$	operator$_{56}$
$goal_{231}$	problem space$_1$	state$_{19}$	operator$_{202}$

1. Generation corresponds to the addition of new candidate objects to the available stock. Productions match against the current context and can create new objects for the stock. For example, a means-ends production can test the current state and goal, and retrieve into working memory an operator that reduces the difference between the state and the goal. Productions that perform generation are called *elaboration* productions, and they fire in parallel because they only add objects to working memory. In addition to creating new objects, elaboration productions can also augment the objects in the current context with additional information, such as computing an evaluation of a state.

2. Selection corresponds to the replacement of an object in the current context slot. Replacement is guided by *decision* productions, which cast votes for or against objects in working memory. Thus, search-control knowledge is encoded as decision productions. The votes for the context slots are totaled starting with the goal, then problem space, state, and operator. If the votes suggest a change to the context, the new object is installed and the remaining slots are emptied. For example, if the goal changes, the current problem space and all the candidate problem spaces are possibly no longer appropriate. The same is true when a new state is selected—the existing operator and the candidate operators may not be appropriate. Therefore, in Soar 1, all of the unprocessed slots and proposed objects are emptied, to be rebuilt with appropriate candidate and selected objects through future elaboration and selection. Ties are broken arbitrarily if they arise.

3. Operator application corresponds to the creation of a new state. Application is performed by *application* productions, which are sensitive to the current context state and operator. Thus, knowledge about the execution of the domain is encoded as application productions. In contrast to STRIPS-like operators, this approach allows for a continuum of declarative representation of operators. It is possible to have productions that

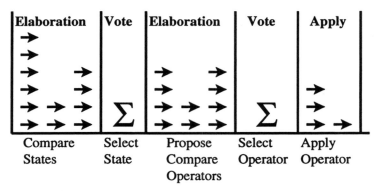

FIG. 1.1.   Processing cycle of Soar 1.

interpret a general declarative representation of the operator; for example, operators can be generated with explicit declarative lists of preconditions, additions and deletions. It is also possible to have ad hoc representations for operators in working memory, in which case the vast majority of the knowledge about performing the operator is represented as productions that are sensitive tó the name of the selected operator.

The basic processing cycle consists of elaboration, followed by decision as shown in Fig. 1.1. If there is no operator selected, the cycle repeats with elaboration. Once an operator is selected, an application phase occurs so that a new state is generated. Then elaboration begins again. Elaboration provides the agent with the ability to perform limited, monotonic inference, and consists of firing all matched productions in parallel. Elaboration continues as long as new productions are matched. Although this could be unbounded in theory, in practice, elaborations last only two or three production cycles.

With this architecture, the selections of the goal, problem space, state, and operators are open at each step of the problem solving to the agent's long-term knowledge. The typical trace of problem solving starts with the initial goal being selected, followed by the creation during elaboration of possible problem spaces. Decision productions cast votes that lead to the selection of a current problem space, followed in turn by the generation and selection of an initial state. Once the state is selected, operators are suggested during elaboration, followed by the selection of one based on votes by decision productions. This selection can be based on means-ends knowledge or other heuristics that are encoded in long-term memory. Following the selection of the operator, the application phase is entered and a new state is created and added to the stock. At this point, knowledge can be used to select between the various states in the stock. Once one is selected, operators are suggested and the search continues. If a state is ever reached that achieves the goal, elaboration productions can recognize this fact, augmenting the goal appropriately, and trigger decision productions that can select a new goal to work on.

Implementation Level

Soar 1 was implemented in XAPS2 (Rosenbloom & Newell, 1987), a parallel production system implemented in Lisp. XAPS2 also supported activation-based matching and an early task-specific version of chunking, but these features were not used in Soar 1.

Results

The major success of Soar 1 was its ability to support a universal weak method (UWM) for a variety of simple puzzles and tasks. The UWM was demonstrated by encoding nine different tasks in Soar 1, and then demonstrating that as knowledge was added about the tasks, the behavior of the agent changed and was consistent with well-known weak methods. Table 1.2 summarizes these results. The methods demonstrated include exhaustive search (ExS), avoiding duplicate states (ADS), heuristic search (HS), means-ends analysis (MEA), breadth-first search (BrFS), depth-first search (DFS), simple hill climbing (SHC), steepest ascent hill climbing (SAHC), best-first search (BFS), modified best-first search (MBFS), and A*.

The tasks were encoded as productions that generated the appropriate goals, problem spaces, initial states, and operators. The knowledge encoded in these productions was necessary to even attempt the problem and did not include any control knowledge. In addition to these tasks productions, there was a set of productions for default control—making decisions when there was no other knowledge available. These productions, together with the architecture, provided the essence of the universal weak method. Additional control knowledge was then encoded as elaboration and decision productions. These productions encoded additional knowledge about the task, such as when one state or operator was more desirable than another. We called these productions *method increments* because they could be freely added in combination for a given task and together they determined the method performed on a task. For example, the method increments for simple hill climbing were:

- If the current state is not acceptable or has an evaluation worse than the ancestor state, vote for the ancestor state.
- If the current state is acceptable and has an evaluation better than the ancestor state, vote for the current state.

TABLE 1.2
Soar 1 Methods Versus Tasks

Task	ExS	ADS	HS	MEA	BrFS	DFS	SHC	SAHC	BfS	MBFS	A*
Eight Puzzle	+	+	+	+	+	+	+	+	+	+	+
Tower of Hanoi	+	+	+		+	+					
Missionaries and Cannibals	+	+	+	+	+	+	+	+	+	+	+
Water Jug	+	+	+		+	+					
Picnic Problem I	+										
Picnic Problem II	+	+	+	+	+	+	+	+	+	+	+
Picnic Problem III	+	+	+	+	+	+	+	+	+	+	+
Syllogisms	+			+							
Wason Verification	+		+		+						
Three Wizards	+		+			+	+		+		
Root Finding I	+	+	+								
Root Finding II	+										

Not all methods arise for all tasks. For example, many of the tasks do not demonstrate means-ends analysis. This is because there is no available means-ends knowledge for the task. Similarly, knowledge about comparing intermediate states can be formulated for only a subset of the tasks (Eight Puzzle, Missionaries and Cannibals, the Picnic Problem, and Root Finding).

SOAR 2 (1983)

The big conceptual advance in going from Soar 1 to Soar 2 was adding subgoaling. Once this was in place, Soar's fundamental problem solving structure was set. The next 10 years were spent refining this structure, and combining it with learning abilities (in Soar 3) and an ability to interact with external worlds (Soar 5). Soar 2 is described in detail in Laird (1984).

Knowledge Level

The advances of Soar 2 were mostly at the problem space and symbolic architecture levels. However, Soar 2 did expand the range of control knowledge that could be encoded for a task in two ways. It expanded the expressiveness of knowledge for selecting context objects as well as allowing for the expression of general metaknowledge.

The Soar 1 decision scheme restricted the expression of knowledge about making decisions to simple votes for or against proposed alternatives. Many types of knowledge are not expressible in this language, such as partial orderings where it is known that one candidate should always be preferred over another. Although knowledge can be added in Soar 1 to vote for a choice, say A, and vote against another choice, say B, in an attempt to prefer A over B, there is no guarantee that other knowledge will not contribute enough votes for B so that it is selected. Thus, the voting scheme might not always maintain the underlying semantics behind why a vote might be made (or more accurately, the actual semantics of a vote were unclear). To remedy this problem, the representation of selection knowledge was changed so that it corresponded more closely to the semantics of preference and goal achievement.

A second restriction in Soar 1 was that all of the knowledge was directly related to the generation or selection of objects for the task. It was not possible to encode knowledge about general (*metalevel*) principles for generating operators or determining which operator was best, such as by making analogies with similar cases, or by performing a look-ahead search. Although Soar 1 allowed multiple goals and problem spaces, it lacked the key reflective ability of allowing the processing in one goal/problem-space to examine and modify the processing in another. Thus, for example, it was not possible to link the results of a look-ahead search in one space with the control of an operator selection in another.

Problem Space Level

The major thrust for change at the problem space level was the desire to introduce subgoals into Soar. We knew when writing Soar 1 that subgoals were necessary, but we delayed introducing them until we understood the basics of integrating production systems and problem spaces.

The guiding principles behind introducing subgoals are quite similar to the ones we used for developing the universal weak method: Soar should be able to generate any and all types of goals. That is, an agent should be able to create goals for achieving operator preconditions, as in GPS and STRIPS. It should also be able to create goals for performing operators. It should even be able to create goals for deciding which operator to select, so-called *metagoals*. Thus, the agent should be able to create all types of goals. We called this property *universal subgoaling*.

A related but separable property is the way in which goals are created and terminated. We posited, in parallel with actually building the agent, that it is possible to create an agent that generates its goals automatically when they are required by problem solving. An agent that creates goals automatically does not have to encode knowledge about when to generate goals, but instead bases the creation of goals on an inability to make progress on its task. We called this property *automatic subgoaling*. GPS had automatic subgoaling, but for only a limited class of goals.

Universal subgoaling and automatic subgoaling are obviously desirable properties, but how is it possible to build an agent that incorporates them? For universal subgoaling, what is the space of all possible goals? For automatic subgoaling, how can we insure that goals are generated whenever they are required? The answers to both of these questions came from using the problem space computational model (PSCM) as a framework for problem solving. The PSCM defines a set of functions—generation, selection, and application—from which all behavior is constituted. These functions in turn determine the types of subgoals that can be generated by the agent.

For the agent to support automatic subgoaling, the goals have to be architecturally generated. That is, the subgoals have to be generated in situations that can be detected in a domain independent manner, no matter what knowledge is available for the task. For example, in GPS, the architecture could automatically detect when the preconditions of an operator did not match the current state and create a subgoal. In contrast, operator selection could never fail—the table of connections was always available to determine which operator should be selected. Similarly, every operator had a directly executable definition, so it was never problematic to implement

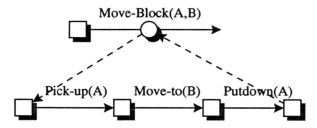

FIG. 1.2.   Soar 2 hierarchical execution subgoal.

an operator. Thus, GPS supported automatic subgoaling, but only for a single problem space function. Most problem space functions were never problematic, and functions were never open to new knowledge. As a result, GPS could only be applied to tasks with a single problem space that had simple operators and for which there existed a complete table of connections.

Soar expands automatic subgoaling to universal subgoaling because every problem space function is an open decision that is made while the task is being performed. The knowledge for these decisions, such as operator selection, is not precompiled into a table of connections before the task is attempted. Instead, the decisions are made based on the preferences retrieved during the elaboration phase. Ironically, opening up the decision procedure at run time to more knowledge also opens up the possibility that the knowledge will be incomplete or inconsistent and that more knowledge will be required before a decision can be made. We called the situations under which progress cannot be made because of incomplete or inconsistent knowledge *impasses*.[1] In Soar 2, the architecture automatically created a subgoal whenever an impasse arose. In later versions of Soar, the architecture would also automatically terminate the subgoal when the impasse was resolved.

Figure 1.2 shows a graphical trace of Soar as it encounters impasses in applying operators, leading to hierarchical execution. The task is to stack blocks, where multiple problem spaces are used to control the problem solving. The top problem space has a single operator for moving blocks. It has two parameters, the first being the block being moved and the second being the location of its destination (either the top of another block or the table). For a given state, this operator may have many instantiations. For this specific example, the goal is to get the blocks stacked in alphabetical order (A on top of B, which in turn is on top of C). The other problem space has operators that pick up, move, and put down a

---

[1]They were originally called *difficulties*, but we then adopted the word *impasses* from Brown and VanLehn's work (1980). Recently it became clear that VanLehn meant dead ends in problem solving, as opposed to architectural inabilities to make progress.

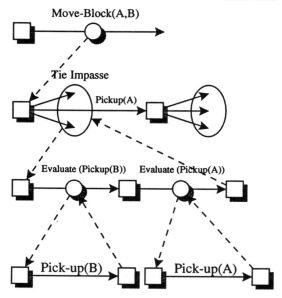

FIG. 1.3. Soar 2 search control and planning subgoals.

specific block. We assume that there is sufficient knowledge to select and apply of operators in this space (pick up, move, put down) directly.

At the top left of Fig. 1.3, the initial state is shown, followed by the selection of MOVE-BLOCK(A,B). Once MOVE-BLOCK(A,B) is selected, it can be applied, but in this case, there is no directly available knowledge for performing the operator. It must be decomposed into simpler steps. Thus, there is an impasse. To resolve this impasse, the second problem space is selected, and its operators are applied to implement MOVE-BLOCK(A,B).

If we remove the assumption that there is sufficient search-control knowledge for the subgoal, we could get the trace shown in Fig. 1.3. Here, the candidate operators are generated, but there is insufficient knowledge to select between them, leading to another impasse. In response to this impasse, the goal becomes to select the best operator. This is a control or meta-subgoal. The operators for the selected problem space evaluate and compare the task operators. In the example, an operator (*evaluate*) is selected to evaluate the operator PICK-UP block. The evaluation is computed in a subgoal. In general, any method for gaining more knowledge could be used, and in this case a limited look-ahead is employed to determine how well PICK-UP contributes to the original task goal. This demonstrates how for a single problem, many different types of subgoals and problem spaces may be generated and used.

How does Soar 2's approach to subgoals differ from AI systems that deliberately create goals? In Soar 1, and for many of the initial versions of Soar 2, goals could be deliberately created by productions suggesting new goals and having them be selected. In the final versions of Soar 2, this was eliminated so that all goals had to be generated by the architecture. It took us a long time to convince ourselves that the impasse-driven subgoaling mechanism in Soar 2 was sufficient by itself, for it eliminated deliberate goals. Where would such functionality now come from? The answer turned out to be simple. When the agent attempts to apply an operator but is unable to do it directly, that is the same as a deliberate goal. Thus, if an agent wants to decompose a single goal into a set of conjuncts and attempt each one individually, that would be cast as a goal with a problem space that had operators for each of the conjuncts. When a conjunct was selected, it would then lead to the creation of a goal, unless it was so simple that it could be performed directly. The functions of generating and selecting between the conjuncts map directly onto generating and selecting the operators that represent the conjuncts. Thus, Soar replaces deliberate subgoals with operators. What is the advantage of Soar's approach? In addition to having a uniform approach to execution control and goal management, Soar provides a graceful path from a knowledge-lean system with lots of goals, to a knowledge-rich system with lots of rules. If knowledge is available to perform the operator/deliberate-goal directly, no goal has to be created. This becomes more important when learning is added so that an operator that originally requires problem solving as a goal becomes one that the agent is able to perform directly without any problem solving.

This combination of universal and automatic subgoaling leads to two hypotheses about the relationships among goals in an intelligent agent:

1. The relationships between goals and subgoals is that of lack of knowledge. A subgoal is created to obtain knowledge so that problem solving in the goal can continue.
2. The functions for creating and selecting goals are embedded within the architecture.

In addition to automatic and universal subgoaling, Soar's subgoaling has many unique properties.

1. Subgoals and goals are simultaneously active. Thus, if some changes are made in a supergoal, possibly through perception or through intermediate results of a subgoal, the problem solving in the supergoal can proceed immediately without waiting for a termination signal from the subgoal.

2. The parameters to a subgoal are not prespecified. Unlike a procedure call, where the parameters to a procedure must be specified in advance, the exact set of parameters is determined dynamically by the needs of the

problem solving in the subgoal. Thus, the supergoal does not need to know what information is going to be relevant to the subgoal.

3. The results of a subgoal are not prespecified. In a traditional procedure call, the type of result is known before the procedure is called. In Soar, a subgoal can create any type of result it deems necessary. For many impasses, preferences will be created as results to resolve the impasse. However, other structures can be created as results, which in turn trigger the creation of preferences in the supergoal that resolve the impasse. Similarly, it may be "expected" that a subgoal return as a result a preference that allows selecting between two alternative operators, whereas the subgoal may actually return results that reject both of the existing alternatives and generate a new operator, which may then be selected.

These properties of Soar's subgoaling allow the problem solving in the subgoal free range as to how the subgoal is achieved and the impasse is resolved. In actuality, Soar's subgoals act more like open calls to the metalevel than restricted calls to subprocessing (Rosenbloom, Laird, & Newell, 1988).

Symbolic Architecture Level

The Basic Problem-Solving Cycle

The basic problem-solving cycle of elaboration-decision-application in Soar 1 was simplified in Soar 2 to be just elaboration-decision. Application was eliminated as a separate phase. The creation of a new state by an operator was performed during the elaboration phase following the selection of the operator.

Preferences and the Decision Procedure

The symbolic preference scheme developed for Soar 2 had the following types of preferences:

- Acceptable: The object mentioned is a candidate for selection.
- Reject: The object mentioned must not be selected.
- Better (Worse): The first (second) object mentioned should not be selected if the second (first) object mentioned is a viable candidate.
- Best: The object mentioned should be selected unless it is rejected or worse than some other object.
- Worst: The object mentioned should not be selected unless there are no other viable alternatives.

- Indifferent: The object mentioned can be selected at random in comparison to other indifferent objects.

In Soar 2, decision productions would interpret these preferences and translate them into a voting scheme that selected the appropriate object. In later versions of Soar, the processing of the decision productions was incorporated directly into the architecture and decision productions were eliminated. This was possible because the semantics of the preferences are fixed and do not change, even when learning was introduced.

Given the semantics of the preferences, four types of impasses could arise for each of the four types of context slots (goal, problem space, state, and operator). These corresponded to different types of incomplete or conflicting knowledge:

1. Tie: The control knowledge is incomplete as to which object is the appropriate selection. For example, if three operators are acceptable without any other preferences, there would be a tie. (Note: If there is knowledge that a choice can be made freely among the three operators, there would be indifferent preferences.) This impasse can be resolved by preferences that cause one choice to dominate (such as by rejecting the alternatives or preferring a single choice), or by making the tieing candidates indifferent.

2. Conflict: The control knowledge is conflicting. For example, if there are two acceptable operators, A and B, and there is one preference that A is better than B, and a second preference that B is better than A, then there is a conflict. This impasse can be resolved by rejecting one of the alternatives.

3. All-rejects: The control knowledge is incomplete in providing a viable alternative. All acceptable candidates are also rejected. This impasse can be resolved by the creation of an acceptable preference for another candidate object.

4. No-change: No new candidates are suggested, so no new decision is made. This impasse can be resolved by the creation of an acceptable preference for another candidate object. This impasse typically arises when new objects must be generated, such as generating a new state when applying an operator.

All of these impasses can be resolved by creating new preferences for the impassed decision. For example, if there is a tie among three operators, creating reject preferences for two of the operators will break the tie. These impasses can also be resolved by changing a decision higher in the context stack. For example, if there is a tie for the operator, the selection of a new state will eliminate the current preferences for the operator slot and lead to the creation of new preferences for operators relevant to the new state.

Subgoals

The symbol level implementation of automatic subgoaling was straightforward given the scheme developed for Soar 1. There were four major changes. The first three were implemented in Soar 2, with the last being part of Soar 3.

1. The architecture automatically created new contexts when an impasse was encountered. Thus, instead of a production voting for a new goal, the architecture would automatically create a context whenever there was an impasse in the decision procedure.

2. Multiple contexts were represented in working memory at the same time. Thus, when a new context was created, the context that gave rise to it would stay in working memory. In Soar 1, there was only a single context, and when a new goal was suggested it would replace the current goal. When a subgoal terminated, the original context had to be reconstructed. In Soar 2, the original context was maintained and the subgoal had a pointer back to it. By maintaining the complete context stack, subgoals had much better access to the state of problem solving that led to the impasse, and returning to the original context no longer required any reconstruction.

3. The results of a subgoal were determined automatically by the graph structure in working memory. If a working memory element was created in the subgoal but was linked through other working memory elements to a supercontext, it was a result and would be maintained after the subgoal terminated.

4. The architecture continually monitored the decisions for all context slots in working memory. Whenever a preference was created for a context slot, during the next decision phase the decision procedure would redecide that slot. If that resolved an impasse, the subcontext was removed from working memory, along with any structures that were not accessible to higher contexts.

Implementation Level

Soar 2 was implemented as a modification to OPS5 (Forgy, 1981), which was implemented in Lisp. The major changes centered on the conflict resolution scheme of OPS and the addition of the preference and decision schemes. There were no changes made to the RETE production matcher.

Using the RETE matcher greatly improved the efficiency of matching productions in Soar.

Results

In Soar 2, the set of weak methods and tasks was expanded. Figure 1.4 shows the relationship among these methods. The lines indicate that a method was derived from an earlier method by adding more knowledge.

Also in Soar 2, programs were built to demonstrate the coverage of universal subgoaling. More important, the first large task, R1-Soar was built

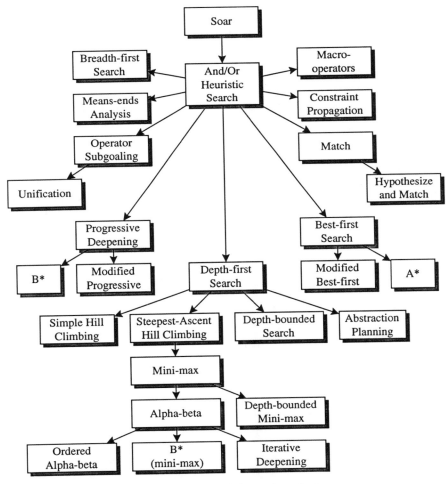

FIG. 1.4. Structure of the weak methods.

in Soar 2. R1-Soar was developed to demonstrate that Soar was sufficient for expert-level performance. We analyzed the knowledge in a key fragment of R1, the computer configuration expert system developed by John McDermott for Digital Equipment Corporation, and developed a system in Soar that had the same functionality. This is discussed in more detail with Soar 3.

SOAR 3 (1984)

In parallel with the development of Soar 1 and 2, Paul Rosenbloom and Allen Newell were creating computational theories of learning. The original goal was to model the ubiquitous power law of practice (Newell & Rosenbloom, 1981). By the beginning of summer in 1982, they had built an initial task-specific model of procedural "chunking," where processing in a goal would be summarized by a set of three productions (Rosenbloom & Newell, 1982). This model was implemented in the XAPS2 production system architecture, that is, the same architecture upon which Soar 1 was based. Over the next year the model was extended and made task independent, and became a central part of Rosenbloom's thesis (Rosenbloom, 1983; Laird, Rosenbloom, & Newell, 1986b). This extended, task-independent chunking model was implemented as part of a new productions system architecture that was designed specifically to support it—XAPS3. During the summer and fall of 1983, we discussed how to incorporate chunking into Soar, and finally in January 1984 we extended Soar 2 to include chunking (Laird, Rosenbloom, & Newell, 1984). At the time, the modifications to the architecture were minor and thus did not lead to a new version of Soar. Soar 3, implemented during the summer of 1984, was a partial rewrite of Soar 2, refining the subgoaling scheme, eliminating decision productions, and moving the decision procedure into the architecture (where it was more efficient). For this chapter, we take a revisionist approach and consider the major contribution of Soar 3 to be the addition of chunking, which is described in Laird, Rosenbloom, and Newell (1986a, 1986b).

Knowledge Level

At the knowledge level, learning is only relevant if it changes the knowledge available to the agent as it attempts to select actions to achieve its goals. Chunking, as it was originally formulated, cached the results of subgoal-based problem solving as productions. The productions, called chunks, summarized the problem solving of the subgoals, and in the future, the chunks would fire in situations that previously would have led to subgoals. Thus, chunking is a form of speed-up learning, moving knowledge from where deliberation in a subgoal is required, to productions, where it is directly available. Although this type of learning affects performance at the problem space and symbol levels, it has been argued that along with explanation-based learning (EBL; Mitchell, Keller, & Kedar-Cabelli, 1986; DeJong & Mooney, 1986), to which chunking is closely related (Rosenbloom & Laird, 1986), it does not produce learning at the knowledge level (Dietterich, 1986). However, the argument is based on the mistaken notion that, at the knowledge level, a system "knows" everything that it can derive at the symbolic architecture level from its symbol structures and the processes that can operate on them (i.e., everything in the "implicational closure"). If, at the symbolic architecture level, the system can generate a wide variety of structures that the system doesn't necessarily know represent true knowledge about the world—for example, imagine that it can generate all possible representational structures within some language (just like the monkeys in the British Museum algorithm can generate all possible strings of English)—then experience can determine which of these structures are actually useful and should be learned. If it is possible to distinguish what has been learned (and thus experienced) versus what could possibly occur, this splits the implicational closure into a segment encoding knowledge (because it has been experienced) versus a segment that does not. Chunking over experiences moves knowledge from the latter segment to the former, thus performing learning at the knowledge level (Rosenbloom, Laird, & Newell, 1987; Rosenbloom & Aasman, 1990).

Problem Space Level

Within the problem space computational model, learning plays a communicative role. It is not one of the basic functions required for making progress, but instead moves knowledge into a problem space from the world and from other problem spaces (in subgoals). It thus enables direct performance of problem space functions that previously required consulting the world or other spaces. For example, if there is a subgoal to select an operator, the subgoal's problem will be to determine which operator is the best for the current situation. Once a determination has been made, a preference will be created to select the best operator. A chunk will be built that summarizes the processing in the subgoal and creates the appropriate preference. The chunk encodes search control knowledge that, in the future, can directly contribute to operator selection. In similar situations, a subgoal will not arise because the chunk will fire and create the preference, thus avoiding any impasse.

A central aspect of the design of chunking in Soar is that it does not interfere with the regular problem space functions. Instead, it is a background process that is invoked automatically whenever a subgoal result is produced, The problem solving has no direct control or sensing of chunking—learning occurs in parallel with problem solving. The intent is for Soar to learn unobtrusively, incrementally, and continually on all tasks.

Although chunking is a fixed architectural mechanisms, the actual semantic content of what is learned can be as varied as the types of reasoning and problem solving that can be encoded in the problem spaces of subgoals. Also, because chunks arise from subgoals, and subgoals themselves can arise for any problem space function, chunks can encode any of the problem solving functions. Thus, chunks can be learned for the following:

1. Problem space proposal and selection.
2. Initial state proposal and selection.
3. Operator proposal, selection, and application.

Moreover, separate learning mechanisms are not required for learning control knowledge, operator creation and application knowledge, or problem formulation knowledge. However, knowledge must be encoded within the system as problem spaces that can generate the appropriate results, either from underlying domain knowledge or from generation spaces constrained by external observations. The result of a subgoal can be success, failure, or some intermediate data structure. Chunking captures the processing leading to the result, independent of the semantic content of the result.

Symbolic Architecture Level

At the symbol level, the challenge is to create an architecture in which the processing of any subgoal can be captured by a production and, conversely, anything represented in a production can be learned through chunking the problem solving of a subgoal. Over the years, there have been significant refinements of chunking and other aspects of the architecture to eliminate most of the cases where the processing in a subgoal cannot be accurately and precisely represented within productions and vice versa.

The following is a chronology of some of the early developments in chunking.

- *Initial implementation:* The first implementation of chunking in Soar kept track of all production firings during a subgoal, as well as all results produced during the subgoal. When the subgoal terminated, all working memory elements that were tested by productions that fired in the subgoal, and existed before the subgoal, became the basis for conditions. These working memory elements, together with the results (which became the actions), were variablized and then reordered to form the conditions and actions of chunks.

- *Backtracing:* Based on a talk by Tom Mitchell on goal-dependent learning, which would later become explanation-based generalization, we modified chunking so that traces of each production firing within a subgoal were saved. We also separated the results into groups that were independent so that more than one chunk could be learned for a subgoal. The conditions of productions were then determined by tracing back from results, through the production traces, to those working memory elements that were connected to a supercontext. This increased the generality of the chunks by eliminating conditions that were not necessary for generating the results that became the actions of the chunk.

• *Condition ordering:* The order in which the conditions of a production are matched can have an enormous impact on the cost of the match (as with other systems that perform conjunctive queries). In standard production systems, all productions are written by hand, so the programmer has the opportunity to provide an appropriate ordering on the conditions of the productions they write. With chunking, we were faced with productions that were created automatically. Initial implementations ordered the conditions of learned productions arbitrarily, and very quickly led to severe performance problems. In response, an automatic condition reorderer was developed to attempt to minimize matching time (Scales, 1986).

• *Incremental chunking:* Chunks were originally built only upon subgoal termination, but there was actually no functional restriction that forced this approach. We modified chunking so that chunks were built for a result as soon as it was generated in a subgoal. This led to increased transfer because some chunks could fire immediately, eliminating the need for further duplicate problem solving within a subgoal.

• *Incorporation of path constraints:* One issue that arose with EBL-style chunking was whether all productions that contributed to producing a result should be included in the dependency analysis. The final decision was that search-control productions, those that created desirability preferences, would be not be included in the backtrace. These productions should affect the speed with which a solution is found, but not the correctness of the results. However, we also recognized that sometimes control knowledge might be used to influence the correctness of a result; for example, a rule that prefers the cheaper of two partial computer configurations could be used to drive the system toward the goal of a cheap full configuration, rather than explicitly comparing the costs of the full configurations as part of the goal test. In response to this, we introduced two additional preferences: require and prohibit. The semantics of *require* were that the object (usually an operator) must be selected for the goal to be achieved. If the object cannot be selected (because there is more than one required, or it is also prohibited), then there is an impasse. The semantics of *prohibit* were that the object must not be selected for the goal to be achieved. The traces for these productions were included in deriving chunks because they encoded goal completion knowledge and not just efficiency knowledge.

- *Match cost:* As more and more productions are learned, a serious issue is whether Soar's matcher slows down. This was called the utility problem (Minton, 1990). In response, the development of efficient, and bounded, matching strategies was a significant path of research within Soar (Gupta, 1986; Gupta, Tambe, Kalp, Forgy, & Newell, 1988; Tambe et al., 1988; Tambe, Newell, & Rosenbloom, 1990). Most recently, Bob Doorenbos studied systems that learn large numbers of productions (100,000) and demonstrated that for some tasks there is no utility problem (Doorenbos, 1993; Doorenbos & Tambe, 1992).

Implementation Level

Little changed at the implementation level in moving from Soar 2 to Soar 3 other than porting it to additional versions of Lisp, thus allowing it to run on a broader set of machines.

Results

The major result of Soar 3 was the integration of chunking with Soar. The demonstration of transfer with chunking in Soar was done for simple toy tasks, such as the Eight Puzzle, Tower of Hanoi, and TicTacToe (Laird, 1984). We also demonstrated that chunking could learn macro-operators similar to Korf's work (Korf, 1983). One interesting result was that instead of representing macro-operators as monolithic structures as in a macro table, each macro-operator was composed of chunks that selected each substep of the macro. The advantage of this approach is that there is transfer of subparts of some macro-operators to other macro-operators, thus decreasing the number of cases that must be learned (Laird et al., 1986a).

The last demonstration of chunking in Soar 3 was within the context of R1-Soar, a re-implementation of part of the original R1 expert system for computer configuration (Rosenbloom, Laird, McDermott, Newell, & Orciuch, 1985). R1-Soar was the first knowledge-rich task encoded in Soar. In R1-Soar, the knowledge for configuring computers was encoded within a hierarchy of problem spaces. Through chunking, the system was able to reduce the time to configure computers, not only for later runs, but also for the initial run. The reason was that some of the configuration work was duplicated during a single run, and chunks learned during the initial part of the configuration transferred to later parts. One way to describe the action of chunking is that it compiled the deep general knowledge encoded in the hierarchy of problem spaces into more specialized but efficient surface knowledge.

Since Soar 3, chunking has been an inherent part of Soar, with many systems using it for a variety of purposes. Some of the types of learning that have been demonstrated via chunking include strategy acquisition, macro-operator acquisition, learning from advice (Golding, Rosenbloom, & Laird, 1987; Laird, Hucka, Yager, & Tuck, 1990), learning from instruction (Huffman & Laird, 1993, 1994), learning from abstraction (Unruh & Rosenbloom, 1989), task acquisition (Yost & Newell, 1989), inductive learning (Miller, 1993; Miller & Laird, 1991; Rosenbloom & Aasman, 1990), constraint compilation (Newell, 1990), explanation-based learning (Rosenbloom & Laird, 1986), learning by analogy, and recovery and relearning (Laird, 1988). The early work on these was summarized in Steier et al. (1987).

SOAR 4 (1986)

The goal of Soar 4 was to create a version of Soar that could be released to users outside of the development group. This involved porting Soar to Common Lisp, fixing lots of bugs, improving the interface, and writing a manual (Laird, 1986). Although Soar continued to be relatively hard to use and learn, the number of applications and users grew rapidly, so that by 1988 there were approximately 50 users of Soar 4. To maintain cohesion, especially because the project had become distributed across the country, workshops on Soar were started, originally every 6 months, and then every 8 months so that by the spring of 1994 there have been a total of 13 Soar workshops.

With the increase in the number of users, there was significant activity in creating new applications of Soar. On the AI side this included applications such as algorithm design (Designer-Soar and Cypress-Soar; Steier, 1987; Steier & Newell, 1988), medical diagnosis (Washington & Rosenbloom, 1989), blood analysis (Johnson, Smith, Johnson, Amra, & DeJongh, 1992), production-line scheduling (Hsu, Prietula, & Steier, 1989), chemical process modeling (Modi & Westerberg, 1989), natural language understanding (Lehman, Lewis, & Newell, 1991), and intelligent tutoring (Ward, 1991).

The year 1986 was also the start of one of the major research directions of Soar. It was at this time that Allen Newell proposed that many of the assumptions embedded in Soar were an appropriate basis for modeling human cognition. Newell's proposal was also based on the assumption that the time had come to consider *unified theories of cognition* (UTC), that is, theories that attempt to cover a broad range of psychological behavior. He proposed that the basis of such theories would be architectures, such as Soar or ACT* (Anderson, 1983). The investigation of Soar as a UTC was spurred by Newell's presentation of the William James Lectures at Harvard in 1987 (Newell, 1987). In preparation for these lectures, the Soar group set out to model a variety of human behavior in Soar. Newell's book, *Unified Theories of Cognition* (1990), captured his vision of a unified theory and proposed Soar as a candidate. Work on Soar as a UTC continued and became one of the major thrusts of research within the Soar community (Lewis et al., 1990; Newell, 1992). Areas of research include immediate reasoning tasks (Polk, Newell, & Lewis, 1989), syllogisms (Polk & Newell, 1988), verbal reasoning (Polk, 1992), number conservation (Simon, Newell, & Klahr, 1991), problem solving (Ruiz & Newell, 1989), instruction taking (Lewis et al., 1989; Huffman & Laird, 1993), visual attention (Wiesmeyer, 1991, 1992), concept acquisition (Miller & Laird, 1991), and natural language understanding (Lehman et al., 1991; Lewis, 1993).

SOAR 5 (1989)

Although Soar 4 led to a greater use of Soar, it still had significant weaknesses. One was that for problem spaces with large state descriptions, the application of an operator and the ensuing creation of a new state would require computationally expensive copying of all of the unchanged state information. A second, seemingly unrelated problem was that programs in Soar 4 had difficulty interacting with external environments. Almost all of the tasks encoded in Soar 4 were internal to the system itself. If it was solving blocks-world problems, it solved them in an internal model of the blocks world. The crux of the problem was that there was no theory as to how Soar systems should interact with the world. There were some basic facilities from OPS5 for reading and writing text; however, the production system would stop running while waiting for the completion of the input (and chunking couldn't appropriately capture these interactions).

The remedy to both of these problems was to adopt a new symbol-level approach to operator application and state maintenance, called *destructive state modification*. This in turn led to a revision of the problem space computational model through the adoption of the *single state principle*: At any point in time there should be at most one state active for each goal (i.e., a stock of one state). Newell observed that this principle was based on both functional and psychological grounds. Psychologically, search strategies such as progressive deepening arise because of the trouble people have in maintaining more than one internal state (plus the external one that is available via perception). Functionally, it was a burden on Soar's matching capabilities to maintain so many states in working memory.

The Soar 5 manual provides the most complete description of Soar 5 (Laird, Congdon, Altmann, & Swedlow, 1990).

Knowledge Level

At the knowledge level, the changes made to Soar 5 were meant to expand the types of tasks to which Soar could be applied and, in turn, to expand the range of knowledge that the system could encode and use. In Soar 4, the problem solver had access to the complete state of a problem and had complete control of changes to the current state. These changes could be made instantaneously, with complete certainty. Moreover, if the problem solver ever found itself in an undesirable state, it could always backtrack to some earlier state and continue from there.

In contrast, interaction with external environments violates many of these assumptions. In general, the problem solver can perceive only a limited portion of the current state of the problem, and the data it receives may have errors. The problem solver has only limited ability to modify the external environment, and the environment has its own dynamics, possibly including other agents. The actions of the problem solver may require time to execute and their effects may be difficult to predict. The dynamics of the world imply that the problem solver cannot simply backtrack out of undesirable situations in an external world, but must press ahead from its current state.

Problem Space Level

The characteristics of external environments listed earlier challenge not only Soar but also the standard formulation of problem spaces as used by most of AI. This in turn has led to dissatisfaction by many with symbolic AI for external interaction. One response has been to abandon the problem space model for interaction with external environments, sometimes denying any internal representation of the problem (Brooks, 1991). Often, when the problem space model is used, it is disassociated from execution and used only for planning activity, with the actual execution performed by separate "customized" modules (Fikes, Hart, & Nilsson, 1972; Gat, 1992). The challenge for Soar 5 was to develop an approach that maintained a single formulation of problem spaces for both execution and planning.

Soar 4's formulation of operators and states was the source of its incompatibilities with external interaction. In Soar 1–4, every operator application created a new state, which was then usually selected to be the current state. All previously generated states were available within the problem space. For Soar 5, we adopted the single state principle, with the result being that there is a single state—the current state—available within a goal at any time. Adopting this principle has a number of ramifications, as listed next.

State Selection

In previous versions of Soar, the decision to select the current state was one of the problem space functions. Under the single state principle, once the initial state is selected, there is no further state selection within a goal.

Backtracking

In earlier versions of Soar, the ability to select previously generated states allowed the system to "backtrack" during problem solving within a single subgoal. Under the single state principle, such backtracking is no longer possible. Surprisingly, little backtracking of this sort actually ever occurred in Soar programs. The reason is that whenever there was a uncertainty in a decision, there would be an impasse, and a look-ahead search across a series of subgoals would determine which was the best choice. This look-ahead search might generate multiple states, but these states were always the single current state in some goal in the context hierarchy. Figure 1.4 shows that all of the choice points during planning are initial states of evaluation goals. Thus, most backtracking was across goals and not within goals. The single state principle still allows this behavior, so that Soar can still search, as long as it is across goals using internal states.

Operator Termination

In previous versions of Soar, the termination of an operator was signaled by the selection of a new state. Thus, there was no need to explicitly signal that an operator had terminated. Also, all operator applications were under complete control of the system, so if it had the knowledge to apply an operator, then and only then was the operator completed. In contrast, Soar 5 has no state selection, so that once an operator is selected, there must be some signal that the operator is complete so that a new operator can be selected. In addition, it is possible that completion of an operator requiring interaction with the external environment will be uncertain. There must be an explicit test that the postconditions of the operator have been achieved. Merely wishing that a block is stacked on another does not make it come true, and conversely, it is possible that the stacking of a block will be carried out by another agent, even before the system has a chance to work on it. These factors combined to lead to the requirement for a new problem space function: termination.

Interaction

In previous versions of Soar, it was difficult to incorporate changes from the outside into the problem space model. Because all state transitions led to new states, conceptually, any input from the outside would have to lead to a new state. This was handled by not allowing asynchronous input; all input came in by explicit request during an operator application. In contrast, in Soar 5, it is easy to extend the problem space model so that the input from sensors dynamically changes the state. As the environment changes, the internal representation of those aspects of the environment sensed by the system also change. Under this model, the top problem space includes a representation of the external environment, although only a portion of the state is directly available to the system. Changes in that problem space can be effected by the agent, through actions on the environment and its own internal structures, as well as other processes in the environment.

Hierarchical Execution

In previous versions of Soar, a subgoal to implement an operator could perform arbitrary processing, but it would always terminate by generating a new state. It was not possible for the subgoal to incrementally modify the current state. Thus, it was not possible to have complex operators that required incremental interaction with an environment. In Soar 5, the implementation of a complex operator, such as "pick up the block," can be performed in a subgoal via more primitive operators, such as "move gripper," as shown in Fig. 1.3. The state of the subgoal is the same as the state to which the "pick up the block" operator is being applied. The problem solving in the subgoal can incrementally perform the operator. This problem solving can be time-dependent, require feedback from the environment, or even involve planning.

Symbolic Architecture Level

To support the single state principle, and thus support interaction with external environments and eliminate extensive state copying, the architecture level was significantly changed. The most significant of these changes was *destructive state modification*. Adopting this led to addition changes to the architecture, including implementation of an automatic persistence scheme, a modification to the elaboration/decision cycle, and the explicit signaling of operator termination via a new preference.

Destructive State Modification

In previous versions of Soar, an operator applied by creating a new state symbol, copying over much of the prior state, and then adding in those aspects of the state required by the application of the operator. This is essentially the situation variable model adopted in many logic-based problem solvers. Unfortunately, it requires a large amount of copying, especially for large states. Under the single state principle, the creation of completely new states is not possible, and instead, the current state is modified in place, a process called *destructive state modification*.

In terms of frame axioms, the previous versions of Soar required axioms as to what stayed the same between states. In contrast, Soar 5 requires axioms as to what changes between states (like STRIPS, but more flexible in representation).

By adopting the single state principle and the associated destructive state modification approach to operator application, it was necessary to devise an approach to applying operators that was still consistent with encoding the actions of the operators in an associative long-term memory. We were still committed to having operators whose executions were composed at run time by relevant productions, as opposed to being limited to fixed declarative descriptions of the actions and postconditions of the operator (as in STRIPS). On the positive side, productions as well as impasse-driven subgoals promised to provide a rich medium for representing conditional and time-dependent actions. On the negative side, all previous Soar systems assumed that all production firings were monotonic so as to avoid conflicts between actions. This was critical to avoid arbitrary action resolution schemes where some source of knowledge (a production) is masked. The only nonmonotonic changes were made by the decision procedure—to select new problem spaces, states, or operators—where they could be directly influenced by the system's knowledge.

To support destructive changes to the state, we extended the preference scheme and decision procedure to apply to all working memory elements, not just the context slots. Thus, a production no longer directly changes working memory, but instead creates preferences for how working memory should be changed. This maintains the monotonic nature of production actions, thus avoiding action conflicts. The productions still only create structures, but the structures they create have a nonmonotonic effect on working memory (through the decision procedure). If there is a conflict between preferences, this also can be represented in working memory as an impasse, but not one that necessarily prevents progress in problem solving, as does an impasse on a context slot. Instead such an impasse represents indecision as to the value of a particular structure. If progress (context decisions) can be made without resolving this indecision, that is fine.

Persistence

Although the preference scheme allows for nonmonotonic changes to working memory, by changing a state in place instead of creating a new one from scratch, we were faced with issues of the consistency and persistence of structures in the state. In previous versions of Soar, a new state was created from scratch. If a part of the state was an entailment from other parts of the state, it would be computed anew for any new state. Thus, although there was duplication in the derivation of the entailment of a state, a new state would be consistent. In Soar 5, structures in the state could be based on data that were later modified by an operator. These structures would have to be removed or recomputed to retain the consistency of the state. In order to avoid requiring domain knowledge to explicitly remove these structures, the semantics of production was changed so that their actions would "retract" when their conditions no longer matched. Thus, a production that calculated an evaluation would retract its result when the aspects of the state it was based on changed (and possibly, independently add a new evaluation based on the updated information). Surprisingly, this "truth maintenance" calculation is provided at no additional computational cost by the RETE match algorithm employed by Soar.

However, retraction semantics cannot be adopted by all productions. Specifically, productions that participate in applying an operator must test existing portions of the state and assert preferences to change them. Such changes must persist beyond the match of the production's conditions, or the change would retract as soon as it was generated. Thus, preferences must have two different classes of persistence. The first class persists as long as the production matches from which the preferences were created are still satisfied, and the second persists independent of the satisfaction of the productions that created them.[2]

A key issue is how to determine which preferences should fall in which persistence class. Such decisions cannot be done solely by a manual labeling of a production because productions can be learned via chunking. Similarly, manual labeling of actions will not work, because even though the actions of a chunk are based on the actions of an existing production, the exact role the action plays—operator application or entailment—can be different in a subgoal, where the operator may participate in the application of a operator, and in the goal where the chunk applies, where the action might be an entailment that should retract when its enabling conditions are no longer satisfied.

It is difficult to determine the exact right way of doing this; however, for Soar 5, we adopted the strategy of using the problem space function of the action to determine its persistence. This is possible in Soar by examining the types of working memory elements tested in the condition of the production, and the type of object the preference is for. These factors determine whether or not the production fulfills the function of operator application. For example, if a preference is generated by a production that tests a state and an operator and modifies the state, then it is part of operator application and does not retract. This is an example where the problem space formulation plays a central role in the architecture.

In previous versions of Soar, the result of a subgoal would persist until the supergoal structure to which it was linked was removed from working

---

[2]The complete details of the persistence scheme are available in the Soar 5.2 manual (Laird, Congdon, Altmann, & Swedlow, 1990) and the Soar 5 specification (Milnes, 1992).

memory. In Soar 5, some preferences must retract when the conditions of the production that created them no longer match (discussed earlier). However, the result of a subgoal should not be retracted when the conditions of the production that created it (i.e., the production in the subgoal) are retracted. Instead, its persistence must be equivalent to what it would have been if it had been created by the chunk learned from the subgoal (otherwise results would retract as soon as the subgoals that created them disappear). Therefore, a new structure must be built for each result: a *justification* that can be added to the matcher to represent the persistence of the result. The matcher then detects when any of the conditions of the justification are no longer satisfied and retracts the result.

Overlapped Application and Selection

In previous versions of Soar, the basic cycle of progress was select a state, propose and select an operator, apply an operator, and then select a state. This is shown in the top of Fig. 1.5. In Soar 5, the process compacts so that following the selection of the initial state, operators are proposed and the current operator is selected, the operator is applied until termination, when a new operator is selected, and so on. Under this scheme,

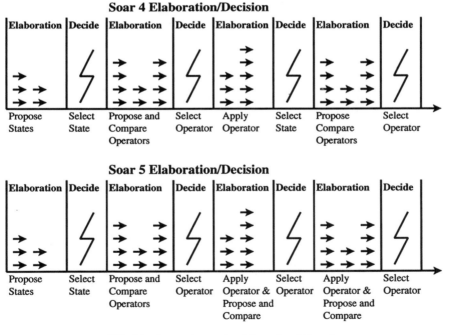

FIG. 1.5.   Processing cycle of Soar 4 and Soar 5.

knowledge to select a future operator is applied in parallel with the application of the current operator.

Maintaining the Coherence of Problem Spaces

In previous versions of Soar, the current state was always a "valid" state in the problem space. During operator application, the new state being constructed was not the current state. The system would "jump" from one valid state to the next. However, in Soar 5, once an operator is selected, the state changes in place. During application, the state may be in a state that is not valid within the problem space. For example, if the state consisted of a set of blocks, during application, a block might temporarily not have a location because its old location was deleted and a new location is being computed. However, when the operator is terminated, the state must be valid. That must be one of the postconditions of the operator. The fact that the state can be temporarily invalid would be cause for concern if a decision were based on it; however all operator decisions are held off until operator termination, so that when a new operator is selected, it is for a valid state of the problem space.

In order to implement the new "termination" problem space function, a new preference was added called *reconsider*. The existence of this preference for a context slot (problem space, state, operator) signifies that a decision can be made for that slot. When a decision is made for the operator slot, it signifies that the current operator has terminated.

Implementation Level

Soar 5 was built on top of the existing implementation of Soar 4 in Common Lisp. Although it provided new functionality, the dynamic creation of justifications led to significant slowdowns, even though time was saved by eliminating most state copying.

Results

Soar 5 was successful in supported interaction with external environments. Input could be asynchronous, and the recognition nature of the production system allowed systems to be built that could be reactive to changes in their environment. In addition, it supported interruption, planning, hierarchical execution, and learning that converted planning into reactive execution (Laird & Rosenbloom, 1990). However, problems—and controversies—still remain in understanding exactly how learning should occur in the presence of external interaction so that behavior after learning maintains appropriate properties with respect to timing and semantic penetrability.

Another way of looking at Soar 5 as an architecture to support external interaction comes from looking at increasing time scales of activities, as

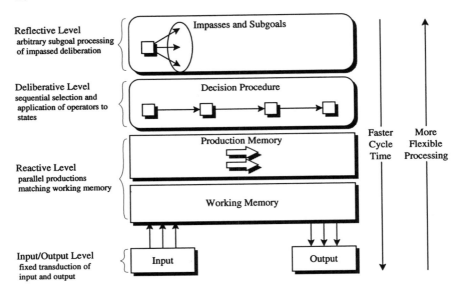

Reflective Level
arbitrary subgoal processing
of impassed deliberation

Impasses and Subgoals

Deliberative Level
sequential selection and
application of operators to
states

Decision Procedure

Reactive Level
parallel productions
matching working memory

Production Memory

Working Memory

Faster   More
Cycle   Flexible
Time   Processing

Input/Output Level
fixed transduction of
input and output

Input

Output

FIG. 1.6. Multiple levels of Soar architecture.

shown in Fig. 1.6. At the fastest time scale, fixed input and output modules interface Soar to its external environment. Input modules install data from sensors into working memory. Output modules detect motor commands in working memory and transfer them to the motor system.

The next level is the reactive level, at which productions match in parallel to the situation in working memory. This level provides for quick reflexive responses to changes in the environment, but does not allow for the integration of knowledge—a production is an isolated piece of knowledge.

The third level is the deliberative level, at which the functions of problem spaces are performed, such as selecting and applying operators. This level is less immediately responsive than the reactive level, as it is implemented by sequences of parallel production firings, plus a decision; however, it makes up for this by enabling two forms of knowledge integration in its action generation: first, through sequences of production firings, where the actions of one production are conditional on the actions of those that fired before it; and second through the combination of preferences in the decision procedure. The fact that the elaboration phase runs until quiescence means that there is an exhaustive access of all directly available knowledge in long-term memory. Thus, as new productions are added to long-term memory, the deliberative level automatically will use them when they are relevant. This is the base level of knowledge-intensive behavior— behavior where the system knows exactly what to do at each step.

The fourth, and final, level is the reflective level, at which the functions of problem spaces can themselves be the object of problem solving in subgoals. This level is the least responsive time wise, but it also provides the most flexibility, by allowing arbitrary problem solving in producing its results. It can involve planning, reasoning by analogy, hierarchical decomposition, and other complex problem-solving methods. It is also the source of new knowledge, because all results of subgoals lead to the creation of new productions that augment the other levels.

Taking these levels together, Soar 5 can be viewed as a combination real-time and planning system. The real-time system consists of the three lower levels, whereas the reflective level allows unlimited planning. These levels can execute in parallel, and knowledge about activity (usually represented as preferences) is transferred from the planning/reflective level to the others through chunking. This makes Soar looks similar to multilevel agent architectures such as Atlantis (Gat, 1992) and Circa (Musliner, Durfee, & Shin, 1992), but with some key differences (many of which are shared with Theo; Mitchell et al., 1991): Soar's levels are all based on a single underlying representation of knowledge (productions), its levels arise dynamically based on the needs of the problem, and its learning leads to a gradual transition from a reflective to a reactive system.

The range of tasks to which Soar 5 was applied included a number of robotic control systems: high-level control of a Puma arm using camera input for vision (Laird, Yager, Hucka, & Tuck, 1991), control of a Hero mobile robot (Laird & Rosenbloom, 1990), navigation in a two-dimensional simulated mobile robot domain (Stobie, Tambe, & Rosenbloom, 1993), control of simulated aircraft (Pearson, Huffman, Willis, Laird, & Jones, 1993), and video game control (John, Vera, & Newell, 1990). Another class of systems was built that interacted with other software systems (Newell & Steier, 1991) including databases, symbolic mathematics packages, chemical process simulators, drawing packages, tutorial environments (Ward, 1991), building-design tools (Steier, 1990), and physical-world simulators. A full summary of the domains tackled with Soar 5 can be found in the introduction to Rosenbloom, Laird, and Newell (1993).

SOAR 6 (1992)

Although Soar 5 broadened the types of domains that Soar could be applied to, it was not without cost. Soar 5 was created by modifying Soar 4, which in turn was based on the code for Soar 3 and Soar 2. There was still some of the original Lisp code for the RETE matcher from OPS5. The patchwork nature of the code made maintenance difficult. In addition, many of the algorithms and implementations developed for those earlier versions were extremely inefficient under the new architecture. Many programs ran a factor of three slower under Soar 5 than under Soar 4. Thus Soar 6 was generated as a complete reengineering and reimplementation of Soar 5.

Implementation Level

Once it was clear that a complete reimplementation was called for, the next decision to be made was whether it should be in Lisp or some other language (in particular, C). Driven by concerns about portability and efficiency, the decision was eventually made to reimplement in C. In addition to the reimplementation, a formal specification of Soar 5 in Z was created (Milnes, 1992) to aid in constructing a correct implementation. The new implementation was designed not only for speed and maintainability, but also for scalability so that very large numbers of productions could be learned. To preserve the ability to compare systems in both Soar 5 and Soar 6, only a few relatively minor conceptual changes were made to the underlying architecture.

The resulting system has the following characteristics:

1. Soar 6 is 15–20 times faster than Soar 5 for medium-size tasks (1,000 productions).
2. Soar 6 learns over 1,000,000 productions without significant performance degradation for certain tasks (Doorenbos, 1994).
3. Soar 6 has run over 4,000,000 production firings on a single task (simulated aircraft control; Pearson et al., 1993) without significant performance degradation.

The performance improvements of Soar 6 have opened up new classes of tasks, such as real-time simulated aircraft control (Pearson et al., 1993) and tactical behavior (Jones et al., 1993; Rosenbloom et al., 1994), and interactive natural language instruction (Huffman & Laird, 1993).

CONCLUSION

Our efforts over the last 12 years have been focussed on the scientific issues surrounding the development of a general cognitive architecture. This focus has been useful in the development and evolution of Soar in terms of functionality, but it has also not come without cost. For years we ignored software engineering, user interface, and learnability issues that have made learning and using Soar sometimes more than a small challenge. In the reimplementation of Soar 6 we addressed many of the software engineering problems, but Soar is still difficult for novices to learn and use—an issue we continue to struggle with.

These problems aside, where are we on our quest for creating an architecture that supports general intelligence? We have come a long way from the eight puzzle and hill climbing, but clearly we have a long way to go, with the need to generalize and extend many of the capabilities in Soar that are currently ad hoc and incomplete. For example:

1. Some essential forms of learning, such as episodic (especially autobiographical) and declarative (especially inductive) are still more complex and difficult, and less routine, than it seems they ought to be.
2. Learning is still fragile. Problems remain of overgeneralization, undergeneralization, utility, and working appropriately in the presence of a dynamic environment.
3. Ways of coping with multiple interacting goals are still rather ad hoc and not routine.
4. Spatial and temporal reasoning (and more generally, dealing with nonsymbolic inputs and outputs) are still rather ad hoc and incomplete.
5. Soar is still radically incomplete with respect to being a full unified theory of cognition, and incorrect in a number of obvious ways (such as having an unbounded working memory).

Although there is a lot left to be done (thus guaranteeing that we will have no problem finding research projects for our graduate students for the foreseeable future), Soar has been a successful vehicle in our quest, as evidenced by the range of systems that have been built with it. Our belief is that this success can be traced to the central idea in Soar, which is that there are two distinct sources of knowledge for controlling behavior. One source is the system's long-term memory. This memory is under the architecture's control and can be organized for efficient retrieval of knowledge relevant to the current situation. Thus, *memory search* need not be inherently combinatorial, and the associative retrieval of a production system is a useful way to organize long-term knowledge.

The second source of knowledge is the system's explicit inferences about the problem—that is, its search through an appropriate problem space. For novel problems, that search can generate new situations, that is, new states, that the system has never previously considered. Thus, problem search can generate new knowledge and new options to consider, making it impossible for the architecture to avoid combinatorial search in all novel problems. However, this search can itself be controlled by any knowledge available to the agent (from memory or additional problem search); by learning, the agent can convert problem search to memory search.

These distinctions are not unique to Soar, and go all the way back to the first AI systems developed in the 1950s. What is unique to Soar is that it is structured so that all problems that Soar attempts can use either type of knowledge when it is available, preferring knowledge in memory when it is available. That is, in Soar, standard, nonproblematic decision making is controlled directly by continual retrieval of preferences from production memory, and problem search only arises when memory search fails.

The biggest surprise in our investigation of Soar is that Soar is still with us (or possibly more correctly we are still with it) after 12 years. In AI, architectures are typically built, tested, used for one, maybe two systems, and then discarded so that the lessons learned can be incorporated in a new, better architecture that is built from scratch. Maybe Soar's longevity is just a testimony to our own stubbornness and perseverance. However, at the time Soar was created, we did not expect it to last this long. During the summer following the initial development and success of Soar, we (John Laird, Paul Rosenbloom, and Allen Newell) decided to form a project for the continued investigation of general cognitive architectures. We needed a name, but Allen knew that the name of the project could not be Soar. Soar was just the name of our current architecture, and clearly we wanted the project to last longer than a transitory piece of software. We are happy that on this account, Allen was wrong.

One explanation for Soar's longevity may be rooted in a second surprise, which concerns our understanding of the role of problem spaces in producing intelligent behavior. Originally, Allen Newell and Herb Simon conceived of problem spaces as an arena for search (Newell & Simon, 1972). Allen's original statement of the problem space hypothesis was that "all symbolic goal-oriented activity could be cast as search in a problem space" (Newell, 1980). This statement became more and more awkward as many of our systems did less and less search, but still successfully solved problems using problem spaces. Instead of searching, they relied on the "situatedness" inherent to Soar. That is, each decision in Soar combines the available knowledge by retrieving preferences for action from production memory based on its sensing of the environment, its current goals, and its interpretation of the environment in light of the goal. Thus, we rely more and more on knowledge search, and the surprise was that the least-commitment, run-time control of behavior inherent in problem spaces is actually more important than the more traditional function of search. We are happy that on this second account, Allen (and Herb) were right (about the importance of problem spaces), but possibly for the wrong reason.

ACKNOWLEDGMENTS

As should be clear from this chapter, we owe a great debt to Allen Newell for his contributions to the development of Soar and our own careers. We also thank the Soar community for its vigor and support of Soar over the years.

REFERENCES

Anderson, J. R. (1983). *The architecture of cognition.* Cambridge, MA: Harvard University Press.

Bell, C. G., & Newell, A. (1971). *Computer structures: Readings and examples.* New York: McGraw-Hill.

Brooks, R. A. (1991). Intelligence without representation. *Artificial Intelligence, 47,* 139–159.

Brown, J. S., & VanLehn, K. (1980). Repair theory: A generative theory of bugs in procedural skills. *Cognitive Science, 4*(4), 379–426.

Davis, R. (1980). Meta-rules: Reasoning about control. *Artificial Intelligence, 15*(3), 179–222.

DeJong, G., & Mooney, R. (1986). Explanation-based learning: An alternative view. *Machine Learning, 1*(2), 145–176.

Dietterich, T. G. (1986). Learning at the knowledge level. *Machine Learning, 1*(3), 287–315.

Doorenbos, R. (1993, July). Matching 100,000 learned rules. *Proceedings of the Eleventh National Conference on Artificial Intelligence* (pp. 290–296). Menlo Park, CA: AAAI Press.

Doorenbos, R. (1994, March). Recent results on matching. *Thirteenth Soar Workshop* (pp. 62–72). Columbus, OH. (Charts presented at the workshop)

Doorenbos, R., Tambe, M., & Newell, A. (1992, July). Learning 10,000 chunks: What's it like out there? *Proceedings of the Tenth National Conference on Artificial Intelligence* (pp. 830–836). Menlo Park, CA: AAAI Press.

Fikes, R. E., Hart, P. E., & Nilsson, N. J. (1972). Learning and executing generalized robot plans. *Artificial Intelligence, 3*(1–4), 251–288.

Fikes, R. E., & Nilsson, N. J. (1971). STRIPS: A new approach to the application of theorem proving to problem solving. *Artificial Intelligence, 2,* 189–208.

Forgy, C. L. (1981). *OPS5 user's manual* (Technical Rep. No. CMU-CS-81-135). Pittsburgh: Carnegie-Mellon University, Computer Science Department.

Forgy, C. L. (1982). Rete: A fast algorithm for the many pattern/many object pattern match problem. *Artificial Intelligence, 19*(1), 17–38.

Forgy, C. L., & McDermott, J. (1977, August). OPS, a domain-independent production system language. *Proceedings of the Fifth International Joint Computer Conference* (pp. 933–939). Cambridge, MA: MIT AI Laboratory.

Gat, E. (1992, July). Integrating planning and reacting in a heterogeneous asynchronous architecture for controlling real-world mobile robots. *Proceedings of the Tenth National Conference on Artificial Intelligence* (pp. 809–815). San Jose, CA: AAAI Press.

Genesereth, M. (1983, August). An overview of meta-level architecture. *Proceedings of the Third National Conference on Artificial Intelligence* (pp. 119–123). Washington, DC.

Golding, A., Rosenbloom, P. S., & Laird, J. E. (1987). Learning general search control from outside guidance. *Proceedings of the Tenth International Conference on Artificial Intelligence.* Milano, Italy.

Gupta, A. (1986). *Parallelism in production systems.* Los Altos, CA: Kaufmann.

Gupta, A., Tambe, M., Kalp, D., Forgy, C. L., & Newell, A. (1988). Parallel implementation of OPS5 on the Encore multiprocessor: Results and analysis. *International Journal of Parallel Programming, 17*(2), 95–124.

Hsu, W., Prietula, M., & Steier, D. (1989). Merl-Soar: Scheduling within a general architecture for intelligence. *Proceedings of the Third International Conference on Expert Systems and the Leading Edge Production and Operations Management* (pp. 467–481).

Huffman, S. B., & Laird, J. E. (1993). Learning procedures from interactive national language instructions. In P. Utgoff (Ed.), *Machine learning: Proceedings of the Twelfth National Conference on Artificial Intelligence* (pp. 506–512). Amherst, MA.

Huffman, S. B., & Laird, J. E. (1994). Learning from highly flexible tutorial instruction. *Proceedings of the National Conference on Artificial Intelligence.* Seattle, WA.

John, B. E., Vera, A. H., & Newell, A. (1990). *Towards real-time GOMS* (Tech. Rep. No. CMU-CS-90-195). Pittsburgh: School of Computer Science, Carnegie Mellon University.

Johnson, T. R., Smith, J. W., Johnson, K., Amra, N., & DeJongh, M. (1992). *Diagrammatic reasoning of tabular data* (Tech. Rep. No. OSU-LKBMS-92-101). Columbus: Laboratory for Knowledge-Based Medical Systems, Ohio State University.

Jones, R. M., Tambe, M., Laird, J. E., & Rosenbloom, P. S. (1993). Intelligent automated agents for flight training simulators. *Proceedings of the Third Conference on Computer Generated Forces and Behavioral Representation* (pp. 33–42). Orlando, FL.

Korf, R. E. (1983). *Learning to solve problems by searching for macro-operators.* Unpublished doctoral dissertation, Carnegie-Mellon University. Available as Carnegie-Mellon University Computer Science Tech. Rep. 83-138.

Laird, J. E. (1984). *Universal subgoaling.* Unpublished doctoral dissertation, Carnegie-Mellon University. Available as Carnegie-Mellon University Computer Science Tech. Rep. 84-129.

Laird, J. E. (1986). *Soar user's manual: Version 4.0.* Palo Alto, CA: Xerox Palo Alto Research Center.

Laird, J. E. (1988). Recovery from incorrect knowledge in Soar. *Proceedings of the Seventh National Conference on Artificial Intelligence* (pp. 618–623). St. Paul, MN.

Laird, J. E., Congdon, C. B., Altmann, E., & Swedlow, K. (1990). *Soar user's manual: Version 5.2* (Tech. Rep. No. CSE-TR-72-90). Ann Arbor: Electrical Engineering and Computer Science Department, University of Michigan. Also available from the Soar Group, School of Computer Science, Carnegie Mellon University, as Tech. Rep. No. CMU-CS-90-179.

Laird, J. E., Hucka, M., Yager, E. S., & Tuck, C. M. (1990). Correcting and extending domain knowledge using outside guidance. In B. W. Porter & R. J. Mooney (Eds.), *Proceedings of the Seventh International Conference on Machine Learning* (pp. 235–243). Austin, TX.

Laird, J. E., & Newell, A. (1983a). *A universal weak method* (Tech. Rep. No. CMU-CS-83-141). Pittsburgh: Carnegie-Mellon University, Computer Science Department.

Laird, J. E., & Newell, A. (1983b). A universal weak method: Summary of results. *Proceedings of the Eighth International Joint Conference on Artificial Intelligence* (pp. 771–773). Karlsruhe, West Germany.

Laird, J. E., & Rosenbloom, P. S. (1990, July). Integrating execution, planning, and learning in Soar for external environments. *Proceedings of the Eighth National Conference on Artificial Intelligence* (pp. 1022–1029). Boston.

Laird, J. E., Rosenbloom, P. S., & Newell, A. (1984, August). Towards chunking as a general learning mechanism. *Proceedings of the Fourth National Conference on Artificial Intelligence* (pp. 188–192). American Association for Artificial Intelligence.

Laird, J. E., Rosenbloom, P. S., & Newell, A. (1986a). Chunking in Soar: The anatomy of a general learning mechanism. *Machine Learning, 1*(1), 11–46.

Laird, J. E., Rosenbloom, P. S., & Newell, A. (1986b). *Universal subgoaling and chunking: The automatic generation and learning of goal hierarchies.* Hingham, MA: Kluwer.

Laird, J. E., Yager, E. S., Hucka, M., & Tuck, C. M. (1991). Robo-Soar: An integration of external interaction, planning and learning using Soar. *Robotics and Autonomous Systems, 8,* 113–129.

Lehman, J. F., Lewis, R., & Newell, A. (1991). *Natural language comprehension in Soar: Spring 1991* (Tech. Rep. No. CMU-CS-91-117). Pittsburgh: Carnegie Mellon University.

Lewis, R., Newell, A., & Polk, T. (1989, August). Toward a Soar theory of taking instructions for immediate reasoning tasks. *Proceedings of the Eleventh Annual Conference of the Cognitive Science Society* (pp. 514–520). Ann Arbor, MI.

Lewis, R. L. (1993). *An architecturally-based theory of human sentence comprehension.* Unpublished doctoral dissertation, Carnegie Mellon University, Pittsburgh.

Lewis, R. L., Huffman, S. B., John, B. E., Laird, J. E., Lehman, J. F., Newell, A., Rosenbloom, P. S., Simon, T., & Tessler, S. G. (1990, July). Soar as a unified theory of cognition: Spring 1990. *Proceedings of the 12th Annual Conference of the Cognitive Science Society* (pp. 1035–1042). Cambridge, MA.

McDermott, J. (1982). R1: A rule based configurer of computer systems. *Artificial Intelligence, 19*(1), 39–88.

Miller, C. (1993). *Modeling concept acquisition in the context of a unified theory of cognition.* Unpublished doctoral dissertation, University of Michigan, Ann Arbor.

Miller, C. S., & Laird, J. E. (1991). A constraint-motivated model of concept formation. *Proceedings of the Thirteenth Annual Meeting of the Cognitive Science Society* (pp. 827–831). Hillsdale, NJ: Lawrence Erlbaum Associates.

Milnes, B. G. (1992). *A specification of the Soar cognitive architecture in Z* (Tech. Rep. No. CMU-CS-92-169). Pittsburgh: Carnegie Mellon University, School of Computer Science.

Minton, S. (1990). Quantitative results concerning the utility of explanation-based learning. *Artificial Intelligence, 42,* 363–391.

Mitchell, T. M., Allen, J., Chalasani, P., Cheng, J., Etzioni, O., Ringuette, M., & Schlimmer, J. (1991). Theo: A framework for self-improving systems. In K. VanLehn (Ed.), *Architectures for intelligence* (pp. 323–355). Hillsdale, NJ: Lawrence Erlbaum Associates.

Mitchell, T. M., Keller, R. M., & Kedar-Cabelli, S. T. (1986). Explanation-based generalization: A unifying view. *Machine Learning, 1*(1).

Modi, A., & Westerberg, A. (1989). *Integrating learning and problem solving within a chemical process designer.* Paper presented at the Annual Meeting of the American Institute of Chemical Engineers.

Musliner, D. J., Durfee, E. H., & Shin, K. G. (1993). CIRCA: A cooperative intelligent real-time control architecture. *IEEE Transactions on Systems, Man, and Cybernetics, 23*(6), 1561–1574.

Newell, A. (1955). The chess machine: An example of dealing with a complex task by adaptation. *Proceedings of the 1955 Western Joint Computer Conference* (pp. 101–108). Western Joint Computer Conference (RAND P-620).

Newell, A. (1969). Heuristic programming: Ill-structured problems. In J. Aronofsky (Ed.), *Progress in operations research* (Vol. III, pp. 360–414). New York: Wiley.

Newell, A. (1972). A theoretical exploration of mechanisms for coding the stimulus. In A. Melton & E. Martin (Eds.), *Coding processes in human memory* (pp. 373–434). Washington, DC: Winston and Sons.

Newell, A. (1973). Production systems: Models of control structures. In W. C. Chase (Ed.), *Visual information processing* (pp. 463–526). New York: Academic Press.

Newell, A. (1980). Reasoning, problem solving and decision processes: The problem space as a fundamental category. In R. Nickerson (Ed.), *Attention and Performance VIII* (pp. 693–718). Hillsdale, NJ: Lawrence Erlbaum Associates.

Newell, A. (1982). The knowledge level. *Artificial Intelligence, 18,* 87–127.

Newell, A. (1987). *Unified theories of cognition: 1987 William James lectures.* Available on videocassette from Harvard Psychology Department.

Newell, A. (1990). *Unified theories of cognition.* Cambridge, MA: Harvard University Press.

Newell, A. (1992). Unified theories of cognition and the role of Soar. In J. Michon & A. Akyurek (Eds.), *Soar: A cognitive architecture in perspective* (pp. 25–79). Cambridge, MA: Kluwer.

Newell, A., & Rosenbloom, P. (1981). Mechanisms of skill acquisition and the law of practice. In J. R. Anderson (Ed.), *Learning and cognition* (pp. 1–55). Hillsdale, NJ: Lawrence Erlbaum Associates.

Newell, A., Rosenbloom, P. S., & Laird, J. E. (1989). Symbolic architectures for cognition. In M. I. Posner (Ed.), *Foundations of cognitive science* (Chapter 3). Cambridge, MA: Bradford Books/MIT Press.

Newell, A., Shaw, J. C., & Simon, H. A. (1957). Empirical explorations of the logic theory machine: A case study in heuristics. *Proceedings of the 1957 Western Joint Computer Conference* (pp. 218–230). Western Joint Computer Conference. Reprinted in E. Feigenbaum & J. Feldman (Eds.). (1963). *Computers and thought* (pp. 109–133). New York: McGraw-Hill.

Newell, A., Shaw, J. C., & Simon, H. A. (1958). Chess-playing programs and the problem of complexity. *IBM Journal of Research and Development, 2*, 320–325. Reprinted in E. Feigenbaum & J. Feldman (Eds.). (1963). *Computers and thought* (pp. 39–70). New York: McGraw-Hill.

Newell, A., & Simon, H. A. (1956). The logic theory machine: A complex information processing system. *IRE Transactions on Information Theory, IT-2*, 61–79.

Newell, A., & Simon, H. A. (1961). GPS, a program that simulates human thought. In H. Billing (Ed.), *Lernende Automaten* (pp. 109–124). Munich: Oldenbourg. Reprinted in E. Feigenbaum & J. Feldman (Eds.). (1963). *Computers and thought* (pp. 279–293). New York: McGraw-Hill.

Newell, A., & Simon, H. A. (1972). *Human problem solving.* Englewood Cliffs, NJ: Prentice Hall.

Newell, A., & Steier, D. (1991). *Intelligent control of external software systems* (Tech. Rep. No. EDRC 05-55-91). Engineering Design Research Center, Carnegie Mellon University, Pittsburgh.

Newell, A., Yost, G. R., Laird, J. E., Rosenbloom, P. S., & Altmann, E. (1991). Formulating the problem space computational model. In R. F. Rashid (Ed.), *Carnegie Mellon Computer Science: A 25-year commemorative* (pp. 259–293). Reading, MA: ACM Press/Addison-Wesley.

Pearson, D. J., Huffman, S. B., Willis, M. B., Laird, J. E., & Jones, R. M. (1993). Intelligent multilevel control in a highly reactive domain. *Proceedings of the International Conference on Intelligent Autonomous Systems* (pp. 449–458). Pittsburgh, PA.

Polk, T., Newell, A., & Lewis, R. (1989). *Toward a unified theory of immediate reasoning in Soar.* Unpublished.

Polk, T. A. (1992). *Verbal reasoning.* (Tech. Rep. No. CMU-CS-92-178). Pittsburgh: Carnegie Mellon University, School of Computer Science.

Polk, T. A., & Newell, A. (1988). Modeling human syllogistic reasoning in Soar. *Proceedings of the 10th Annual Conference of the Cognitive Science Society* (pp. 181–187). Montreal.

Rosenbloom, P. S. (1983). *The chunking of goal hierarchies: A model of practice and stimulus-response compatibility.* Unpublished doctoral dissertation, Carnegie-Mellon University, Pittsburgh.

Rosenbloom, P. S., & Aasman, J. (1990). Knowledge level and inductive uses of chunking (EBL). *Proceedings of the Eighth National Conference on Artificial Intelligence* (pp. 821–827). Boston: AAAI, MIT Press.

Rosenbloom, P. S., Johnson, W. L., Jones, R. M., Koss, F., Laird, J. E., Lehman, J. F., Rubinoff, R., Schwamb, K. B., & Tambe, M. (1994, May). Intelligent automated agents for tactical air simulation: A progress report. *Proceedings of the Fourth Conference on Computer Generated Forces and Behavioral Representation* (pp. 69–78). Orlando, FL.

Rosenbloom, P. S., & Laird, J. E. (1986, August). Mapping explanation-based generalization onto Soar. *Proceedings of the Fifth National Conference on Artificial Intelligence* (pp. 561–567). Philadelphia: AAAI.

Rosenbloom, P. S., Laird, J. E., McDermott, J., Newell, A., & Orciuch, E. (1985). R1-Soar: An experiment in knowledge-intensive programming in a problem-solving architecture. *IEEE Transactions on Pattern Analysis and Machine Intelligence, 7*(5), 561–569.

Rosenbloom, P. S., Laird, J. E., & Newell, A. (1987). Knowledge-level learning in Soar. *Proceedings of AAAI-87.* American Association for Artificial Intelligence.

Rosenbloom, P. S., Laird, J. E., & Newell, A. (1988). Meta-levels in Soar. In *Meta-level architectures and reflection* (pp. 227–240). Amsterdam: North Holland.

Rosenbloom, P. S., Laird, J. E., & Newell, A. (Eds.). (1993). *The Soar papers: Research on integrated intelligence.* Cambridge, MA: MIT Press.

Rosenbloom, P. S., & Newell, A. (1982, August). Learning by chunking: Summary of a task and a model. *Proceedings of the Second National Conference on Artificial Intelligence* (pp. 255–257). Pittsburgh.

Rosenbloom, P. S., & Newell, A. (1987). Learning by chunking: A production-system model of practice. In D. Klahr, P. Langley, & R. Neches (Eds.), *Production system models of learning and development* (pp. 221–286). Cambridge, MA: Bradford Books/MIT Press.

Rosenbloom, P. S., & Newell, A. (1993). Symbolic architectures: Organization of intelligence. In T. A. Poggio & D. A. Glaser (Eds.), *Exploring brain functions: Models in neuroscience* (pp. 225–231). Chichester, England: Wiley.

Rosenbloom, P. S., Newell, A., & Laird, J. E. (1991). Towards the knowledge level in Soar: The role of the architecture in the use of knowledge. In K. VanLehn (Ed.), *Architectures for intelligence* (pp. 75–111). Hillsdale, NJ: Lawrence Erlbaum Associates.

Ruiz, D., & Newell, A. (1989). Tower-noticing triggers strategy-change in the Tower of Hanoi: A Soar model. *Proceedings of the 11th Annual Conference of the Cognitive Science Society* (pp. 522–529). Ann Arbor, MI.

Rychener, M. D., & Newell, A. (1977). An instructable production system: Basic design issues. In D. A. Waterman & F. Hayes-Roth (Eds.), *Pattern-directed inference systems* (pp. 135–153). New York: Academic Press.

Scales, D. (1986). *Efficient matching algorithms for the Soar/OPS5 production system* (Tech. Rep. No. KSL-86-47). Computer Science Department, Stanford University.

Simon, T., Newell, A., & Klahr, D. (1991). A computational account of children's learning about number conservation. In D. Fisher, M. Pazzani, & P. Langley (Eds.), *Concept formation: Knowledge and experience in unsupervised learning* (pp. 423–461). San Mateo, CA: Morgan Kaufmann.

Steier, D. M. (1987, August). Cypress-Soar: A case study in search and learning in algorithm design. *Proceedings of the Tenth International Joint Conference on Artificial Intelligence* (pp. 8–13). Milano, Italy: Morgan Kaufmann.

Steier, D. M. (1990). Intelligent architectures for integration. *Proceedings of the IEEE Conference on Systems Integration.*

Steier, D. M., Laird, J. E., Newell, A., Rosenbloom, P. S., Flynn, R. A., Golding, A., Polk, T. A., Shivers, O. G., Unruh, A., & Yost, G. R. (1987). Varieties of learning in Soar: 1987. In P. Langley (Ed.), *Proceedings of the Fourth International Workshop on Machine Learning* (pp. 300–311). Irvine, CA: Kaufmann.

Steier, D. M., & Newell, A. (1988, August). Integrating multiple sources of knowledge into Designer-Soar, an automatic algorithm designer. *Proceedings of the Seventh National Conference on Artificial Intelligence* (pp. 8–13). St. Paul, MN.

Stobie, I., Tambe, M., & Rosenbloom, P. S. (1993). Flexible integration of path-planning capabilities. In W. J. Wolfe & W. H. Chun (Eds.), *Mobile robots VII* (pp. 52–61). *Proceedings SPIE 1831.* Boston.

Tambe, M., Kalp, D., Gupta, A., Forgy, C., Milnes, B., & Newell, A. (1988, July). Soar/PSM-E: Investigating match parallelism in a learning production system. *Proceedings of the ACM/SIGPLAN Symposium on Parallel Programming: Experience with applications, languages, and systems* (pp. 146–160). New York: ACM Press.

Tambe, M., Newell, A., & Rosenbloom, P. S. (1990). The problem of expensive chunks and its solution by restricting expressiveness. *Machine Learning, 5*(4), 299–348.

Unruh, A., & Rosenbloom, P. S. (1989). Abstraction in problem solving and learning. *Proceedings of the Eleventh Joint Conference on Artificial Intelligence* (pp. 681–687). Detroit.

Ward, B. (1991). *ET-Soar: Toward an ITS for theory-based representations.* (Tech. Rep. No. CMU-CS-91-146). Pittsburgh: Carnegie Mellon University.

Washington, R., & Rosenbloom, P. S. (1989). *Applying problem solving and learning to diagnosis.* Unpublished manuscript, Computer Science Department, Stanford University.

Whitehead, A., & Russell, B. (1935). *Principia mathematica.* Cambridge: Cambridge University Press.

Wiesmeyer, M. (1991). An operator-based model of rapid visual counting. *Thirteenth Annual Conference of the Cognitive Science Society* (pp. 552–557). Chicago.

Wiesmeyer, M. (1992). *An operator-based model of covert visual attention.* Unpublished doctoral dissertation, University of Michigan, Ann Arbor.

Yost, G., & Newell, A. (1989). A problem space approach to expert system specification. *Proceedings of the Eleventh Joint Conference on Artificial Intelligence* (pp. 621–627). Detroit.

Chapter 2

The Study of
Cognitive Architecture

Zenon W. Pylyshyn
Rutgers University
University of Western Ontario

Although much psychological theorizing has always been implicitly concerned with architectural issues—for that is what we are concerned with when we ask "what kind of a physical system is the mind?"—Allen Newell was arguably the first scientist to try to say something in detail about the nature of this architecture. In my reading of the history of the field this began with his 1973 paper on production systems as models of control structures (Newell, 1973a). It was here that the idea of proposing a new primitive architecture and discovering the constraints that it imposes on processes first took shape in what we then referred to as a theory-laden programming language. I have more to say about this as a research strategy later. But I begin by reviewing the concept of cognitive architecture and summarizing some things I have already written about why it is such a fundamental problem in cognitive science. In fact, in my view, it is the central problem of cognitive science and must be addressed from the start or the science will continue to develop fragmented and ad hoc models for small domains of data.

I develop this claim by sketching some ideas I have argued at greater length elsewhere. Whether or not there is a distinct level of organization of an intelligent system that can be called its architecture is a long-term empirical question. What is not an empirical question, however, is whether the computational view of mind requires such a level. The very notion of computation, if taken literally, presupposes the existence of mechanisms whose variability is circumscribed in certain particular ways. Computation presupposes a fixed point in the organization of a system. This organization provides the physical mechanisms that carry out algorithmic processes which, in turn, manipulate symbol structures. How fixed this structure is and with respect to which parameters it is fixed or changeable is itself a fundamental question I address.

For any particular computational process there is only one level of the system's organization that corresponds to what we call its cognitive architecture. That is the level at which the states (datastructures) being processed are representational, and where the representations correspond to the objects of thought[1] (including percepts, memories, goals, beliefs, etc.). Notice that there may be many other levels of system organization below this, but that these do not constitute different cognitive architectures because their states do not represent cognitive contents. Rather, they correspond to various kinds of implementations, perhaps at the level of some abstract neurology, that realize (or implement) the cognitive architecture[2] or to biological (e.g., anatomical) or physical organizations. Similarly, there may be various levels of organization above this, but these need not constitute different cognitive architectures. They may represent the organization of the cognitive process itself, say in terms of hierarchies of subroutines, not a different level of the system structure. Also, various regularities in a system's behavior may result from the particular experience or knowledge that the system has or the way that knowledge was acquired and organized. On the other hand, they may also be genuinely architectural—they may represent different macroarchitectural organizations, as is the case with what Fodor (1983) called mental modules. Such organizations are fixed in a way that qualifies them as architectural properties—that is, they are cognitively impenetrable (discussed later).

I argue that for purposes of cognitive science, the difference between cognitive architecture and other levels of system organization is fundamen-

---

[1]It is nontrivial to specify what constitutes an "object of thought" as opposed to some other hypothetical construct or intervening variable—such as the internal stimuli of behaviorist theories (e.g., Osgoode's s_m; Osgoode, 1953). Roughly, objects of thought are intentional states in the sense of Fodor (1980) or Pylyshyn (1984), which represent equivalence classes of brain states characterized by semantic properties—that is, by what they are about. These semantic properties then appear in broad generalizations that capture the systematicity of behavior.

[2]Connectionists (e.g., Smolensky, 1988) sometimes talk about distributed representations as involving a level somewhere between implementation and full semantic representations—a sort of subcognitive level of representation. But this is a very misleading way of speaking. What so-called distributed representations do is encode some semantic objects in terms of sets of features (or "microfeatures," frequently statistically derived). They do this as a way of (i.e., in lieu of) representing the concepts or objects themselves. This is a feature-decomposition or a componential view of representation. However, in this case the components into which the represented objects are decomposed *are* the semantically interpreted symbols, they are not some special lower level of quasi-representation.

tal; without an independently motivated theory of the functional architecture, a computational system cannot purport to be a literal model of some cognitive process. There are three important reasons for this, which I sketch next:

- Architecture-relativity of algorithms and strong equivalence. For most cognitive scientists a computational model is intended to correspond to the cognitive process being modeled at what might roughly be characterized as the level of the *algorithm*[3] (this view of the proper level of correspondence is what is referred to as "strong equivalence"). Yet we cannot specify an algorithm without first making assumptions about the architecture: Algorithms are relativized to architectures. An algorithm can only be realized on an architecture that provides the appropriate primitive operations and functional organization. For example, the discrimination-tree algorithm can only be realized in what is called a register architecture, in which items are stored in registers and retrieved by address. Similarly, a binary search algorithm can only be realized in an architecture that provides primitive arithmetic operations (or at least an ordering over addresses and an operation for deciding the order of a pair of items). Because an algorithm always presuppose some architecture, this means that discovering the cognitive architecture of the mind must be a central concern of a cognitive science that takes its goal to be the discovery of mental processes or the algorithms used by the mind, or in other words the development of strongly equivalent models of cognition.

- Architecture as a theory of cognitive capacity. Another way of looking at the role of architecture is as a way of understanding the set of possible cognitive processes that are allowed by the structure of the brain. This means that to specify the cognitive architecture is to provide a theory of the *cognitive capacity* of an organism. The architecture provides the *cognitive constants*, whereas the algorithms and representations provide the free empirical parameters set by the incoming variable information. This allows one to explain both individual differences and differences across occasions and contexts as differences in *methods*, with architecture held constant (at least to a first approximation).

- Architecture as marking the boundary of representation-governed processes. Finally, for many of us, a fundamental working hypothesis of

---

[3]I use this term in order to build on the general understanding most of us have of a certain level of description of a process—for example, the level at which rules and basic operations are applied to encoded representations. The notion of algorithm, however, needs to be explicated with some care in cognitive science (see Pylyshyn, 1984), especially as the architecture of the mind is very likely to be quite different from that of modern computers, and hence mental algorithms will likely look very different from conventional ones as well.

cognitive science is that there exists an autonomous (or at least partially autonomous) domain of phenomena that can be explained in terms of representations (goals, beliefs, knowledge, perceptions, etc.) and algorithmic processes that operate over these representations. Another way to put this is to say that cognitive systems have a real level of organization at what Newell (1982) has called the "knowledge level." Reasoning and rational knowledge-dependent principles apply at this level. Because of this, any differences in behavioral regularities that can be shown to arise from such knowledge-dependent processes do not reveal properties of the architecture, which remain invariant with changes in goals and knowledge. Although this is really another way of saying the same thing that was already said earlier, the different emphasis leads to a novel methodological proposal, namely, that the architecture must be cognitively impenetrable. Differences in knowledge and goals do not lead directly to differences in architectures, although they can do so indirectly, as when one decides to take actions that themselves lead to such changes, such as deciding to ingest drugs.

I have discussed these claims in various places in the past decade. For present purposes I want to concentrate on the notion of architecture as defining cognitive capacity and then to discuss what approaches a scientist might take in understanding cognition if the distinction between architecture and process or representation is taken seriously. I begin with some general points about the purpose of theories.

One of the more insidious metascientific tenets of psychology (and social science generally) is the idea that our principle goal is to build theories that "account for variance" or make statistically reliable predictions. The main problem with that view is that it fails to distinguish what type of variance is theoretically relevant and it fails to distinguish the different ways in which statistical prediction can be accomplished. Two ways of predicting the same behavior need not be equivalent from the point of view of their explanatory adequacy. This is a point I argued in several places, including in my dispute with John Anderson (Anderson, 1978; Pylyshyn, 1979) concerning his claim that the form of mental representation is not empirically decidable. Consider the following examples.

Suppose you wished to model some cognitive phenomenon, such as perhaps reading. Among the data you might wish to account for is the way in which task latency varies with changes in the task (say, reading time as a function of certain aspects of grammatical structure). You might also wish to predict subjects' eye movements—both their latencies and their loci. Let us suppose there are several models that make approximately equivalent quantitative and qualitative predictions in this case. Is there anything to choose among them? Consider the following different ways in which the predictions might arise. (Each of these models is assumed to be implemented in a computer and takes ASCII encodings of the reading text as input. What it prints out and in what order varies with the model.)

1. The first model is a form of table lookup. It makes its predictions by storing a corpus of text in some form along with mean measurements obtained from previous subjects. (Or if storing the actual text seems like a cheat, imagine storing some skeletal information such as strings of form classes rather than the actual words.) This model prints out time-stamped gaze positions that constitute predictions of subjects' behavior while reading the input text.

2. A second model is based on an elaborate multivariate statistical predictor with a number of parameters whose values are estimated from independent data. The input to the predictor could be words, phrases, parenthesized word strings, n-gram frequency tables, or any other parameters shown to be correlated with the relevant dependent variables. As with the first model, this one also prints out a list of time-stamped gaze positions.

3. A third model actually goes through a sequence of states each of which specifies where the subject's gaze would be in that state, as well as the time that elapsed since the previous state. In this model the sequence of intermediate states that the model goes through in its processing corresponds to the sequence of states that a subject goes through. Thus the time associated with each gaze position is computed in the order in which the modeled process actually unfolds. The computation itself could be based on a stochastic mathematical model of state transitions—such as a Markov model used by the Harpy speech recognition system (Reddy, 1975).

4. A fourth and final model not only goes through the same sequence of states as the process it is modeling, but also the transitions from state to state are governed by the same information and the same principles or rules that determines the human process. In particular, what the model examines at gaze location L_i determines where its gaze will saccade to on the next location L_{i+1}, and the time between fixations is related in some systematic way to the number and nature of the operations performed during each state transition.

Clearly these models are not equivalent from the point of view of their explanatory power even if they are equally predictive over some particular body of data. There are two morals I wish to draw from this simple example. The first is that explanatory power is measured relative to a *set* of behaviors. The set need not even be representative—it need not be an ecologically valid sample. The reason is that when an organism is in its ecological niche the range of behaviors that it exhibits can be highly restricted by the range of environmental variations, whereas a general theory ought to account for the set of possible behaviors over different environments. In other words a general and principled cognitive theory must be able to account for the organism's *cognitive capacity*. This capacity is, by hypothesis, something that does not change over specified kinds of environmental variation (in particular, informational variation). Hence the capacity fixes certain parameters while others are fit to the particular circumstances. What models 1 and 2 fail to do is fix certain parameters while fitting a more restricted set to a specific situation.

The difference between the third and fourth models is more subtle and perhaps even more important. The reason we intuitively prefer the fourth model is that we implicitly accept that a computational model should do more than just mimic the behavior actually observed—even a sufficiently large sample of behavior. It ought to also model the *way* in which the behavior is caused in the organism. Even going through the same intermediate states as the organism being modeled is not enough unless the state changes occur for the same reason. This point has been central to some of my disagreements with models of mental imagery phenomena. I review some of these arguments for illustrative purposes because they are central to the issue of which regularities are due to the architecture and which are due to knowledge-dependent processes.

When subjects reason using images, they appear to be constrained in various ways; for example, the sequence and timing of various representational states appears to be regular and predictable. In fact, because the sequence is very much like that which unfolds in a real physical situation, this is often taken to suggest that there are architectural properties that mimic nature. For example, there are models that postulate mental analogs of space and other properties—a sort of natural harmony view of the mind.

I have discussed the shortcomings of this view at length. What I have objected to has been the particular assumptions about the architecture that are made in various models, rather than the idea that there may be something special (although unspecified) going on in imagery-based reasoning. I believe there is a lesson to be learned in these arguments concerning what architecture is supposed to be doing for us and how its properties show through in empirical phenomena.

A revealing example is the Shepard and Feng (1972) study of mental paper folding. In this experiment, subjects were shown a sheet of paper cut so that it could be folded to form a box. The sheets had marks on two edges and the subject's task was to say whether the two marks would join when the paper was folded along indicated edges. The reliable finding was that the amount of time to do the mental task increased linearly with the number of folds that it would actually take to bring the two relevant edges physically together. What Shepard and Feng concluded is that a "second order isomorphism" exists between the way subjects had to imagine the task and the way that physical constraints require it to be performed in reality. They further took this to be evidence that imagery mimics real actions in the world—a property that they refer to as "analogue."

Subjects in this task doubtlessly go through a sequence of mental representations corresponding to a sequence of individual folds. But the question still remains: Why do they do so? Or why does that constraint on the sequence of mental events hold? In the physical case it holds because of how the task must be done by hand and because of physical properties of real surfaces (e.g., they cannot interpenetrate without tearing). In the mental case it could hold for a number of quite different reasons, several of which are worth enumerating. Which one holds—that is, what the reason is for the observed constraint holding—is always an empirical issue. My point here is simply to indicate that it matters which interpretation is true because they each tell us something quite different about the nature of mind and of the mental process underlying the observation. Consider the following three options and their implications.

1. The observed constraint on the sequence of mental states that subjects go through might hold because that's one of the properties of mind— of the architecture deployed in image-based reasoning. This is certainly the way that many people interpret this and other similar results (e.g., Kosslyn, 1980). Another way of putting this is to attribute the regularity to properties of the medium in which the imaginal representation is embedded. Note, however, that if that were the case then the constraint could not be made to disappear by merely changing the way the task is understood, or the subjects' goals, or the knowledge that they have concerning the way that folding operations work. This would be the strongest and most interesting reason for the observed regularity because it would lead directly to specifying certain properties of the cognitive architecture—the basic mechanisms and resources of cognition.

2. Another reason that subjects might have gone through the sequence that they did is that they might have chosen to do the task this way for any of several reasons. On this story, subjects could equally have chosen to do it some other way, but instead chose to mimic the way the paper would have been folded in reality. I am not claiming that this is in fact the correct explanation in this case, but it is a logical possibility and would constitute quite a different interpretation of the observer constraint. I have, moreover, claimed that this is precisely the correct explanation for a variety of other imaginal processes that have been studied chronometrically in the literature.

For example, it has been widely observed that the amount of time it takes to switch attention from one place on an imagined map to another is a linear function of the actual distance on the corresponding real map. I have argued (Pylyshyn, 1981) that the best explanation for this is that subjects take the task to be the simulation of what would happen if they were looking at a map and scanning it for specified places. Because subjects know what would happen—for example, in order to look from A to B one has to scan the intermediate locations—they make this happen in their imagining. In other words, they imagine a sequence of events in which attention is first at A, then a small distance away from A, and so on as it approaches B. We showed empirically that if the subjects do not take their task to be the mimicking of such a scan, then the linearity constraint no longer holds. The same is true for a variety of other results—such as the finding that it takes longer to report features on an object imagined as small than on the same object imagined as large (Kosslyn, 1975).

3. A third possible reason for the sequence of mental representations being constrained as it is in the paper-folding task is that subjects' knowledge of the task domain is organized in such a way that the observed sequence is a natural consequence. For example, in order to do the paper-folding task one needs to know what happens when a sheet of paper is folded about a given line. But suppose, as seems reasonable, that people ordinarily only know what will happen when a single fold is made. In other words, knowledge of the results of folding is indexed to individual applications of the fold operator. Why should that be so? It could arise because of experience (we only experience the results of one fold at a time) or as a result of a general economy of storage (it would be wasteful to store the result of pairs of folds when this is rarely needed and it can be reconstructed from knowing the result of individual folds). However, in this case the architecture does not *require* this particular way of representing the knowledge of paper folding, and other organizations could also arise (e.g., origami experts who deal with folding problems on a frequent basis may well represent their knowledge in terms of clusters of folds).

The difference between explanation 1 and the other two is that the constraint in the latter two emerges from much more general properties of mind—for example, the property of being able to represent beliefs and to reason with them, and the property of tending to minimize memory demands for rarely needed information. If, however, the correct explanation of the constraint is 1—that it is due directly to a property of the cognitive architecture—then discovery of such constraints would provide important evidence for the nature of mind. Unfortunately, it turns out more often than not that observed regularities do not directly reflect the cognitive architecture, but rather the way that general architectural features interact with task demands and the structure of knowledge representation.

The problem is that human behavior is remarkably flexible. Almost no behavior (putting aside its physical form, which is clearly circumscribed by the laws of physics) can be excluded under all possible sets of beliefs and goals. In physics one can, at the very least, claim that certain motions or states are impossible. But within the domain of cognitive behaviors, almost nothing can be so excluded. It is because of this that the mind is better modeled by some form of resource-limited Turing machine than as any kind of a noncomputational physical device—including a biological machine—even though it is clearly implemented in tissue, just as a Turing machine must be implemented in some physical form to produce actual instances of behavior. When we undertake to specify a cognitive architecture what we are doing is attempting to discover *which* variant of a Turing machine corresponds to the mind. But because of the intimate way that architecture and encoded knowledge interact in generating behavior, it is a highly nontrivial matter to infer the architecture from behavioral regularities. In my observation there are three distinct approaches to this goal.

The first approach is to set boundary conditions on the architecture. This can serve as a powerful way of excluding putative architectural proposals. For example, the work sketched earlier criticizing certain imagery models (Pylyshyn, 1973, 1981) is in this category. By showing that observed regularities can be altered in a rational way by changing subjects' beliefs about the world or about the task (i.e., by showing that the regularities are cognitively penetrable), we demonstrate that the regularities do not reveal properties of the architecture.

The second approach is to attempt to uncover pieces of the architecture in areas where the behavioral regularity is modular or cognitively impenetrable. A considerable degree of success has been achieved in the study of early vision, preattentive perceptual processes, and arguably even the syntactic aspects of language processing in this way. In these areas provisional proposals have been made concerning properties of the architecture.

The third approach is by far the most ambitious. It is to use all one's intuitive appreciation of the computational problems and the primitive operations that human cognition might possess, to try to postulate a complete and uniform architecture for cognition. Allen Newell is the only person to have attempted so grand and ambitious a scheme. The reasons for taking this high road were also well articulated by Newell (1973b). They are that cognition cannot be adequately analyzed piecemeal by building models of little fragments of phenomena, because understanding cognition is highly holistic, and the small questions cannot be addressed without embedding them in a larger picture of what cognitive phenomena we ultimately hope to explain. This is not only the high road, it is also the most treacherous, because any mistaken assumptions one makes in the initial axioms will tend to permeate the rest of the theory.

And finally, as a generalization of the high road, one of the novel methodologies I have attempted to exploit is called the *minimal mechanism strategy* (Pylyshyn, 1989). This strategy attempts to find the apparently simplest mechanism (or set of operations) that are sufficient for carrying out a task that one has independent reason to believe must be carried out as part of the larger process being studied. To my mind Newell's (1973a) postulation of a production system (PSG) as a component of the rapid memory search task was one of the first examples of this strategy. My own attempt to postulate a set of primitive mechanisms that would allow one to build up a pattern-description and perceptual-motor coordination system is another example of this strategy.

In what follows, I attempt a quick analysis of these strategies and the general problem of methodology in the study of cognitive architecture.

DESIGN QUESTIONS ABOUT ARCHITECTURES

If we accept the importance of specifying the architecture in building models of the mind, we will sooner or later be faced with a number of important design decisions.

The Problem of Control Structure

This was not even seen as a problem for cognitive science until Newell's 1973 paper (Newell, 1973a). Where is there a problem about the control structure? It might seem that if you have a model in the form of a program in some language, you have specified all you need to; you don't have to worry about something called its "control structure." After all, the process unfolds as it does because of the sequence of commands you write down, including commands for branching on various conditions. What more is there? Newell argued very persuasively that such a program presupposes a particular (unstated) control structure that may not be empirically warranted. There are processes being carried out and memories being used that do not appear explicitly in the model presented in this way. Binding variables, passing arguments, tracking return addresses for subroutines and dynamic environments associated with individual subroutine calls involves considerable run-time resources and an elaborate machinery that remains hidden from view and unexamined. Newell proposed production systems in the first instance as a way to minimize the run-time mechanisms and to make explicit the assumptions concerning what controls the sequencing of the basic operations of a process.

The Problem of Choosing the Primitives

Choosing the basic operations in an architecture involves taking a position on certain general organizational structures and trade-offs, such as the discipline for invocation of operators, computation versus lookup, top-down versus bottom-up guidance, fetch-execute versus recognize-act cycle (see Newell, 1973a), constraints on message and argument passing, parallelism, synchronization, and so on. These are issues that have to be faced in the course of designing an architecture and are likely to be approached on an incremental or even trail-and-error basis.

The Problem of Uniformity Versus Multiplicity of Architectures

On the face of it there appears to be a need for different architectures whenever very different forms of representation are involved. For example, in early vision the representation appears to be somatotopic and the processing runs off as a parallel relaxation process across the image. Similarly, perceptual-motor coordination becomes almost reflexive and highly stratified for certain kinds of functions. There has also been a lot of speculation concerning whether imagery and other central functions that are sometimes found dissociated in pathological cases might not involve separate architectures. There is very little detailed study of these cases from a computational perspective, so the case for distinct architectures, although tempting, has not been made. At some level we know that something special is going on in these different skills. Yet at another level (say at the neural level) they are made of the same ingredients. Whether at the special level we call *cognitive architecture* they are distinct remains to be seen as more detailed theories are worked out—although I have some cautionary comments to make about this later.

The Problem of What Is Explicitly Represented

Behavior of a system can arise from the way it is structured or from the representations it contains. The distinction between these two was raised earlier in connection with the decision as to which aspects of behavior are attributable to the architecture and which to the knowledge that is represented. But sometimes the distinction is not empirically so clear, especially in the case of "rules." Here the question arises: Are the rules that are appealed to in explaining the behavior themselves represented, or do they merely describe how the system behaves? Are they explicit or implicit? Does the system "follow the rule" or merely "behave in accordance with the rule"? The difference is an important one because different entities are posited in each case. If a system "follows a rule" then the rule must be explicitly represented and accessed in generating the behavior. To use computer terminology, such a rule is being used in "interpreted" mode. Some encoding of the inscription of the rule is actually accessed and evaluated to generate an action. If the rule is explicitly encoded then the form of the rule is empirically significant. Consequently, the theory must assume some internal encoding scheme (or language) and hypothesize that the rule is encoded using this scheme. If the rule is implicit, or if it merely describes the behavior, then the form of the rule or the notation in which it is written has no empirical consequences. That is the case with, for example, the laws of physics. It is only the regularity that the laws describe that is significant, not their form. Any *extensionally equivalent* form is equally valid, though some may be more parsimonious or easier to compute or more transparent, and so on.

Given this distinction, the question then arises whether the rules that are hypothesized for human behavior are explicitly represented or are implicit. For example, are the rules of arithmetic, or grammar, or of social conduct, explicitly represented? The answer is not always so clear. Of course, if people can tell you the rule they are following (as in the case of such mathematical procedures as taking a square root, or in the case of traffic rules) then one can be reasonably sure that the rule is explicitly represented. But when the rule is tacit and not reportable by the subject, the issue is more difficult. There we need additional evidence that the form of the rule is important. Even in the case of grammar, where the realist view was promoted most strongly by Chomsky (see Pylyshyn, 1991b) the issue remains unclear. Whether or not the rules of grammar are explicitly represented and accessed in the course of speaking or comprehending remains an empirical question, the evidence for which is still tenuous (but see Pinker & Prince, 1988). On the other hand it is clear that at least some of what we call beliefs and goals are explicitly represented, and that the representational form must meet certain boundary conditions, such as compositionality and systematicity (see Fodor & Pylyshyn, 1988, for detailed arguments). This, in turn, places certain strong requirements on the nature of the architecture—requirements that are met by architectures that, like the original Turing machine, read and write symbolic expressions. Whether they can also be met by other classes of architecture remains to be seen—although none that have been proposed so far (e.g., connectionist or analogue architectures) meets these minimal conditions.

The Problem of Change

Human behavior is highly plastic. There are almost no behaviors of which a person is physically capable that could not be elicited under *some* circumstances, under some beliefs and goals. Changes in behaviors may have short- or long-term consequences on patterns of behavior. Some of these are rational responses to decisions taken with certain information and certain beliefs and utilities. Others are the result of more subtle manipulation of information and memory and the often tacit discovery of utilities of different actions (there is good reason to think that a great deal of human conditioning is of this sort—see Brewer, 1974). Others are the result of self-observation, playful discovery, or even trial and error. Others may be the result of a reorganization of knowledge into more efficient form—as occurs when explicitly represented knowledge of novices becomes compiled into larger automated structures ("chunks") in experts. And finally, some may be the result of changes in aspects of the architecture. The latter are changes that need not bear an informational or logical relation to the causal events. They may, for example, result from the effects of mere repetition or from simple exposure to triggering events—such as happens, for example, when instinctive behavior is released by appropriate triggers. Very little is known about which changes are architectural and which are a form of knowledge induction. For example, it is widely assumed that both natural concepts and linguistic competence are acquired through knowledge-induction rather than architecture-changing processes (see Piatelli-Palmarini, 1980). Historically, psychologists have referred to all of these forms of long-term behavior alterations as "learning." But a science that takes cognitive architecture as a central concern has to make distinctions among them, because they may represent quite different ways in which an architecture interacts with an environment to produce changes in state. The study of learning has been a sad chapter in the history of psychology, with the ironic consequence that the most studied problem in psychology remains the least understood.

SOME WAYS TO STUDY ARCHITECTURE

There is no formula for discovering the architecture of mind, any more than there is a formula for uncovering the secrets of the physical world. We cannot afford to leave out any source of evidence, including direct neurophysiological evidence. Indeed, we need to explore the space of options even more than we do in a mature science. It is in this spirit that I want to discuss some ways that people have studied cognitive architecture.

First there is the obvious distinction between the high road and the low road—between those, like Alan Newell, who would build large-scale unified theories of the mind, and those who take the approach much more common in psychology and build computational models that closely fit a set of fairly restricted empirical data. The minimodel builders very nearly have a monopoly in cognitive science, and perhaps there is good reason for it. It is here that the methodology of information-processing psychology is most developed (methods such as chronometric analysis, protocol analysis, stage analysis, and so on), and it is here that models lend themselves most readily to experimental tests. Over the past 50 years experimental psychology has been at its most innovative in the development of experimental paradigms for deciding between such binary properties as serial-versus-parallel, attentive-versus-preattentive, self-terminating versus exhaustive, and so on (Newell lists a much larger number of such oppositions).

I do not pass judgment on the relative merits of these two approaches (Allen Newell did a good job of that in his "Twenty Questions" paper; Newell, 1973b). However, I do want to comment on a couple of disadvantages of the low road. One problem with it, which David Marr (1982) was most articulate in pointing out, is that if we attempt to study mechanisms outside of their more general functional context, we are quite likely to misidentify the reason for a regularity—in the way I wrote about earlier when I referred to discovering why some regularity holds. In fact, if we look at a narrow range of behavioral contexts, it is entirely natural to postulate an architectural mechanism that generates each observed regularity. But the regularity may not reveal the constraints of a mechanism at all. It may simply reveal the existence of a very general capacity and the way it interacts with a particular task. John Anderson (1991) also argued for this point using some specific examples (see also the response by Simon, 1991). The principle that behavioral regularities may be attributable to interactions with the demands of the environment (or more precisely, with task demands) has been made in various contexts by ecological psychologists as far back as Egon Brunswick (1956) and reiterated by Simon (1969) in his famous ant-on-the-beach parable, as well as in Newell and Simon (1972). It is also the principal point behind my critique of a large class of experiments on "mental imagery" that purport to show that certain special (sometimes "analog") mechanisms are involved in reasoning with mental images (Pylyshyn, 1981). The lesson ought to have become etched in the minds of information-processing modelers, but it has not.

The reason for raising this issue at this time is that if one is concerned with methodologies for discovering properties of the cognitive architecture, one must be acutely aware of the fact that not all empirical regularities transparently reveal properties of the architecture. That's why injunctions such as "first find out what function is being computed" can have a salutary effect.

What this all leads to is that in attempting to understand the larger architectural problems, one is faced with a dilemma. If we look at particular experiments and try to model them, we run the risks already alluded to. But is there any other way to proceed? All I can do is reiterate a general injunction concerning minimizing commitment too early and avoiding the temptation to posit a mechanism for each reliable empirical regularity. We have already seen—in discussing the mental imagery research—that many robust behavioral regularities do not reveal properties of the architecture because they can be shown to be cognitively penetrable, and hence knowledge dependent. Cognitive penetrability remains a major diagnostic tool in determining whether a regularity arises from some architectural feature or at least in part from a knowledge-based cognitive process. The earliest application of this criterion (although not under that name) was the demonstration that the psychophysical threshold (see the historical review of this notion by Corso, 1963) did not reveal a property of the architecture, but was confounded with a cognitive decision process that could be penetrated by changes in beliefs and utilities. This was the important contribution of signal detection theory (Green & Swets, 1966).

In what follows, I sketch some ideas about the high road for inferring aspects of the architecture. In doing this I refer to two general case studies. The first comes from Newell's own work (as described mainly in Newell, 1990) and shows how as a theory matures, more and more of the empirical phenomena that were assumed to directly reflect architectural properties may turn out to be interaction effects among other factors. The second example is from my own work on visual location indexes and illustrates a research strategy that I call the *minimal mechanism strategy*.

WHEN AND WHY TO POSIT PARTICULAR ARCHITECTURAL PROPERTIES

Newell (1990) distinguished between what he called "technological limitations" of an architecture and designed-induced functional limitations. The difference is subtle but important. Technological limitations are arbitrary brute facts about such things as resources available to the computational machinery. There is no point asking why such a limitation occurs—beyond perhaps asking for neural substrates. If we say that short-term memory (STM) has a certain size, say seven plus or minus two symbols, then we are claiming such a brute fact about how the brain happens to be structured.[4] On the other hand, it may also be possible to explain the phenomena of STM by appealing to the way that task requirements interact with the design principles of an intelligence system—principles that are independently motivated because of what the system has to be able to accomplish in dealing with the world, solving problems, learning, and so on. In the case of Soar, STM phenomena occur as a side effect of other more principled design properties, for example, because symbols must be kept available as long as

---

[4]Asking why STM has a capacity of seven symbols rather than nine would be just like asking why we have five fingers on each hand instead of four or six. The best answer may well be that it had to be some number and five did not put us at a survival disadvantage. Many people believe there has to be a teleological or evolutionary explanation for all properties of an organism. But that is patently false, because there are indeterminately many properties that will always remain unaccounted for after all evolutionary factors are taken into account.

a relevant subgoal is active and they disappear because the working memory changes with each new production cycle, and so on.

Whether or not this particular story is correct, the idea of allowing shortcomings—deviations from normative or optimality principles—to derive from interacting functional requirements is surely a good strategy. It's much like the strategy I have always advocated with respect to appealing to stochastic mechanisms: Although some psychological mechanisms and processes may be inherently stochastic, a reasonable research strategy is to resist appealing to stochastic notions until forced to do so because of the inability of deterministic structural hypotheses to deal with the phenomena. The reason for such a conservative strategy in the case of stochastic mechanisms is the same as the reason for resisting positing arbitrary technological limitations as a first move, namely, that it is too easy to merely stipulate properties that map directly onto empirical phenomena and in so doing miss deeper principles that have a wider domain of applicability but that relate to the phenomena in question by interacting with particulars of the task at hand. We have already seen examples of this principle in connection with the discussion of hypotheses concerning analogue mechanisms for visual imagery phenomena.

Before moving on to my own work, I want briefly to elaborate this claim that empirical observations may not directly reflect properties of underlying mechanisms. One example that Newell commented on some years ago (Newell, 1986) concerns the modularity of cognition. The first-order evidence suggests that the cognitive system may be completely interdependent—with perception, language processing, and other cognitive skills all talking to one another and all depending on reasoning. Subsequent refinement of the evidence suggests a second-order view that when the proper distinctions are made (say, between detection and response selection or between parsing and understanding sentences) there is much reason to believe that the cognitive system is architecturally highly restricted with respect to which processes can talk to which. This leads naturally to a stage view wherein certain subprocesses must be completed without the intervention of sources of knowledge outside those designated for that stage (or perhaps stored inside that module). Although I believe that something like that is true of vision, I acknowledge that some forms of apparent modularity (cognitive impenetrability of certain subprocesses) need not arise directly from architectural constraints. They may arise indirectly from requirements that the architecture imposes on such things as argument passing, as well as on task-induced requirements on ordering of processes, on clustering of expert knowledge in subprocesses, and so on. Of course, in the end these do depend on the architecture, because without an appropriate architecture none of the observed behavior would occur. The point is that the observed regularities need not reveal properties of the architecture directly because the observations may arise from the way some (perhaps accidental) architectural feature interacts with knowledge, habits, task demands, and other factors.

As Newell (1990) pointed out, certain phenomena of encapsulation, although real enough, may in the end be compatible with a uniform architecture that exhibits modularity as a consequence of the way that the general architectural constraints interact with other factors. For example, modularity may result from (a) the development of compiled expertise through chunking of past experience (which itself depends on the architecture, though in a less direct way) and (b) the temporal order in which processes are executed, which itself may be a product of both architecture and knowledge represented (as I suggested in discussing the Shepard and Feng experiment). The last word is not in on exactly how architectural constraints manifest themselves in what appears to be clearly a "fragmented" system of processing. But the possibility that it too is an interaction effect remains a serious contender here, as it is in the case of other phenomena like STM. Of course, what is needed is not just the recognition of a logical possibility but a specific proposal as we have in the case of STM. For what it's worth, my own bet is that in areas such as early vision and certain perceptual-motor effects, the encapsulation is a symptom of real architectural differences, although in other putative areas (e.g., face recognition, mental imagery) they are interaction effects. But only time will tell.

THE MINIMAL MECHANISM STRATEGY AND FINST INDEX THEORY

Finally, I want to devote some time to the question of methodology for taking the high road in designing a cognitive architecture. In recent years I adopted a strategy I believe bears a resemblance to that which motivated Newell's first exploration in the design of a general cognitive architecture. In doing this I confined myself to relatively early stages in vision—in particular to the interface between the early stage in vision that is preattentive, automatic, impenetrable, and perhaps parallel, and later stages where processes become serial and under at least some minimal voluntary control. The strategy I have adopted is one I refer to as a *minimum mechanism strategy*, which represents at least one relatively high-road approach toward the difficult but crucial problem of inferring aspects of the cognitive architecture.

The approach is something like that taken by Alan Turing in his famous paper on the Entscheidungsproblem. In that paper, Turing asked himself, What are the minimal essential operations that a mathematician must perform in doing proofs? Turing then postulated a mechanism based on these minimal operations: The mechanism can write symbols on a tape, it can move the tape by one unit, and it can change its state as a function of its current state and the symbol currently under its read head. The reasoning that went into this design was actually made explicit in Turing's paper.

Newell (and earlier Newell and Simon) also considered what the very least was that could be assumed in building a system that did not presuppose a hidden run-time control structure. This led to the idea of building an architecture based on a recognize-act cycle—an idea that turned out to have many interesting side effects. For example, in attempting to design a process that would run on such an architecture and produce the observed behavioral regularity in a rapid memory search task, Newell (1972a) was led to a novel hypothesis concerning the locus of the serial exhaustive search observations. This hypothesis (called the *decoding hypothesis*) was totally natural in the production system architecture, although it would have seemed unmotivated in a conventional architecture.

Another example of this minimalist strategy was Marr and Nishihara's (1976) proposal for a mechanism that brings a three-dimensional representation of an image into correspondence with a canonical model of the object for purposes of recognition. The problem they addressed is how a viewer-centered image (with depth information) could be placed into canonical orientation in order to be looked up in a table of shapes so the object could be identified. This proposal postulates a simple and primitive piecewise image-rotation mechanism. This mechanism takes a pair of vectors in the three-dimensional representation and computes their projection after they have been rotated by a small angle about a reference axis called a Spasar. Using this simple idea they were able to offer the beginnings of a theory of object recognition by shape, as well as suggest an account of the Shepard and Metzler (1971) mental rotation experiments.

In all these cases, what is involved is the postulation of a mechanism that is extremely primitive yet appears to be sufficient for the task at hand. Because the notion of simplicity is not well defined, such mechanisms are not unique and their utility ultimately depends on how well the complexity of processes built out of them matches the empirically observed complexity of psychological processes. Despite the nonuniqueness of the selection of a primitive basis, the minimal mechanism strategy represents a departure from the usual way of building models to account for experimental findings. It follows the principle of least commitment in the design of an architecture. If the evidence requires a more complex basis, this can be provided without abandoning the original model, because complex operators can be built out of the simpler ones if the latter are appropriately chosen to be complete.

This is not the time nor the place to go into details of the mechanism we have proposed as part of an early vision process. However, a brief sketch may provide a flavor of what is involved. The mechanism in question is one that binds internal variables to primitive features in a visual scene. In so doing it individuates these features without necessarily recognizing their type nor encoding their location in some coordinate frame of reference. Because the binding is assumed to be sticky and once assigned remains with the feature independent of its retinal location, the postulated pointer (called a FINST) provides a way to refer to occupied places in a scene.

Although the idea is extremely elementary, it turns out to have broad implications for a number of visual phenomena, including parallel tracking of multiple targets, stability of the visual world with eye movements, certain image scanning experiments, subitizing, and the beginnings of a view of cross-modality binding of locations for perceptual-motor coordination. These implications are discussed in Pylyshyn (1989). I do not have space here to do more than sketch the basic idea and suggest why it has the broad ramifications.

A simple way to illustrate what is intended by such an indexing mechanism is to describe an experiment showing that multiple items can be tracked simultaneously. In these studies, which have now been repeated in dozens of ways and by several investigators (Pylyshyn & Storm, 1988; Yantis, 1992), subjects are shown a set of 10–15 identical objects on a screen. A subset of 3–5 of them is briefly distinguished, say, by flashing them. Then all objects begin to move about in random noncolliding motion (Brownian motion). Subjects are required to track the subset (usually with instructions not to move their eyes). Some time later a response is required that depends on subjects' having successfully tracked all the moving objects. For example, in a typical experiment one of the items flashes or changes shape. Subjects' task is to say whether it was a member of the previously distinct subset. Subjects are able to perform better than chance under a variety of conditions where they are unlikely to have been tracking by continuously scanning all targets in round-robin fashion. We concluded (Pylyshyn & Storm, 1988) that they must have tracked all 4 (or perhaps 5) objects simultaneously.

The model we have in mind is extremely simple, although it has wide ramifications. It is just this. Some small number of primitive visual features attract indices from a finite pool of available internal names or pointers. These indices provide a way to access the objects in the visual field—even if the objects are in motion. Such access is primitive and occurs despite the fact that the indexed objects need not be classified nor their locations encoded in an explicit (e.g., Cartesian coordinate) fashion. What the index provides is a way to strobe the indexed places for additional properties (a network model of a possible mechanism is presented in Acton & Eagleson, 1993). The basic assumption is that no visual properties of a scene can be computed unless the features involved are first indexed in this primitive way.

What indices allow the visual system to do is leave some of the memory in the scene instead of having to encode all the details. In that sense it provides a primitive way of "situating" vision (to use currently popular jargon). It also provides a way to convert visualization phenomena (e.g., "mental scanning" results such as already discussed) into partially visual phenomena. By indexing places in a real visual field, subjects can actually scan their attention to those places and hence generate what appears to be "mental scanning" phenomena (Kosslyn, 1973). But without indices, no relative locations can be computed and no directed movement of attention or eye movements can be carried out, thus explaining the instability of vision in the ganzfeld (Avant, 1965).

Similarly, the phenomenon of *subitizing* can be viewed as counting the number of indexes in use. According to this view, when determining the cardinality of features in the subitizing range subjects need not search for the features in the visual scene—providing they are already indexed. That is why subitizing is faster than counting, relatively insensitive to spatial layout, and not possible when the features do not induce indices (i.e., when they are not what are called "popout" features), as reported in Trick and Pylyshyn (1994).

Many experiments have been done to explore the conditions under which indices are automatically attracted to features (e.g., it appears that onsets and luminance changes attract indexes but equiluminant color changes do not). Also, in computing certain relational properties that require serial processing (e.g., what Ullman, 1979, calls "visual routines"), the relevant places in the scene must first be indexed, otherwise there is no way to direct processing serially to these features.

If we do assume the existence of such indices, however, we also have a way to understand what happens when a "mental image" is "superimposed" on a visual scene. These experiments include the "mental scanning" phenomena studied by Kosslyn (which remain robust when an actual visual display is involved), as well as a variety of superposition phenomena—ranging from motor adaptation to imagined arm locations (Finke, 1979), to comparison of seen and imagined patterns (Hayes, 1972; Shepard & Podgorny, 1978), to illusions produced by imagining features superimposed on visual ones (Bernbaum & Chung, 1981). In these and other such cases, what appears to be happening is that imagined patterns are being superimposed on visually present ones. This experience of visual projection notwithstanding, however, we do not need to posit a pictorial object (the mental image) superimposed upon another pictorial object (the perceived image) in order to obtain the visual-like effects observed in these experiments. As long as we have a way of binding representations of features (regardless of the form that this representation takes) to particular places in a scene, we provide a way for actual space to act as a framework for locating imaginal features. Because of this, we make it possible to convert aspects of the process of inspecting the merged information into an actual visual process. Take, for example, the image-scanning experiment. As long as subjects can think "*this place* is where the lighthouse is and *that place* is where the beach is . . ." (where the locatives are replaced by FINST indices to features in the scene), they can move attention or even their gaze to the indexed places—thereby taking more time when the distance is greater. Other examples were discussed in Pylyshyn (1989).

Finally, indices form the basis for perceptual motor control. According to our working hypothesis, they are the mechanism by which places in space can be bound to internal arguments both for visual predicates and for cross-modality binding of arguments in motor commands. Thus the FINST mechanism is an aspect of the architecture of early vision and motor control—a part of the cognitive system that Newell (1990) speculated might require special mechanisms.

The minimal mechanism strategy suggests that even when it is not possible to obtain direct evidence for a particular mechanism, such as FINSTs (at least, no more direct than the multiple-object tracking results), positing such a mechanism is justified when it allows one to construct certain processes that otherwise would remain a mystery. This is in fact just an instance of the hypothetico–deductive method, with the additional twist that we are giving particular weight to the sufficiency criterion, and attempting to begin with the simplest set of operations sufficient for the task—even if we might expect that the actually mechanisms are more complex and contain the hypothesized operations as just one logical component.

CONCLUSION

Psychologists have typically been a timid bunch, unwilling to make bold hypotheses or sharp distinctions. I have argued that progress in cognitive science depends crucially on making at least one critical distinction. It's the distinction between cognitive process and cognitive architecture. There are many ways to view this distinction. Moreover, as with any empirical distinction, we find that it leaks at its edges and its joints and has to be patched carefully in order to continue providing insights without getting bogged down in border disputes.

The message of this chapter has been that the very possibility of a strong form of computational psychology—where the computational process literally mirrors, or is *strongly equivalent* to, the cognitive process being modeled— depends on our being able to independently motivate the properties of the architecture that supports the processes we are modeling. Without such independent motivation, the processes that we postulate are implicitly conditioned by the computer languages and architectures that we happen to have around—which were not designed with psychological modeling in mind.

Having said that, we now are faced with the enormity of the task at hand. For to design a cognitive architecture is to develop a theory of the mind's relatively fixed capacities—those capacities whose modification does not follow the same principles as the modification of behavior produced by the mind's apprehension of new information, knowledge and goals. The border between architectural change and knowledge-based (or inductive) change is difficult enough to adjudicate in practice. But the task of inferring the architectural structure that underwrites cognitive processes is even more difficult insofar as it must be quite indirect—although no more difficult that the task of uncovering the fixed principles in any domain. We can approach this task in various ways. We can develop small-scale models as we have been doing over the past half century, and remain wary that any architecture we hypothesize (or implicitly assume) must meet certain boundary conditions—such as being cognitively impenetrable. We can then subject our assumed architectural mechanisms to these criteria and see if they stand up to scrutiny (as was done in Pylyshyn, 1981, 1991a).

Alternatively, we can take the bold step of attempting to design a complete architecture from whole cloth and subject it to the widest range of possible investigations by attempting to build working models of many different tasks. This is the strategy that Allen Newell took. An architecture posited de novo is bound to be wrong both in detail and likely even in more basic ways, and we must be prepared to iterate the process of refinement tirelessly. But unless we take on that task, we may be relegating psychology to the ranks of taxonomic and descriptive sciences, like botany and zoology. I am not suggesting that this would be a terrible disaster—it may even be the only option that will work in the end and it may have considerable practical importance. But for those of us who hope that cognition and computation are both natural scientific domains for which common causal laws may eventually be formulated, this seems like a poor working hypothesis. From this perspective, Newell's seminal works seem like a proper step, although perhaps a small step, in the right direction.

REFERENCES

Acton, B. J., & Eagleson, R. A. (1993). A network model of spatial indexing. *Investigative Opthalmology and Visual Science, 34* (item 413), p. 784.

Anderson, J. R. (1978). Arguments concerning representations for mental imagery. *Psychological Review, 85*, 249–277.

Anderson, J. R. (1991). The place of cognitive architecture in a rational analysis. In K. VanLehn (Ed.), *Architectures for intelligence* (pp. 1–24). Hillsdale, NJ: Lawrence Erlbaum Associates.

Avant, L. L. (1965). Vision in the Ganzfeld. *Psychological Bulletin, 64*, 246–258.

Bernbaum, K., & Chung, C. S. (1981). Muller-Lyer illusion induced by imagination. *Journal of Mental Imagery, 5*, 125–128.

Brewer, W. F. (1974). There is no convincing evidence for operant or classical conditioning in adult humans. In W. B. Weiner & D. S. Palermo (Eds.), *Cognition and symbolic processes* (pp. 1–33). Hillsdale, NJ: Lawrence Erlbaum Associates.

Brunswick, E. (1956). *Perception and the representative design of psychological experiments.* Berkeley, CA: University of California Press.

Corso, J. F. (1963). A theoretico-historical review of the threshold concept. *Psychological Bulletin, 60,* 356–370.

Finke, R. A. (1979). The functional equivalence of mental images and errors of movement. *Cognitive Psychology, 11,* 235–264.

Fodor, J. A. (1980). *Representations.* Cambridge, MA: MIT Press.

Fodor, J. A. (1983). *The modularity of mind: An essay on faculty psychology.* Cambridge, MA: MIT Press.

Fodor, J. A., & Pylyshyn, Z. W. (1988). Connectionism and cognitive architecture: A critical analysis. *Cognition, 28,* 3–71.

Green, D. M., & Swets, J. A. (1966). *Signal detection theory and psychophysics.* New York: Wiley.

Hayes, J. R. (1972). On the function of visual imagery in elementary mathematics. In W. Chase (Ed.), *Visual information processing* (pp. 177–211). New York: Academic Press.

Kosslyn, S. M. (1973). Scanning visual images: Some structural implications. *Perception and Psychophysics, 15,* 90–94.

Kosslyn, S. M. (1975). The information represented in visual images. *Cognitive Psychology, 7,* 341–370.

Kosslyn, S. M. (1980). *Image and mind.* Cambridge, MA: Harvard University Press.

Marr, D. (1982). *Vision.* San Francisco: W. H. Freeman.

Marr, D., & Nishihara, H. K. (1976). *Representation and recognition of spatial organization of three-dimensional shapes* (A.I. Memo 377). Cambridge, MA: MIT Artificial Intelligence Laboratory.

Newell, A. (1973a). Production systems: Models of control structures. In W. Chase (Ed.), *Visual information processing* (pp. 463–515). New York: Academic Press.

Newell, A. (1973b). Why you can't play twenty questions with nature and win. In W. Chase (Ed.), *Visual information processing* (pp. 283–305). New York: Academic Press.

Newell, A. (1982). The knowledge level. *Artificial Intelligence, 18,* 1, 87–127.

Newell, A. (1986). General discussion of modularity of mind. In Z. W. Pylyshyn & W. Demopoulos (Eds.), *Meaning and cognitive structure: Issues in the computational theory of mind* (pp. 153–156). Norwood, NJ: Ablex.

Newell, A. (1990). *Unified theories of cognition.* Cambridge, MA: Harvard University Press.

Newell, A., & Simon, H. A. (1972). *Human problem solving.* Englewood Cliffs, NJ: Prentice Hall.

Osgoode, C. E. (1953). *Method and theory in experimental psychology.* New York: Oxford University Press.

Piatelli-Palmarini, M. (Ed.). (1980). *Language and learning: The debate between Jean Piaget and Noam Chomsky.* Cambridge, MA: Harvard University Press.

Pinker, S., & Prince, A. (1988). On language and connectionism: Analysis of a parallel distributed processing model of language acquisition. *Cognition, 28,* 73–194.

Pylyshyn, Z. W. (1973). What the mind's eye tells the mind's brain: A critique of mental imagery. *Psychological Bulletin, 80,* 1–24.

Pylyshyn, Z. W. (1979). Validating computational models: A critique of Anderson's indeterminacy of representation claim. *Psychological Review, 86,* 4, 383–394.

Pylyshyn, Z. W. (1981). The imagery debate: Analogue media versus tacit knowledge. *Psychological Review, 88,* 16–45.

Pylyshyn, Z. W. (1984). *Computation and cognition.* Cambridge, MA: MIT Press.

Pylyshyn, Z. W. (1989). The role of spatial indexes in spatial perception: A sketch of the FINST spatial indexing model. *Cognition, 32,* 65–97.

Pylyshyn, Z. W. (1991a). The role of cognitive architecture in theories of cognition. In K. VanLehn (Ed.), *Architectures for intelligence* (pp. 189–224). Hillsdale, NJ: Lawrence Erlbaum Associates.

Pylyshyn, Z. W. (1991b). Rules and representations: Chomsky and representational realism. In A. Kashir (Ed.), *The Chomskian turn* (pp. 231–251). Oxford: Basic Blackwell.

Pylyshyn, Z. W., & Storm, R. W. (1988). Tracking multiple independent targets: Evidence for a parallel tracking mechanism. *Spatial Vision, 3*(3), 1–19.

Reddy, D. R. (1975). *Speech recognition.* New York: Academic Press.

Shepard, R. N., & Feng, C. (1972). A chronometric study of mental paper folding. *Cognitive Psychology, 3,* 228–243.

Shepard, R. N., & Metzler, J. (1971). Mental rotation of three-dimensional objects. *Science, 171,* 701–703.

Shepard, R. N., & Podgorny, P. (1978). Cognitive processes that resemble perceptual processes. In W. K. Estes (Ed.), *Handbook of learning and cognitive processes* (Vol. 5, pp. 189–229). Hillsdale, NJ: Lawrence Erlbaum Associates.

Simon, H. A. (1969). *The sciences of the artificial.* Cambridge, MA: MIT Press.

Simon, H. A. (1991). Cognitive architectures and rational analysis: comment. In K. VanLehn (Ed.), *Architectures for intelligence* (pp. 25–40). Hillsdale, NJ: Lawrence Erlbaum Associates.

Smolensky, P. (1988). On the proper treatment of connectionism. *Behavioral and Brain Sciences, 11,* 1–74.

Trick, L. M., & Pylyshyn, Z. W. (1994). Why are small and large numbers enumerated differently? A limited capacity preattentive stage in vision. *Psychological Review, 101*(1), 1–23.

Ullman, S. (1979). Visual routines. *Cognition, 18,* 97–159.

Yantis, S. (1992). Multielement visual tracking: Attention and perceptual organization. *Cognitive Psychology, 24,* 295–330.

DISCUSSION

Architecture Matters:
What Soar Has to Say
About Modularity

Richard L. Lewis
Princeton University

According to Zenon Pylyshyn, Allen Newell took the high road in psychology by working on a theory of the mind intended to cover a wide range of cognitive behavior. Both Newell and Pylyshyn have put forth convincing arguments about the merits of such a research path, and the central role that cognitive architecture plays in it (Newell, 1973a, 1973b, 1990; Pylyshyn, 1984, and Chapter 2, this volume). Theories of architecture allow one to develop detailed models of local phenomena while addressing global issues about the mind. One such issue that Pylyshyn has raised with respect to Soar is modularity (Pylyshyn, 1991, 1993). The challenge is clear: How can a uniform theory such as Soar be right in the face of evidence that the mind is, in at least some respects, modular? As Pylyshyn points out, Newell (1990) began to answer this in his discussion of Fodor's 1983 monograph. There are two major parts to the answer. First, Soar can indeed admit additional processing modules because it is a bus-oriented system (the working memory is the bus); Newell (1990) speculated that imagery, for example, might require such a special system. Second, the present set of mechanisms underlying central cognition in Soar already exhibit some features of modularity. The purpose of this chapter is to further explore modularity and Soar along this path by considering in some detail one area of psycholinguistics—sentence processing—where modularity has been a central concern, and asking how Soar could account for the pattern of results that has accumulated.

MODULARITY IN SENTENCE PROCESSING

In sentence processing (online parsing and comprehension), the basic modularity issue is whether there is an *autonomous syntactic parser* that operates automatically without appeal to semantic or contextual knowledge sources (Garfield, 1989). Such a component would be a prime example of a cognitive module (or an *input analyzer* in Fodor's terms). The alternative view is that comprehension is an interactive process (Marslen-Wilson, 1975) in which multiple knowledge sources (including syntax) interact to produce the meaning. The critical issue is not whether knowledge sources are applied, but how. Modularity does not claim that semantics and context are unnecessary parts of the comprehension process, but simply that syntactic processing occurs independently of the other knowledge sources. Similarly, an interactive account does not deny the importance of syntactic knowledge, but does not grant it distinguished status as a separate module.

The primary way psycholinguists have attempted to address this issue is to study local ambiguity resolution. How are knowledge sources applied to resolve ambiguities? The logic is as follows: If online syntactic structuring of ambiguous material is unaffected by context or semantics, then this suggests an autonomous syntax module. If online resolution is affected by nonsyntactic information, then this suggests an interactive comprehension architecture.

Do the data favor a modular or interactive architecture? Consider briefly just a few studies. Tyler and Marslen-Wilson (1977) presented striking evidence in favor of an interactive architecture by demonstrating the rapid effect context can have on syntactic processing. Subjects heard sentence fragments like the following, ending with ambiguous strings (in italics):

(1) (a) If you walk too near the runway, *landing planes* . . .
    (b) If you've been trained as a pilot, *landing planes* . . .

At the offset of the final word in the ambiguous phrase (*planes*), a probe word was visually presented. The word was a verb that was a continuation of the sentence. The subject's task was to name the verb. The contextually appropriate continuation is *are* for (1a) and *is* for (1b). Appropriate continuations had a naming latency advantage over inappropriate continuations, indicating that the context had a rapid effect on the initial analysis of the ambiguous string. Further evidence of context effects came from Crain and Steedman (1985), who used a different technique (rapid grammaticality judgment) to show that the number of referents established in the context can affect the perceived grammaticality of a locally ambiguous sentence.[1]

---

[1]Although these experiments have been criticized for not measuring immediate online processing, they still present challenging data for a modular approach; see Steedman and Altmann (1989).

Evidence for syntactic modularity has accumulated as well. One well-known study by Ferreira and Clifton (1986) presented evidence that ambiguous noun phrase-verb (NP-V) strings are always interpreted as subject-verb, regardless of the implausibility or contextual inconsistency of this reading. Material included sentences such as:

(2) (a) The evidence examined by the lawyer turned out to be unreliable.
     (b) The defendant examined by the lawyer turned out to be unreliable.

In (2a), the inanimacy of *evidence* makes it implausible that the evidence was doing the examining. Yet, increased reading times (over unambiguous controls) were detected in both cases at the disambiguating region (the *by*-phrase), suggesting that subjects incorrectly interpreted the first verb as the main verb, regardless of the animacy of the initial NP.

Are we still waiting for the conclusive experiment to settle the modularity debate? The equivocal nature of the data is reflected in two relatively recent reviews of the sentence-processing field (Altmann, 1989; Frazier, 1987). The reviewers came to rather different conclusions concerning modularity, a difference hardly due to the 2-year gap in publication. Should the field have taken more seriously Newell's warnings about pursuing simple binary oppositions in the absence of more complete processing theories (Newell, 1973b)? There has been indication that researchers are acknowledging that things are probably more complex than a modular/interactive dichotomy. For example, Britt, Perfetti, Garrod, and Rayner (1992) explored the possibility that the processing is different depending on the kind of syntactic construction. Holbrook, Eiselt, and Mahesh (1992) described a model with a single processor and independent knowledge sources. The resulting theories look like a mix of interactive and modular approaches.

In fact, Just and Carpenter (1992) may have come close to providing that debate-settling experimental data, though it settles the debate by rendering it moot. Using material identical to (2), they found that some subjects did use semantic information online (appearing nonmodular), whereas some subjects did not (appearing modular). These data seem hard to reconcile with either a purely modular or purely interactive theory, if such theories are taken to posit universal architectural principles. The first-order characterization to be drawn from these data, along with the rest of the apparently conflicting data from the past two decades, is that human sentence processing can exhibit both modular and interactive effects.[2]

---

[2]The main point of the Just and Carpenter study was to demonstrate a correlation between subject performance on the modularity task and the reading span task, and subsequently to explain the data by differences in working memory capacity. I do not address this correlation here. It is not yet clear to what extent all modular/interactive effects can be attributed to capacity constraints. See also Just, Carpenter, and Hemphill (Chapter 5) and Young (Discussion following Chapter 5) in this volume.

LANGUAGE COMPREHENSION IN SOAR

Consider now how Soar (Laird, Newell, & Rosenbloom, 1987; Newell, 1990) comprehends language. Soar must map an incoming utterance to its contextualized meaning. It does this by applying *comprehension operators* to the words as they come in, producing a temporary meaning structure in working memory. Given the real-time immediacy constraint (Just & Carpenter, 1987), Soar must accomplish this mapping with just a few (about two to five) operators per word. There is not time for more processing, given the temporal mapping of Soar onto human cognition (operators take ~50–100 ms). Furthermore, the comprehension operators must bring all the relevant knowledge sources to bear—syntactic, lexical, semantic, contextual—because there are no other online processes that will apply this knowledge. Finally, these operators must arise via chunking over more deliberate comprehension spaces that represent the multiple knowledge sources. Soar treats language as a skill that gets better over time.

Figure 1 shows the basic structure of NL-Soar, a model that has the characteristics just sketched (Newell, 1990; Lehman, Lewis, & Newell, 1991a, 1991b; Lewis, 1993). The figure also shows that, in addition to a meaning representation (the situation model), NL-Soar also produces a representation of the syntactic structure of the utterance (the utterance model), for all the familiar functional reasons.

What is the nature of the comprehension operators? Given that two different models are built up by these operators during comprehension, one natural scheme is to have two different kinds of operators: *u-constructors*, which build the utterance model, and *s-constructors*, which build the situation model. The u-constructors take as input the results of lexical access and the current utterance model, and produce an updated utterance model. The s-constructors take as input the current utterance and situation models and produce an updated situation model.[3]

It is now possible to describe the distribution of knowledge in the system in terms of problem space functions. Syntactic knowledge resides primarily in the *proposal* and *application* of the u-constructors. Semantic interpretation knowledge resides in the proposal and application of the s-constructors; in linguistic terms, this includes the knowledge that maps syntactic configurations or relations to thematic roles. Decomposing the knowledge this way across different operators (as opposed to a single fully integrated comprehension operator) increases the generality of the resulting proposal rules, thereby increasing the asymptotic efficiency of the system (Lewis, 1993).

How does ambiguity arise? Choice points arise in problem spaces when multiple operators are applicable at a given state. Thus, syntactic ambiguity in NL-Soar arises when multiple u-constructor operators (corresponding

---

[3]There is additional processing for reference resolution as well, not discussed here.

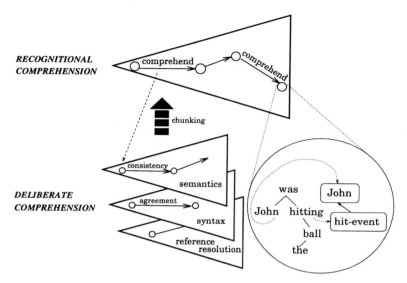

FIG. 1. The basic structure of NL-Soar.

to different syntactic paths) propose themselves. This generation of multiple alternatives occurs in parallel. The selection of the appropriate operator may now be effected by search control rules that encode semantic and contextual knowledge (see Fig. 2). For example, in (2), a pair of u-constructors might be proposed in parallel at *examined*, corresponding to the main verb and reduced relative readings. A selection rule sensitive to the animacy of the initial NP might then fire, guiding comprehension down the appropriate path.

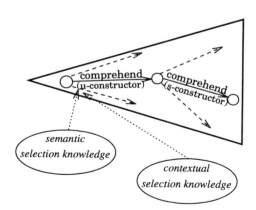

FIG. 2. Resolving ambiguity in NL-Soar.

IS NL-SOAR MODULAR?

Viewed in terms of its relationship to central cognition, NL-Soar is unmistakably nonmodular. Comprehension processes are embedded in the same architectural mechanisms that effect all cognition. NL-Soar appears to be a classic example of a functionality implemented in a *horizontal* architecture (Fodor, 1983), an architecture that shares mechanisms and resources across domains. Yet there is clearly a syntactic module. The set of associations (productions) that realize the proposal and implementation of the u-constructor operators comprise a processing system with many of the distinguishing characteristics of modules. The operators are informationally encapsulated—they encode nothing but syntactic knowledge. The proposal and implementation is automatic (once chunked). The operators are sensitive only to the particular class of inputs that they recognize (via their specialized conditions), and perform one function only (parsing), with a fixed kind of representation as output (the utterance model). The application of the operators is mandatory (unless other equally practiced operators can be made available). Finally, the operators are fast (on the order of 100 ms; see Newell, 1990, for a similar discussion).

Consider how NL-Soar might exhibit both interactive and modular behavior. The critical issues are the time course of comprehension, and what knowledge is available recognitionally. During normal to rapid comprehension, with only a few operators per word available, each problem space function—the proposal, selection, and application of the comprehension operators—must occur essentially by recognition. This means that the associations required to directly implement these functions must already have been learned. If the relevant semantic or contextual associations are in place to guide the selection of u-constructors (see again Fig. 2), then NL-Soar will behave as an interactive system, with all knowledge sources immediately participating. If the relevant semantic or contextual associations are not in place, that is, they haven't been learned yet, then NL-Soar will behave as a modular system, resolving the local ambiguity without recourse to these knowledge sources.[4] Note that NL-Soar is modeless—it is not waiting for its "interactive switch" to be turned on. Rather, the behavior it exhibits will span a continuum of modularity and interactivity depending on the current state of its operator selection knowledge, which consists of a large number of very specific associations.

The processing organization that emerges here is similar to other proposals in which a syntax module generates alternative structures in parallel,

---

[4]What this doesn't explain is why there might still be strong syntactic preferences (such as minimal attachment or right association) when other knowledge sources are lacking. The extent to which there actually are such preferences is a complex issue that I cannot address here.

and semantic and contextual knowledge sources decide among them via a restricted interface (Altmann & Steedman, 1988; Warner & Glass, 1987). As Altmann (1988) pointed out, such fine-grained control over a syntax module preserves the modularity hypothesis while still predicting interactive effects. These models, along with NL-Soar, make clear the problem of experimentally falsifying modularity.

If the present model is so similar to these existing proposals, what else does it have to offer? Has Soar not contributed anything to the venture? In fact, Soar contributes a great deal:

1. The parallel proposal of multiple syntactic alternatives is a direct result of Soar's massively parallel recognition memory. All proposal associations for u-constructors fire in parallel.

2. The fine-grained control over the syntactic module is a direct result of embedding the processing in Soar's control structure. Because control in Soar is obtained at the level of the operator (decision cycle), it makes the prediction that syntactic processing is controllable at that level. Temporally, this means on the order of 100 ms—at least at the word level, as opposed to, say, the phrasal or clausal level.

3. The restricted interface between the syntax module and the other knowledge sources is a direct result of Soar's representation of search control. Operator selection occurs via a fixed set of preferences that define a partial ordering among the proposed alternatives.

4. NL-Soar makes some novel qualitative predictions about the effect that learning and experience have on modular behavior. First, the more novel the semantic content and context for an utterance, the more likely modular effects will arise. This is because the more novel the context, the less likely that the appropriate selection chunks will have been created beforehand. The corollary prediction is that modularity effects can be reduced with experience. There is even the possibility that modularity effects can be reduced with instruction, finally providing an explanation for how people are able to comprehend severe garden paths once they are carefully explained (a phenomenon also noted by Gibson, 1991).[5]

5. Just as important as these gross predictions is the fact that NL-Soar permits posing questions about the impact of learning in the first place.

---

[5]Fodor (1983) dismisses such evidence as irrelevant to studying the normal operation of the language processor, noting that processing a garden path sentence "even feels different" from normal comprehension. This is just what one would expect from Soar given that the processing must first be deliberate, becoming recognitional only after some practice. Anyone who has worked in the area of garden path sentences can attest to the fact that over time the severe garden path effects can disappear (they can also *reappear* in otherwise unexpected places).

Where do the comprehension operator selection rules come from (i.e., from what set of problem spaces could these associations have emerged by chunking)? What are the limits to the effects that large amounts of practice can have on the processes of language comprehension?

6. Finally, NL-Soar is embedded in a theory of cognition. NL-Soar must be a functional comprehender, not just a parsing module. This permits exploring comprehension in the service of actual tasks such as instruction taking (Huffman & Laird, in press; Lewis, Newell, & Polk, 1989), as well as considering general questions concerning the relationship of language and thought (Lehman, Lewis, & Newell, in press; Lehman, Newell, Polk, & Lewis, 1993).

Although this account is promising, many important questions remain. One major gap in NL-Soar's modularity story regards the acquisition of language and the nature of innate content. Although NL-Soar presently lacks an acquisition theory, the general notion of innate problem spaces is perfectly consistent with Soar. Indeed, they are functionally required if Soar is to ever begin learning anything. For example, the initial spaces that give rise to the u-constructors must contain something that might be recognizable as representing innate universal grammatical principles. Another gap in the theory concerns neural specificity. Soar does not have a theory of neural implementation, so issues of localization and selective impairment cannot be adequately addressed.

THE MODULARITY OF SOAR: REPRISE

We started with a concern that perhaps Soar was too uniform and horizontal to be consistent with evidence suggesting some aspects of mind were in fact modular. By considering the Soar language faculty, NL-Soar, we discovered that not only was NL-Soar consistent with many of the desirable properties of modular theories, but that in fact, these properties were largely derived from embedding comprehension within the Soar architecture. The resulting model pushes the state of the science (along with models such as CC-Reader; Just & Carpenter, 1992) by beginning to address both modular and interactive effects as well as allowing us to explore the relationship between modularity and learning.

One possible conclusion we could draw from this is that language comprehension, perhaps along with other apparently modular processes, is just another variety of general cognition, implemented in a universal architecture capable of doing essentially anything. But consider the following switch in perspective. Instead of asking how Soar characterizes modularity in terms of general cognition, ask how Soar characterizes general cognition in terms of modularity. The aspects of the architecture which led to a language system with modular features—the parallel recognition memory, the recognize-decide-act control structure, chunking—are in place to support all cognitive activity. What Soar suggests, then, is that the same mechanisms that underly fast, modular processing are what central cognition consists of *all the way down* (cf. Fodor, 1983). In sum, apparently nonmodular cognitive theories such as Soar may help capture important general principles of mental architecture, even if the mind is modular in significant ways. Onward down the high road!

REFERENCES

Altmann, G. (1988). Ambiguity, parsing strategies, and computational models. *Language and Cognitive Processes, 3*, 73–97.

Altmann, G. (1989). Parsing and interpretation: an introduction. *Language and Cognitive Processes, 4*, SI1–19.

Altmann, G., & Steedman, M. (1988). Interaction with context during human sentence processing. *Cognition, 30*, 191–238.

Britt, M. A., Perfetti, C. A., Garrod, S., & Rayner, K. (1992). Parsing in discourse: Context effects and their limits. *Journal of Memory and Language, 31*, 293–314.

Crain, S., & Steedman, M. (1985). On not being led up the garden path: The use of context by the psychological syntax processor. In D. R. Dowty, L. Karttunen, & A. M. Zwicky (Eds.), *Natural language parsing* (pp. 320–358). Cambridge: Cambridge University Press.

Ferreira, F., & Clifton, C., Jr. (1986). The independence of syntactic processing. *Journal of Memory and Language, 25*, 348–368.

Fodor, J. A. (1983). *Modularity of mind: An essay on faculty psychology.* Cambridge, MA: MIT Press.

Frazier, L. (1987). Sentence processing: a tutorial review. In M. Coltheart (Ed.), *Attention and performance XII: The psychology of reading* (pp. 559–586). East Sussex, UK: Lawrence Erlbaum Associates.

Garfield, J. L. (Ed.). (1989). *Modularity in knowledge representation and natural-language understanding.* Cambridge, MA: MIT Press.

Gibson, E. A. F. (1991). *A computational theory of human linguistic processing: Memory limitations and processing breakdown* (Tech. Rep. No. CMU-CMT-91-125). Pittsburgh: Carnegie Mellon University, Center for Machine Translation.

Holbrook, J. K., Eiselt, K. P., & Mahesh, K. (1992). A unified process model of syntactic and semantic error recovery in sentence understanding. *Proceedings of the Fourteenth Annual Conference of the Cognitive Science Society* (pp. 195–200).

Huffman, S. B., & Laird, J. E. (in press). Flexibly instructable agents. *Journal of Artificial Intelligence Research (JAIR).*

Just, M. A., & Carpenter, P. A. (1987). *The psychology of reading and language comprehension.* Boston: Allyn & Bacon.

Just, M. A., & Carpenter, P. A. (1992). A capacity theory of comprehension: Individual differences in working memory. *Psychological Review, 99*(1), 122–149.

Laird, J. E., Newell, A., & Rosenbloom, P. S. (1987). Soar: An architecture for general intelligence. *Artificial Intelligence, 33*, 1–64.

Lehman, J. F., Lewis, R. L., & Newell, A. (1991a). Integrating knowledge sources in language comprehension. *Proceedings of the Thirteenth Annual Conference of the Cognitive Science Society* (pp. 461–466). (Also in P. S. Rosenbloom, J. E. Laird, & A. Newell (Eds.). (1993). *The Soar papers: Research on integrated intelligence* [pp. 1309–1314]. Cambridge, MA: MIT Press.

Lehman, J. F., Lewis, R. L., & Newell, A. (1991b). *Natural language comprehension in Soar: Spring 1991* (Tech. Rep. No. CMU-CS-91-117). Pittsburgh: Carnegie Mellon University, School of Computer Science.

Lehman, J. F., Lewis, R. L., & Newell, A. (in press). *Architectural influences on language comprehension.* In Z. Pylyshyn (Ed.), *Cognitive architecture.* Norwood, NJ: Ablex.

Lehman, J. F., Newell, A., Polk, T. A., & Lewis, R. L. (1993). The role of language in cognition: A computational inquiry. In G. Harman (Ed.), *Conceptions of the human mind* (pp. 39–58). Hillsdale, NJ: Lawrence Erlbaum Associates.

Lewis, R. L. (1993). *An architecturally-based theory of human sentence comprehension.* (Tech. Rep. No. CMU-CS-93-226). Pittsburgh: Carnegie Mellon University.

Lewis, R. L., Newell, A., & Polk, T. A. (1989). Toward a Soar theory of taking instructions for immediate reasoning tasks. *Proceedings of the Eleventh Annual Conference of the Cognitive Science Society* (pp. 514–521). Ann Arbor, MI. Also in P. S. Rosenbloom, J. E. Laird, & A. Newell (Eds.). (1993). *The Soar papers: Research on integrated intelligence* (pp. 719–726). Cambridge, MA: MIT Press.

Marslen-Wilson, W. D. (1975). Sentence perception as an interactive parallel process. *Science, 189,* 226–227.

Newell, A. (1973a). Production systems: Models of control structures. In W. G. Chase (Ed.), *Visual information processing* (pp. 463–526). New York: Academic Press.

Newell, A. (1973b). You can't play 20 questions with nature and win: Projective comments on the papers of this symposium. In W. G. Chase (Ed.), *Visual information processing* (pp. 283–308). New York: Academic Press.

Newell, A. (1990). *Unified theories of cognition.* Cambridge, MA: Harvard University Press.

Pylyshyn, Z. W. (1984). *Computation and cognition.* Cambridge, MA: Bradford/MIT Press.

Pylyshyn, Z. W. (1991). The role of cognitive architecture in theories of cognition. In K. VanLehn (Ed.), *Architectures for intelligence* (pp. 189–223). Hillsdale, NJ: Lawrence Erlbaum Associates.

Steedman, M., & Altmann, G. (1989). Ambiguity in context: A reply. *Language and Cognitive Processes, 4,* SI105–122.

Tyler, L. K., & Marslen-Wilson, W. (1977). The on-line effects of semantic context on syntactic processing. *Journal of Verbal Learning and Verbal Behavior, 16,* 683–692.

Warner, J., & Glass, A. L. (1987). Context and distance-to-disambiguation effects in ambiguity resolution: Evidence from grammaticality judgments of garden path sentences. *Journal of Memory and Language, 26,* 714–738.

Chapter 3

Learning Analytically
and Inductively

Tom M. Mitchell
Carnegie Mellon University

Sebastian B. Thrun
University of Bonn

LEARNING

Learning is a fundamental component of intelligence, and a key considera-tion in designing cognitive architectures such as Soar (Laird, Rosenbloom, & Newell, 1986). This chapter considers the question of what constitutes an appropriate general-purpose learning mechanism. We are interested in mecha-nisms that might explain and reproduce the rich variety of learning capabili-ties of humans, ranging from learning perceptual-motor skills such as how to ride a bicycle, to learning highly cognitive tasks such as how to play chess.

Research on learning in fields such as cognitive science, artificial intelli-gence, neurobiology, and statistics has led to the identification of two distinct classes of learning methods: inductive and analytic. Inductive methods, such as neural network backpropagation, learn general laws by finding statistical correlations and regularities among a large set of training examples. In contrast, analytical methods, such as explanation-based learning, acquire general laws from many fewer training examples. They rely instead on prior knowledge to analyze individual training examples in detail, then use this analysis to distinguish relevant example features from the irrelevant.

The question considered in this chapter is how to best combine inductive and analytical learning in an architecture that seeks to cover the range of learning exhibited by intelligent systems such as humans. We present a specific learning mechanism, explanation-based neural network learning (EBNN), that blends these two types of learning, and present experimental results demonstrating its ability to learn control strategies for a mobile robot using vision, sonar, and laser range sensors. We then consider the analytical learning mechanism in Soar, called chunking, and recent attempts to complement chunking by including inductive mechanisms in Soar. Finally, we suggest a way in which EBNN could be introduced as a replacement for chunking in Soar, thereby incorporating inductive and analytical learning as architectural capabilities.

The following section provides an overview of inductive and analytic principles for learning, and argues that both are necessary for a general learning mechanism that scales up to handle a broad range of tasks. The subsequent section presents the EBNN learning mechanism, together with experimental results illustrating its capabilities. Finally, we consider the general learning mechanism for Soar, and the question of how to best incorporate both inductive and analytic learning within this architecture.

WHY COMBINE ANALYSIS AND INDUCTION?

At the heart of the learning problem is the question of how to successfully generalize from examples. For instance, when people learn to ride a bicycle or learn to play chess, they learn from specific experiences (e.g., riding a specific bicycle on a particular day in a particular place). Somehow they are able to generalize away from the myriad details of specific situations, to learn general strategies that they expect to apply in "similar" subsequent situations. In doing this, they must differentiate between the many irrelevant details of the situation (e.g., the angle of the sun on that particular day, the color of the bicyclist's shirt), and the few essential features (e.g., the velocity and tilt angle of the bicycle). This section provides brief overviews of analytical and inductive methods for generalizing from examples, then considers the complementary benefits of these two learning paradigms.

Analytical Learning

Analytical learning uses the learner's prior knowledge to analyze individual training examples, in order to discriminate the relevant features from the irrelevant. The most common analytical learning method is explanation-based learning (DeJong & Mooney, 1986; Mitchell, Keller, & Kedar-Cabelli, 1986). To illustrate, consider the problem of learning to play chess. More specifically, consider the subtask of learning to recognize chess positions in which one's queen will be lost within the next few moves. A positive example of this class of chess positions is shown in Fig. 3.1.

As explained in the figure caption, this is a positive example of a chess position in which black can be forced to lose its queen. To learn a general rule from this example, it is necessary to determine which board features

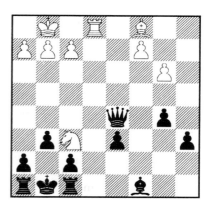

FIG. 3.1. A positive example of the concept "chess positions in which black can be forced to lose its queen within two moves." Note the white knight is attacking both the black king and queen. Black must therefore move its king, enabling white to capture the black queen.

are relevant to losing the queen, and which are irrelevant details to be ignored. Inductive learning methods generalize by collecting multiple training examples, then determining which features are common to the positive examples but not to the negative examples. In the chess example just given, there are many features that happen to be true (e.g., the feature "four white pawns are still in their original positions"), but only a few that are relevant (e.g., "the black king and queen are simultaneously under attack"). In this chess example, inductive techniques will require hundreds or thousands of training example chess boards to statistically determine which features are relevant and to generalize appropriately.

In analytical learning such as explanation-based learning, a justifiable generalization of the chess position can be derived from just this one training example. This is accomplished by the learner explaining how the training example satisfies the target concept, then identifying the features mentioned in the explanation as relevant. Given prior knowledge of the legal moves of chess, it is possible for the learner to construct an explanation of why the black queen is lost in the particular training example of Fig. 3.1. The explanation is given in the figure caption. Notice this explanation mentions the feature that "the white knight is attacking both the black king and queen." This feature is thus determined to be relevant in general, and forms a condition under which black will in general lose its queen. In contrast, other irrelevant features that would be considered in inductive learning (e.g., "four white pawns are still in their original positions") are not even considered, because they play no part in the explanation. Explanation-based learning generalizes through explaining and analyzing training instances in terms of prior knowledge. Although our purpose here is to examine computer learning algorithms, it is interesting to note that research on human learning provides support for the conjecture that humans learn through such explanations (see, e.g., Ahn & Brewer, 1993; Chi & Bassok, 1989; Qin, Mitchell, & Herbert, 1992).

Analytical learning methods have been used successfully in a number of applications—notably for learning rules to control search. For example, Prodigy (Minton et al., 1989) is a domain-independent framework for means–ends planning that uses explanation-based learning to acquire search control knowledge. Prodigy learns general rules that characterize concepts, such as "situations in which pursuing subgoal ?x will lead to backtracking." Given a specific problem solving domain defined by a set of states, operators, and goals, Prodigy learns control rules that significantly reduce backtracking when solving problems in this domain. It has been demonstrated to learn search control rules comparable to hand-coded rules in a variety of task domains (Minton et al., 1989).

The chunking mechanism in Soar (Laird et al., 1986) also provides an example of analytical learning, as explained in Rosenbloom and Laird (1986). In Soar, problem solving corresponds to search in problem spaces (a problem space is defined by problem states and operators). Whenever Soar has no control knowledge to choose its next search step, it reflects on the current situation by using a higher level problem space, resulting in a choice of an appropriate search step. The trace of reasoning performed in this higher level space forms an explanation of why the selected search step is appropriate in this specific instance. The Soar architecture automatically records this explanation whenever it reflects in this fashion, and the chunking mechanism forms a new control rule (called a *production*) by collecting the features mentioned in the explanation into the preconditions of the new rule. Soar's analytical chunking mechanism has been shown to learn successfully to speed up problem solving across a broad range of domains. For example, Doorenbos (1993) presented results in which over 100,000 productions are learned from such explanations within one particular domain.

Inductive Learning

Although analytical learning can produce appropriate generalizations by analyzing single training examples, it requires strong prior knowledge about its domain in order to construct appropriate explanations. Its determination of which features are relevant will only be as correct and complete as the prior knowledge from which explanations are formed. In many domains, such complete and correct prior knowledge is unavailable. For example, consider learning the concept "stocks that double in value over the next year." In this case, an explanation of a training example would require explaining which features were responsible for the increase in value. Unlike the chess domain, in which the effects of each possible move are known perfectly in advance, the stock-market domain cannot be modeled so correctly and completely. In such cases, inductive techniques that identify empirical regularities over many examples are useful.

To illustrate inductive learning, consider the task of learning to drive a motor vehicle. Pomerleau (1989) described the computer system ALVINN that learns to steer a vehicle driving at 55 mph on public highways, based on input sensor data from a video camera. Notice this task involves learning control knowledge, much like the control knowledge learned by Prodigy and Soar. In this domain, however, a complete and correct model of the effects of different steering actions is not known a priori. Therefore an inductive learning method, neural network backpropagation (Rumelhart, Hinton, & Williams, 1986), is used to learn a mapping from the camera image to the appropriate steering direction. Thousands of training examples are collected by recording camera images and steering commands while a human drives the vehicle for approximately 10 minutes. These human-provided training examples of visual scenes and corresponding steering commands are generalized by the neural network to acquire a general mapping from scenes to steering commands. The resulting network has been demonstrated to drive unassisted for intervals up to 100 miles at speeds of 55 mph on public highways. The neural network learning technique is a method for fitting hundreds of numeric parameters in a predefined but highly expressive nonlinear functional form. These parameters are fitted by performing a gradient descent search to minimize the error between the network output and the desired output for the training example set.

Why Combine Analytical and Inductive Learning?

Analytical and inductive learning offer complementary approaches to identifying correct hypotheses during learning. In domains where strong prior knowledge is available, such as chess, analytical methods such as explanation-based learning can generalize correctly from single examples. In domains where such strong prior knowledge is not available, inductive methods such as neural network backpropagation offer a means of identifying empirical regularities over large sets of training data. In the chess example given earlier, analytical learning offers a means of generalizing correctly by analyzing single examples, whereas inductive learning would probably require thousands of examples to find appropriate regularities given the large number of possible features. In the driving task, however, it is difficult to imagine how to program in sufficient prior knowledge to allow explaining why a particular steering direction is appropriate, in terms of the individual pixels of the camera image. In this case, inductive learning can sort through the large number of potential features by finding regularities among thousands of training examples.

Methods for combining inductive and analytical learning have been the subject of considerable recent research. For example, Shavlik and Towell (1989) described a method called KBANN for using prior symbolic knowledge to initialize the structure and weights of a neural network, which is then inductively refined using the backpropagation method. A similar method has been reported by Fu (1989). Pazzani, Brunk, and Silverstein (1991) described a combined inductive/analytical method called FOCL for learning sets of horn clauses, demonstrating its ability to operate robustly given errors in the initial domain knowledge. Ourston and Mooney (1994) described a method called EITHER for refining domain theories in the light of additional empirical data. Although research in this area is very active, the question of how to best blend inductive and analytical learning is still open. Desired properties for a combined mechanism include the following:

- Given a perfect domain theory, learn as effectively as explanation-based learning.
- Given an incorrect theory, or no theory, learn as effectively as the best inductive methods.
- Operate robustly over the entire spectrum of domain theory quality.
- Accommodate noisy data.
- Support sufficiently rich representations for hypotheses.
- Refine the domain theory with experience, at the same time as using it to learn the target function.

A COMBINED INDUCTIVE–ANALYTICAL LEARNING MECHANISM

The explanation-based neural network (EBNN) learning mechanism integrates inductive and analytic learning. As the name suggests, EBNN is based on an artificial neural network representation of knowledge. Neural networks are used to draw inferences about the domain, just as rules are used to draw inferences in symbolic representations. By using a neural network representation, pure inductive learning algorithms such as the backpropagation algorithm Rumelhart et al. (1986) become applicable. In addition, EBNN includes an analytic learning component, based on explaining and analyzing training instances in terms of other, previously learned networks.

In what follows we describe the EBNN learning mechanism. We also present some results obtained in the domain of mobile robot navigation. Based on these we discuss the role of inductive and analytical learning in EBNN.

Introduction to EBNN

To understand the EBNN learning mechanism, consider the example given in Fig. 3.2, adapted from Winston, Binford, Katz, and Lowry (1983) and Towell and Shavlik (1989). Suppose we are facing the problem of learning

(a) Training examples

is light	has handle	made of Styrofoam	upward concave	color	open vessel	flat bottom	is expensive	is_cup?
yes	yes	no	no	blue	yes	yes	yes	yes
no	no	yes	yes	red	no	yes	no	no
yes	no	yes	yes	red	yes	no	no	no
no	no	yes	yes	green	yes	yes	no	yes
⋮	⋮	⋮	⋮	⋮	⋮	⋮	⋮	⋮

(b) Target concept

is_cup?	:-	*is_liftable, holds_liquid*
is_liftable	:-	*is_light, has_handle*
is_liftable	:-	*made_of_Styrofoam, upward_concave*
holds_liquid	:-	*open_vessel, flat_bottom*

FIG. 3.2.   The cup example.

to classify cups. More specifically, imagine we want to train a network, denoted by *f*, that can determine whether an object is a cup based on the features *is_light, has_handle, made_of_Styrofoam, color, upward_concave, open vessel, flat_bottom,* and *is_expensive.* One way to learn the new concept is to collect training instances of cups and noncups, and employ the backpropagation procedure to iteratively refine the weights of the target network. Such a learning scheme is purely inductive. It allows learning functions from scratch, in the absence of any domain knowledge.

Now let us assume one has already learned a *neural network domain theory,* which represents each individual inference step in the logical derivation of the target concept. In our example, such a domain theory may consist of three networks, the network f_1, which predicts whether an object is liftable, the network f_2, which predicts whether an object can hold a liquid, and a third network, f_3, that predicts whether an object is a cup as a function of the two intermediate concepts *is_liftable* and *holds_liquid* (cf. Fig. 3.3). This set of networks forms a complete domain theory for the classification of a cup, as it allows classifying any object as a cup or not. However, it is not necessarily correct, as the domain theory networks themselves may have been constructed from examples.

How can this neural network domain theory be employed to refine the target network f? EBNN learns analytically by explaining and analyzing each training example using the following three-step procedure:

1. Explain

The domain theory is used to explain training instances by chaining together multiple steps of neural network inferences. In our example, the domain theory network f_1 is used to predict the degree to which the object is liftable, network f_2 is employed to predict whether the object can hold a liquid, and finally network f_3 uses these two predictions to estimate whether the object is a cup. This collection of neural network inferences, which we refer to as the *explanation*, explains why a training instance is a member of its class in terms of the domain theory. The explanation sets up the inference structure necessary for analyzing and generalizing this training instance.

2. Analyze

The preceding explanation is analyzed in order to generalize the training instance in feature space. Unlike symbolic approaches to EBL, which extract the weakest precondition of the explanation, EBNN extracts slopes of the target function. More specifically, EBNN extracts the output–input slopes of the target concept by computing the first derivative of the neural network explanation. These slopes measure, according to the domain theory, how infinitesimal changes in the instance feature values will change the output value of the target function.

In the cup example, EBNN extracts slopes from the explanation composed of the three domain theory networks f_1, f_2, and f_3. The output–input derivative of f_1 predicts how infinitesimal changes in the input space of f_1 will change the degree to which f_1 predicts an object to be liftable. Likewise, the derivatives of f_2 and f_3 predict the effect of small changes in their input spaces on their vote. Chaining these derivatives together results in slopes that measure how infinitesimally small changes of the individual instance features will change the final prediction of cupness.

Slopes guide the generalization of training instances in feature space. Notice that irrelevant features, whose values play no role in determining whether the object is a cup (e.g., the features *color* and *is_expensive*), will

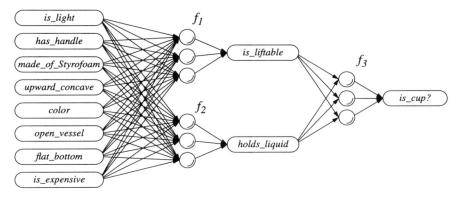

FIG. 3.3. A neural network domain theory for the classification of a cup.

have approximately zero slopes. On the other hand, large slopes indicate important features, because small changes in the feature value will have a large effect on the target concept according to the neural network domain theory. Notice that the extraction of slopes relies on the fact that artificial neural networks are differentiable, real-valued functions.

3. Refine

Finally, EBNN refines the weights and biases of the target network both inductively and analytically. Figure 3.4 summarizes the information obtained by the inductive and the analytical component. Inductive learning is based on the target value for each individual training instance, whereas analytical learning is based on the target slopes extracted from the explanation. When updating the weights of the network, EBNN minimizes a combined error function that takes both value error and slope error into account.

$$E = E_{values} + \alpha E_{slopes} \qquad (1)$$

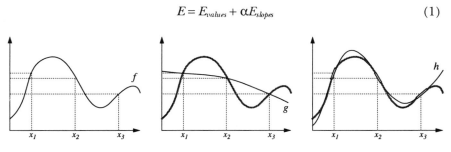

FIG. 3.4. Fitting values and slopes in EBNN. Let f be the target function for which three examples $<x_1, f(x_1)>$, $<x_2, f(x_2)>$, and $<x_3, f(x_3)>$ are known. Based on these points the learner might generate the hypothesis g. If the slopes are also known, the learner can do much better: h.

Here α is a parameter that trades off value fit versus slope fit, and that therefore determines the relative impact of inductive versus analytical components of learning. Gradient descent is employed to iteratively minimize E. Notice that in our implementation we used a modified version of the Tangent-Prog algorithm (Simard, Victori, LeCun, & Denker, 1992) to refine the weights and biases of the target network (Masuoka, 1993).

What is a reasonable method for weighting the contributions of the inductive versus analytical components of learning—that is, for selecting a value for α? Because the domain theory might be incorrect, the analytically extracted slopes for a particular training example might be misleading. In such cases, one would like to suppress the analytical component ($\alpha = 0$), relying only on the inductive component. For other training examples the domain theory and explanation might be correct, and $\alpha = 1$ might be more useful. EBNN dynamically adjusts the value of α for each individual training example, based on the observed accuracy of the explanation: The more accurately the domain theory predicts the known target value of the training instance, the higher the value of α for this training example.

The accuracy, denoted by δ, is measured as the root-mean-square difference between the true target value and the prediction by the domain theory. When refining the weights and biases of the target network, δ determines the weight of the target slopes α according to the following formula:

$$\alpha = 1 - \frac{\delta}{\delta_{max}} \qquad (2)$$

Here δ_{max} denotes the maximum prediction error, which is used for normalization. This weighting scheme attempts to give accurate slopes a large weight in training, while ignoring inaccurate slopes. This heuristic weighting scheme, called LOB* (Mitchell & Thrun, 1993), is based on the heuristic assumption that the accuracy of the explanation's slopes are correlated to the accuracy of the explanation's predictions.

Summary

This completes the description of the EBNN learning mechanism. To summarize, EBNN refines the target network using a combined inductive–analytical mechanism. Inductive training information is obtained through observation, and analytical training information is obtained by explaining and analyzing these observations in terms of the learner's prior knowledge. Inductive and analytical learning are dynamically weighted by a scheme that estimates the accuracy of the domain theory for explaining individual examples.

Both components of learning, inductive and analytical, play an important role in EBNN. Once a reasonable domain theory is available, EBNN benefits from its analytical component, because it gradually replaces the pure syntactical bias in neural networks by a bias that captures domain-specific knowledge. The result is improved generalization from less training data. Of course, analytic learning still requires the availability of a domain theory that allows explaining the target function. If such a domain theory is weak or not available, EBNN degrades to a purely inductive neural network learner. It is the inductive component of EBNN that ensures that learning is possible even in the total absence of domain knowledge.

Experimental Results

EBNN has been applied to various domains, including classification, prediction, game playing, perception, and robot control. Here we report an application of EBNN to learning mobile robot navigation using Q-learning (Watkins, 1989).

Xavier (O'Sullivan, 1994), the robot at hand, is shown in Fig. 3.5. Xavier is equipped with a ring of 24 sonar sensors, a laser range finder, and a color camera mounted on a pan/tilt head. Sonar sensors return approximate echo distances along with noise. The laser range finder measures distances more accurately, but its perceptual field is limited to a small range in front of the robot. The task of the robot was to learn to navigate to a specifically marked target location in a laboratory environment. In some experiments, the location of the marker was fixed throughout the course of learning; in others it was moved across the laboratory and only kept fixed for the duration of a single training episode. Sometimes parts of the environment were blocked by obstacles. The marker was detected using a visual object tracking routine that recognized and tracked the marker in real time using the pan/tilt head. The robot was rewarded if it managed to stop in front of the marker. It was penalized for losing sight of the marker.

Sensor input was encoded by a 46-dimensional vector, consisting of 24 sonar distance measurements, 10 distance measurements by the laser range finder, and an array of 12 values coding the angle of the marker position relative to the robot (cf. Fig. 3.6). Every 3 seconds the robot could choose one of seven possible actions, ranging from sharp turns to straight motion. In order to avoid collisions, the robot employed a precoded obstacle avoidance routine based on potential field navigation (Khatib, 1986). Whenever the projected path of the robot was blocked by an obstacle, the robot decelerated and, if necessary, changed its motion direction (regardless of the commanded action). Xavier was operated continuously in real time. Each learning episode corresponds to a sequence of actions that starts at a random initial position and ends either when the robot loses sight of the target object, for which it is penalized, or when it halts in front of the marker, in which case it is rewarded.

color camera
pan/tilt head

range finder

sonar ring

structured light

bump detectors

radio link

computers

FIG. 3.5. The Xavier robot.

In order to learn to generate actions from delayed reward, we applied EBNN in the context of Q-learning (Watkins, 1989). In essence, Q-learning constructs utility functions $Q(s, a)$ that map sensations s and actions a to task-specific utility values. The Q values will be positive for final successes and negative for final failures. In between, utilities are calculated recursively using an asynchronous dynamic programming technique (Barto, Bradtke, & Singh, 1991). More specifically, the utility $Q(s_t, a_t)$ at time t is estimated through a mixture of the utilities of subsequent observation–action pairs, up to the final utility at the end of the episode. The exact update equation used in the experiments, combined with methods of temporal differencing (Sutton, 1988), is:

$$Q^{\text{target}}(s_t, a_t) \leftarrow \begin{cases} +100 & \text{if } a_t \text{ final action, robot reached goal} \\ -100 & \text{if } a_t \text{ final action, robot lost sight of the marker} \\ \\ \gamma[(1-\lambda \cdot \max_{a \text{ action}} Q(s_{t+1}, a) + \lambda \, Q^{\text{target}}(s_{t+1}, a_{t+1})] & \text{otherwise} \end{cases} \tag{3}$$

Here γ $(0 \le \gamma \le 1)$ is a discount factor that, if $\gamma < 1$, favors rewards reaped earlier in time, and λ $(0 \le \lambda \le 1)$ is a gain parameter trading off the recursive component and the nonrecursive component in the update equation. Once the function Q has been learned, steepest descent in the utility space results in optimal paths to the goal. Hence, learning control amounts to learning appropriate Q functions. In our implementation, the Q function was represented by a collection of artificial neural networks that mapped sensations s to utility values, one for each action a.

Q-learning and other related dynamic programming algorithms have been applied successfully to game playing domains (Tesauro, 1992) and robotics (Gullapalli, 1992). In these previous approaches, the update of the target networks was purely inductive. EBNN, applied to Q-learning, extends inductive learning by an analytical component. Just as for the classification example given in the previous section, EBNN requires the availability of an appropriate neural network domain theory. Here the learner is given a collection of *predictive action models* f_a, one for each action a, that allow predicting the sensation and reward at time $t + 1$ from the sensations of time t. Such a neural network domain theory allows explaining (post-facto predicting) sensations and final outcomes of each individual learning episode. In Xavier's case, each action model maps 46 input values to 47 output values. The models were learned beforehand using the back-propagation training procedure, employing a cross-validation scheme to prevent overfitting the data. Initially, we used a training corpus of approximately 800 randomly generated actions, which was gradually increased through the course of this research to 3,000 actions, taken from some 700 episodes. These training examples were distributed roughly equally among the seven actions.

Xavier's predictive action models face a highly stochastic situation. There are many unknown factors that influence the actual sensations. First, sensors are generally noisy—that is, there is a certain likelihood that the sensor returns corrupted values. Second, the obstacle avoidance routine is very sensitive to small and subtle details in the real world. For example, if the robot faces an obstacle, it is often very hard to predict whether its obstacle avoidance behavior will make it turn left or right. Third, the delays in communication, imposed by the radio Ethernet link, turned out to be rather unpredictable. These delays, which influenced the duration of actions, were anywhere in the range of 0.1 to 3 seconds. For all these reasons, the domain theory functions f_a captured only typical aspects of the world by modeling the average outcome of actions, but were clearly unable to predict perfectly. Empirically we found, however, that they were well suited for extracting useful slopes. Figure 3.6 gives an example of a slope array extracted from a domain theory network applied to a typical world state.

Having trained the domain theory networks, we finally attacked the primary goal of learning, namely, learning Q. The explanation and analysis of episodes in Q-learning is analogous to the analysis of training instances in the cup example. EBNN explains episodes by chaining together predictive action models. For each state–action pair in the episode, EBNN extracts target slopes of the utility function via the first derivative of the explanation of the episode:

$$\Delta_{s_t} Q^{\text{target}}(s_t, a_t) \leftarrow \begin{cases} \partial \dfrac{f_{a_t}}{\partial s} & \text{if } a_t \text{ final aciton} \\[2ex] \gamma \left[(1-\lambda) \left. \dfrac{\partial Q_a}{\partial s} \right|_{s_{t+1}} + \lambda \, \Delta_{s_{t+1}} Q^{\text{target}}(s_{t+1}, a_{t+1}) \right] \left. \dfrac{\partial f_{a_t}}{\partial s} \right|_{s_t} & \text{otherwise} \end{cases} \quad (4)$$

We performed five complete learning experiments, each consisting of 30–40 episodes. When training the Q networks, all training data were memorized and a recursive replay technique was used, similar to "experience replay" described in Lin (1992). The update parameter γ was set to 0.9, and λ was set to 0.7.

In all cases Xavier learned to navigate to a static target location in less than 19 episodes, each of which was between 2 and 11 actions in length. It consistently learned to navigate to arbitrary target locations (which was required in 4 out of 5 experiments) always in less than 25 episodes. Although the robot faced a high-dimensional sensation space, it always managed to learn the task in less than 25 episodes, which is less than 10 minutes of robot operation, and, on average, less than 20 training examples per Q network. This training time does not include the time for collecting the

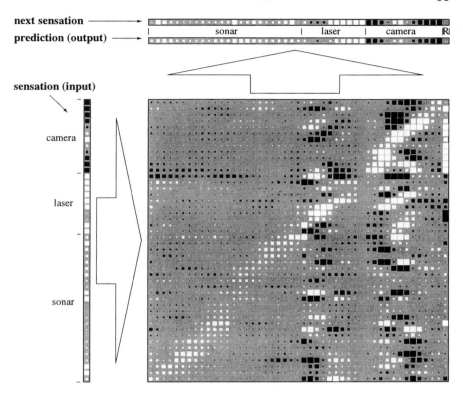

FIG. 3.6. Prediction and slopes. A neural network action model predicts sensations and reward for the next time step. The large matrix displays the output-input slopes of the network. White boxes refer to negative and black boxes to positive values. Box sizes indicate absolute magnitudes. Notice the positive gradients along the main diagonal.

training data to learn the domain theory action models. In general, we assume the cost of learning such domain-specific but task-independent action models can be amortized over many control learning tasks faced by the robot within its environment. Hence, only a small fraction of this cost should be considered as relevant to this task.

When testing the robot, we also confronted it with situations that were not part of its training experience. In one experiment, we kept the location of the marker fixed and moved it only in the testing phase. In a second experiment, we blocked the robot's path with large obstacles, even though it had not experienced obstacles during training. It was here that the presence of an appropriate domain theory was most important. Although without domain theory the robot almost always failed to approach the marker under these new conditions, it reliably (>90%) managed this task when it was trained with the help of the domain-theory networks. This is because the domain theory provides a knowledgeable bias for generalization to unseen situations.

In order to investigate and characterize EBNN more thoroughly, we applied EBNN to a simulated robot navigation task, depicted in Fig. 3.7(a). The robot, indicated by the small circle, has to navigate to the fixed goal location (large circle) while avoiding a collision with the obstacle and the surrounding walls. Its sensors measure the distances and the angles to both the center of the obstacle and the center of the goal, relative to the robot's view. At any time, five different actions are available to the robot, depicted in Fig. 3.7(b). Note that this learning task is completely deterministic.

The learning setup was analogous to the robot experiments described earlier. Before learning an evaluation function, we trained five neural network action models, one for each individual action. Subsequently, five Q functions were trained to evaluate the utility of each individual action.[1] In a first experiment, we were interested in the merit of the analytic learning component of EBNN. We trained the model networks using a large training corpus of 8,192 training instances each. EBNN was then applied to the task of learning control. Figure 3.8 displays the performance as a function of the number of training episodes. As can easily be seen, standard inductive learning requires more training examples than the combined inductive and analytic learning in EBNN. This is because the analytic component of EBNN provides a knowledgeable, domain-dependent bias, which partially replaces the purely syntactical, inductive bias. Of course, asymptotically, with an unlimited amount of training data, both approaches might be expected to exhibit equivalent performance.

Clearly, EBNN outperformed pure inductive learning because it was given a domain theory trained with a large number of training examples. In order to test the impact of weaker domain theories on EBNN, we conducted a series of experiments in which we trained different sets of domain-theory networks using 5, 10, 20, 35, 50, 75, 100, and 150 training examples per action network. As shown in Fig. 3.7(c), the number of training examples determines the accuracy of the resulting domain theory. Figure 3.9 displays the performance graphs resulting from using these different domain theories. As can be seen, EBNN degrades gracefully to the performance of a pure inductive learner as the accuracy of the domain theory decreases.

The graceful degradation of EBNN with decreasing accuracy of the domain theory is due to the fact that misleading slopes are identified and their influence weakened (cf. Eq. 2). In other experiments reported else-

---

[1]In this implementation we used a real-valued approximation scheme using nearest neighbor generalization for the Q functions. This scheme was empirically found to outperform the backpropagation algorithm.

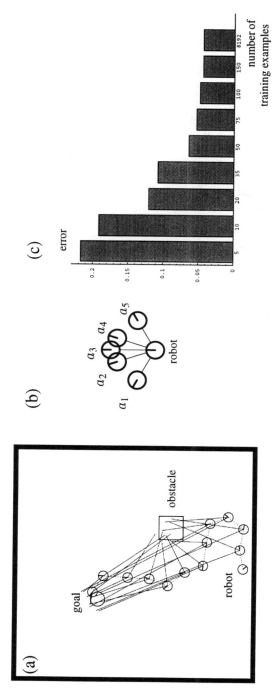

FIG. 3.7. (a) The simulated robot world. (b) Actions. (c) The squared generalization error of the domain theory networks decreases monotonically as the amount of training data increases. These nine alternative domain theories were used in the experiments.

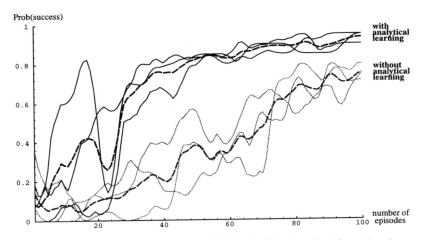

FIG. 3.8. Performance curves for EBNN with (black) and without (gray) analytical training information (slope fitting) for three examples each, measured on an independent set of problem instances. The dashed lines indicate average performance. In this experiment, the agent used well-trained predictive action models as its domain theory.

where (Thrun & Mitchell, 1993) it was demonstrated that EBNN will fail to learn control if the domain theory is poor and α is kept fixed. These results also indicate that in cases where the domain theory is poor a pure analytical learner would be hopelessly lost. In the experiments reported here EBNN recovered from poor domain theories because of its inductive component, which enabled it to overturn misleading bias extracted from inaccurate prior knowledge.

Why Are Both Induction and Analysis Needed?

The inductive component of learning in EBNN is the standard backpropagation algorithm for updating network weights to fit observed training example values. The analytical component of learning in EBNN is the use of prior knowledge to explain observed training examples, and the use of slopes extracted from these explanations to further update the weights of the target network. EBNN blends these two mechanisms, weighting the contribution of analytical learning on an example-by-example basis, depending on the accuracy of the domain theory in explaining the particular observed training example.

The importance of analytical learning lies in its ability to generalize more correctly from fewer examples. As demonstrated by the experimental results from EBNN, prior knowledge leads to a significantly steeper learning curve. This in turn allows scaling up the learning system to more complex learning tasks. We conjecture that with increasing task complexity, the

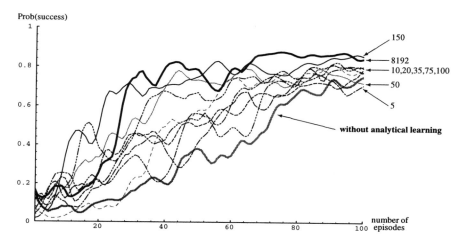

FIG. 3.9. How does domain knowledge improve generalization? Averaged results for EBNN domain theories of differing accuracies, pretrained with 5 to 8,192 training examples. In contrast, the bold gray line reflects the learning curve for pure inductive Q-Learning. All curves are averaged over 3 runs and are also locally window-averaged. The performance (vertical axis) is measured on an independent test set of starting positions.

analytic component of learning will gain in importance. This is because for each inductively derived target value, the analytic component of EBNN will generate n target slopes, where n is the input dimension of the target network. In the ideal case, a single training example in EBNN might therefore be as effective as $n + 1$ training examples in pure inductive learning. These numbers match very roughly our empirical findings.

The importance of inductive learning lies in its ability to extend the system's knowledge beyond that which can be inferred from its starting knowledge. It is obvious in domains such as robot control and speech recognition that manually developing a perfect domain theory is unrealistic. In the case of Xavier, for example, one would have to apply an incredible effort to manually input action models that would meet the requirements of purely analytical learning. An appropriate domain theory would have to include accurate descriptions of the particular sensor noise of ultrasonic and visual sensors, as well as the physics of the robot and its environment. Even the communication delay caused by heavy network traffic would have to be explainable, because it plays a crucial role in determining the outcome of the robot's actions. Although past research has illustrated the feasibility of hand-coding models for idealized and usually noise-free learning scenarios (Laird & Rosenbloom, 1990; Mitchell, 1990), in a domain as complex and as stochastic as Xavier's world this will be an unreasonably difficult undertaking. The importance of induction is that it enables learning observed empirical regularities that can contradict prior knowledge.

INDUCTION AND ANALYSIS IN SOAR

Because Soar is intended as a general architecture for intelligent systems, the question of how to best incorporate both learning mechanisms within Soar seems central to its success. The following subsection briefly summarizes current approaches, and the subsequent subsection considers the possibility of incorporating EBNN within Soar.

Current Learning Mechanisms in Soar

Soar has a single, analytical learning mechanism embedded in the architecture: chunking. Chunking is a variant of explanation-based learning, as discussed in Rosenbloom and Laird (1986). For the current discussion, the key points regarding learning in Soar are:

- Chunking is the only architectural learning mechanism in Soar. It has been claimed (Laird et al., 1986) that chunking is a sufficient architectural learning mechanism.

- The chunking mechanism preserves the correctness of Soar's prior knowledge. More precisely, each production rule created by chunking follows deductively from previous rules in the system. If the prior knowledge is correct, any rule learned by chunking will also be correct. If prior knowledge is incorrect, learned rules may be incorrect.

- In cases where Soar's initial knowledge is incorrect and internally inconsistent, chunking may learn contradictory rules when given multiple examples. In this case, the ill effects of one incorrect rule may be screened by a second (contradictory) rule that applies to some of the same situations (e.g., Rosenbloom, Laird, & Newell, 1987). Whether this beneficial screening will occur depends on the form of the initial knowledge, and on the sequence in which training examples are presented. Thus, while learning of individual rules is a truth-preserving step, learning sets of rules from inconsistent initial knowledge can lead to behavior that improves over the behavior of the initial inconsistent knowledge. This is possible because of the screening of incorrect rules. Because this effect depends on the observed training examples and can result in behavior not produced by the initial knowledge, we consider this an inductive effect.

- Explicit inductive learning methods have also been implemented on top of the Soar architecture by providing problem spaces that perform induction (e.g., Miller & Laird, 1991; Rosenbloom & Aasman, 1990). The detailed implementation of this inductive mechanism relies on the already described effect of screening incorrect rules by learning new rules that better fit the observed data. The explicit programming of induction in problem spaces is accomplished by providing a problem space in which reasoning traces follow the general-to-specific ordering of possible concepts, and in which chunking provides the mechanism for creating new rules from reasoning traces in this problem space. The initial knowledge in this problem space is general enough to "explain" any example observed by the system, so that the particular sequence of examples encountered determines which reasoning traces are produced, and hence which productions are learned.

As the preceding summary indicates, Soar's chunking mechanism provides a form of analytical learning, and the screening effect of new learned rules on inconsistent prior knowledge allows for an inductive component to Soar's learning. Although the capabilities of Soar's analytical learning mechanism have been convincingly demonstrated in a variety of domains (e.g., Tambe, Doorenbos, & Newell, 1992), its inductive learning capabilities have yet to be demonstrated on the same scale.

Our assessment is that although combining inductive and analytical learning will be important to the goal of Soar as a general model of learning, we foresee two difficulties with the current strategy of combining an architectural chunking mechanism with explicit programming of inductive mechanisms in problem spaces. First, it is not clear whether an inductive process that produces new rules but does not refine old rules can efficiently support statistical induction in which each example contributes a small change to a continuously evolving hypothesis. For example, consider the problem of learning to drive Pomerleau's ALVINN system. To succeed, Soar would have to acquire control knowledge from training data involving many hundreds of noisy, complex images, for which inductive regularities emerge only from the statistics of thousands of training examples. In this kind of application, initial knowledge is difficult to derive, so that analytical learning is inapplicable and the burden falls on inductive mechanisms. Here, it appears that Soar's inductive mechanism would require producing a new production each time a new training example was encountered that was inconsistent with the current hypothesis, leading to an enormous number of generated rules that are later screened. Second, it is not clear how Soar's current inductive processes would behave in the face of noise in the training data. Because new rules screen old, one can imagine a scenario in which noisy data first leads the system to learn rule A, then to screen it by rule B (which is consistent with the new example), then to relearn A, and so forth. Although it has not been demonstrated that such difficulties are insurmountable by the proposed Soar inductive methods, neither has it been demonstrated that Soar and chunking can successfully deal with these difficulties.

Because EBNN has been demonstrated to successfully learn statistical regularities from high-dimensional, noisy data, guided by approximate domain knowledge, it is worthwhile to consider the feasibility of incorporating it within a Soar-like architecture for problem solving and learning. This possibility is considered next.

Embedding EBNN in Soar

Here we consider the possible incorporation of the EBNN learning mechanism within a Soar-like architecture. The benefit of such a union would be to combine the inductive–analytical learning capabilities of EBNN with the architectural capabilities of Soar to organize learning and problem solving. One way to incorporate EBNN within Soar would be to substitute EBNN for chunking, with the following correspondences:

- The problem solving traces that provide dependencies used by chunking would become the explanations used by EBNN.
- As with chunking, EBNN would be invoked each time a problem-solving impasse occurs (i.e., whenever the next search action is not obvious). The types of information learned (to preempt subsequent impasses) would be the same as for chunking.
- Unlike chunking, in which a distinct rule is learned from each explanation, in EBNN a distinct network would be learned only for each distinct type of impasse for each distinct problem space. When future impasses of the same type occurred for the same problem space, the existing network would be refined (both analytically and inductively) using the EBNN algorithm.
- In order for the explanations to provide derivative information for EBNN, the production rules on which they were based would be modeled by separate neural nets—one for each type of rule. In general, for each Soar production rule concluding some value for attribute A, a corresponding network for concluding A would be created and would be used to provide derivative information whenever the corresponding rule was involved in some explanation.
- In Soar, an impasse is resolved once deliberation chooses how to continue beyond the search impasse (e.g., by selecting which operator to apply next in the search). At this point, chunking is invoked. In order to support the inductive component of EBNN learning, and to allow for the possibility that deliberation was based on incorrect knowledge, a separate empirical evaluation of the impasse resolution will be required (e.g., to determine whether the selected operator truly succeeds). This empirical evaluation might be obtained, for example, by monitoring the final outcome of the search, or by estimating its likelihood of success based on independent knowledge (e.g., as in reinforcement learning).

Let us refer to such a system as EBNN-Soar, and to the current version of Soar as Chunking-Soar. Key differences between these two systems would include:

- Learning in EBNN-Soar would support pure induction at the architecture level, as well as analytical learning and blends of these two. We expect this would provide more robust learning in the face of approximate prior knowledge and noise in the training data.
- Analytical learning in EBNN-Soar will be slower than in Chunking-Soar. More precisely, analytical learning in EBNN-Soar will incrementally refine the neural network that encodes knowledge for a particular impasse/problem-space pair, mediated by the companion inductive learning component of EBNN. This will lead to less abrupt changes to system knowledge than in Chunking-Soar, where a complete rule is formulated based solely on the analysis of a single example. Others have noted (Rosenbloom, 1983) that learning in Chunking-Soar may be too abrupt to be a correct model of human learning.
- EBNN-Soar may avoid the average growth effect encountered by Chunking-Soar (Tambe et al., 1992), in which the large number of learned chunks can lead to significant slowdown in processing. By representing knowledge using a bounded collection of neural nets (one per <impasse, problem-space> pair), the cost of applying such knowledge cannot grow indefinitely.
- Because it would use a bounded set of networks for representing learned knowledge, EBNN-Soar may encounter limitations in representational expressiveness that are not present in Chunking-Soar. In particular, its bounded-space representation of control knowledge may have too little capacity to accurately represent complex control knowledge. As a result, it may be necessary to develop a more elaborate memory organization than the simple approach sketched here.

SUMMARY AND CONCLUSIONS

We began this chapter with the question of how to best combine inductive and analytical learning in an architecture that seeks to cover the range of learning exhibited by intelligent systems such as humans. Although this question is far from answered, the EBNN algorithm described here provides a general learning method for robustly combining these two types of learning. We presented experimental results showing the use of EBNN for learning mobile robot control strategies, guided by approximate, previously learned knowledge. We also considered briefly the way in which Soar achieves analytical and inductive learning, and the possibility of incorporating EBNN within a Soar-like architecture. The main points of this chapter include:

- Both inductive and analytical learning mechanisms will be needed to cover the range of learning exhibited by humans and other intelligent systems. Analytical mechanisms are required in order to scale up to learning complex concepts, and to handle situations in which available training data is limited. Inductive mechanisms are required in order to learn in situations where prior knowledge is incomplete or incorrect.

- Explanation-based neural network (EBNN) learning provides a means of smoothly combining inductive and analytical learning. Experimental results demonstrate that EBNN can learn to control a mobile robot, from noisy data including vision, sonar, and laser range sensors, and based on approximate knowledge that was previously learned by the robot itself. Given strong prior knowledge, EBNN learns from considerably less data than pure induction (exemplified by the neural network backpropagation algorithm). As the accuracy of this prior knowledge decreases, EBNN's ability to generalize degrades gracefully until it reaches the same level of performance as pure induction.

- Soar's architectural learning mechanism, chunking, is a purely analytical mechanism. Recent research on Soar has explored ways of incorporating inductive learning mechanisms by including problem spaces that, when coupled with chunking, result in inductive learning within Soar. We suggested an alternative way to combine analytical and inductive learning within a Soar-like architecture: Replace Soar's chunking mechanism by EBNN. We believe such an architecture would have significant advantages in handling statistical learning from noisy data. Such a change would introduce changes to the architecture's representation (neural network vs. symbolic productions), memory organization (one neural network replaces multiple productions), and scaling properties (reducing the average growth effect problem, but raising new problems stemming from the bounded expressive capability of fixed-size networks). Although the details of such an architecture remain to be designed, we believe the demonstrated abilities of EBNN warrant further exploration of this alternative.

ACKNOWLEDGMENTS

This chapter has benefited from a number of discussions over the years with Allen Newell, John Laird, and Paul Rosenbloom regarding the sufficiency of chunking and the potential role of inductive learning in Soar.

This research is sponsored in part by the National Science Foundation under award IRI-9313367, and by the Wright Laboratory, Aeronautical

Systems Center, Air Force Materiel Command, USAF, and the Advanced Research Projects Agency (ARPA) under grant F33615-93-1-1330. Views and conclusions contained in this document are those of the authors and should not be interpreted as necessarily representing official policies or endorsements, either expressed or implied, of NSF, Wright Laboratory, or the U.S. government.

REFERENCES

Ahn, W.-K., & Brewer, W. F. (1993). Psychological studies of explanation-based learning. In G. DeJong (Ed.), *Investigating explanation-based learning* (pp. 295–316). Boston: Kluwer.

Barto, A. G., Bradtke, S. J., & Singh, S. P. (1991, August). *Real-time learning and control using asynchronous dynamic programming* (Tech. Rep. COINS 91-57). Department of Computer Science, University of Massachusetts, Cambridge.

Chi, M. T. H., & Bassok, M. (1989). Learning from examples via self-explanations. In L. B. Resnick (Ed.), *Knowing, learning, and instruction: Essays in honor of Robert Glaser*. Hillsdale, NJ: Lawrence Erlbaum Associates.

DeJong, G., & Mooney, R. (1986). Explanation-based learning: An alternative view. *Machine Learning, 1*(2), 145–176.

Doorenbos, R. E. (1993). Matching 100,000 learned rules. *Proceeding of the Eleventh National Conference on Artificial Intelligence AAAI-93* (pp. 290–296). Menlo Park, CA: AAAI Press/MIT Press.

Fu, L.-M. (1989). Integration of neural heuristics into knowledge-based inference. *Connection Science, 1*(3), 325–339.

Gullapalli, V. (1992). *Reinforcement learning and its application to control.* Unpublished doctoral dissertation, Department of Computer and Information Science, University of Massachusetts, Cambridge.

Khatib, O. (1986). Real-time obstacle avoidance for robot manipulator and mobile robots. *International Journal of Robotics Research, 5*(1), 90–98.

Laird, J. E., & Rosenbloom, P. S. (1990). Integrating execution, planning, and learning in soar for external environments. In *Proceeding of the Eighth National Conference on Artificial Intelligence AAAI-90* (pp. 1022–1029). Menlo Park, CA: AAAI Press/MIT Press.

Laird, J., Rosenbloom, P., & Newell, A. (1986). Chunking in SOAR: The anatomy of a general learning mechanism. *Machine Learning, 1*(1), 11–46.

Lin, L.-J. (1992). *Self-supervised learning by reinforcement and artificial neural networks.* Unpublished doctoral dissertation, School of Computer Science, Carnegie Mellon University, Pittsburgh.

Masuoka, R. (1993, October). Noise robustness of EBNN learning. *Proceedings of the International Joint Conference on Neural Networks.*

Miller, C. S., & Laird, J. E. (1991). A constraint-motivated lexical acquisition model. *Proceedings of the Thirteenth Annual Meeting of the Cognitive science Society* (pp. 827–831). Hillsdale, NJ: Lawrence Erlbaum Associates.

Minton, S., Carbonell, J., Knoblock, C. A., Kuoka, D. R., Etzioni, O., & Gil, Y. (1989). Explanation-based learning: A problem solving perspective. *Artificial Intelligence, 40,* 63–118.

Mitchell, T. M. (1990, August). Becoming increasingly reactive. *Proceedings of 1990 AAAI Conference.* Menlo Park, CA: AAAI Press/MIT Press.

Mitchell, T. M., Keller, R., & Kedar-Cabelli, S. (1986). Explanation-based generalization: A unifying view. *Machine Learning, 1*(1), 47–80.

Mitchell, T. M., & Thrun, S. B. (1993). Explanation-based neural network learning for robot control. In S. J. Hanson, J. Cowan, and C. L. Giles (Eds.), *Advances in Neural Information Processing Systems 5* (pp. 287–294). San Mateo, CA: Morgan Kaufmann.

O'Sullivan, J. (1994, January). *Xavier manual*. Carnegie Mellon University, Learning Robot Lab Internal Document.

Ourston, D., & Mooney, R. (1994). Theory refinement combining analytical and empirical methods. *Artificial Intelligence, 66*, 311–344.

Pazzani, M. J., Brunk, C. A., & Silverstein, G. (1991, June). A knowledge-intensive approach to learning relational concepts. *Proceedings of the Eighth International Workshop on Machine Learning* (pp. 432–436). Evanston, IL.

Pomerleau, D. A. (1989). *ALVINN: An autonomous land vehicle in a neural network* (Tech. Rep. No. CMU-CS-89-107). Pittsburgh: Carnegie Mellon University, Computer Science Department.

Qin, Y., Mitchell, T. M., & Herbert, S. (1992, April). Using EBG to simulate human learning from examples and learning by doing. *Proceedings of the Florida AI Research Symposium* (pp. 235–239).

Rosenbloom, P. (1983). *The chunking of goal hierarchies: A model of practice and stimulus-response compatibility* (Tech. Rep. No. CMU-CS-83-148). Pittsburgh: Carnegie Mellon University, School of Computer Science.

Rosenbloom, P. S., & Aasman, J. (1990). Knowledge level and inductive uses of chunking (ebl). *Proceedings of the Eighth National Conference on Artificial Intelligence* (pp. 821–827). Boston: AAAI, MIT Press.

Rosenbloom, P. S., & Laird, J. E. (1986). *Mapping explanation-based generalization onto soar* (Tech. Rep. No. 1111). Stanford, CA: Stanford University, Department of Computer Science.

Rosenbloom, P. S., Laird, J., & Newell, A. (1987). *Knowledge level learning in soar* (Tech. Rep. No. AIP-8, Artificial Intelligence and Psychology Project). Pittsburgh: Carnegie Mellon University.

Rumelhart, D. E., Hinton, G. E., & Williams, R. J. (1986). Learning internal representations by error propagation. In D. E. Rumelhart & J. L. McClelland (Eds.), *Parallel distributed processing* (Vols. I and II). Boston: MIT Press.

Shavlik, J. W., & Towell, G. G. (1989). An approach to combining explanation-based and neural learning algorithms. *Connection Science, 1*(3), 231–253.

Simard, P., Victorri, B., LeCun, Y., & Denker, J. (1992). Tangent prop—A formalism for specifying selected invariances in an adaptive network. In J. E. Moody, S. J. Hanson, & R. P. Lippmann (Eds.), *Advances in neural information processing systems* (Vol. 4, pp. 895–903). San Mateo, CA: Morgan Kaufmann.

Sutton, R. S. (1988). Learning to predict by the methods of temporal differences. *Machine Learning, 3*.

Tambe, M., Doorenbos, R., & Newell, A. (1992). *The match cost of adding a new rule: A clash of views* (Tech. Rep. No. CMU-CS-92-158). Pittsburgh: Carnegie Mellon University.

Tesauro, G. J. (1992). Practical issues in temporal difference learning. In J. E. Moody, S. J. Hanson, & R. P. Lippmann (Eds.), *Advances in neural information processing systems* (Vol. 4, pp. 259–266). San Mateo, CA: Morgan Kaufmann.

Thrun, S. B., & Mitchell, T. M. (1993, July). Integrating inductive neural network learning and explanation-based learning. R. Bajcsy (Ed.), *Proceedings of IJCAI-93*. San Mateo, CA: Morgan Kaufmann.

Towell, G. G., & Shavlik, J. W. (1989). *Combining explanation-based learning and neural networks: An algorithm and empirical results* (Tech. Rep. No. 859). University of Wisconsin-Madison, Computer Science, Madison.

Watkins, C. J. C. H. (1989). *Learning from delayed rewards*. Unpublished doctoral dissertation, King's College, Cambridge, UK.

Winston, P. H., Binford, T. O., Katz, B., & Lowry, M. (1983). Learning physical descriptions from functional definitions, examples, and precedents. *Proceedings of the National Conference on Artificial Intelligence* (pp. 433–439). Washington, DC: Morgan Kaufmann.

DISCUSSION

Learning Matters

Paul S. Rosenbloom
University of Southern California

In chapter 3 of this volume, Mitchell and Thrun focus on one of the key issues in the construction of an autonomous agent—how such an agent can learn to control its behavior through direct interaction with its environment. Although the chapter does not explicitly highlight specific hypotheses, it seems safe to extract from it three underlying hypotheses: one top-level and two subordinate. The actual expression of these hypotheses is mine, but the intent here is to capture the essence of what Mitchell and Thrun intended, and then to use these hypotheses to focus a discussion from the intertwined perspective of our experience with Allen Newell and Soar (which are often hard to disentangle). One thread that will be implicit through much of the material in this discussion is particularly identified with Newell's research philosophy: Working with an integrated architecture means looking deeply at its consequences for new phenomena or capabilities before hypothesizing new mechanisms to account for them, and in the process the architecture will often teach you what you couldn't have anticipated.

Mitchell and Thrun's top-level hypothesis focuses on a necessary condition for effective learning of control by an autonomous agent.

Hybrid-learning hypothesis: Learning to control behavior from external interaction requires a blend of analytical and empirical techniques.

Analytical techniques, such as explanation-based learning (EBL; DeJong & Mooney, 1986; Mitchell, Keller, & Kedar-Cabelli, 1986), focus on using

111

background knowledge in interpreting the agent's interactions with its environment. Such techniques can learn quite effectively from even a small number of interactions if the agent is endowed with appropriate background knowledge. Empirical techniques, such as the wide range of induction algorithms that have so far been developed (Weiss & Kulikowski, 1991), make up for an almost total lack of background knowledge by searching for regularities over large sets of interactions. A good blend of analytical and empirical techniques would maximize learning effectiveness by using whatever background knowledge it could, but also coping with inadequacies in this knowledge by searching for regularities over larger sets of interactions.

The two subordinate hypotheses draw implications from the hybrid-learning hypothesis for Soar (Laird, Newell, & Rosenbloom, 1987; Newell, 1990; Rosenbloom, Laird, Newell, & McCarl, 1991) and explanation-based neural network (EBNN) learning (chapter 3).

Chunking-insufficiency hypothesis: Chunking is not a sufficient learning mechanism for an autonomous agent; in particular, Soar will need to be augmented with an inductive learning mechanism that includes some form of statistical capability.

EBNN-utility hypothesis: EBNN is a useful means of blending analytical and empirical techniques for learning to control an autonomous agent.

The chunking-insufficiency hypothesis follows directly from the hybrid-learning hypothesis, and from the facts that (1) chunking is an analytical learning mechanism and (2) it is Soar's only learning mechanism. The EBNN-utility hypothesis follows from the hybrid-learning hypothesis and EBNN's demonstrated ability to blend background knowledge with multiple external interactions.

HYBRID-LEARNING HYPOTHESIS

The top-level, hybrid-learning hypothesis is the least controversial of the three. If anything, it appears to understate the case. In his work on the knowledge level, Newell identified intelligence with the extent to which an agent uses its knowledge in selecting actions in service of achieving its goals (Newell, 1982). According to this definition, any failure to use knowledge that is both available and relevant in controlling action selection may thus reflect a lack of intelligence. Such knowledge could be embodied in the domain theories typically used in analytical learning, or in the examples typically used in empirical learning. However, critical knowledge may also be embodied in a variety of other forms, such as manuals, fragments of

advice, and descriptions of similar problems and situations.[1] Standard analytical and empirical learning techniques are not able to handle such
sources of knowledge, even when hybridized, and so exhibit lowered standards of intelligence, and relatively inferior performance, in the presence
of such knowledge. What is really needed is an extension of the hybrid-
learning hypothesis—and a corresponding extension of our learning systems—to cope with this wider range of available knowledge sources.

One formulation of the extended hypothesis might be as follows.

Intelligent-learning hypothesis: Intelligence requires learning from whatever
sources of knowledge are both available and relevant.

This hypothesis doesn't directly say what kinds of learning mechanisms are
needed, but does provide a strong constraint on their requisite functionality.

CHUNKING-INSUFFICIENCY HYPOTHESIS

The chunking-insufficiency hypothesis evaluates Soar with respect to the
hybrid-learning hypothesis, yielding a negative result, at least with respect to
its (lack of) embodiment of induction. If we look just at the bottom line, Soar
has indeed not yet reached state-of-the-art levels of performance in induction
tasks. Work based on Miller and Laird (1991) is reaching such levels,
although key parts of the algorithm are currently represented outside of
Soar. Other investigations, such as Unruh and Rosenbloom (1989) and
Rosenbloom and Aasman (1990), have made significant progress on a
number of the basic issues in Soar-based induction—such as how to make
inductive leaps and how to integrate the information embodied by many
examples into a coherent structure—but have not yet led to state-of-the-art
inductive performance. Mitchell and Thrun's hypothesized explanation for
this shortfall is Soar's lack of an architectural induction mechanism that
embodies a statistical capability. However, the following quote makes it clear
that our perspective on this is a bit different.

Deduction, induction, and *abduction* have always seemed to me a particularly
superficial way to classify types of reasoning (Newell 1969, 1973b). *Induction*
plays no special role in my thinking and it never occurred to me to address
whether Soar could do induction. Of course it can, just as it can do syllogisms
or design algorithms or play video games. (Newell, 1992, p. 478)

So let's first review the progress that has been made on the aforementioned
basic issues in Soar-based induction in the absence of specific architectural

---

[1]One possible categorization of the different knowledge sources that might be available
for learning can be found in Huffman, Pearson, and Laird (1993).

mechanisms for induction, and then return to the questions of statistical and architectural mechanisms.

Chunking is not an inherently inductive mechanism, except when it overgeneralizes (Laird, Rosenbloom, & Newell, 1986). Instead, its function is to derive generalized rules analytically from traces of the system's goal-based performance. Induction primarily comes about in Soar through inductive leaps (either deliberate or implicit) that occur while attempting to achieve goals; problem spaces are not themselves either inherently deductive or inductive, but can exhibit either form of behavior as a function of their contents. Chunking then creates "inductively generalized" rules by analyzing the traces of this inductive problem solving. For example, in Unruh's work on abstraction, the problem solving is able to deliberately ignore particular operator preconditions (Unruh & Rosenbloom, 1989), leading to the acquisition of control chunks that test fewer conditions than they otherwise would. These generalized rules effectively act as segments of abstract plans.

Although the ability to make inductive leaps is crucial, it is not all there is to induction from multiple examples. Also crucial is the ability to integrate the information embodied by many examples into a coherent structure—for example, a representation of the concept underlying the set of examples—as demonstrated in Soar, for example, in Rosenbloom and Aasman (1990) and Miller and Laird (1991). For incremental learning this requires repeatedly accessing and updating the structure representing what has been learned from earlier examples. In Soar, such prior structure is accessed either by direct memory access (Rosenbloom & Aasman, 1990)— that is, by production firing—or by search in problem spaces (Miller & Laird, 1991). Modification occurs by learning new structure and effectively suppressing (all or part of) the old structure so that the new structure is used in its place. This suppression is accomplished at present either by masking the old structure (Miller & Laird, 1991)—by, for example, ensuring that during search the new structure will be found prior to the old structure—or by explicitly rejecting it (Rosenbloom & Aasman, 1990).

Statistical measures are used by induction programs to identify potentially meaningful trends across sets of examples. This helps in coping with stochastic aspects of the examples, as well as in ferreting out relationships that may otherwise be hidden in the complexity of the interactions. However, despite this acknowledged role, we remain rather ambivalent about the role of statistics in intelligent behavior in general, and in Soar in particular. One part of this ambivalence is wondering whether the amount of precision provided by such measures is particularly useful. For example, the MYCIN experiments showed that, at least in the space of rule certainties, having very few partitions on the space was more than adequate (Buchanan & Shortliffe, 1984). Another part of this is noticing that practice effects, such as those produced by chunking, can yield a number of psychological phenomena that are typically attributed to statistical measures, such as frequency and typicality effects (Miller & Laird, 1991). Although it remains to be shown whether this can provide the full range of such phenomena, such as probability matching, it begins to raise the question as to whether explicit statistical measures are even necessary.

In addition to the belief that deduction and induction are not fundamentally different, the philosophy underlying the overall approach to induction in Soar includes that inductive leaps are inherently risky, and should therefore be made as intelligently as possible; that is, they should be guided by whatever knowledge is both available and relevant. In Pylyshyn's terms, this means induction should be cognitively penetrable (Pylyshyn, 1984), and not part of the architecture. Placing induction above the architecture, and providing Soar's full capabilities in guiding it, enables Soar to be a particularly good vehicle for pursuing the intelligent-learning hypothesis—at least to the extent that explicit statistical mechanisms are not implicated—and is, in fact, a significant current focus within the project. However, by making induction an object of deliberation, this approach also raises the key question of how induction could ever be straightforward and ubiquitous in Soar. This is, I think, the heart of the question Mitchell and Thrun are asking about Soar and its ability to be inductive (and thus match the requirements of the hybrid-learning hypothesis).

At the moment we only have a tentative response to this question, and that is to focus on the comprehension abilities that are being added to Soar (Lehman, Lewis, & Newell, 1991). Comprehension involves taking a new item, such as a natural-language utterance or a visual scene, and bringing it together with what is already in memory to yield a coherent model of the situation. Incremental generalization is just a particular stylized version of such a comprehension process, where the new item is an example and the existing memory structures represent a concept. At each step, the new example is comprehended with respect to the existing concept representation, resulting in modifications to the representation that capture what new information is conveyed by the example.

If comprehension were to be a pervasive activity in Soar, then it may be that chunking over this activity will yield induction that is not only straightforward and ubiquitous, but also guided by whatever knowledge is used during comprehension. Although investigations of comprehension in Soar began within the relatively narrow scope of natural language text, it is clear that such activity is implicated in processing all input from the external environment, whether it be verbal, visual, or any other input modality. We (with Ben Smith) have also begun to investigate the idea that comprehension is ubiquitous as well in internal communication among multiple problem spaces. A simple example of this might be a situation in which one problem space creates its initial state based on comprehending an impasse that occurred in the parent space. A more involved example might be a situation in which one problem space selects an action to perform through comprehending a (possibly analogical) solution produced in a subspace.

All of this still leaves open the accuracy of the chunking-insufficiency hypothesis, but does highlight the questions that must be addressed in Soar for it to be laid to rest.

EBNN-UTILITY HYPOTHESIS

The EBNN-utility hypothesis indicates a positive evaluation of EBNN with respect to the hybrid-learning hypothesis. As I understand it, EBNN learns from a performance trace—an interleaved sequence of actions and states—augmented with state evaluations (reinforcements). The overall problem is to learn to predict the reinforcement that will result from applying particular actions to particular states. When combined with a gradient-ascent (hill-climbing) method, these learned predictions enable actions to be selected that increase later reinforcement.

EBNN's inductive method learns from only part of the information in the performance trace: associations between state–action pairs and later reinforcements. It ignores all of the information embodied by the portion of the trace between the state–action pair and the reinforcement, and thus fails to perform as intelligently as it could. The hybrid method overcomes this limitation by learning action models—that is, predictions of the states that result from applying particular actions to particular states—from the otherwise neglected portions of the trace, and then using slopes derived from chains of these action models to guide the overall inductive process.

The experimental results with this method provide strong support for the EBNN-utility hypothesis (chapter 3), so the remaining comments are not focused directly on its validity, but instead on two related questions, one more specific and one more general.

The more specific question is, why it is necessary to modify the basic learning algorithm—to use slope information—in order to utilize the extra knowledge that is embodied by the action models? Could something deeper instead have been learned by looking more intensively at the existing architecture? Standard neural-network algorithms can incorporate additional knowledge into the induction process via either of two routes: through additional training examples synthesized from the additional knowledge, or through direct setting of weights (or network topology).[2] Could the knowledge embodied by the action models have been incorporated into the overall

---

[2]Additional knowledge could also theoretically be incorporated through the setting of parameters in the learning equations, but we ignore this possibility here.

inductive process via either of these existing two routes, or was the creation of a new route—that is, slope information—necessary? The first of these existing routes does turn out to underlie how one other reinforcement learning system utilizes the action models that it also acquires (Sutton, 1990). It is also analogous to how some symbolic learning algorithms combine multiple sources of knowledge in induction; for example, incremental version space merging (IVSM) uses explanation-based learning to generate abstract training instances, which are then processed normally by the induction algorithm (Hirsh, 1989). Use of the second existing route could involve the construction of a single decomposable network in which subregions of weights are trained based on the extra knowledge, and then frozen during normal inductive learning (as, for example, in Jordan & Rumelhart, 1992). Alternatively, it could involve some sort of compilation technique—quite analogous to chunking—that takes a neural network with an arbitrary number of layers and, based on analyzing the network of weights, compiles it into the weights of a standardized one or two-layer network. For EBNN, this would consist of compiling the network that is defined by chaining together a sequence of action networks directly into the weights of the evaluation network. It isn't clear whether either of these existing routes would work well in Mitchell and Thrun's task; however, if they wouldn't, it would be quite interesting to understand why.

The more general question is how EBNN stands with respect to the intelligent learning hypothesis; that is, to what extent can it form the basis of an intelligent system that can make use of the broader range of knowledge sources that may often be available and relevant for learning to control behavior? Pure inductive algorithms fall far short of what is required. By providing a new route for knowledge incorporation EBNN may be moving in the right direction, but if so, how much further has it moved? Does its new route enable it to cope with anything beyond action models, or is it still dramatically limited by being such a hardwired learning architecture?

ACKNOWLEDGMENT

The preparation of this commentary was sponsored by the National Aeronautics and Space Administration under cooperative agreement NCC 2-538. I would also like to thank Haym Hirsh, John Laird, and Craig Miller for helpful comments and discussions on this material.

REFERENCES

Buchanan, B. G., & Shortliffe, E. H. (1984). *Rule-based expert systems: The MYCIN experiments of the Stanford Heuristic Programming Project.* Reading, MA: Addison-Wesley.

DeJong, G., & Mooney, R. J. (1986). Explanation-based learning: An alternative view. *Machine Learning, 1,* 145–176.

Hirsh, H. (1989). Combining empirical and analytical learning with version spaces. *Proceedings of the Sixth International Workshop on Machine Learning.* Cornell.

Huffman, S. B., Pearson, D. J., & Laird, J. E. (1993). Correcting imperfect domain theories: A knowledge-level analysis. In S. Chipman & A. L. Meyrowitz (Eds.), *Foundations of knowledge acquisition: Cognitive models of complex learning* (pp. 209–244). Hingham, MA: Kluwer.

Jordan, M. I., & Rumelhart, D. E. (1992). Forward models: Supervised learning with a distal teacher. *Cognitive Science, 16,* 307–354.

Laird, J. E., Newell, A., & Rosenbloom, P. S. (1987). Soar: An architecture for general intelligence. *Artificial Intelligence, 33,* 1–64.

Laird, J. E., Rosenbloom, P. S., & Newell, A. (1986). Overgeneralization during knowledge compilation in Soar. In T. G. Dietterich (Ed.), *Proceedings of the Workshop on Knowledge Compilation* (pp. 46–57). Otter Crest: AAAI/Oregon State University.

Lehman, J. F., Lewis, R. L., & Newell, A. (1991). Integrating knowledge sources in language comprehension. In *Proceedings of the Thirteenth Annual Meeting of the Cognitive Science Society* (pp. 461–466). Hillsdale, NJ: Lawrence Erlbaum Associates.

Miller, C. S., & Laird, J. E. (1991). A constraint-motivated model of concept formation. In *Proceedings of the Thirteenth Annual Meeting of the Cognitive Science Society* (pp. 827–831). Hillsdale, NJ: Lawrence Erlbaum Associates.

Mitchell, T. M., Keller, R. M., & Kedar-Cabelli, S. T. (1986). Explanation-based generalization: A unifying view. *Machine Learning, 1,* 47–80.

Newell, A. (1969). Heuristic programming: Ill-structured problems. In J. Aronofsky (Ed.), *Progress in Operations Research, III* (pp. 360–414). New York: Wiley.

Newell, A. (1973). Artificial intelligence and the concept of mind. In R. C. Schank & K. M. Colby (Eds.), *Computer models of thought and language* (pp. 1–60). San Francisco: W. H. Freeman.

Newell, A. (1982). The knowledge level. *Artificial Intelligence, 18,* 87–127.

Newell, A. (1990). *Unified theories of cognition.* Cambridge, MA: Harvard University Press.

Newell, A. (1992). SOAR as a unified theory of cognition: Issues and explanations. *Behavioral and Brain Sciences, 15,* 464–488.

Pylyshyn, Z. W. (1984). *Computation and cognition: Toward a foundation for cognitive science.* Cambridge, MA: Bradford.

Rosenbloom, P. S., & Aasman, J. (1990). Knowledge level and inductive uses of chunking (EBL). In *Proceedings of the Eighth National Conference on Artificial Intelligence* (pp. 821–827). Boston: AAAI, MIT Press.

Rosenbloom, P. S., Laird, J. E., Newell, A., & McCarl, R. (1991). A preliminary analysis of the Soar architecture as a basis for general intelligence. *Artificial Intelligence, 47,* 289–325.

Sutton, R. S. (1990). Integrated architectures for learning, planning, and reacting based on approximating dynamic programming. In B. W. Porter & R. J. Mooney (Eds.), *Proceedings of the Seventh International Conference on Machine Learning* (pp. 216–224). Austin, TX: Morgan Kaufmann.

Unruh, A., & Rosenbloom, P. S. (1989). Abstraction in problem solving and learning. In *Proceedings of the Eleventh International Joint Conference on Artificial Intelligence* (pp. 681–687). Detroit: IJCAII.

Weiss, S. M., & Kulikowski, C. A. (1991). *Computer systems that learn.* Los Altos, CA: Morgan Kaufmann.

Chapter 4

Meaning Matters:
Problems in Sense Resolution

George A. Miller
Princeton University

I want to discuss some problems in sense resolution that I have run into in trying to get computers to understand human language. (Actually, my real interest is in how people understand human language, but trying to explain it to a computer provides a severe test for my ideas.) I think that Soar might suggest some solutions to these problems, but before I can even ask sensible questions, I need to explain where I am coming from.

Thinking about my work in relation to Soar is a new challenge for me, and I may need help to get it right. Usually I talk to people who try to draw flowcharts for language processing by a human nervous system. If you examine the hypotheses advanced by scientists who study the language of people who have suffered brain injuries, you will find that they have a lot of boxes scattered about with arrows between them—boxes for hearing speech or reading print, short-term buffers for storing speech or storing print, output boxes for uttering speech or writing, and so on. And somewhere in the center of all these boxes there will usually be one labeled "cognition" or "meaning," where a miracle is assumed to occur. The arrangement of the boxes is intended to explain data obtained from simple tests of various defects of listening or reading or speaking or writing, or tests of the relations between and among these several different kinds of defects. What I try to say to those who think of language processing in this way is that their meaning box is really a large swamp full of complicated and interesting things.

In presenting my ideas to an audience interested in computer simulations of cognitive processes, however, the picture is just the reverse. That is to say, they tend to view language as a transducer, as a peripheral process that transforms linguistic signals into the concepts that a goal-oriented problem-solving system can deal with. Their diagrams have two little boxes, one at either end: an input transducer labeled "comprehend" and an output transducer labeled "generate," with an elaborately developed flow-chart of the cognitive processes intervening between these two transducers. The goal is to process such sentences as "Put the red block on the green block" or "Some artists are barbers." What I want to say to those who think of language processing in this way is that their peripheral boxes are really a large swamp full of complicated and interesting things.

Both groups agree on a modular analysis of language processing, but they put their emphases on very different modules. This difference seems to be a consequence of what I call the transparency of the signal. As long as everything is working well, the peripheral boxes do their work quietly, out of conscious awareness. If you are simulating normal cognition, as in artificial intelligence, the signal is transparent; it is easy to take the peripheral processing for granted and to look right past it at the concept it encodes. Only when something fails to work properly, as in the case of brain damage, do we notice the complicated machinery that is involved in language comprehension. Peripheral failures are clearly linguistic, and lead to neurolinguistic studies of the formal aspects of language; central failures are conceptual and fall outside the domain of neurolinguistics. So the two enterprises go their separate ways.

You might think that a simple solution to all the problems of language understanding would be to combine the elaborate peripheral modules of a neuropsychologist with the elaborate central modules of a cognitive simu-lator. The idea is right in general, but sadly lacking in specifics. When you contemplate the combination seriously, you quickly realize that it cannot work. There is a serious mismatch between the peripheral boxes of the neuropsychologists and the central boxes of the problem solvers. Elimi-nating the mismatch is not a simple matter, because neither team under-stands the problems that the other is trying to solve.

What I would like to see—what I think most workers in computational linguistics would like to see—is a robust system that would accept any spoken or written language and would "understand" it well enough to perform accurately certain superficially simple processes: to answer ques-tions, to carry out commands, to retrieve information, to paraphrase or summarize passages, to translate into another language, to explain concepts to young learners, and so on. These are, of course, precisely the linguistic processes that students of artificial intelligence have been trying to simulate for many years, but with discouragingly limited success. That is to say, computers can perform such functions, although not as well as people can, as long as the topic is restricted to a narrow domain and some plausible constraints are put on the complexity of the sentences and the signal-to-noise ratio. But they do not scale up well to real applications.

I certainly do not want to minimize the considerable progress that has been made, but neither do I want to minimize the problems that remain. The principle problem is that a great deal of knowledge is required in order to correlate linguistic forms with their meanings. It is generally assumed that both world knowledge and linguistic knowledge are needed. But the question remains: How should we give a computer the kind of knowledge that is required in order to relate forms and meanings?

WORLD KNOWLEDGE VERSUS LINGUISTIC KNOWLEDGE

The need for world knowledge to support language comprehension is well recognized. I have in mind ambiguous sentences like "Sam walked into the library." Some people have trouble recognizing that "Sam walked into the library" is ambiguous. "Sam walked into the tree" is also ambiguous, and in the same way. One explanation of how people resolve such ambiguities is that they draw on their knowledge of the world. It is common knowledge that libraries are things you go inside of whereas trees (generally) are not, and that trees are things you bump into whereas libraries (generally) are not. That is to say, people know about libraries and about trees, and what they know resolves the potential ambiguity so rapidly that it is not even noticed.

That is a plausible approach. But world knowledge is so huge and amorphous that I have never had the courage to tackle it. Nothing less than a system as sophisticated as Soar could possibly encompass it, and even Soar might not suffice. So I have tried to take a shortcut. I have tried to imagine what linguistic knowledge would be required and how it might be organized. Indeed, many of the problems that seem to require world knowledge could be handled well enough if only our systems had more linguistic knowledge. The ambiguous sentence just discussed, "Sam walked into the library," can serve as an example. Suppose our system—the system that we design to map linguistic forms into their meanings—knows that *walk into* is a phrasal verb with more than one sense. Then the problem would be to use the linguistic context to determine which sense of *walk into* is appropriate in any given case. This is the kind of linguistic relation between a verb and its context that is called a selectional restriction (or a selection preference): A verb selects certain nouns that can serve felicitously as its direct object.

Because linguistic knowledge is a part of world knowledge, an appeal to linguistic knowledge might seem parsimonious. But the sheer bulk of information that is involved is still forbidding. To get a rough estimate, take the 1,700-page grammar by Quirk, Greenbaum, Leech, and Svartvik (1985) and pile it on top of the 1,500-page *Webster's Ninth New Collegiate*

Dictionary (1987). And even that is an underestimate—there is much that speakers of English know about their language that the authors of these great books have not yet described. But it is less than, say, *The Encyclopedia Britannica*, which might be taken as a comparable estimate of the amount of world knowledge a system would require.

Whether linguistic knowledge, defined to include lexical as well as grammatical information, could suffice to answer all of the questions for which a need for world knowledge has been invoked is not something I hope to settle here. My point is merely that more and better linguistic knowledge could be a great help. In any case, I am going to discuss only linguistic knowledge—there are enough problems involved with that to overflow the space I have available.

One obvious linguistic need is for a good, robust parsing program. In spite of remarkable progress in syntactic theory and in parser construction during the past quarter century, we still do not have a computer system capable of parsing correctly every grammatical sentence that comes its way. It is a difficult problem, but in order to get ahead with my present concerns I am going to assume that it has been solved.

THE LEXICAL MATRIX

I want to begin at a level simpler than syntax, at the level of words. (I say *words*, although more complex grammatical constituents involve the same problems—but that would require more syntax than I want to introduce at this point.) A *word* is an association between an utterance and a concept that has a syntactic function. It is that association that we need to understand.

The three major problems that I see at the level of words are *synonymy* (when two words express the same sense), *polysemy* (when two senses are expressed by the same word), and *coreference* (when two words have the same referent). In information retrieval, for example, synonymy can cause you to miss those items filed under a synonym of the term you happened to use in your request. Polysemy, on the other hand, can result in false drops; the word used in your request can retrieve items on topics other than the one you had in mind. And mistakes in coreference (as between words in successive requests) can garble the retrieval completely. Although all three are important, here I intend to discuss only the first two, synonymy and polysemy.

At the word level, the association between the peripheral boxes and the central boxes can be thought of as a mapping between word forms and word meanings. Actually, there are several mappings between levels of representation. To keep matters as simple as possible, I consider only inscriptions—written word forms. And I assume that word senses are given by the kind of brief semantic explanations that are found in a standard (monolingual) dictionary. I concentrate on the mapping between written forms and the meanings that they can be used to express. If you imagine this mapping as a large (and largely empty) matrix with the word forms labeling the columns and the word meanings labeling the rows, then an entry in a cell of the matrix means that the word in that column can (in some appropriate context) be used to express the meaning in that row.

One advantage to thinking of a dictionary as a lexical matrix is that synonymy and polysemy are seen to be complementary ways of looking at the same thing. That is to say, the mapping between forms and senses is many : many. If a row has more than one entry, it means that more than one word can be used to express that sense, that is, the word forms are synonymous. If a column has more than one entry, it means that more than one sense can be expressed by that form, that is, the word form is polysemous.

The mapping between word forms and word senses does not exhaust the lexical knowledge our system must have. There are also many morphological relations between and among the word forms, and many semantic relations between and among the word senses. There is much of interest to say about both formal and semantic relations, but the lexical matrix is concerned specifically with relations between forms and meanings.

It is possible to assume that the same lexical matrix is consulted for both input and output—that is to say, for both the "comprehend" and the "generate" transducers of a model of central processes. In language generation, you enter the lexical matrix with a sense and search for the best word to express it. The output problem is to choose among synonyms. In language comprehension, on the other hand, you enter the lexical matrix with a word and search for the sense that it expresses in that context. The input problem is to choose among meanings.

The assumption of a single lexical matrix is more convenient than plausible, however. It has long been known that people's comprehension vocabularies are much larger than their production vocabularies, and neurolinguistic evidence is accumulating that specific semantic deficits are more readily observed on the output side than on the input. At least two lexical matrices seem to be indicated. But then the question arises as to how two or more lexicons can be coordinated while still remaining independent mental modules.

However the number of lexical matrices is settled, the fact remains that synonymy is primarily an output problem and polysemy is primarily an input problem. Let me discuss each of them in turn.

SYNONYMY

What kind of linguistic knowledge should an output system have in order to choose appropriately among synonyms? The question presupposes that the system already knows which words are synonymous. How is that knowledge represented? One possible answer (usually attributed to Leibniz) is that the system must know which pairs of words can be interchanged without changing the meaning of any sentence in which they occur. The trouble is that, if you take this definition of synonymy literally, there are very few synonyms in any natural language. Even words like *snake* and *serpent* that have very similar referents are not completely interchangeable—*serpent* tends to be reserved for literary and biblical contexts. The clear fact is that two words may be interchangeable in some contexts, but not in others. And almost no words are interchangeable in every context of use.

It is generally agreed, therefore, that synonymy involves semantic similarity, not semantic identity. But this transformation from identity to similarity raises a host of theoretical problems. Although an identity theorist could imagine a simple list of identical pairs, a similarity theorist needs a theory complicated enough to explain why some pairs are more similar than others: why, say, *shore* and *coast* seem more similar than *duck* and *goose*, but not as similar as *car* and *automobile*. It is a familiar fact that people can judge the semantic similarity of pairs of words quickly and easily, and that the judgments of different persons are highly correlated. Psychologists have made use of this ability, but no one has a good explanation of how people do it. Perhaps similarity of the referents—based on world knowledge—is involved. Or perhaps linguistic knowledge is sufficient. Unfortunately, an appeal to linguistic knowledge is only slightly less forbidding than an appeal to world knowledge.

Knowing what meanings a word can be used to express is necessary, but not sufficient. People also know how to use the word in order to express a given meaning. That is to say, people know how the context of a word affects its meaning. Miller and Charles (1991) suggested that, other things being equal, judgments of semantic similarity are closely related to the variety of linguistic contexts in which the words can be interchanged. They propose that every word sense is associated with what they call a *contextual representation*, a representation of the contexts in which the word form can be used with that sense. Words with similar contextual representations are judged to be similar in meaning. Knowing contextual representations for every sense of every word we know is, clearly, a large amount of linguistic knowledge that takes people years to master, but it must somehow be built into any computer system that hopes to use language the way people do.

POLYSEMY

The input problem arises from polysemy, from the existence of words with multiple senses. Scientists and engineers take considerable pains to avoid polysemy in their technical notations, but natural languages do not. It is a perverse design feature of natural languages that not only do they allow the use of words with many alternative senses, but the most polysemous words are the words we use most frequently. General usage is riddled with potential ambiguities. Throughout the centuries many wise men have noticed this feature of language and have proposed measures to eliminate it.

The fascinating fact is, however, that polysemy does not interfere with people's use of natural language as a means of communication. Sense resolution is such a natural and easy cognitive process that most people do not even realize they are doing it. Indeed, when I tell friends that I am studying sense resolution, they have trouble seeing what the problem is. So I use the following elementary example. If I say, "He nailed the board across the window," nobody notices that *board* has more than one sense. People recognize immediately that a wooden board is involved. On the other hand, if I say, "He nailed the board for corruption," people think of an entirely different sense of *board*, the sense that is similar to *committee* (and also a different sense of *nail*). But they still do not realize that they are making rapid and accurate decisions as to which meaning should be retrieved and used to construct the interpretation of this sentence. What I would like to do, I tell my friends, is to explain to a computer how to make such decisions. Those who are unfamiliar with computers find it hard to believe that this is so complicated.

It is easy to overlook problems of sense resolution. For example, when Winograd (1970, 1972) programmed a computer to process such sentences as "Put the cylinder on the block," the fact that the domain of discourse was limited to his block world relieved him of the need to reject such alternative readings as, "Offer the cylinder for sale at auction," or "Install the cylinder in the engine." If you do not limit yourself to the block world—if you try to deal with language as it is used more generally—you must learn how to distinguish among many different senses of "block":

auction block	block plane	mental block
block and tackle	block print	road block
block diagram	cell block	starting block
block grant	cinder block	stumbling block
block head	city block	ventricular block
block house	cylinder block	trap block
block letter	engine block	wood block
block party	heart block	writer's block

to list a few of those you can find in dictionaries. And those are only the nouns. The larger world of blocks is surprisingly complex.

A dictionary will give you descriptions of the different senses that a polysemous word can be used to express, but many dictionaries are weak on describing the contexts in which these different senses are understood. Good dictionaries will often give illustrative sentences, either chosen from literature or composed by the lexicographer, but one or two sentences is hardly enough to insure mastery. It is this contextual description—what Miller and Charles have called a contextual representation—that is needed in order to determine the intended sense of a polysemous word.

Polysemy poses special problems for machine translation, because concepts that are expressed by the same word in one language are usually expressed by different words in another language. Consequently, computational linguists have tried a variety of strategies for automating sense resolution (or "disambiguation," as it is frequently called). Too many studies of sense resolution have been done to review here, but I can give the flavor of this work by describing a comparison we are presently conducting.

SENSE RESOLUTION: AN EXPERIMENTAL COMPARISON

At the Princeton Cognitive Science Laboratory we have compared three different ways of giving a computer contextual representations—that is to say, giving it information about contexts that it needs in order to choose between alternative senses of a polysemous word. We chose the noun *line*, which we believe has at least 25 distinguishable senses. From various bodies of text that are available to us we collected about 18,000 sentences containing the nouns *line*, *lines*, *Line*, or *Lines*. Claudia Leacock began sorting these sentences into 25 separate bins, one for each sense. By the time she had classified about 11,000 of them, she had accumulated several hundred instances of each of three senses: queue, text, and product.

We then enlisted the collaboration of three scientists who have different approaches to this problem. The first is Ellen Voorhees, of the Siemens Laboratory in Princeton. Voorhees is an expert in information retrieval; her approach is an adaptation of Salton's vector method of retrieval (Salton, 1991). The second is Kenneth Church, of the Bell Telephone Laboratories, who uses Bayesian statistics (Gale, Church, & Yarowsky, 1992). And the third is Geoffrey Towell, who uses a neural net that learns to classify sentences with a backpropagation algorithm.

The general idea of all three is to identify particular words that can be used as indicators—words that co-occur frequently with one sense but infrequently with the others. For example, *wait* turns out to be a good indicator for the queue sense, *write* for the text sense, and *sell* for the product sense. In order to find such indicators, the first step is to define a vector over all of the words that occur in training sets of sentences. The size of the training set is, of course, one of the parameters we wanted to explore. Once the words have been counted, weights can be assigned according to how discriminating each word is. Then the words in any new test sentence can be weighted and the weights summed for each sense;

the sense giving the largest sum is taken to be the sense of the word in that sentence. The three techniques that we compared differ in how the vectors are weighted. Features to note are, first, that all three methods are statistical; second, that all three were applied to the same test materials; and third, that they were required to distinguish among three senses (most previous studies have tried to distinguish only two).

For all three approaches, subsets of the sentences using *line* in each of these three senses were used for training. Training sets of 50, 100, and 200 sentences were selected at random; the remaining sentences were used to test the effectiveness of the training. Without going into details (which are reported by Voorhees, Towell, & Leacock, 1992), there was a learning curve—performance improved as the size of the training set increased—and after seeing 200 instances of each of the three senses, all three methods could classify correctly about 75% of the new sentences that it had not been trained on. When only two senses are to be distinguished, these methods do much better: Almost 90% are classified correctly.

I have mixed feeling about these results. On the one hand, I am disappointed that none of the methods achieved a level of accuracy I would expect of a practical system for automatic sense resolution. But on the other hand, I am encouraged by the fact that such crude methods are as successful as they are. I think the best perspective is provided by comparing these methods with what we think people are doing when they recognize different senses of *line*.

I think it is apparent that none of these methods is a close model of human performance. Consider a number of comparisons.

1. Rate of learning: Evidence about human performance is not as clear as one would like, but the best we have suggests that people can learn a new sense for a word after seeing it used about 15 or 20 times, roughly 10 times faster than these methods, and with better learning.

2. Ease of resolution: Even after the learning process is completed, the resolution process, which involves comparing the words in a new sentence with the list of some 2,700 weights for all of the different words that occur in the training sets, is computationally intensive, suggesting that the rapid and easy performance of humans must be achieved in some different way.

3. Degree of polysemy: The performance of these methods seems to decline rapidly as the number of alternative senses to be discriminated increases, whereas there is no evidence that increasing the degree of polysemy impairs human performance. Indeed, there is some evidence that polysemous words (perhaps because they are more familiar) are actually processed faster than monosemous words.

4. Simultaneous resolution: The statistical methods that we have looked at focus on the meaning of a single word in the context of a test sentence, whereas people are able to resolve the senses of several polysemous words

simultaneously. For example, there are three ambiguous words in the following sentence:

The	wire	upset	the	coach
	message	tripped		teacher
	filament	worried		carriage

so there should be at least eight possible interpretations, but people quickly determine that only three of the eight are plausible messages. That is to say, people seem able to solve a more difficult problem than the statistical methods have been asked to solve.

5 Use of word order: These statistical methods ignore word order and assign the same weight to words occurring near the polysemous target that they give to words occurring at a distance, whereas people who read these sentences report strong convictions that they base their decisions almost entirely on local context, on the order of words occurring just before or just following the polysemous word. Note that if two senses of a polysemous word occur in the same context, these methods will not distinguish them. We used a complete sentence as the contextual unit, which means that if two senses of *line* occur in the same sentence—"She wrote the last line of the play as she waited in the check-out line at the supermarket"—then it is impossible to get both senses right because when word order is ignored they have identical contexts.

In short, alphabetized lists of 2,700 words and their relative weights are not a satisfactory model of the contextual representations that Miller and Charles wanted to associate with each sense of every word. At present, therefore, we are preparing to explore a different approach.

CONTEXTUAL TEMPLATES

One conclusion I have drawn from our experiences with these statistical techniques is that you cannot resolve senses accurately without syntax. My hope is that it can be done with something less than a full, definitive parsing of every sentence. Because people claim that they make most of their decisions about sense on the basis of very local context, we might hope to succeed with nothing more than that.

In an effort to incorporate word order, Michael Colon and I used the same training sets to create a list of the local contexts preceding and following 200 sentences using *line* in each of these three senses. When a test sentence had the same leading or following context as one or more of the training sentences, it was assigned that sense. We found that test sentences that embed *line* in a local context that occurred in the training set are recognized with remarkable accuracy, but that far too many of the test sentences (roughly 50%) are undecidable—they occur in contexts that the system has never seen before. A truly enormous training set would be required before all of the possible preceding and following sequences were encountered.

If you ask someone to read these sentences and to highlight just those words that they use to determine the meaning of the polysemous word, the results suggest that there are local patterns, or contextual templates, associated with each sense. This was the general lead that Kelly and Stone (1975) pursued. They constructed a large lexicon in which each polysemous word was associated with a hand-coded decision algorithm. The algorithms looked at surface syntax and morphology, simple selectional restrictions on neighboring words, and the exact neighboring words themselves. After an energetic attempt to apply these templates to human language, they became convinced that such a strategy cannot succeed on a broad scale.

In spite of Kelly and Stone's discouraging results, we are preparing to pursue this approach once again. We think we have a secret weapon that they did not have. We have a lexical database, WordNet, that should enable us to formulate templates with variables in them.

What is WordNet? Let me first explain what I mean by a template with variables. The simplest example I can think of is the following: If we were trying to distinguish *table* as a piece of furniture from *table* as an array of printed data, one strong indication that *table* is referring to data is when the word *table* is followed immediately by a number: "Table 3," for example, will almost always be a reference to a tabulation of information. People will treat "Table 3" as an instance of the more general template, table + (number), where "number" is the name of a variable. If our learning system could deal with such variables, it would not have to learn separately about "Table 1" and "Table 2" and "Table 3" and so on indefinitely.

Our current program, therefore, is first, to formulate templates that incorporate variables; second, to test these templates on appropriate collections of sentences that have been classified by hand; and then third, if the results show that these contextual templates are a satisfactory form of contextual representation, to develop automatic procedures for finding suitable contextual templates. Our hope is that by basing the contextual templates on large textual corpora and by incorporating variables we will be able to succeed where Kelly and Stone did not.

But now I owe you an explanation of where we expect to get the variables to substitute into our templates. That brings me to WordNet, the lexical database that we have been developing at Princeton.

WORDNET

If you look in any introductory book on cognitive psychology, you will probably find a diagram illustrating the assumed organization of lexical knowledge in long-term memory. Usually some 20 or 30 words are included for illustrative purposes. The words will be represented as nodes, and relations between words will be represented by labeled arcs between nodes. It is assumed (usually implicitly) that the thousands of other words a person knows can be represented the same way.

WordNet (Miller & Fellbaum, 1991) is an online lexical database for English based on the assumption—designed to test the assumption—that knowledge of the entire lexicon is organized by such a network of semantic relations. The fundamental semantic relation is synonymy, which is required in order to define the lexicalized concepts that words can be used to express. Sets of synonyms (synsets) representing a lexicalized concept provide the nodes. They are organized into a network by such semantic relations as antonymy (opposition), hyponymy (class inclusion or subordinate/superordinate), meronymy (part/whole), troponymy (manner), and entailment. That is to say, if synset A is superordinate to synset B, pointers between those synsets will indicate that A is the hypernym of B, and that B is the hyponym of A.

In the course of building WordNet, we discovered that no single organizational structure is adequate for the entire lexicon: nouns, verbs, adjectives, and adverbs each have their own semantic relations and their own organization, determined by the role they play in the construction of linguistic messages. Thus, nouns are organized hierarchically by the class inclusion relation, whereas antonymy is the basic relation organizing the adjective lexicon. At present, there are more than 79,000 entries (words and collocations) in WordNet Version 1.3, expressing some 60,000 lexicalized concepts that are organized into networks by 83,000 pointers between concepts. Those numbers are steadily growing as we continue to edit and expand it.

How can WordNet be used in sense resolution? Philip Resnik, at the University of Pennsylvania, defines a selectional preference as a relation between a verb and a set of nouns that frequently serve as the direct object of that verb (Resnik, 1992). He has found that such sets of nouns are closely related in WordNet, suggesting that the hyponyms of a generic noun might provide the kind of variable we want to include in contextual templates.

Suppose, for example, that we are trying to distinguish between two senses of the verb *draw*, one being to pull something, and the other being to create a pictorial representation. Suppose further that we can parse sentences well enough to identify phrases and subject-verb-object relations, and that we have found that when the direct object of the verb *draw* is a noun phrase containing the noun *cord*, the odds are very good that the pulling sense of draw is intended. Then we can treat *cord* as a variable. That is to say, we can retrieve from WordNet a great variety of cords—hyponyms, such as *twine, string, drawstring, line, clothesline, yarn, thread, lace, shoelace*, etc. When any of these words occur as part of the direct object of the verb *draw*, we will assume that the pulling sense of the verb is intended.

The same selectional preference should work in reverse. That is to say, if the problem is to decide whether the noun *lace* is intended to refer to a cord or a decorative fabric, if it is part of the direct object of *draw*, we can opt for the cord sense.

At present we are only beginning to explore this technique for resolving word senses. That is to say, we have not yet discovered its shortcomings and so are still relatively enthusiastic about the prospects. But even if we can make a convincing case that selectional preferences of this kind offer the best approach, we will still face the problem of discovering a suitable set of such preferences, and extracting them automatically from standard corpora of English. That is to say, the computer will have to think about the contexts it encounters, and that is where I look hopefully to those who want to use Soar to process natural language.

CONCLUSION

It will surely not escape this audience that what I have been referring to as contextual templates in particular, and contextual representations more generally, are simply the conditional antecedents of productions rules, and that the whole problem of sense resolution can be cast as the problem of creating an appropriate production system. So our program of research could be described as an experiment to discover whether the problem (or this part of the problem) of language comprehension can be phrased in terms compatible with Soar. I hope so. Sense resolution is difficult, and those of us struggling with it would appreciate any help we can get.

ACKNOWLEDGMENTS

Preparation of this chapter was supported in part by grant N00014-91-J-1634 from the Defense Advanced Research Projects Agency and the Office of Naval Research, and by a grant from the James S. McDonnell Foundation. The views expressed are those of the author, who wishes to acknowledge his indebtedness to all members of the team at the Princeton University Cognitive Science Laboratory who have worked on the lexical project, but particularly to Richard Beckwith, Ross Bunker, Michael Colon, Christiane Fellbaum, Benjamin Johnson-Laird, Philip N. Johnson-Laird, Claudia Leacock, Katherine Miller, Daniel Teibel, Randee Tengi, Pamela Wakefield.

REFERENCES

Gale, W., Church, K. W., & Yarowsky, D. (1992). A method for disambiguating word senses in a large corpus. *Statistical Research Reports, 104*, 1–34. Murray Hill, NJ: AT&T Bell Laboratories.

Kelly, E., & Stone, P. (1975). *Computer recognition of English word senses.* Amsterdam: North-Holland.

Miller, G. A., & Charles, W. C. (1991). Contextual correlates of semantic similarity. *Language and Cognitive Processes, 6,* 1–28.

Miller, G. A., & Fellbaum, C. (1991). Semantic networks of English. *Cognition, 41,* 197–229.

Quirk, R., Greenbaum, S., Leech, G., & Svartvik, J. (1985). *A comprehensive grammar of the English language.* London: Longman.

Resnik, P. (1992, June). A class-based approach to lexical discovery. *Proceedings of the 30th Annual Meeting of the Association for Computational Linguistics* (pp. 327–329). Newark, DE: University of Delaware.

Salton, G. (1991). Developments in automatic text retrieval. *Science, 253,* 974–980.

Voorhees, E. M., Towell, G., & Leacock, C. (1992, August). Learning context to disambiguate word senses. *Proceedings of the 3rd International Workshop on Computational Learning Theory and Natural Learning Systems.* University of Wisconsin.

Webster's Ninth New Collegiate Dictionary. (1987). Springfield, MA: Merriam-Webster.

Winograd, T. A. (1970). *Procedures as a representation for data in a computer program for understanding natural language.* Doctoral dissertation, Massachusetts Institute of Technology, Department of Mathematics.

Winograd, T. A. (1972). *Understanding natural language.* New York: Academic Press.

DISCUSSION

Meaning Matters:
Response to Miller

Jill Fain Lehman
Carnegie Mellon University

George Miller has laid out an interesting and fundamental problem in language comprehension. My intention is to take seriously his question of whether Soar can help him with the problem of sense resolution. Before I can do that, however, I need to rephrase the problem a bit in terms that are more useful to developing my response.

As I understand it, Miller is looking for an automatic procedure for learning *contextual templates*. The procedure should combine information from two sources—a large corpus of sentences and WordNet—to produce rules that suggest appropriate word senses in relevant contexts. To use one of his examples, consider a corpus that contains sentences with two senses of *lace*, one as a cord (e.g., a shoelace) and the other as a decorative fabric. If sentences in which *lace* is the direct object of *draw* tend to correspond to instances of the first meaning, then our procedure should produce a rule that looks something like:

> IF the sentence contains a verb that is a pull-like act and
>   the object of the verb is *lace*
> THEN use the sense of *lace* as a cord-like thing

What do each of the corpus and WordNet contribute to the process? What the corpus contributes is, first, indices into the set of word senses and semantic relationships that is WordNet. Second, it gives a set of correlations between word senses that is supposed to be indicative of broader usage (if

133

pull-like act predicts cord-like thing in the corpus, then it is assumed to predict the same sense in general usage as well). WordNet contributes the set of possible senses for each word. It also contributes the method of generalization (or induction) for the learning component of the procedure. It does this by providing an operational definition of, for example, what a pull-like act is. That operational definition is grounded in the synonym, hypernym, and hyponym relations that allow us to navigate through Word-Net, starting at the pull-like sense of *draw* and moving outward to all the other pull-like acts. The purpose of this inductive step is to compensate for lack of coverage in the corpus—a comprehension system that uses our templates may still choose the right sense for *lace* when it encounters sentences with *pull* or *drag*, despite not having seen those words previously.[1]

So Miller's question is, essentially, can Soar help him in this endeavor of creating an automatic procedure? I'd like to give an unequivocal answer to that question, but I can't. The best I can do is reply, "no, yes, and maybe."

"NO"

Understanding the "no" in my reply requires understanding NL-Soar, a set of problem spaces that act as Soar's language comprehension capability. The output of NL-Soar is two models: the utterance model, which captures the structure of the utterance, and the situation model, which captures the meaning of the utterance. Because we're concerned here with the resolution of meaning, I'll confine my remarks to the creation of the situation model, assuming the existence of the utterance model to guide that creation without explaining its origin or representation (see Richard Lewis's Discussion following Chapter 1 for a discussion of the utterance model).

There are two features of NL-Soar's processing that are key to understanding the "no" argument. The first feature is that NL-Soar is a single-path comprehender, maintaining only a single interpretation of the utterance at all times. This means that the system makes a commitment to a particular word sense for every word, as it is encountered. It makes its commitment based on the context available at the time. That context includes syntactic information, represented by the current state of the utterance model. It may also include situational information, in that there may be objects in the world that are being referred to in the utterance, and the existence of those objects partially defines the context. Given the available context, the system always makes a single word sense commitment, and having made that commitment, moves on.

---

[1]Note that nothing dictates that the induction be performed when *lace* is encountered. We could equally well imagine a system that built a rule relating *draw* and *lace* explicitly, then generalized its preference for the pulling sense of *draw* when it encountered *pull* or *drag* at some point in the future (a lazy form of induction, recognizable as analogy).

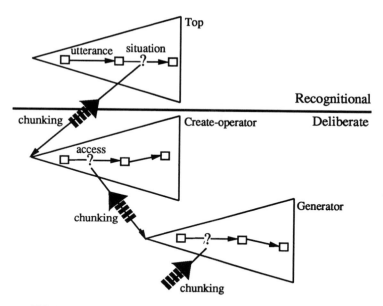

FIG. 1. Recognitional and deliberate comprehension in NL-Soar.

The second important feature of NL-Soar is that it contains two different comprehension processes: a recognitional process and a deliberate process. Figure 1 shows the difference graphically. Recognitional behavior occurs in the Top problem space. There, a comprehension operator simply brings all the relevant knowledge to bear to produce the situation model directly. In other words, the system has a set of associations in long-term memory that map the current problem-solving context into modifications to the situation model that incorporate the appropriate meaning of the current word. Recognitional comprehension arises in NL-Soar via learning over impasses. Impasses arise when the system cannot recognize exactly how to build the situation model just by looking at the current context of the word (no association is available in long-term memory). To resolve the impasse, the system must gather knowledge from a variety of problem spaces. The operators in these problem spaces sequentially bring to bear different knowledge sources. At the end of the deliberative comprehension process, when the system has found a meaning for the new word that is consistent with the context, the impasse is resolved and a new association, or chunk, is added to long-term memory. The chunk integrates the different knowledge sources that led to the appropriate meaning. The next time the system encounters a similar context, the chunk makes the modifications to the situation model available recognitionally. Thus, recognitional comprehension represents the eventual performance of the system; it is the performance of the system reached asymptotically via learning over a long period of time.

Consequently, most of the time NL-Soar behaves with a mix of recognitional and deliberate comprehension, constantly moving its knowledge from diffuse to integrated form.

What does word sense resolution look like in NL-Soar? Let's go back to our example of drawing a lace. NL-Soar will have already made a commitment to a meaning for *draw* when it reaches *lace*. Although the system can repair a wrong commitment, for simplicity we will assume that it made the right commitment. We'll also assume that NL-Soar has never seen the current context before. When the impasse arises the system must comprehend *lace* deliberately, that is, it applies operators in its lower problem spaces to explore each of the meanings of *lace* in turn, until it finds one that is syntactically, semantically, and pragmatically consistent with the current context. One of the operators it uses during this search triggers a semantic rule that looks very much like the rule given in the previous section. Once the system has found a consistent meaning, the impasse that led to deliberate comprehension is resolved and the different knowledge sources are integrated into a new comprehension operator. The comprehension operator is an association between the elements of the context that led to the selection of the meaning and the changes to the situation model that represent that meaning.

If we now look only at the system's comprehension behavior in the recognitional problem space, it appears that NL-Soar contains a procedure by which a contextual template does arise automatically through learning. Unfortunately, such a myopic view belies Miller's original intent. In reality, the contextual templates that he is interested in already exist in the system in the form of hand-coded associations available via operators in a semantic problem space. Given that the system is not automatically learning those semantic rules, my answer to Miller's question, "Can NL-Soar help?" must be "No."

"YES"

On the other hand, Miller actually gave two criteria for recognizing a successful solution to his problem. The first criterion, was, of course, to demonstrate an automatic procedure for building sense resolution rules. The second criterion, however, was to show that the procedure had the same behavioral regularities exhibited by our most flexible and robust sense resolvers (people). As the Princeton Cognitive Science Laboratory's experimental comparison demonstrated, to meet the former criterion is not to guarantee the latter. The three statistical approaches they studied did, indeed, learn sense resolution knowledge, but they performed poorly with respect to the behavioral criteria. NL-Soar, on the other hand, does not acquire sense resolution knowledge, but seems to meet some of the behavioral criteria quite well, nonetheless. Let's consider each regularity in turn, and examine whether NL-Soar meets it.

1. *Rate of learning.* People learn better and faster than the statistical methods, apparently requiring only about 15–20 occurrences of a new sense to achieve mastery. There are multiple subproblems in acquiring a new word sense, including (at least) (a) recognizing which word is being used in a new way, (b) using prior knowledge and current context to reason about the new meaning, and (c) learning the set of contexts that correlate with the new sense. The kind of procedure we've been discussing addresses only the last of these points. It seems unlikely that human learning rates can be achieved without solutions for all subproblems. Still, as we've seen, NL-Soar doesn't address even (c). What it does do, however, is suggest an architecture into which we can fit processes that overcome each of these subproblems. The key feature of this architecture is that it treats each subproblem as a lack of recognitionally available knowledge in a step of either an acquisition or comprehension procedure. In so doing, it creates a variety of situations in which impasses will arise and learning can occur (whether the rate of learning will be human-like is an empirical question that remains to be answered). The dynamic in such an architecture will be a constant flow of knowledge "upward" from the lowest problem spaces (which do the initial acquisition of word sense), to the deliberate problem spaces (which reason over multiple knowledge sources, including lexical knowledge), to the recognitional space (which applies knowledge in its integrated form).

2. *Ease of resolution.* People show ease of resolution after learning; the statistical methods remain computationally intensive. Increasing ease of resolution over time is predicted by the extended structure of NL-Soar outlined earlier. Each context for a new word sense must be uncovered during deliberate comprehension before it can be recast into recognitional form. The deliberate process is computationally intensive; the recognitional process is not. Once the knowledge has flowed upward, utterances with that word sense will be comprehended easily.

3. *Degree of polysemy.* People handle highly polysemous words easily, often processing them more quickly than monosemous words; performance of the statistical methods declines rapidly with the number of alternative senses. Miller makes the additional point here that there is a correlation in English between polysemy and frequency. In a system like NL-Soar, such a correlation would have a causal role in explaining the regularity. The more frequently a word is encountered, the more likely it is that the recognitional knowledge is available, with the deliberation having been performed on prior instances. With a higher likelihood of recognitional processing, polysemous words will be comprehended more quickly.

4. *Simultaneous resolution.* People are able to resolve the senses of several polysemous words in a sentence easily; statistical methods cannot. At first glance, this regularity would seem problematic for NL-Soar because the system maintains only a single interpretation. If it commits to a wrong interpretation, however, it can undo that commitment when disconfirming evidence appears. A full description of the repair mechanism would be inappropriate here, but can be found in Lehman, Lewis, and Newell (1991). The relevant aspect of the repair process is that it is achieved via operators in the problem spaces for deliberate comprehension. As a result of chunking, the repair then becomes recognitionally available. Consequently, handling multiple polysemies can appear effortless in NL-Soar even if the action of a comprehension operator involves undoing a previous commitment.

5. *Use of word order.* People seem to differentiate the usefulness of parts of the context based on locality, whereas statistical methods do not. NL-Soar's knowledge causes it to rely primarily on local information as well, allowing it to differentiate parts of the context based on word order, syntactic relations, and so forth. Of course, to the extent that the required context for making a decision isn't local (e.g., a distant verb particle), then NL-Soar will take advantage of the more distal context as well.

The point here is simple. I believe some of the behavioral regularities that Miller seeks arise not from the sense resolution procedure per se, but from the transformation of deliberate knowledge to recognitional form that pervades the entire acquisition/comprehension process. Although there is no question that we need an automatic procedure for building sense resolution rules, that procedure must reside within a framework like NL-Soar's to meet his second criterion. So, "yes," perhaps we have something to offer after all.

"MAYBE"

Looking at the current NL-Soar led us to the conclusion that although we do not yet have the procedure Miller desires, we have the right sort of framework in which to build it. This seems to me an unsatisfying response. So let's explore, hypothetically, what it would take to get NL-Soar to do what he actually wants it to do.

What we're after is an automatic procedure for finding contextual templates, where a contextual template is a rule that looks something like: If there's a verb that is a pull-like act and the object of that verb is *lace*, then the right sense of *lace* is a cord-like thing. Abstractly, the rules should map a meaning and a word playing a particular functional role into a meaning for that word. NL-Soar has a problem space that has rules of this sort hand-coded in. The question, then, is how would such a rule arise? The answer in Soar is always the same: through chunking. Having said that, which is a fairly trivial response, we are led to the real questions. Chunking over what? What is the processing going on in the subspaces below the impasse? What kind of impasse would it be, such that the right chunk would result?

One way to produce the rules we're after would be to cast the problem as lack of knowledge for proposing a lexical-access operator. Lack of knowledge results in an impasse. The pre-impasse problem space would contain both the current word and the situation model built up by accessing the meanings of previous words. The character of the lower space (or spaces) would be that of a lexically indexed meaning generator. It would contain, at the very least, a generate operator to bring the senses to choose from into working memory, and a recognition operator to allow the system to decide when it has the right sense. The scheme clearly makes use of one of the resources Miller has given us—the word senses would come from WordNet. The role of the corpus is less clear. What sorts of associations does the recognition operator trigger? Memories of sentences previously encountered? I don't think so. I think those memories are of experiences that arise from observing and acting in the world. They're the sorts of experiences such that when the pre-impasse situation model and a candidate meaning are juxtaposed by the recognition operator, it is equivalent to asking, "Have I ever been in this situation, where I'm trying to pull on a shoelace?" (not, "Have I ever been in this situation, reading about pulling on a shoelace?"). Recognizing the situation as having occurred in the world justifies the candidate meaning in context. Does this imply that there is no role left for the corpus? Not necessarily. We could imagine treating the corpus as a stimuli for producing the simulation of experiences that would give rise to "memories" such as the ones just described, or as a stimuli for asking whether such a simulation is possible.

Now suppose you have no experiences with shoelaces. Then the problem devolves into finding an experience similar enough to justify the cord-like meaning. That search cannot be conducted haphazardly, however. Thus, our lower problem space needs operators that could start at a particular meaning and move to other meanings in some principled fashion. With a structure like WordNet in long-term memory, operators like hyponym and hypernym would give exactly the sort of operational definition that is needed. Applying recognition operators to a hypernym is like asking, "Do I have the experience of pulling a cord?" If that question is not evocative, the hyponym operator moves you back down through WordNet enabling you to ask, "Have I pulled a rope? a string? a thread?"

In short, a lexically indexed meaning generator would allow the system to do a certain amount of problem solving using the word senses and relations in a structure like WordNet to control the search through the set of possibilities. Problem solving is terminated in the lower space when a candidate meaning is justified by a recognition memory of events in the world—experience dictates semantics. When the impasse in the upper space resolves, the chunk that results maps a meaning and a word playing a particular functional role into a meaning for that word, exactly the sort of rule Miller is looking for.

Of course, this is all very hypothetical. It remains to be seen whether it will play out in the implementational details. The good news, for Miller at least, is that WordNet could be key to making a scheme like this work. The bad news, for Miller at least, is that there also appears to be no way out of answering questions like: Where does the knowledge evoked by the recognition operator come from? How are our experiences in the world remembered in a form that is accessible to linguistic processes? These are questions that set us squarely down in the great morass of world knowledge George had hoped to avoid.

REFERENCE

Lehman, J. F., Lewis, R., & Newell, A. (1991). *Natural language comprehension in Soar* (Tech. Rep. No. CMU-CS-91-117). Pittsburgh: Carnegie Mellon University.

Chapter 5

Constraints on Processing Capacity: Architectural or Implementational?

Marcel Adam Just
Patricia A. Carpenter
Darold D. Hemphill*
Carnegie Mellon University

Under appropriate conditions, many adults show impressive problem-solving skills, as indicated by their ability to learn algebra, assemble toys from instructions, or devise plans for a complex event, such as moving a household. In spite of these impressive problem-solving skills, it is neither difficult nor surprising to demonstrate that under some circumstances, these same adults can appear much more limited in their problem-solving skills. Hesitations and errors are easily evoked even in familiar tasks like mental arithmetic or syllogistic reasoning when they exceed the problem solver's ability to compute and maintain information online, without the aid of pencil and paper. Errors in such reasoning tasks are often accepted as manifestations of the limitation of short-term or working memory. In this chapter, we examine in detail the processes that fail in one type of reasoning task in order to characterize the underlying limitation on working memory. We describe a range of cognitive phenomena that indicate performance constraints, phenomena such as a limit on how much information can be stored in a given situation, or on how fast it can be processed. We present an integrated account of these phenomena in terms of a unified theory of capacity constraints (or resource limitations) in cognition.

We start by considering why constraints on performance should be of relevance to a unified theory of cognition. There are some performance constraints that provide some of the main input to a unified theory. (The

---

*Darold Hemphill is currently at Bellcore, Piscataway, NJ.

other main input is a task analysis or rational analysis.) One such constraint is that some forms of a task are more difficult than other forms (e.g., mentally squaring a three-digit number takes longer and is more subject to error than squaring a two-digit number) and that within tasks, some steps take longer and are more subject to error than others. Note that these performance constraints relate some task characteristic to a qualitative or quantitative change in performance. We call them *task-related performance constraints*, and relate them to other classes of performance constraints. We argue that some of the different classes of performance constraints have a common basis, and therefore should be accorded a common account in a unified theory of cognition.

The other classes of performance constraints that we consider are those imposed by certain systematic differences among individuals, differences within each individual related to ancillary demands of a task (such as a superimposed secondary task), and differences within individuals related to increases in age in adulthood. Our main argument is that some of these classes of variation can be explained in terms of a single underlying construct, namely, capacity constraints on working memory.

A second argument is that some of these variations in performance can indicate which facets of the performance are consequences of the common human cognitive architecture, and which are a function of resource limitations. We argue that any characterization of human performance based exclusively on the performance of a single individual, or on the average or modal performance of a group of individuals, is inherently unable to distinguish architectural from implementational constraints. More specifically, we argue that characterizations of processing strategy that fail to take such variation into account cannot be informed about such issues as modularity of system components and about major alternative processing strategies.

The chapter has two main sections. The first provides an overview of the theory of working memory and describes several experimental studies of reasoning in the Tower of Hanoi puzzle, along with a simulation that tests the specific predictions of the model for this task. The second section generalizes the theory by examining individual differences in reasoning more broadly. In this section, we first review the psychometric results that have emerged from the analysis of intercorrelations of scores from test batteries that have been administered to large populations of adults (typically college-age or military-age subjects). Then we review some data on the effects of aging that compare the performance of younger and older subjects on various reasoning tasks. In both cases, the pattern of correlations supports the argument that variation in working-memory limitations accounts for individual differences in certain online problem-solving tasks.

PERFORMANCE CONSTRAINTS AND THE NATURE OF WORKING MEMORY

The characterization of working memory that we offer pertains to the limitation on the ability to perform information operations (symbolic processing) while simultaneously keeping some small amount of information in an activated state (Baddeley, 1986). We refer to this constraint as the *limited working-memory capacity.* We cannot stress enough the focus on the conjunction of processing and storage as the way to characterize the limitation. The limitation is intended to apply to the operational capacity or throughput of immediate thought. There are undoubtedly other limitations in the system; for example, it has been convincingly demonstrated that there is a passive phonological buffer and an articulatory loop of limited duration that participates in rehearsal; these peripheral systems play a major role in explaining the limits observed in word span or digit span tasks (Baddeley, 1986). Our focus, however, is not on the more peripheral storage systems, but on working-memory capacity, which we argue is better construed as a constraint on computation as well as storage during cognitive processing.

Another constraint on processing is the amount of declarative and procedural knowledge available to the individual, and perhaps its compactness (i.e., how well chunked it is). Knowledge or expertise has been successfully invoked to explain differences among individuals in problem-solving domains such as mnemonic expertise (Chase & Ericsson, 1982) and chess (Chase & Simon, 1973; de Groot, 1965). For example, in the domain of mechanical reasoning, individuals who had formal training or extensive mechanical experience differ from less knowledgeable people in three ways (Hegarty, Just, & Morrison, 1988). They are more likely to know the relevant attributes of a mechanical system, and consequently, less likely to be misled by irrelevancies. They are also more likely to know how the relevant features are related to mechanical advantage, and they are more likely to have rules for quantitatively integrating the effects of multiple features. These three types of knowledge differences, when instantiated in a Soar-based simulation model, are sufficient to account for the more knowledgeable individuals' better accuracy in mechanical reasoning problems. The knowledge differences also account for the different types of explanations of the problems given by more and less knowledgeable subjects. The research on mechanical reasoning is a clear example of how declarative and procedural knowledge can be a source of differences among individuals.

The demonstrations of knowledge effects raise the more general issue of when performance differences among individuals should be ascribed to differences in knowledge and when to something else. At a methodological level, the nature and existence of differences in declarative knowledge can sometimes be directly assessed; or it can be minimized through the use of novel tasks; or knowledge differences can be equated through instruction and prior practice. One or another of these approaches is used in most of the problem-solving tasks that are examined in this chapter, all of which makes plausible the search for alternative sources of variation in constraining performance.

COMPUTATIONAL INSTANTIATION: CAPACITY-CONSTRAINED CAPS

Central to the computational model is the idea that a common resource, namely, activation, mediates both information maintenance and computation, and that working-memory constraints exist in the amount of activation available for its allocation to storage and computation. In the domain of sentence comprehension, the account is instantiated in a particular simulation model called CC READER; its initials reflect the assumption that comprehension processes are capacity constrained (Just & Carpenter, 1992). The more general simulation system is an interpreter called 3CAPS (for Capacity Constrained CAPS), a modification of CAPS, which in turn is constructed on top of OPS5. We first briefly describe the reading model and then the capacity-constrained production system interpreter.

Like the original READER model (Thibadeau, Just, & Carpenter, 1982), CAPS is a hybrid of a production system (Newell, 1973) and an activation-based connectionist system. Consequently, the model takes the production system formalism as the basic architecture, as suggested by Newell. As is the case with conventional production systems, the procedural knowledge in CAPS consists of a set of productions, each of which is a condition–action contingency that specifies what symbolic manipulation should be made when a given information condition arises in working memory. For example, a typical condition is, "if the current word is a determiner (e.g., *the*)"; the associated action is, "expect that the current phrase is a noun phrase." The execution of the production can change the contents of working memory, thereby enabling another production. CAPS, however, deviates in many important ways from conventional production systems by incorporating mechanisms that are common to activation-based parallel connectionist models (Cottrell, 1989; Waltz & Pollack, 1985; St. John & McClelland, 1990).

The first way that CAPS differs from a conventional production system is that each element, which can represent a word, phrase, grammatical structure, or thematic structure, has an associated activation level so that the element can have varying degrees of activation. The condition part of a production specifies not just the presence of an element but also the minimum activation level at which the element satisfies the condition (the threshold). Only if the activation level of an element is above the threshold is it effectively "in" working memory and, consequently, available to initiate other computational processes. Second, productions change the activation level of an element by propagating (copying) activation from a source element to the output element. Third, productions can fire reiteratively over successive cycles so that the activation levels of the output elements become gradually incremented until they reach some threshold. In other words, the symbolic manipulation occurs as a reiterative action with cumulative effects. Finally, CAPS allows multiple productions to fire in parallel on a given cycle, as long as their conditions are met. Hence, a model for sentence processing can work on different levels of language comprehension, such as syntactic, semantic, and referential, at the same time, and can generate new partial computational products simultaneously from different levels.

In 3CAPS, the capacity constraint is imposed by the interpreter by limiting the amount of activation that can be consumed at any given time. If the total demand for activation for both storage and processing exceeds the allowable maximum (some number of units of activation, called the *cap*), then both the storage and processing functions are scaled back (deallocated). Our initial deallocation scheme limits both functions proportionately, akin to an across-the-board cut. This scaling-back of activation has important consequences for both the time course and the content of processing. First, the deallocation of the activation to computation can slow down processing by increasing the number of cycles required for an element to reach the threshold. Second, the deallocation of activation to the maintenance of earlier elements produces forgetting, because the activation levels of some of the elements are continuously decremented with each new cycle of processing that exceeds the activation quota. An allocation parameter determines the relative extent to which computation or information maintenance suffers when the demands for storage and processing exceed the activation quota.

Grain Size

When working memory is viewed as a computational arena, it becomes clear that its capacity should be construed not just as a storage capacity (perhaps measured in chunks), but as operational capacity, or throughput. By analogy, consider how the capacity of a hospital to perform surgery might be measured in terms of throughput, such as the number of surgical procedures of a given type that can be performed per day, rather than in some static terms, such as the number of surgical theatres. Of course, the surgical capacity of a hospital depends on what types of procedures are involved, what instrumentation is available, the skill of the surgeons and support personnel, and so on. So operational capacity must be specified in terms of the number of procedures of a given type per unit time, such as the number of appendectomies that can be performed per day. Similarly, any measure of working memory's operational capacity must take into account the nature of the information being processed and the nature of the operations that are being applied.

We claim that working-memory capacity is a good level of aggregation for characterizing the constraint on immediate thought. The basis of this claim is empirical. Measures of working-memory capacity that operationalize the concept of both storage and computation provide higher correlations with individual differences in performance or age-related changes in performance than do measures of pure storage, such as standard digit or word span (Daneman & Carpenter, 1980). There may also be more constancy at this level than at finer levels, such as the time course of activation or inhibition. An analogy concerning grain size can be made here to the concept of signal-to-noise ratio in some types of computational models, like connectionist models. The lower the signal/noise ratio is, the poorer the performance of a model will be. There can be many different determinants of the signal/noise ratio acting individually or collectively to lower the ratio (e.g., amount of noise in the input, amount of noise in the connection weights, etc.) But irrespective of the source, the decrements in performance will often be similar for a given decrement in the signal/noise ratio. Similarly, in the model we propose, there can be a variety of determinants of the relation between the supply and the demand for resources (e.g., inherent amount of resources, task demands, chronological age), but it is this relation that will be useful in characterizing resource constraints on performance. In addition to the resource-limitation constraints, we reiterate the point that relevant domain knowledge (declarative and procedural) will also be partial determinants of performance.

Experimental Data on Problem Solving

In this section, we describe some studies of people performing the Tower of Hanoi puzzle. We show that their ability to make a given move correctly is determined in part by (a) the size of their inherent working-memory capacity, (b) the demand placed on working-memory resources at that moment by the need to generate and store problem subgoals, and (c) the demand placed on working-memory resources imposed by a secondary task (visual letter categorization). We argue that all of these determinants affect performance similarly, and invite a common explanation of the performance constraint.

At a higher level, this task may share an important characteristic of many online reasoning tasks that have been used in psychometric studies, such as visual analogies or numerical sequence extrapolation. Although these tasks differ in their domain (visual vs. numerical), they share the characteristic of requiring subjects to generate and maintain multiple goals while simultaneously doing other computations. Moreover, performance on such tasks is often highly intercorrelated, meaning that subjects who perform well on one such task tend to perform well on other such tasks, even though the tests are dissimilar on the surface. The general argument is that one source of the intercorrelation may be some general constraint on the ability to generate and maintain goals while simultaneously performing computations. Consequently, an analysis of the precise nature of constraints in performing the Tower of Hanoi puzzle may illuminate which aspects of problem solving reflect individual differences in capacity constraints.

The Tower of Hanoi puzzle is useful for studying the role of working memory, particularly when the problem is solved using a strategy that draws heavily on working-memory resources. The Tower of Hanoi puzzle consists of three pegs and a stack of disks of increasing size arranged on one of the pegs in the form of a pyramid, with the largest disk on the bottom and smallest disk on the top. A four-disk puzzle is shown in the top part of Fig. 5.1. The subject's task is to reconstruct the pyramid, moving one disk at a

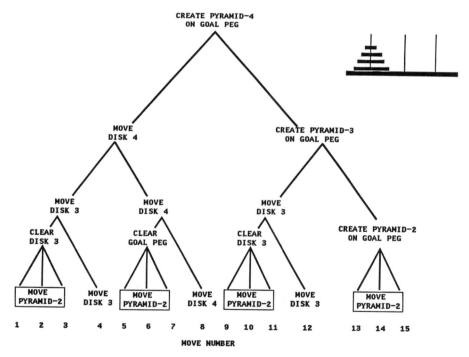

FIG. 5.1. The problem structure generated by the goal-recursion strategy for the four-disk Tower of Hanoi puzzle. The tree is traversed depth first, from left to right, generating the 15 successive moves. The phrase "Move pyramid-2" treats the two smallest disks as a single goal planning unit, although this assumption is not crucial to the analysis.

time, onto another peg (called the goal peg), without ever putting a larger disk on top of a smaller disk. In this example, the puzzle's four disks are arranged on the leftmost peg, and the goal is to reconstruct them on the goal peg; in this case, the peg that is designated as the goal is the rightmost peg. A unique sequence of moves will solve any puzzle in the minimum path. In the four-disk puzzle, this sequence consists of 15 moves, or more generally, the optimal solution path consists of $2^d - 1$ moves, where d is the number of disks.

The motivation for studying working memory in the Tower of Hanoi puzzle arose from previous research on the Raven Progressive Matrices Test, which suggested a large role of working memory in accounting for the individual differences in that test (Carpenter, Just, & Shell, 1990). The Raven Progressive Matrices Test problems consist of a 3×3 visual array with one element of the array (the bottom right) missing. The subject is required to pick a correct completion from among eight alternatives. Figure 5.2 is an isomorph of such a problem. To solve any problem, subjects must determine the nature of the variation among the elements in a row in order to select the correct response from among the depicted alternatives. The 36 problems in the test are arranged actuarially in terms of increasing difficulty, from those problems that most adults correctly solve to those items that relatively few solve. Our analysis of the test indicates that a small number of relatively simple rules describes the variation among elements in most problems. In general, the rules are not particularly difficult or abstract. Rather, in accounting for the differential difficulty of various problems in the Raven test, we find that error rates across problems increase with the number of dimensions of variation in a Raven problem. This result suggests that the sheer keeping track of figural attributes and rules in those problems might be a substantial source of problem differences in the test. "Keeping track" refers to processes such as generating subgoals in working memory, recording the attainment of subgoals, and setting new subgoals as others are attained. Furthermore, the result suggests that differences among individuals in the Raven test might also be accounted for in terms of individual differences in working-memory capacity.

The general hypothesis is that the capacity to compute relations and generate goals while simultaneously maintaining previous goals and information about the problem state might be a general ability that impacts on other problem-solving tasks that share these characteristics. Consequently, subjects who are successful at goal management in the Raven test should also perform well on other cognitive tasks involving extensive goal management, such as the Tower of Hanoi puzzle. When subjects use a working-memory intensive strategy on the Tower of Hanoi puzzle, the errors should correlate with errors on the Raven test, to the extent that both tasks require goal management. This is the result that we previously reported in an abbreviated form (Carpenter et al., 1990). The general argument is that goal manage-

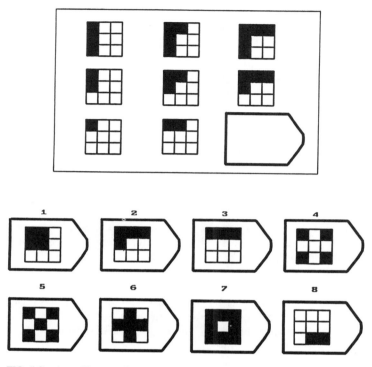

FIG. 5.2.   A problem to illustrate the format and types of rules in the Raven Progressive Matrices Test. Each problem consists of a 3 × 3 array with a missing entry on the bottom. The subject must determine the rules that relate the elements to select the correct completion. This problem is solved by a simple progression rule, in which the number of black squares in the top of each row increases by one from the first to the second column and from the second to the third column. The number of black squares along the left remains constant within a row, but changes between rows from three to two to one. (The correct answer is number 3.)

ment and computation in reasoning tasks may stress working memory capacity and hence, are a source of error in similar types of reasoning tasks. To examine this hypothesis, we analyze performance in the Tower of Hanoi in more detail, report additional experiments on the role of working memory in the Tower of Hanoi task, and present a simulation model that accounts for the capacity constraints on problem-solving performance.

Goal Generation and Errors in the Tower of Hanoi

Although the Tower of Hanoi puzzle can be solved using several different strategies, one of the commonly used strategies is called the goal-recursion strategy (Kotovsky, Hayes, & Simon, 1985; Simon, 1975). With this strategy, the puzzle is solved by first setting the goal of moving the largest disk from the bottom of the pyramid on the source peg to the goal peg, then moving the second-largest disk directly on top of the largest disk, and so on. But before the first goal can be satisfied, the disks constituting the subpyramid above the largest disk must be moved out of the way. This goal is recursive because in order to move the subpyramid, its largest disk must be cleared, and so on. Thus, to execute this strategy, a subject must set up a number of hierarchically embedded subgoals and remember his or her place in the hierarchy while executing successive moves.

The hierarchy of subgoals that must be generated or retained in solving the Tower of Hanoi puzzle can be depicted as a goal tree. Figure 5.1 shows a diagram of the goal tree when the goal recursion strategy is used in a four-disk problem. Each branch corresponds to a subgoal, and the terminal nodes correspond to individual moves. (This particular goal tree assumes that the goal of moving pyramid-2 [consisting of the smallest and second-smallest disks] can be treated as a single chunk, which appears to be the case for subjects with just a few practices on the puzzle [Kotovsky & Fallside, 1989]; but this assumption is not critical to the main argument.) The subject can be viewed as doing a depth-first traversal of the goal tree. In order to achieve a goal listed at a particular node, a subject is taught to construct the two subgoals corresponding to the two branches emanating from that node. Thus, each move can be classified according to the number of goals that must be generated to execute the move. For example, Move 1 entails generating four subgoals, whereas Move 9 entails generating three subgoals. Moves 1, 5, 9, and 13 entail generating one or more subgoals before executing the move; in contrast, no new subgoals need to be generated before any of the other moves are made. However, the execution of the other moves does entail either maintaining or attaining various subgoals.

Generating goals, as well as keeping track of them, is a process that makes considerable demands on working memory. Consequently, the likelihood of an error on a move should increase with the number of goals to be generated to enable that move. Evidence consistent with this prediction comes from a study in which subjects were taught a variety of different solution strategies for solving the six-disk Tower of Hanoi, including the goal-recursion strategy (Egan & Greeno, 1974). In general, errors on different moves increase with the number of generated goals in the move.

If goal generation requires working-memory resources, then generating multiple goals should be particularly taxing for individuals who have fewer resources. This is the rationale for expecting that problems in the Raven Progressive Matrices Test that require more goal generation and maintenance would be a source of individual differences. This rationale also leads to a prediction that performance on the Tower of Hanoi using the goal-recursion strategy should correlate with performance on the Raven test, because both tasks may rely on generating and maintaining goals in working memory.

Procedure. To ensure that subjects used the goal-recursion strategy, they were given extensive instruction and practice on this strategy with the two-disk and three-disk versions of the puzzle. Then, they were given Tower of Hanoi problems of increasing size, from three disks to seven disks, and were reminded before each puzzle to use the goal-recursion strategy. To minimize the adoption of other strategies, the start and goal pegs were selected at random. In place of a physical Tower of Hanoi, subjects were given practice with a computer-generated (Vaxstation II) graphics display, with disks that moved when a source and destination peg were indicated with a mouse. After the source and destination of a selected move had been indicated by two appropriate mouse clicks, the to-be-moved disk disappeared from the source peg and reappeared on the destination peg. Although subjects seldom tried to execute illegal moves (placing a larger disk on a smaller one), the program disallowed it by not changing the display and signaling the illegality.

The main performance measure of interest was the occurrence of a move that was inconsistent with the goal-recursion strategy (a move that we call a *stray* from the minimum path). When a subject made a stray move, then the move was displayed, but the computer also sounded a tone and would not allow another move until the subject had retracted the stray move. Thus, a subject could not stray more than one move from the optimal solution path.

The subjects who participated in the experiment were 45 undergraduates from Carnegie Mellon, the University of Pittsburgh, and the Community College of Allegheny County. In addition to the Tower of Hanoi problems, they were also given the Raven Progressive Matrices Test, Sets I and II, using standard psychometric procedures. For analysis purposes, they were divided into five groups that spanned the range of the Raven scores from medium to very high (out of 36 possible points): 12–19 ($n = 9$), 20–24 ($n = 9$), 25–29 ($n = 14$), 30–32 ($n = 9$), 33–36 ($n = 4$).

Results. A prediction of the theory is that errors on the Tower of Hanoi puzzle should occur on moves that impose a greater burden on working memory and that the effect should depend, in part, on the capacity to maintain goals in working memory, as assessed by the Raven test. For any given move, the likelihood of making a stray move should correlate with the number of new goals to be generated on that move. These predictions were supported. Figure 5.3 shows the probability of an error on moves that require the generation of zero, one, or two or more subgoals, for the Disk-3 to Disk-7 puzzles. The curves are for four subject groups who are classified according to their Raven test score. (The lowest scoring group, which had the highest error rate, is not shown.)

Because of its extensive dependence on goal management, overall performance of the goal-recursion strategy in the Tower of Hanoi puzzle was

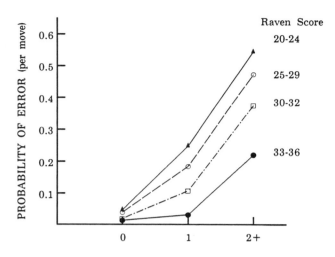

NUMBER OF GENERATED SUBGOALS

FIG. 5.3. The probability of an error for moves in the Tower of Hanoi puzzle as a function of the number of subgoals that are generated to enable that move. The curves represent four groups of subjects who are sorted according to their Raven test scores, from best (33–36 points) to low-median (20–25 points) performance. From Carpenter, Just, and Shell (1990). Reprinted by permission.

predicted to correlate highly with the Raven test. More specifically, the correlation between errors on the Raven test and total number of errors on the six Tower of Hanoi puzzles was $r(43) = .77$, $p < .01$, a correlation that is close to the test–retest reliability typically found for the Raven test (Court & Raven, 1982). A subanalysis of the 34 higher scoring subjects (that is, eliminating the group of the 9 lowest scoring subjects) still resulted in a significant correlation between errors on the Tower of Hanoi puzzles and the Raven test, $r(32) = .57$. These correlations support the thesis that the execution of the goal-recursion strategy in the Tower of Hanoi puzzle and the performance on the Raven test are both related to the ability to generate and maintain goals in working memory. Moreover, it is extremely unlikely that any substantial portion of the correlation is due to variation in the procedural or declarative knowledge of the two tasks.

A more detailed analysis examined the error rates of each group as a function of the number of subgoals generated in order to make a move, whether zero, one, or two or more subgoals. The specific hypothesis is that the error rates should differ more on moves that are more demanding of working memory capacity. As predicted, and as shown in Fig. 5.3, error rates were low and comparable for moves that did not require the generation of additional subgoals. By contrast, lower scoring subjects made significantly more errors as the number of subgoals to be generated increased, as reflected in a significant interaction between the subject groups and whether there were zero or one or more subgoals to be generated. Even when the analysis is restricted to the four better scoring groups, the lower scoring groups of these four had significantly more difficulty when they had to generate one or more goals. Also as expected, the errors increased with the number of subgoals to be generated in working memory. The error rates also can be compared to chance performance. On all but the first move, there are two possible legal moves in addition to the correct move; however, one of the two legal alternatives is to take back the previous move. This is an uncommon mistake and so the effective guessing rate is 50%. Thus, the three lowest scoring groups performed at close to chance level when they had to generate two or more subgoals. In all, these results support the hypothesis that errors in the Tower of Hanoi puzzle reflect the difficulty of constructing subgoals in working memory. The systematic interaction between the move difficulty and the Raven scores, as an index of working memory capacity, suggests that both the extrinsic task load and the intrinsic variable may reflect similar limitations on working memory.

A Continuous-Load Secondary Task

On Tower of Hanoi moves in which performance is affected by a lack of working-memory resources, performance should be further impaired by a concurrent task that also draws on working-memory resources. Of course, a concurrent task would be expected to cause decrements in performance overall. But the current model leads to the specific hypothesis that moves that require the generation of multiple goals should be more impaired than those that require no new goals be generated. To test this hypothesis, we introduced a concurrent monitoring task during the solution of some Tower of Hanoi puzzles. In the dual task situation (the "load" condition), subjects monitored either of two locations in the base of a visually presented Tower of Hanoi puzzle where every 2 seconds, a different randomly selected letter of the alphabet was displayed at both locations. Subjects monitored the changing letter and pressed the space bar whenever a vowel was displayed. (There was approximately 1 vowel for every 10 consonants and the letter "Y" was excluded.) Although subjects monitored for vowels, in fact, the analysis excluded moves on which a vowel was actually presented in the load condition; hence, any decrement in performance cannot be attributed to disruption caused by actually detecting and responding to a target.

Procedure. As in the previous study, subjects were given extensive instructions and practice with the goal-recursion strategy for the two- and three-disk Tower of Hanoi puzzle, and then practice with the "load" condition for the two-, three-, and four-disk Tower of Hanoi puzzles. In the test phase, subjects solved the five-disk Tower of Hanoi puzzle four times, across which we counterbalanced the presence or absence of the load condition.

Forty-five Carnegie Mellon students participated, but five subjects were not included because they failed to respond to at least 30% of the vowels in the load task, indicating that they may not have been performing the problem-solving task under load. Subjects were also partitioned into three groups (high, medium, or low scoring) based on their performance on a subset of problems from the Raven Progressive Matrices Test that had been selected for discriminating among subjects in the first experiment.

Results. As predicted, the presence of a load caused a particularly high number of strays (deviations from the optimal path) if the move involved generating multiple new goals (2+), but not if there were no new goals or only one, as shown in Fig. 5.4. Supporting the hypothesis that goal generation draws on working memory, the data show that the presence of a load is especially deleterious when there are multiple new goals, resulting in a significant interaction of the number of new goals and the presence of a load. As predicted, the number of strays increased significantly with the number of new goals to be generated, from .01, to .05, and .41, for zero, one, and two or more new goals, respectively. This result, which replicates that of Experiment 1, supports the hypothesis that moves that require generating more new goals are more demanding of working memory capacity. In fact, the high error rate (.41) when two or more new goals must be generated is close to random performance. Although the effects of load and the interaction with subject groups (more errors by lower

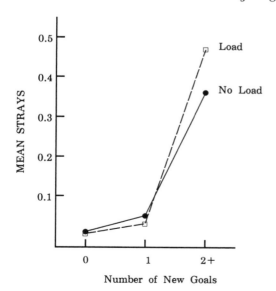

FIG. 5.4. The probability of an error for moves in the Tower of Hanoi puzzle as a function of the number of subgoals that are generated, and whether the task was administered by itself (no-load condition) or accompanied by another demanding task (load condition). The greater increase in errors for moves requiring more subgoals in the load condition suggests that both manipulations require working-memory resources.

ability subjects) were in the predicted direction, due to the variability within and between groups, the interaction effect was not significant. In general, the pattern of results supports the hypothesis that executing the goal recursion strategy to solve the Tower of Hanoi puzzle in the current situation requires working-memory capacity to generate goals. The correlation between performance here and on the Raven Matrices Test and the predicted effects of load are both consistent with the hypothesis that it is goal generation that mediates the similar effects.

Pupillometric Responses During Goal Generation

One technique for measuring the demand on cognitive resources is pupillometry, the measurement of changes in pupil size, as espoused by Kahneman (1973). Previous studies suggest that the greater the demand on capacity, the greater the change in pupil size (Ahern & Beatty, 1979; Beatty, 1982). For example, pupil change is greater during more difficult mental multiplication (e.g., $14 \times 19 = ?$) than simpler multiplication (e.g., $6 \times 12 = ?$). The neurophysiological basis for the relation between pupil dilation and the consumption of cognitive resources, according to Beatty, may be the cortical modulation of the reticular formation, which may also modulate some peripheral systems, such as the pupillary control system. The implication is that the pupillary response is only a correlate of cognitive intensity, and hence the marker is indirect and not causally linked. In addition, there is a temporal lag between the resource consumption and the pupillary response. Nevertheless, there is reason to believe that pupillary response may be sensitive to cognitive demand, such as goal generation. For instance, earlier studies have indicated that pupillary response may be sensitive to resource demands in language processing. For example, pupils dilate more if a subject must repeat nonstructured linguistic strings rather than more structured ones (Schluroff, 1982). Also, pupil dilation increases with the processing of sentences containing lexical ambiguities compared to sentences with comparable nonambiguities (Ben-Nun, 1986; Schluroff et al., 1986). More recently, pupillary responses have been shown to be sensitive to variation in syntactic demands during reading comprehension (Just & Carpenter, in press). Readers processed sentences that varied in syntactic complexity and then answered true–false verification questions to ensure that they had comprehended the sentences. Pupillary dilation was larger for the more complex constructions, sentences containing object relative clauses, such as "The reporter that the senator accused walked to the building" than for simpler sentences containing subject relative clauses, such as, "The reporter that accused the senator walked to the building." Readers showed significantly greater changes in pupillary size when processing the more complex construction, specifically after encountering the more complex relative clause. Cumulatively, the research suggests that there are small but consistent effects of processing demands on pupillary response that may reflect the consumption of cognitive resources.

Procedure. The most relevant characteristic of the pupillary response is the peak amplitude of the dilation, which tends to occur approximately 1,200 ms after the first encounter with the demand (Ahern & Beatty, 1979; Beatty, 1982; Janisse, 1977). Specifically, in the present study, we compared peak amplitudes in trials that involve differential amounts of goal generation. However, it was necessary to modify the Tower of Hanoi procedure to separate individual moves so that pupil dilations could be associated with particular processing loads. Subjects were shown a single state that was randomly selected from the 32 possible states in the five-disk Tower of Hanoi. A marker indicated which disk was to be moved out, and another marker indicated the final goal peg for the entire stack. The subject's task was to select the next move. Specifically, they pressed one of three buttons corresponding to the destination peg (left, center, or right peg) for the indicated disk. After practice with the goal-recursion strategy and the specific method of indicating movement with the graphic display, each subject solved seven puzzles, with the same type of display as in the first experiment. Forty-two students served as subjects.

Results. As predicted, pupil diameter increased significantly as the number of new goals that had to be generated on a given move increased, as shown in Fig. 5.5. This result further supports the hypothesis that resource demands increase with the number of new goals generated. The result is less compatible with a knowledge-based explanation of the differences in the performance on different move types. In sum, both the patterns of errors across these experiments and the results of this more autonomic measure of resource consumption suggest that goal generation is a significant source of cognitive demand.

The Simulation Model

To examine our proposal that individuals differ in the amount of activation available for storage and processing, a production-system simulation model that solves the Tower of Hanoi puzzle was constructed in 3CAPS. One unconventional aspect of the Tower of Hanoi model is that the number of processing cycles that it takes to make each move depends on the amount of activation that is available. If activation is plentiful, then a given production may be able to activate its action elements to threshold in a single cycle. But if storage or processing demands conjointly exceed the activation maximum, then the production will increment the activation level of its

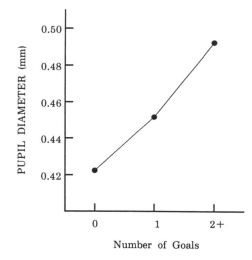

FIG. 5.5. The pupil size (mm) as a function of the number of subgoals to be generated in making a move in the five-disk Tower of Hanoi. The increase in pupil size with goal generation is consistent with the hypothesis that generating more goals is more demanding on resources.

action elements more gradually, requiring more cycles before the level reaches a threshold. At the same time, if the demand on the activation exceeds the maximum, some of the activation that is being used to maintain representational elements in an activated state will be deallocated, resulting in some partial forgetting of previously generated partial products.

The constraint on the total amount of activation in the system conjointly limits how much activation can be propagated per cycle and how many elements can be maintained in working memory. Given a certain maximum on the amount of activation that is available, there are many points along an isoactivation curve that can be adopted. At one extreme, the brunt of an activation shortage could be borne by the storage function, such that at times of peak demand there is a lot of forgetting of partial and final products in working memory, but processing (particularly the time it takes to compute something) remains unchanged. At the other extreme, the brunt could be borne by the processing function, such that at times of peak demand, processing slows down but there is no forgetting. (Limiting the amount of activation available per cycle slows down processing by requiring more cycles of propagation to raise an element's activation to a given level.) The current implementation chooses an intermediate point in this trading relation. Any shortfall of activation is assessed against both the storage and processing, in proportion to the amount of activation they are currently consuming.

There are several implications of this scheme. First, decrementing the activation levels of old elements is a form of continuous forgetting by displacement. This is unlike conventional displacement models that posit one element displacing another from a limited number of storage locations. By contrast, this model posits that the activation that is used to maintain old elements is drawn away by the action of the productions' incrementing the activation levels of other elements. Thus, when the activation demands exceed the constraint, there will be gradual forgetting of old information (or old partial products) with each new cycle of processing that exceeds the activation quota. Second, when the number of partial products is small (say, early in a task), then the forgetting due to displacement will be less than when there are many partial products (say, late in a task that requires storage of partial products). Furthermore, the constraint does not apply until the demand for activation exceeds the quota. Thus, the effects of the constraint will arise at different times for different people. The manifestation of the constraint is some combination of forgetting (decrease in activation of old elements) and a slowdown of processing (more cycles of activation will be required for an element's activation level to reach a given threshold).

The Tower of Hanoi Model. The model solves the Tower of Hanoi puzzle using the goal-recursion strategy. The model tries to make a move that would satisfy the current goal. If that move entails moving a disk that is currently blocked by having other disks on top of it, then the model sets a new subgoal to unblock that disk. Three of the model's productions are responsible for moving disks and for setting subgoals. In conversational form, these rules are:

- Unblock Disk at Source: If the goal is to move a disk between two pegs, and another disk rests on the top of the disk to be moved, then set a subgoal to move the blocking disk to the third peg.
- Unblock Disk's Destination: If the goal is to move a disk between two pegs, and the target peg has a disk that is smaller than the disk to be moved, and this smaller disk rests on a disk that is larger than the disk to be moved, then set a subgoal to move the smaller disk to the third peg.
- Move Disk: If the goal is to move a disk between two pegs, and the disk is not covered, and the topmost disk on the target peg is larger than the disk to be moved, then move the disk.

To illustrate how the model solves a puzzle using these productions, consider which productions fire at the beginning of the solution of a five-disk puzzle. The first production to fire creates a goal to move the base of the pyramid (the largest disk, disk-5) from the start peg to the goal peg. However, this disk is covered by another disk (disk-4), so the Unblock Disk at Source production fires and creates a subgoal to move disk-4 from the start peg (peg A) to the middle peg (peg B). Disk-4 is also covered, by disk-3, and so the Unblock Disk at Source production fires again, and creates another subgoal to move disk-3 from the start peg to the goal peg (peg C) (because the subgoal is to move disk-4 to peg B from peg A). The Unblock at Source production fires twice more, and creates subgoals to move disk-2 and disk-1, in order to unblock disk-3 and disk-2 respectively. Disk-1 is not covered and there are no disks on its destination peg (the goal peg, peg C), so the Move Disk production fires and moves disk-1. In order to move this one disk, the model executed six cycles of production firings, and created five goals.

Forgetting. Every goal element added to working memory has an activation level associated with it. In the 3CAPS architecture, the sum of the activations associated with all the elements in working memory is limited to a specified value, the cap. If a production adds a new element whose additional activation would make the total activation exceed the cap, then the activations of all the elements in working memory (including the new element) are reduced by an amount that will keep the total under the cap. During the course of solving a puzzle, the activation level of a goal element may be decremented several times, and its activation may fall below the level of a threshold at which it can be matched by a production; in other words, the element has been forgotten. If the model reaches a point in its solution where the next goal is below threshold, before continuing, that goal must receive sufficient activation to exceed the threshold. The reactivation of the goal is accomplished by firing a special recovery production that channels a small amount of activation to the goal. The recovery production may have to fire several times in order to bring the goal's activation level above threshold; just how many times depends on how far below threshold it has fallen.

Simulation of Subjects' Performance. To examine whether activation-based capacity differences can account for the differences observed in the subjects' performances, the model was run with a range of values of activation cap. Most of the human performance data concerned stray moves, and that was the primary measure of interest in the model. However, because the model never actually made stray moves, the measure of strays obtained from the simulations had to be less direct. Specifically, if we assume that human stray moves are caused primarily by forgetting of a subgoal, then the number of firings of the recovery production may provide a measure of how much a goal has been forgotten. Hence, the prediction is that the number of recovery productions should be correlated with the frequency of stray moves in the human data.

The general result obtained from the simulations was that decreasing the cap value resulted in an increase in the numbers of normal cycles and recovery cycles per move, particularly on the moves that required the generation of new subgoals. The lower panel of Fig. 5.6 shows the average number of recovery cycles per move, for moves requiring the generation of zero, one, or two or more subgoals. The parameter on the curve is the activation cap. The simulation was run using three different cap values, which changed linearly from a low to a high level. The upper panel of Fig. 5.6 presents the corresponding data for human subjects in one of the previously described Tower of Hanoi experiments. The human data indicate the probability of stray moves as a counterpart to the number of recovery cycles. The parameter on the curve in the human data is the subjects' score on a subset of the problems from the Raven Progressive Matrices Test that had been selected for discriminating among subjects in the first experiment.

The pattern of the simulation results is clearly similar to the pattern of results from the human subjects. There is relatively little forgetting on moves that do not require the generation of subgoals, and hence, little firing of the recovery productions. By contrast, there is considerable forgetting when multiple subgoals must be generated. In addition, the increase in the cap (i.e., available activation) is generally beneficial, and mirrors the decreases in the high ability subjects' strays. This result shows that differences in activation are sufficient to explain the differences in human ability.

In summary, the constrained capacity model accounts for the individual differences, the differences in move difficulty, and the effect of a secondary task on performance, in terms of both the probability of error and changes in pupil size.

INDIVIDUAL DIFFERENCES IN PROBLEM SOLVING

Having demonstrated that working memory limitations play an important role in the Tower of Hanoi puzzle and in the Raven Advanced Progressive Matrices Test, we now return to the issue of why processing constraints in such reasoning tasks are of interest to a general theory of cognition. These two reasoning tasks are well-analyzed examples of a broader class of online reasoning tasks that show consistent individual differences in performance. That is, subjects who perform well on one task tend to do well on another, as we found for the Tower of Hanoi puzzle and the Raven Test. Moreover, the novelty of the tasks (to our subjects) and the striking differences in their content suggest that the basis of the correlation is unlikely to be a function of subjects having acquired expertise separately in each domain. This argues against ascribing these individual differences to domain knowledge. A theory that was based solely on domain knowledge could also have difficulty accounting for the systematic interactions between individual

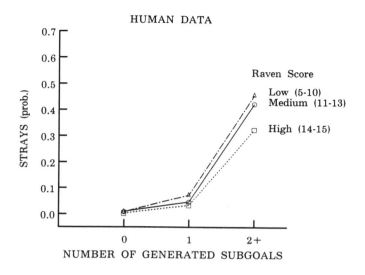

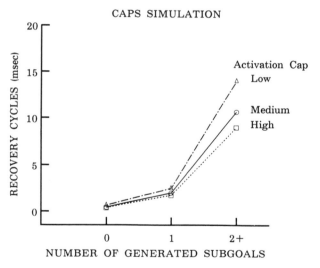

FIG. 5.6. The probability of a stray move for human subjects (upper panel) compared to the simulation model (lower panel) as a function of the number of goals to be generated in a move. The human data are from three subject groups that are classified according to their scores on the Raven Matrices Test, and show the interaction between the number of goals and ability. The simulation data present the number of cycles of the recovery production that reactivates a subgoal to threshold as a function of three different activation caps.

differences and the conditions than manipulated the load on working memory during reasoning. Consequently, the interpretation of the performance constraints is more compellingly made in terms of some more general limitation on reasoning that is manifested in these two very different tasks. In this section, we examine the argument in light of data that are drawn more broadly from other reasoning tasks and other populations, by reviewing the psychometric results within populations of adults (usually college-age or military-age adults) and then examining the differences in reasoning performance between younger and older adults.

Psychometric Data From Young Adults

One premise of the argument that these individual differences are quite general is that subjects who perform well on the Raven also perform well on other complex reasoning tasks that are, at least superficially, quite different (Marshalek, Lohman, & Snow, 1983). This high intercorrelation across different tasks suggests the existence of some general constraints on reasoning in any task. Moreover, the intercorrelation is difficult to account for in terms of knowledge of task-specific rules and strategies because the tasks involve different domains, such as numerical analogies, complex spatial reasoning, and letter series completion. Before returning to this point, we briefly review the nature of the intercorrelation.

One of the most compelling studies that illustrates high intercorrelations among complex reasoning tasks is a series of nonmetric scaling studies that examines interrelations among a large number of ability test scores (Snow, Kyllonen, & Marshalek, 1984). The databases include many archival sources in which large numbers of adults had been tested on a variety of psychometric tests, as well as recent data collected from approximately 100 college students. For each of these databases, a two-dimensional scaling solution captures much of the variance and, at the same time, shows remarkable consistencies in the resulting structure of the solution. Complex reasoning tasks, such as the Raven test, are at the center of the solution; these are tests in which there are typically errors related to the difficulty of the item. An individual's scores across these tests are highly intercorrelated, in spite of marked differences in the tests' formats and content (whether visual, numerical, or linguistic). By contrast, simpler tests, for which performance typically varies in speed, tend to fall in the periphery of the solution, and the correlations are more dependent on the format (whether visual, numerical, or linguistic). The results of the various analyses are summarized in an idealized space, shown in Fig. 5.7. In the idealized solution, the Raven test is in the center of the figure along with other complex tests, including complex spatial visualization tasks, verbal analogy tests, and letter series tests. The typical interpretation of the high intercorrelation is that, in spite of the differences in format, the reasoning tasks in the center of the space draw on

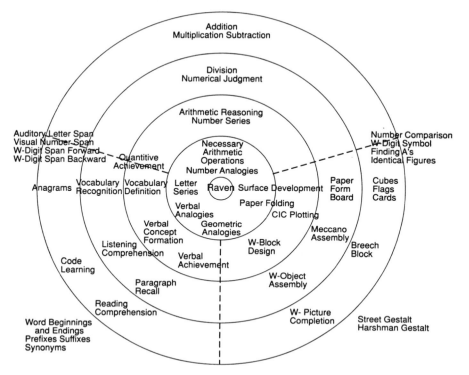

FIG. 5.7. An idealized scaling solution that summarizes the relations among ability tests across several sets of data, illustrating the centrality of the Raven test. The outwardly radiating concentric circles indicate decreasing levels of test complexity. Tests involving different content (figural, verbal, and numerical) are separated by dashed radial lines. The complex reasoning tasks tend to cluster together at the center in spite of their different content. From Snow, Kyllonen, and Marshalek (1984). Adapted by permission.

similar processes. Generalizing from our previous conclusions from the Raven Matrices Test and Tower of Hanoi puzzle, these processes may make large demands on working memory, for example, in generating, maintaining, and updating goals. In fact, a task analysis of some of these tests in the center of the space supports the hypothesis that they also make the extensive demands on working memory. For example, to solve a letter series task, the subject must encode a sequence of letters, determine which pairs of letters might be related by a similar rule, test the adequacy of the (typically simple) rule, determine which remaining letters are related, and hypothesize and verify their relation, all while retaining the earlier rule. Clearly, letter series tasks make demands on working memory (Simon & Kotovsky, 1963).

Complex visualization tasks also often make extensive demands on working memory by requiring the subject to retain intermediate results of initial computations while executing successive steps (Just & Carpenter, 1985). It is sometimes counterintuitive that such demands exist in visually presented problems because of the incorrect assumption that a visual format serves as an external memory; however, a visual presentation does not eliminate extensive demands, as the research on both Tower of Hanoi puzzle and the Raven Matrices Test have demonstrated. The claim, therefore, is that many of the psychometric reasoning tasks that are in the center of the space analyzed by Snow and his colleagues share the property of making extensive demands on working memory, in spite of their superficially different formats.

Psychometric results are correlational, and hence inherently open to alternative causal interpretations. In the current context, one important alternative interpretation is that psychometric tests reflect differences in having acquired relevant previous knowledge. According to this alternative, individuals who tend to do well on the Raven test are those who have had some relevant experience, either on these specific tasks or analogous tasks. This "fortuitous experience" interpretation has another hurdle in explaining the current data, namely, why errors are not general over all moves but instead are primarily associated with the generation of multiple goals in the Tower of Hanoi puzzle and are associated with problems that involve multiple rules in the Raven test. These are the moves and problems that make extensive demands on working memory. Thus, the fortuitous experience explanation would be less parsimonious, and less plausible, than the conclusion that there is some general limitation in working-memory capacity.

Working-memory capacity may also influence the acquisition of problem-solving skill (Kyllonen & Stephens, 1990). The problem-solving skill that these authors analyzed was learning how to trace signals passing through logic gates over an electronic circuit. To control for the possibility of differential prior knowledge of the task, a second experiment used a different set of problems involving rules and colors, which were isomorphic to the logic gates only at the deepest level. A third study examined transfer between the two domains, by first administering one type of task and then another and looking for specific transfer. Working-memory capacity was assessed with two tasks that were specifically designed to require concurrent storage and execution of processes. Using path analysis, the researchers concluded that working-memory capacity was a primary determinant of performance in skill acquisition. Moreover, by analyzing performance when subjects learned both tasks, they found no evidence for the transfer of content-specific skills. Statistically controlling for declarative learning ability, the latent factor representing working-memory capacity played the largest role in governing the rate of skill learning (approximately $r = .7$) in all three large-scale studies.

In sum, a variety of correlational studies, as well as the current analyses of the Tower of Hanoi and Raven Matrices Test performance, suggests that individual differences in problem solving depend crucially and largely on working-memory capacity.

Psychometric Data on Aging

Another type of individual difference that supports a role for working-memory limitations in problem solving comes from an examination of the effects of aging on cognitive performance. Performance in reasoning tasks typically shows consistent declines with age. Such deficits, according to a commonly expressed hypothesis in the area of cognitive gerontology, may be manifestations of increasing limitations in working memory resources (Cattell, 1971; see a review by Salthouse, 1992a). The effects of aging are pertinent in the present context for two reasons. First, if the effects are consistent with a decrement in working-memory capacity, then the characterization of the decrement may provide further constraint on how working memory is modeled. Second, decrements with aging apparently occur in spite of the accumulation of knowledge or expertise, and so provide a challenge to a theory that attributes individual differences primarily to the acquisition of knowledge.

As a background to the characterization, it is important to point out that the negative effects of healthy aging on cognition are somewhat circumscribed, even aside from the fact that the tests do not purport to tap wisdom, but much more superficial aspects of knowledge. Specifically, indices of vocabulary knowledge generally show little or no decreases with aging (Salthouse, 1988b). By contrast, decrements with aging are more apparent in reasoning tasks or, more generally, tasks that have a pronounced computational component (Jones & Conrad, 1933; Salthouse, 1988a). For example, in a 1981 standardization of a widely used intelligence test, the WAIS-R, there is relatively little decrement with age in the multiple-choice vocabulary test. In contrast, there is a marked decrement in the similarities test, a test that also involves vocabulary knowledge but that requires subjects to describe the similarity between two concepts (Salthouse, 1988a). The similarities test involves computation, rather than just retrieval, because it requires considering the features that describe the two concepts and comparing their overlap to arrive at an informative and yet shared characterization of two concepts. Other reasoning tasks that have a marked computational component also tend to show age-related decrements. An extensive review of 28 studies in the aging literature indicates that, on average, there is a moderate correlation (−.44) between chronological age and performance in reasoning tasks (such as the Raven test, series completion tasks, or three-term series problems) and a correlation (−.38) between age and specifically spatial reasoning (as assessed by tests like paper folding, cube comparisons, or the Primary Mental Abilities Spatial test; Salthouse, 1992a).

In such correlational data it is impossible to guard against all other mediating factors. However, aging researchers have tried to assess two factors that are obvious candidates. One candidate factor relates to the "disuse" hypothesis, namely, that performance declines with age because of a lack of use or experience in the relevant domain. Several studies that have directly examined the performance of relevant populations have failed to support this hypothesis. For example, studies of the performance of aircraft pilots and air traffic controllers indicate that their declines in performance on spatial ability tasks with age are comparable to those exhibited by unselected subjects (see the summary in Salthouse, 1992a). In one such study, practicing architects manifest declines in spatial problem solving with age that parallel the declines of adults who have less relevant experience. Figure 5.8 shows data from Salthouse (1992a), who compared the performance of architects to that of other adults, who were rated according to amount of spatially relevant experience. As the curves indicate, more experience is correlated with improved performance; however, experience does not mitigate the effects of aging (Salthouse, Babcock, Mitchell, Skovronek, & Palmon, 1990; Salthouse & Mitchell, 1990; Salthouse, 1992a). Such results support the view

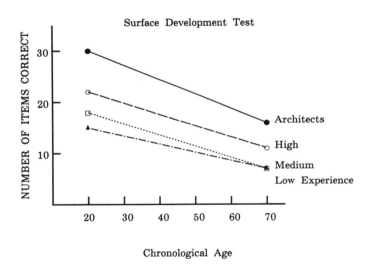

FIG. 5.8. Performance on a spatial reasoning test as a function of chronological age, comparing architects who have a great deal of relevant experience to nonselected subjects, who were classified according to their degree of experience. The positive effect of experience is indicated by the better performance of architects and high-experience individuals. However, all groups show decrements with age, arguing that experience does not mitigate the effect of age on spatial reasoning. Data are from Salthouse (1992a). Adapted by permission.

that experience can contribute to the improvement of performance in reasoning tasks; however, experience is not the only factor and does not ameliorate the deterioration in certain reasoning tasks that occurs with normal aging.

A second factor that seems not to explain the deterioration with age is roughly referred to as generational factors; these can include a variety of more specific cultural or environmental changes that may have occurred with time and influence cross-sectional comparisons. One response to such changes is to assess the same population longitudinally. One such time-lag study of the Primary Mental Abilities Reasoning and Spatial subtests (Schaie, 1988) tested a wide age range of individuals across several decades. In that study, the longitudinal decrement with age was between 25% and 56% as great as that observed in cross-sectional comparisons. Hence, there may be some generational factors, but the conclusion is that there is still considerable decrement as a function of aging, independent of extrinsic factors that may contribute to the differences between older and younger individuals. Although such studies do not eliminate all of the possible interpretations of the causal factors that could contribute to cognitive aging, there is some evidence that more directly supports the interpretation of these deficits in terms of increasing limitations in working-memory capacity.

Importantly, more direct assessments of working-memory capacity show age-related decrements. In these studies, working-memory capacity is typically assessed by the Reading Span task or a listening variant of it, rather than by digit span or word span task. In the Reading Span test, the subject reads and processes a series of sentences and then must recall the sentence final word. The maximum number of sentences that can be processed and final words recalled is typically defined as the span (Daneman & Carpenter, 1980). In the Listening Span variant, the subject listens to the set of sentences, spoken with only a brief pause between successive sentences to allow the subject to verify it as true or false, but to minimize the opportunity for covert rehearsal. The logic underlying the test is that it requires not just storage but also processing.

A survey of 10 studies that directly compares the span scores of older and younger subjects found that in seven of the studies the older subjects have a significantly lower span than the younger subjects (Carpenter, Miyake, & Just, 1993). Similarly, a survey of eight studies that assesses the correlation between chronological age and either Reading or Listening span scores shows significant correlations in seven of the eight, with an average correlation of −.42. These data suggest that older individuals have more difficulty than younger ones in tests that stress working memory. The ability to both hold and manipulate information in working memory is a plausible candidate to account for some of the age-related deterioration in reasoning tasks that have this characteristic.

Further evidence that working-memory limitations may account for some of the aging effects comes from studies that have directly correlated the age-related decrement in performance with measures of working-memory capacity (Salthouse, 1992b, 1992c; Salthouse, Mitchell, Skovronek, & Babcock, 1989). One such study examined the effects of task complexity, which was operationalized as varying the number of times a particular operation had to be performed (Salthouse, 1992b). For example, in a cube assembly task, the subject might have to mentally make one, two, or three folds in order to judge whether or not the two designated sides in a drawing of an unfolded paper cube would meet. In an analogy task, the subject might have to compare one, two, or three elements to judge the validity of the analogy. To perform such multiple operations requires maintaining information while performing the next computation. The deterioration in performance with age, as assessed by errors, is typically greater if there is a larger number of operations. Across a variety of tasks, the results show a significant interaction in error rates between the number of operations and chronological age. An example of the data from one such task, the visual analogy task, is shown in Fig. 5.9. Performance declines with age, particularly for the analogy task that involves three elements. The question addressed in this research is what possible sources of processing difficulty might account for the interaction of age and task complexity. One source was a factor related to working-memory capacity, as assessed by both the Reading Span task and a numerical version of the task. A second source, related to working memory, is processing efficiency (as assessed by the speed of the response in a simple version of the task). A third source is the error rate that is associated with the single execution of an operation; multiple executions of an errorful process may account for additional errors. In the final correlational analysis, several stepwise regressions gave little support for the hypothesis that the errors in the more complex version are simply the multiplicative result of the error rate in the simpler version of the task. The point, which echoes the argument made with respect to the Raven Progressive Matrices Test, is that the operations, when performed alone, are not particularly problematic for these subjects. Rather, the errors arise in the situation that requires the processing in the context of keeping track of other information. More specifically, the analysis suggested that a simple measure of operational speed and working-memory capacity together accounted for all of the reliable variance in decrement associated with aging.

In sum, the correlational analysis suggests that working-memory limitations, which may in part be mediated by the speed of processing, contribute to the deficits manifested by older subjects compared to younger ones in computationally intensive tasks. Moreover, such effects seem not to be easily explained in terms of any simple notion of differential knowledge or expertise. Indeed, the results on aging suggest that knowledge and expertise

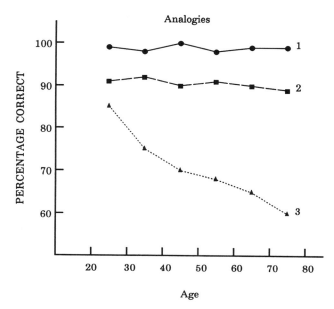

FIG. 5.9. Performance on a visual analogy task as a function of chronological age and the complexity of the analogy task. Data are from Salthouse (1992b). Adapted by permission.

improve performance and do not account for the decrement in reasoning with age.

One Versus Many Pools of Capacity

We have now broached the topic of performance limitations in visually based reasoning and its relation to measures of working-memory capacity that are based, in part, on language processing. The conjunction of these two examples poses a question about the commonality of the source of constraint. Put another way, is there a single working-memory capacity or resource pool, or are there several working-memory capacities or resource pools (such as separate pools for language, spatial thinking, numerical processing, and possibly others)? More importantly, what sources of evidence are useful in helping to answer this question?

One source of evidence has come from correlational studies that bridge the psychometric approach to individual differences with the cognitively oriented analysis of specific cognitive processes and representations. Such studies may examine patterns of intercorrelations among individuals, but use measures from tasks that are motivated by cognitive models. One such series of four studies, each involving approximately 500 Air Force recruits, used structural equation modeling to argue that there is a unitary working-memory capacity, and that it is closely related to reasoning ability (Kyllonen & Christal, 1990). The working-memory tasks involve numerical, logical, or alphabetic computations and, at the same time, some information storage. For example, in the alphabet recoding task, the subjects are given a string of alphabetic characters to remember (e.g., G N C) and then on the second screen, some numerical index (e.g., −2) indicating that they should calculate either the predecessor or successor relations (e.g., E L A). After comparing several possible confirmatory factor analysis models, Kyllonen and Christal concluded that there is evidence for a unitary working-memory capacity, at least one that includes both logical/linguistic and numerical operations. In addition, there is an extremely high correlation between the working-memory factor and the reasoning factor, except that reasoning correlates more with general knowledge, whereas working memory correlated slightly more with processing speed. In addition, there is evidence of some content distinction between verbal and quantitative domains. When multiple measures from a variety of tasks are used to statistically identify a working-memory factor, then it appears that the factor is implicated in a variety of online reasoning tasks, particularly when the task performance is enhanced by efficient processing.

Using a related approach, researchers who have examined the intercorrelations among a variety of tests that appear to require working memory typically find evidence for significant shared variance. For example, working-memory tests patterned after the Reading Span task but involving different content show significant intercorrelation that is sometimes interpreted as reflecting a unitary working-memory capacity (Engel, Cantor, & Carullo, 1992; Salthouse, 1992b). The strength of these approaches, like their psychometric predecessors, is that they analyze data from a variety of tasks, which means that the statistically defined shared variance is broadly implicated.

The Snow et al. analysis, as exemplified in the multidimensional analysis cited earlier, provides a robust and thoughtful guide to this psychometric terrain. The suggestion that emerges from that work is that there is evidence for a central ability (general reasoning), and there are peripheral abilities as well. The more modality- and domain-specific the crucial processes are, the more the individual differences are determined by peripheral abilities. The more conceptually difficult a task is, the more it draws on the central working-memory capacity.

The current research, as well as our earlier research on problem solving and on language (Carpenter et al., 1990; Just & Carpenter, 1985, 1992), differs from these approaches by involving a detailed analysis of the processes in a particular task or small number of related tasks, supported by both simulation modeling and empirical data. Although much more statistically limited, the present approach has the advantage of precisely describing the processes and representations that are the sources of errors, and consequently, the potential sources of differences among individuals. In some cases, such as the present analysis of the Tower of Hanoi and the Raven Matrices Test, the similarity of the microlevel descriptions, in combination with the highly correlated empirical results, strongly supports the interpretation that the underlying processes and representations that are the sources of individual differences are similar in the two tasks.

One proposal that is consistent with both the psychometric and our current data is that there are overlapping pools of central capacity, along with more peripheral pools that represent domain- or modality-specific resources associated with the peripheral input or output systems. This could be construed as a set of small overlapping pools that together define a large pool. Each small pool would correspond to the resources that support a set of related cognitive processes and representations. An example of one of the pools that lies within the large pool defining central capacity might be the pool that supports the processing of embedded clauses. Represented more toward the periphery of the central pool would be the resources that are associated with peripheral input or output systems (such as perceptual matching) or some domain-specific processes (such as numerical processing). The phonological buffer, as well as the articulatory loop discussed by Baddeley, might involve systems that are supported by peripheral resources.

There is an important property of tasks that are of the center of the ability space that is characterized similarly by our capacity approach as well as by these more psychometric type approaches. The tasks that draw on the abilities at the center of the space are more conceptual, and less modality or domain specific. Furthermore, the central tasks are particularly demanding at a conceptual level. The important property is the cause of the conceptual difficulty associated with the tasks at the center. The cause is the multiplicity of processes and representations that must be supported simultaneously, and not their particular properties. For example, a difficult problem in the Raven Matrices Test is difficult not just because it requires an inference to be made, but more because it requires that an inference be made in the midst of storing lots of other partial products and doing other computations before and after making the difficult inference. It is not that the component processes or representations in a particular problem are so difficult, but that they must be dealt with in a context of other representations and processes. We know this because the problems that require the difficult processes and representations to be dealt with in a simpler context are solved by many more people.

Mechanisms That Can Impose Constraint

There are other ways to impose resource constraints on a computational system. For example, there could be resource limitations that constrain the use of procedural or declarative knowledge, such as retrieval failures, long searches, or limitations on chunking. There could also be constraints at a finer grain size, such as a limitation on a variable-binding memory (suggested by Newell as one way to instantiate a type of limitation in working memory). In this section, we briefly examine some alternative hypotheses concerning capacity to examine their relation to the proposal instantiated in 3CAPS.

Total Capacity and Efficiency. The notion of *capacity* traditionally has been interpreted as a structural limit on the number of simultaneously active representations that could be maintained in working memory. Such a limit can be realized in both symbolic and parallel distributed processing (PDP; subsymbolic) models. In symbolic models, the representations are conceptualized as chunks (Miller, 1956). In network models, an analogous concept would be a limit on the number of simultaneously activated nodes or links. The conception of capacity instantiated in 3CAPS extends the limitation beyond a structural limit to also include computation; the cap on activation can impact either on the maintenance of previously activated representations or on the computation of new information. The structural conception, typically assessed by digit or word span, often does not correlate very well with individual differences in more complex tasks (Carpenter et al., 1994; Daneman & Carpenter, 1980). In contrast, the operationalizations of capacity measures that involve both storage and computation do correlate with individual differences in complex tasks such as reading (Carpenter & Just, 1989; Carpenter et al., 1994; Daneman & Carpenter, 1980) and reasoning (Carpenter et al., 1990).

In addition, the model also provides a precise framework in which to express a different, but frequently hypothesized, source of deficit—processing speed or efficiency. The efficiency concept can apply to several computational aspects of processing—the time course with which information is activated from long-term memory, the time course of computing new information (transformation), and the time course of information decay. A generalized efficiency hypothesis has been suggested to explain the deficit among older individuals, with the idea that if their speed is slowed, then their working-memory capacity will effectively decrease (Babcock & Salthouse, 1990).

A related version of this hypothesis is that certain categories of individual differences reside in the allocation or management of resources, rather than in the efficiency of the system in general or the efficiency of some specific process. The efficiency hypothesis is implicated in aphasics' deficits by repeated differences in the temporal parameters of specific processes for some aphasic patients in various priming and judgment tasks. Some studies suggest slower activation in aphasics than in normals (Haarmann & Kolk, 1991), and others suggest faster decay of activation (Friederici & Kilborn, 1989; Haarmann & Kolk, 1992). A comparison of studies suggests that aphasics may have different resource allocation schemes in different tasks, in some cases resulting in relatively slower activation and in other cases decreased maintenance (Haarmann, 1992). In the domain of aging, the speed of information activation, not decay, has been hypothesized to be a source of working-memory limitation, based on a statistical analysis of the covariance between changes in working-memory span tasks and in speeded perceptually based tasks, as a function of age (Salthouse, 1991).

Changes in total resources and in efficiency are not mutually exclusive, although they differ in their intuitive appeal as explanations across various domains. The types of generalized performance changes induced by fatigue, aging, or concentration seem compatible with the concept of total available activation (Kahneman, 1973). In contrast, a change in processing efficiency may be more specific to a specific psychological process (Cohen, Dunbar, & McClelland, 1990; Schneider & Shiffrin, 1977). Moreover, both constructs may be appropriate and useful in accounting for the effects induced by brain trauma.

Inhibition. Another mechanism that could contribute to reductions in the effective capacity of working memory is the generation and maintenance of irrelevant information, due to a lack of inhibition. In the current model, these activities would effectively reduce the resources for more relevant processing. Evidence for a lack of inhibition is most convincing in studies that show systematic intrusions and interference from inappropriate associations in output responses (Dempster, 1992). Various versions of the inhibition hypothesis have been put forward to explain developmental deficits in tasks that have inhibitory components (Bjorklund & Harnishfeger, 1990; Dempster, 1992), comprehension deficits in aging (Hamm & Hasher, 1992; Hasher & Zacks, 1988), individual differences in comprehension among college-age students (Gernsbacher, Varner, & Faust, 1990), and deficits associated with frontal-lobe damage (Dempster, 1992).

In one form, the inhibition hypothesis is closely related to the concept of resource allocation. In this view, the deficit arises because inappropriate information is maintained, rather than forgotten or actively suppressed. Hence, inhibition becomes highly related to the issue of total capacity, as well as efficiency, as described earlier. In another view, the inhibition hypothesis refers to the activation of inappropriate information. According to this construal, capacity is effectively decreased because the task appropriate information must compete with inappropriate information. Intuitively, this latter version seems appealing as a potential source of deficit in semantically richer and less constrained domains, such as text comprehension (Hamm & Hasher, 1992; Hasher & Zacks, 1988). Either the activation of inappropriate information or the maintenance of information that is no longer relevant to the current subgoal could contribute to an effective decrement in capacity.

Resource Allocation Policy. In a system with resource limitations, the deployment of the limited resources can have a large effect on performance, especially when the resource demands greatly outstrip the supply. One immediate consequence of an allocation policy is that it can be the mechanism that brings about the trading relation between speed and accuracy of comprehension processing, where accuracy refers to maintaining and later using partial products appropriately. The current across-the-board percentage deallocation policy produces processing that is both slower and more errorful when resource demands outstrip supply. This is also the performance exhibited by most subjects.

High demand could have a different effect on performance if allocation policy were different. By differentially deallocating activation to either maintenance or processing, the comprehension process can maintain its speed and sacrifice accuracy or sacrifice its speed and maintain its accuracy. Some subjects (low-capacity subjects on high-demand sentences) maintain or even increase speed on high-demand sentences, at the cost of failing to comprehend the sentences (King & Just, 1991). The model provides a mechanism to account for these different "strategies" or allocation policies.

There are other allocation policies that seem plausible and merit future investigation. One alternative is to have different allocations among processes. Specifically, the allocation policy might favor more automatic processes, which presumably consume fewer resources anyway. But in the event of a resource shortfall, the automatic processes might receive a larger proportion of their demand than the higher level, controlled processes. In addition, the allocation policy might be sensitive to the nature of the task or even subject to strategic control. For example, the more costly the loss of a partial product, the greater the relative allocation of storage might be. More generally, the allocation policy elicited by tasks with different characteristics is an important future research issue that is highlighted by the model (see Haarmann & Kolk, 1992, for a related discussion).

SUMMARY AND IMPLICATIONS

The solution processes in solving the Tower of Hanoi puzzle and, more generally, the solution processes in a wide range of reasoning problems require mental bookkeeping. This mental bookkeeping involves generating and maintaining information, such as goals and intermediate solutions, and performing specific reasoning processes. Such simultaneous storage and computation appear to place a burden on working memory. Moreover, it may be the systematic variation in the ability to generate, hold, and process information that accounts for the high intercorrelations in the performance levels achieved by the same individuals across different types of reasoning tasks, intercorrelations that are difficult to ascribe to differences in previous domain knowledge. One compelling piece of evidence for this interpretation is the strong correlation between performance on reasoning tasks and measures designed to specifically assess an individual's working-memory capacity. Another type of support is the ability of a computational model of working-memory limitations, in terms of the activation available for computation and storage, to account for performance limitations in the Tower of Hanoi. This model accounts for the specific patterns of performance within a task as it relates to goal generation and maintenance in the Raven Progressive Matrices Test and the Tower of Hanoi. The model also provides an explanation of the pattern of intercorrelations among superficially different reasoning tasks, whereas a knowledge-based explanation cannot easily do so.

The general conclusion we draw is that a unified theory of cognition must take into account that cognition is often resource bound, and the theory should explain how resource constraints affect the nature of thought. This chapter presents several sources of evidence to indicate that thought is inherently resource limited, even when knowledge is plentiful. An important additional step in this research program is to characterize the precise way in which the resource constraints shape the nature of thought. We have made an initial foray into this topic in the area of sentence comprehension, where we have argued that several types of sentence parsing heuristics (e.g., how to deal with syntactic or lexical ambiguity, when to incorporate pragmatic information into the syntactic parsing) are manifestations of capacity constraints (Just & Carpenter, 1992). It may be that other forms of thought are similarly shaped by considerations of resource availability.

According to this view, resource constraints should take their place along with the two other major determinants of thought, the nature of the task environment and the knowledge (declarative and procedural) available to the system. Any thinking system will be limited by its particular implementation, and a unified theory of cognition will have to account for the effects of those limitations in the case of human reasoning.

ACKNOWLEDGMENTS

We would like to thank David Fallside for his help in developing the simulation model of the Tower of Hanoi puzzle.

This research was partially supported by ONR N00014-92-J-1209 and by NIMH Research Scientist Awards MH-00661 and MH-00662 to the first two authors. Darold Hemphill was supported by a training fellowship on grant NIMH-19102.

REFERENCES

Ahern, S., & Beatty, J. (1979). Pupillary responses during information processing vary with Scholastic Aptitude Test scores. *Science, 205,* 1289–1292.

Babcock, R. L., & Salthouse, T. A. (1990). Effects of increased processing demands on age differences in working memory. *Psychology and Aging, 5,* 421–428.

Baddeley, A. D. (1986). *Working memory.* Oxford, UK: Oxford University Press.

Beatty, J. (1982). Task-evoked pupillary responses, processing load, and the structure of processing resources. *Psychological Bulletin, 91,* 276–292.

Ben-Nun, Y. (1986). The use of pupillometry in the study of on-line verbal processing: Evidence for depths of processing. *Brain and Language, 28,* 1–11.

Bjorklund, D. F., & Harnishfeger, K. K. (1990). The resources construct in cognitive development: Diverse sources of evidence and a theory of inefficient inhibition. *Developmental Review, 10,* 48–71.

Carpenter, P. A., & Just, M. A. (1989). The role of working memory in language comprehension. In D. Klahr & K. Kotovsky (Eds.), *Complex information processing: The impact of Herbert A. Simon* (pp. 31–68). Hillsdale, NJ: Lawrence Erlbaum Associates.

Carpenter, P. A., Just, M. A., & Shell, P. (1990). What one intelligence test measures: A theoretical account of the processing in the Raven Progressive Matrices Test. *Psychological Review, 97,* 404–431.

Carpenter, P. A., Miyake, A., & Just, M. A. (1994). Working memory constraints in comprehension: Evidence from individual differences, aphasia, and aging. In M. Gernsbacher (Ed.), *The handbook of psycholinguistics* (pp. 1075–1122). San Diego, CA: Academic Press.

Cattell, R. B. (1971). *Abilities: Their structure, growth, and action.* New York: Houghton Mifflin.

Chase, W. G., & Ericsson, K. A. (1982). Skill and working memory. In G. H. Bower (Ed.), *The psychology of learning and motivation* (Vol. 16, pp. 1–58). New York: Academic Press.

Chase, W. G., & Simon, H. A. (1973). Perception in chess. *Cognitive Psychology, 4,* 55–81.

Cohen, J. D., Dunbar, K., & McClelland, J. L. (1990). On the control of automatic processes: A parallel distributed processing account of the Stroop effect. *Psychological Review, 97,* 332–361.

Cottrell, G. W. (1989). *A connectionist approach to word sense disambiguation.* San Mateo, CA: Morgan Kaufmann.

Court, J. H., & Raven, J. (1982). *Manual for Raven's Progressive Matrices and Vocabulary Scales* (Research Supplement No. 2, and Part 3, Section 7). London: H. K. Lewis.

Daneman, M., & Carpenter, P. A. (1980). Individual differences in working memory and reading. *Journal of Verbal Learning and Verbal Behavior, 19,* 450–466.

de Groot, A. D. (1965). *Thought and choice in chess.* The Hague: Mouton.

Dempster, F. N. (1992). The rise and fall of the inhibitory mechanism: Toward a unified theory of cognitive development and aging. *Developmental Review, 12,* 45–75.

Egan, D. E., & Greeno, J. (1974). Theory of rule induction: Knowledge acquired in concept learning, serial pattern learning, and problem solving. In L. W. Gregg (Ed.), *Knowledge and cognition* (pp. 43–103). Hillsdale, NJ: Lawrence Erlbaum Associates.

Engel, R. W., Cantor, J., & Carullo, J. J. (1992). Individual differences in working memory and comprehension: A test of four hypotheses. *Journal of Experimental Psychology: Learning, Memory, and Cognition, 18,* 972–992.

Friederici, A. D., & Kilborn, K. (1989). Temporal constraints on language processing: Syntactic priming in Broca's aphasia. *Journal of Cognitive Neuroscience, 1,* 262–272.

Gernsbacher, M. A., Varner, K. R., & Faust, M. (1990). Investigating differences in general comprehension skill. *Journal of Experimental Psychology: Learning, Memory, and Cognition, 16,* 430–445.

Haarmann, H. (1992). *Agrammatic aphasia as a timing deficit.* Unpublished doctoral dissertation, Nijmegen Institute for Cognition and Information.

Haarmann, H. J., & Kolk, H. H. J. (1991). Syntactic priming in Broca's aphasics: Evidence for slow activation. *Aphasiology, 5,* 247–263.

Haarmann, H. J., & Kolk, H. H. J. (1994). On-line sensitivity to subject-verb agreement violations in Broca's aphasics: The role of syntactic complexity and time. *Brain and Language, 46,* 493–516.

Hamm, V. P., & Hasher, L. (1992). Age and the availability of inferences. *Psychology and Aging, 7,* 56–64.

Hasher, L., & Zacks, R. (1988). Working memory, comprehension, and aging: A review and a new view. In G. H. Bower (Ed.), *The psychology of learning and motivation* (Vol. 22, pp. 193–225). New York: Academic Press.

Hegarty, M., Just, M. A., & Morrison, I. R. (1988). Mental models of mechanical systems: Individual differences in qualitative and quantitative reasoning. *Cognitive Psychology, 20,* 191–236.

Janisse, M. P. (1977). *Pupillometry: The psychology of the pupillary response.* Washington, DC: Hemisphere.

Jones, H. E., & Conrad, H. S. (1993). The growth and decline of intelligence: A study of a homogeneous group between the ages of ten and sixty. *Genetic Psychology Monographs, 13,* 223–298.

Just, M. A., & Carpenter, P. A. (1985). Cognitive coordinate systems: Accounts of mental rotation and individual differences in spatial ability. *Psychological Review, 92,* 137–172.

Just, M. A., & Carpenter, P. A. (1992). A capacity theory of comprehension: Individual differences in working memory. *Psychological Review, 99,* 122–149.

Just, M. A., & Carpenter, P. A. (1993). The intensity of thought: Pupillometric indices of sentence processing. *Canadian Journal of Experimental Psychology, 47,* 310–339.

Kahneman, D. (1973). *Attention and effort.* Englewood Cliffs, NJ: Prentice Hall.

King, J., & Just, M. A. (1991). Individual differences in syntactic processing: The role of working memory. *Journal of Memory and Language, 30,* 580–602.

Kotovsky, K., & Fallside, D. (1989). Representation and transfer in problem solving. In D. Klahr & K. Kotovsky (Eds.), *Complex information processing: The impact of Herbert A. Simon* (pp. 69–108). Hillsdale, NJ: Lawrence Erlbaum Associates.

Kotovsky, K., Hayes, J. R., & Simon, H. A. (1985). Why are some problems hard? Evidence from Tower of Hanoi. *Cognitive Psychology, 17,* 248–294.

Kyllonen, P. C., & Christal, R. E. (1990). Reasoning ability is (little more than) working memory capacity?! *Intelligence, 14,* 389–433.

Kyllonen, P. C., & Stephens, D. L. (1990). Cognitive abilities as determinants of success in acquiring logic skill. *Learning and Individual Differences, 2,* 129–160.

Marshalek, B., Lohman, D. F., & Snow, R. E. (1983). The complexity continuum in the radex and hierarchical models of intelligence. *Intelligence, 7,* 107–127.

Miller, G. A. (1956). The magic number seven, plus or minus two: Some limits on our capacity for processing information. *Psychological Review, 63,* 81–97.

Newell, A. (1973). Production systems: Models of control structures. In W. C. Chase (Ed.), *Visual information processing* (pp. 463–526). New York: Academic Press.

Salthouse, T. A. (1988a). Effects of aging on verbal abilities: Examination of the psychometric literature. In L. L. Light & D. M. Burke (Eds.), *Language, memory, and aging* (pp. 17–35). New York: Cambridge University Press.

Salthouse, T. A. (1988b). Initiating the formalization of theories of cognitive aging. *Psychology and Aging, 3,* 3–16.

Salthouse, T. A. (1991). Mediation of adult age differences in cognition by reductions in working memory and speed of processing. *Psychological Science, 2,* 179–183.

Salthouse, T. A. (1992a). Reasoning and spatial abilities. In F. I. M. Craik & T. A. Salthouse (Eds.), *The handbook of aging and cognition* (pp. 167–211). Hillsdale, NJ: Lawrence Erlbaum Associates.

Salthouse, T. A. (1992b). Why do adult age differences increase with task complexity. *Developmental Psychology, 28,* 905–918.

Salthouse, T. A. (1992c). Working-memory mediation of adult age differences in integrative reasoning. *Memory & Cognition, 20,* 413–423.

Salthouse, T. A., Babcock, R., Mitchell, D. R. D., Skovronek, E., & Palmon, R. (1990). Age and experience effects in spatial visualization. *Developmental Psychology, 26,* 128–136.

Salthouse, T. A., & Mitchell, D. R. D. (1990). Effects of age and naturally occurring experience on spatial visualization performance. *Developmental Psychology, 26,* 845–854.

Salthouse, T. A., Mitchell, D. R. D., Skovronek, E., & Babcock, R. (1989). Effects of adult age and working memory on reasoning and spatial abilities. *Journal of Experimental Psychology: Learning, Memory, and Cognition, 15,* 507–516.

Schaie, K. W. (1988). Internal validity threats in studies of adult cognitive development. In M. Howe & C. J. Brainerd (Eds.), *Cognitive development in adulthood* (pp. 241–272). New York: Springer-Verlag.

Schluroff, M. (1982). Pupil responses to grammatical complexity of sentences. *Brain and Language, 17,* 133–145.

Schluroff, M., Zimmermann, T. E., Freeman, R. B., Jr., Hofmeister, K., Lorscheid, T., & Weber, A. (1986). Pupillary responses to syntactic ambiguity of sentences. *Brain and Language, 27,* 322–344.

Schneider, W., & Shiffrin, R. M. (1977). Controlled and automatic human information processing: I. Detection, search, and attention. *Psychological Review, 84,* 1–66.

Simon, H. A. (1975). The functional equivalence of problem solving skills. *Cognitive Psychology, 7,* 268–288.

Simon, H. A., & Kotovsky, K. (1963). Human acquisition of concepts for sequential patterns. *Psychological Review, 70,* 534–546.

Snow, R. E., Kyllonen, P. C., & Marshalek, B. (1984). The topography of ability and learning correlations. In R. J. Sternberg (Ed.), *Advances in the psychology of human intelligence* (Vol. 2, pp. 47–103). Hillsdale, NJ: Lawrence Erlbaum Associates.

St. John, M. F., & McClelland, J. L. (1990). Learning and applying contextual constraints in sentence comprehension. *Artificial Intelligence, 46,* 217–257.

Thibadeau, R., Just, M. A., & Carpenter, P. A. (1982). A model of the time course and content of reading. *Cognitive Science, 6,* 157–203.

Waltz, D. L., & Pollack, J. B. (1985). Massively parallel parsing: A strongly interactive model of natural language interpretation. *Cognitive Science, 9,* 51–74.

DISCUSSION

Functionality Matters:
Capacity Constraints and Soar

Richard M. Young
MRC Applied Psychology Unit, Cambridge, England

> *There are more things in an architecture, Horatio, than are dreamt of in your theorizing.*
>
> —Allen Newell (1990, p. 306)

FUNCTIONAL VERSUS RESOURCE CONSTRAINTS

The idea of *capacity constraints* appears not to sit comfortably with Soar. The basic design of Soar, for example, calls for an essentially unbounded working memory to serve as the changing database for the long-term recognitional memory. Attempts to impose a brute force limitation on the capacity of the working memory—to decide that it cannot hold more than 7 items, say, or 17, or 70—seem not to work, because with the current style of Soar usage there are always tasks that require more working memory elements than the arbitrary limit. This aspect makes many psychologists doubtful about Soar (see, e.g., the commentaries in Newell, 1992), but as we shall see, it does not rule out the possibility that Soar can model and account for the psychological phenomena associated with limited working memory. It does mean that we need to be wary of simplistically identifying Soar's working memory with psychological "working memory," whether in the sense of Just and Carpenter (e.g., Daneman & Carpenter, 1980) or of Baddeley (1986).

In his book *Unified Theories of Cognition* (1990), Allen Newell distinguished between *functional* constraints on the one hand, and *resource* constraints on the other. To take the easy case first, resource constraints arise from the physical or biological substrate out of which an intelligent agent is built. (Newell called them "technological" limitations because of his view that systems are constructed as hierarchical levels of technologies, each level being implemented in terms of the level below.) The general argument is that for routine behavior on a task comfortably within the agent's ability, properties of the implementation are invisible, precisely because the agent has adapted successfully (through evolution and through learning) to the performance of that task. But at the limits of performance, details of the implementation begin to show through, and resource constraints begin to play a role in the resulting behavior.

Functional constraints are a little trickier. The basic idea is that they can be explained in functional terms, that is, by reference to the task that an agent is trying to perform and what it has to do in order to perform it, without any need to appeal to properties of the implementational substrate. This is a fairly broad notion, and one finds in practice a variety of different arguments for functional constraints. One argument sees a constraint as consequential upon, or emergent from, the functional requirements on an agent: the need for it to adapt to and survive in its environment and achieve its goals. In the case of limited (psychological) working memory, this argument tries to show that, given the functional requirements on an intelligent agent, it will necessarily exhibit certain phenomena of limited memory. Another argument views a functional constraint as the result of a trade-off in design, and tries to show, for example, that an alternative design for an agent with a larger working-memory capacity would be necessarily worse off in some other respect, such that it is worse off overall. Limitations of knowledge also fall under the broad heading of functional constraints, especially when contrasted with resource—and hence implementational—constraints.

In Chapter 5 in this volume, Just, Carpenter, and Hemphill present a persuasive case that it is important to understand the constraints on cognitive performance, to understand individual differences in performance, and to understand the relationship between the two. As a discussant, I see the job of this commentary as being not to disagree with their argument, nor to criticize their impressive and admirable work, but to show that Soar's approach to explaining the phenomena would be a little different from theirs. Characteristically, Soar attempts to account for phenomena involving constraints by looking first for functional explanations, and only then appealing to the idea of limited resources. I illustrate this approach by means of three examples based on existing work with Soar. In discussing them, I use the term *resource constraint* or limitation when talking about Soar, and *capacity constraint* (or limitation) when talking about the work of Just and Carpenter, without wishing to prejudge the correspondence between them.

EXAMPLE 1: POLK'S MODEL OF SYLLOGISTIC REASONING

We begin by considering Thad Polk's model of syllogisms. Polk (this volume, Discussion following Chapter 10; Polk, 1992; Polk & Newell, 1995) models human performance on a task requiring subjects to draw conclusions from the two premises of a syllogism, and in particular models sets of systematic data collected by Johnson-Laird and colleagues. Early versions of Polk's model were implemented in Soar (e.g., Newell, Young, & Polk, 1992; Polk & Newell, 1988). More recent versions are still compatible with Soar and are clearly inspired by Soar-like considerations. Polk's work illustrates a number of points. It is convenient to present the discussion through a sequence of assertions about his model.

First, the model is strongly functional. One sense of this claim is simply that the model performs the task, that is, it reads the two premises and attempts to draw a conclusion, and is thus a functional model. (That word *functional* continues to be tricky.) Another sense, more directly relevant here, is that the model draws on general abilities that the subject is known to have, especially skills for comprehending language. Unlike most psychological models, and in particular unlike other models of syllogistic reasoning, Polk does not posit unique processing abilities specialized to the syllogism task. Thus the model is functional in the sense that it draws on abilities, like language skills, that exist in order to provide the agent with certain functional capabilities (e.g., speaking, listening, reading) that are motivated independently of this particular task.

Second, subjects' difficulties with the task are explained as a consequence of this functional basis. Polk points out that although subjects' everyday language skills (e.g., of encoding and comprehension) can serve to perform the syllogism task, they are not perfectly adapted to that task, and so by themselves are not adequate for perfect performance. For example, "language comprehension is not guaranteed to deliver a necessary and sufficient representation of what the premises are about. It just constructs a [mental] model of the situation that is consistent with the premises (i.e. the premises will be true in the model). Such a model can both support conclusions that are not strictly valid . . . and fail to support conclusions that are" (Polk, 1992, p. 38). In this and similar ways, difficulties with the task are explained on the grounds of functional constraints without appeal to the notion of resource constraints.

Third, the model deals with individual differences. The model contains a number of qualitative parameters that determine such things as detailed aspects of how the premises are encoded, for example, whether or not a premise of the form "No X are Y" will be interpreted as also implying "No Y are X." Different choices for the detailed structure generate a whole space of syllogism models, and Polk shows that different models in that space provide a good fit to different individuals. The fit to individual subjects is in fact at least as good as the subjects' test–retest fit to their own performance 1 week later. This parameterized model provides a highly successful knowledge-based, and hence functional, account of individual differences, which makes no reference to resource constraints.

Fourth, the difference between good and bad subjects is greater on the hard problems than on the easy problems, and the model exhibits this same property (T. A. Polk, personal communication). This is an interesting finding, worth detailed discussion. Note to begin with that by "good" (vs. "bad") subjects we mean simply those who get many of the syllogisms right, and that "easy" (vs. "hard") problems are those that many subjects get right.

This sort of interaction of problem complexity with individual performance is cited repeatedly by Just and Carpenter (e.g., Chapter 5, this volume; 1992) as support for their capacity-constrained model, to an extent that it comes close to being treated as a "signature" phenomenon for such a model. However, that degree of reliance on the phenomenon would be misplaced, because in fact only certain broad commitments are needed of a model for it to exhibit this property. It is, for example, a phenomenon "naturally" exhibited by knowledge-based models, such as production systems. The argument is straightforwardly that both good and bad subjects have rules adequate for the easy problems, but only the good subjects have the rules for the hard problems. Hence we expect to see a wider spread of performance on the hard problems than on the easy ones. The argument is a very general one, certainly not specific to syllogisms nor to capacity-constrained models or production systems. The generalization would appear to be that the interaction between difficulty and performance should be expected from any approach in which the model of the good subjects in some appropriate sense subsumes the model of the bad subjects. This means that we should expect the phenomenon to be robust, not only across tasks, but across theories too. And that in turn means that although it is important for a model to predict it, the effect is not a good candidate for a signature phenomenon. It does not discriminate between models. In the present case, if Just and Carpenter were to apply their theory to the syllogism task, they would presumably explain the interaction, as elsewhere, in terms of capacity limitations. But such an explanation is not required. A functional account does just fine.

Fifth, and finally, Polk's functional model offers a better account of the individual data than does a capacity-constrained model. Although Just and Carpenter wrote about "individual differences," they did so by dividing subjects into "high-" and "low-span" groups (e.g., 1992) and continuing to work with aggregate, not individual, data. A model such as Polk's, however, provides a close fit to the behavior of individuals. It does so by modeling individual subjects at a finer grain size. Furthermore, the functional model provides a better account than can be given even in principle by a capacity-constrained model. Just and Carpenter's approach associates individuals with a certain amount of "activation," which is a unidimensional quantity. Consequently, the possible individual models can vary along just a single dimension. Polk's model, by contrast, locates individuals within a multi-dimensional space of possible models, which the data on best-fitting models indicate is needed.

In summary, then, Polk's analysis of syllogistic reasoning illustrates how a functional model can explain subjects' difficulties with a task, and exhibit the characteristic interaction between task difficulty and individual performance, without needing to appeal to resource constraints. It provides an account of individual differences in performance, which we have argued is both actually and in principle better than the account offered by a capacity-constrained model. That is quite a yield from a single example. Our treatment of the other examples is much briefer.

EXAMPLE 2: LEWIS' ANALYSIS OF LINGUISTIC MODULARITY

In his discussion of Pylyshyn's chapter (Chapter 2), Richard Lewis presents a linguistic example that illustrates how the animacy or non-animacy of the subject of a sentence can affect the disambiguation of a locally ambiguous verb. Does a sentence beginning "The defendant examined . . ." continue like (a) ". . . the courtroom" or (b) ". . . by the lawyer shocked the jury"? But if the subject is *evidence* instead of *defendant*, then only one of those continuations is possible.

There is a continuing controversy in the psycholinguistic literature over the question of "modularity," concerning, for example, whether pragmatic considerations such as animacy can affect the course of syntactic parsing. Lewis' example is taken from the work of Just and Carpenter (1992), who in turn drew from earlier experiments by others. The data on processing times from subjects reading such sentences provide Just and Carpenter with a key example of how "syntactic encapsulation [is] an issue of capacity rather than of architecture" (1992, p. 126), and of how a capacity-constrained model can account for both apparently "modular" and apparently "interactive" (i.e., nonmodular) results. According to their argument, high-activation subjects are able to take account of both syntactic and pragmatic information at the same time, and can therefore make use of pragmatic cues to guide them directly to a correct syntactic interpretation. This yields "interactive" performance. Low-activation subjects do not have such an ability, and are therefore unable to take advantage of the pragmatic cue. They generate behavior that looks "modular."

Lewis pointed out that NL-Soar—a program being developed to provide Soar with an ability to understand language (e.g., in his thesis: Lewis, 1993)—can also exhibit behavior ranging from modular to interactive, depending on the familiarity of the text and the setting, that is, on the extent to which Soar has from prior experience already acquired relevant chunks of knowledge. The more novel the content and context of the sentence, the more problem-solving Soar will need to do, and the more it will generate modular behavior in which it is apparently unable to exploit the (in)animacy of the subject to guide initial interpretation of the verb. It may need to explore both interpretations. But in a more familiar situation, where more of the knowledge needed for comprehension has been chunked into an immediately usable form, the performance will be more interactive. For example, the inanimacy of *evidence* can be taken into account for guiding the initial interpretation of the verb form *examined*.

Thus NL-Soar offers an account of the same phenomenon addressed by Just and Carpenter, but without needing to invoke the notion of resource constraints. As was the case with Polk's model of syllogistic reasoning, NL-Soar is a functional model. Given the Soar architecture, NL-Soar is strongly shaped by the need to meet the functional demands on a theory of natural language comprehension, in particular that it cope with a variety of different sentence forms and that it comprehend language in real time. To the extent that the phenomenon can be seen to emerge as a necessary consequence of a language comprehension system that meets those functional requirements, Soar's approach questions whether a separate explanation in terms of capacity limitations is really needed.

EXAMPLE 3: KNOWLEDGE-BASED LOOK-AHEAD

Our third example also draws on the work of Rick Lewis (unpublished, but see Newell, 1992, p. 474). A little while ago he made a start on exploring how Soar models would behave with *ubiquitous chunking*, that is, if all the information in Soar's working memory were encoded into unitary symbols representing familiar concepts. Consider, for example, the representation of a particular car, say a 1990 Subaru Loyale station wagon. Current Soar practice would encode this as a set of properties, something like:

[DATE=1990, MAKE=SUBARU, MODEL=LOYALE, TYPE=STATION-WAGON].

But with ubiquitous chunking, it would be encoded (for me) as a symbol like G274, meaning "a-car-like-mine." Such symbols are "chunks" in the sense of Miller (1956) (which is perhaps an indication that the Soar community is finally beginning to take seriously the famous "7 ± 2" paper!). They form a "mental vocabulary" for representation.

Lewis' story is far from complete, but it seems likely that a Soar model with ubiquitous chunking would exhibit limitations in its ability to represent imagined situations or objects. In essence, the argument is simple. If all your learned abilities to manipulate and reason with an internal representation depend upon its being encoded as a collection of familiar chunks, then you can deal only with internal situations that can be so encoded. Unfamiliar objects and situations require preliminary experience, so that you can first learn chunks to recognize and encode them.

Such an account may well apply straightforwardly to Just and Carpenter's (1985) mental rotation and other similar task. The story would be that subjects bring to the situation a mental vocabulary of more-or-less familiar views of more-or-less familiar kinds of objects, and knowledge of the effects within this representational vocabulary of more-or-less familiar transformations. Subjects should be able to perform tasks whose representational demands lie within the scope of that mental vocabulary, but will encounter increasing difficulty as the task requires representing situations that go beyond it. Individual subjects will differ in their prior experience, and thus in the content and range of their representational capabilities, and hence in their profile of performance on the tasks. As with the previous examples, such an approach provides a functional account of subjects' performance on tasks of mental transformation, and offers the potential for explaining both successful behavior and difficulties without appealing to the idea of capacity or capacity constraints, and for describing individual differences in performance without the need to posit differential resources.

CONCLUSION

One way of summarizing where we now stand is to ask how well Soar might fare on the variety and kinds of tasks analyzed by Just and Carpenter. To start at the more successful end, we have seen that the topic of individual differences is handled well by Soar, as exemplified in a running model of syllogistic reasoning that provides a fit to individual subjects as good as their own test–retest consistency. The domain of sentence processing is addressed by the NL-Soar project, which is shaping up as an integrated account of a wide range of psycholinguistic phenomena. In particular, it offers an explanation of the range of modular to interactive processing behaviors, although not yet an actual simulation of the relevant experiments. For tasks such as mental rotation or Raven Matrices, there are no Soar programs extant, but a set of ideas centering on the interaction between problem solving and ubiquitous chunking holds promise for explaining some of the main empirical phenomena. And then at the bottom of the scale, as we move toward effects that almost certainly have a largely physiological basis, such as those associated with aging, we encounter behaviors that we would not expect Soar to account for. As a Soar model gets "older," the main thing that happens to it is that it learns more, and care has been taken to ensure that further learning helps Soar rather than hinders it. So it is unlikely that Soar by itself will offer explanations of aging effects.[1] Soar is currently weakest in dealing with the correlational data across tasks, such as the correlation of subjects' performance on diverse tasks with their score on the reading-span test that lies at the heart of Just and Carpenter's story. To predict it, Soar would presumably need to posit some elements of processing in common between the different tasks, which is the traditional route to accounting for the correlations across different tasks.

Despite the emphasis in this commentary upon functional constraints, there is nothing in Soar that argues against the existence of resource constraints, and almost certainly it will eventually be necessary to find a way to incorporate them to provide a more complete account of cognition. In the meantime, Soar focuses our attention on a different way of approaching the kind of phenomena discussed by Just and Carpenter. Soar encourages us to understand which of the performance limitations, uncovered by careful and ingenious experiments like those in the preceding chapter, can be explained on functional grounds, that is, those that arise from the architecture's attempt to satisfy the functional requirements on the agent. The phenomena that can be so accounted for, we have argued, do not need any further explanations, such as those offered by appealing to capacity constraints. Soar therefore does not argue directly against the kind of mechanism espoused by Just and Carpenter, but it does suggest that the mechanism is being overextended, that it is being applied where it is not needed because there exist perfectly adequate functional explanations.

Allen Newell famously, and repeatedly, urged us to "listen to the architecture." As the quotation at the beginning of this commentary suggests, what it says can sometimes surprise us.

ACKNOWLEDGMENTS

I thank Rick Lewis, Andrew Howes, and Milind Tambe for much helpful discussion about the subject matter of this commentary and for reactions to an earlier version. This commentary was written while the author was visiting the Department of Psychology, Carnegie Mellon University.

---

[1]There is in fact a concern in the literature on machine learning that learning can worsen an agent's performance (Tambe, 1991). Ironically, one such mechanism is called the average growth effect, known by its acronym as AGE!

REFERENCES

Baddeley, A. D. (1986). *Working memory*. Oxford, UK: Oxford University Press.

Daneman, M., & Carpenter, P. A. (1980). Individual differences in working memory and reading. *Journal of Verbal Learning and Verbal Behavior, 19*, 450–466.

Just, M. A., & Carpenter, P. A. (1985). Cognitive coordinate systems: Accounts of mental rotation and individual differences in spatial ability. *Psychological Review, 92*, 137–172.

Just, M. A., & Carpenter, P. A. (1992). A capacity theory of comprehension: Individual differences in working memory. *Psychological Review, 99*, 122–149.

Lewis, R. L. (1993). *An architecturally-based theory of human sentence comprehension* (Tech. Rep. No. CMU-CS-93-226). Unpublished doctoral dissertation, School of Computer Science, Carnegie Mellon University, Pittsburgh.

Miller, G. A. (1956). The magic number seven, plus or minus two: Some limits on our capacity for processing information. *Psychological Review, 63*, 81–97.

Newell, A. (1990). *Unified theories of cognition*. Cambridge, MA: Harvard University Press.

Newell, A. (1992). Precis of *Unified Theories of Cognition*. *Behavioral and Brain Sciences, 15*, 425–492.

Newell, A., Young, R., & Polk, T. A. (1992). The approach through symbols. In D. E. Broadbent (Ed.), *The simulation of human intelligence* (pp. 33–70). Oxford: Blackwell.

Polk, T. A. (1992). *Verbal reasoning*. Unpublished doctoral dissertation, Carnegie Mellon University, School of Computer Science, Pittsburgh.

Polk, T. A., & Newell, A. (1988, August). Modeling human syllogistic reasoning in Soar. In *Proceedings of the Annual Conference of the Cognitive Science Society* (pp. 181–187). Montreal.

Polk, T. A., & Newell, A. (1995). Deduction as verbal reasoning. *Psychological Review, 102*, 533–566.

Tambe, M. (1991). *Eliminating combinatorics from production match*. Unpublished doctoral dissertation, School of Computer Science, Carnegie Mellon University, Pittsburgh.

Chapter 6

Great and *Big* Ideas
in Computer Structures

Gordon Bell
Microsoft Corp.

DEDICATION

I went to Carnegie Tech after spending my first 6 professional years designing computers at Digital Equipment Corporation to be part of the startup faculty of the computer science department. Allen Newell, Alan Perlis, and Rod Williams, who headed the Electrical Engineering Department, made this career changing choice easy for me.

Like everyone who knew Allen, I feel deeply honored to have known him and was influenced by him in many ways. Allen was the most thoughtful, kind, and gentle gentleman I know. His intellect, coupled with his enthusiasm and smile, virtually always led a group in the right direction. He was the role model for a scientist, teacher, husband, father, and person. I cite Allen as "my ideal" when engineers ask me for career advice because Allen maintained a constant enthusiasm for work, and doing science. He saw no higher state of being. We worked together to research and write *Computer Structures: Readings and Examples* (Bell & Newell, 1971), which was a classic for almost 20 years, or about two hardware generations. We developed the processor-memory-switch (PMS) and instruction-set processor (ISP) notations for describing computers. Although thousands of computers have been introduced since 1971, only a few basically new ideas for computers have emerged since *Computer Structures*. Our taxonomic framework has proved to be equally descriptive of computing alternatives, including the massively parallel computers of the 1990s. Designing taxonomies to generate alternatives still remains my favorite approach for design. This fascination with taxonomies is based on their ability to take a number of artifacts, and relate them in a common framework that shows attributes and relationships. This is a form of generality—one mechanism serves many functions.

Design systems using the PMS and ISP notations were built in the early 1970s by Haney, Knudsen, Siewiorek, and Barbacci, and these influenced languages for simulating digital systems. *Computer Structures: Principles and Examples* (Siewiorek, Bell, & Newell, 1982) further refined and utilized the notations. Our interest in design helped motivate the framework for register transfer level design. We also used the design framework for *Designing Computers and Digital Systems Using PDP16 Register Transfer Modules* (Bell, Grason, & Newell, 1972). For a variety of reasons, the book is hardly known, but everyone who read it was enthusiastic about a book on design. This register transfer level approach allowed Barbacci to build the first computer design system. Commercial systems are just beginning to synthesize digital systems.

I wanted to write this chapter to interact with Allen about what's changed in *Computer Structures* (Bell & Newell, 1971; Siewiorek et al., 1982). *Computer Structures III* hasn't progressed very far because its focus is unclear, given the basic need for a comprehensive architecture book has been satisfied (Hennessy & Patterson, 1990). Being at Carnegie and working with Allen was the most happy and productive time for me. I certainly learned the most. I can only hope the patient time away from Allen's main line of research to work on low-level machines with me was as worthwhile for him as it was for me. I hope these comments will be worthwhile to you.

APPROACH

This chapter combines an approach to explaining the evolution of computer structures that I hope Allen would have enjoyed, but lacks the benefit of his interaction. The chapter has six parts, describing the two revolutionary ideas, the principle of locality, and three sets of design principles. The idea is to show that computer structures have evolved based on just these ideas. The two really big, revolutionary ideas of this century, and possibly of all time, are the stored program computer and the integrated circuit, the crude oil used to implement computers. The principle of locality is a behavioral phenomenon of programs on which many computer mechanism are based. Three general design principles explain many computer structures variants: replicatability provides increased performance,

TABLE 6.1
Two Great Ideas, Locality, and Three Design Principles

1. The stored program computer is one of the great inventions. The variants:
    a. Computers provide an unlimited number of functions and applications—they provide control, memory, switching and processing of information.
    b. Every level of a computer hierarchy is built on a lower level—thus, hardware may be traded for software and vice versa (first two to three levels).
    c. One computer can provide an environment for many computers for multiprogramming and timesharing.
    d. A set of distributed computers can behave as one computer, given enough software.
2. The integrated circuit invention and evolution is equally as important as the computer.
    a. One more bit is needed every 18 months to address physical memory.
    b. A hierarchy of memories exist and can exploit locality and fill economic needs.
3. Principle of locality: Temporal and spatial locality are a property of computation.
    a. Members of the memory hierarchy (e.g., the cache) can exist.
    b. Multiple processors can exist as scalable computers
    c. Distributed workstations (i.e., scalable mCs) can behave as a single system.
4. Replication design principles: Replication provides parallelism for performance, spatially distributed computing, and redundancy for higher reliability.
    a. Replicatability within a computer generates multiprocessors and the opportunity and need for parallel processing
    b. Replicatability of computers generates multicomputers and provides an opportunity and need for them to be used as a single resource
5. Economics design principles: A somewhat rational market based on economic utility, determines the form and function of computation, not elegance, religion, architecture, etc.
    a. The investment in software and computer families motivated the 360 family, the VAX hierarchical computing environment, Intel X86, and scalable computers.
    b. A computer system must be balanced across processing, the memory hierarchy, terminal access including visualization, and networking.
    c. *Amdahl's law* of diminishing returns for fast and slow, serial and parallel use.
    d. Computer size, generation, and problem scalability.
6. Generality design principle
    a. Generality allows resources to be bound late and flexibly (e.g., computation, memory, and bandwidth, as well as hardware and software trade-offs occur).

reliability, and allows physical distribution; economics constrain and provide the objective function for the world, including computer structures; and good designs are based on finding general-purpose mechanisms. These six ideas and the variants of them are given in Table 6.1.

Table 6.2 gives what I believe to be the two great ideas, some big and good ideas together with the machines that embodied the principles. I refrain from enumerating the bad ideas, but these would be instructive. Before looking at the ideas, it's important to note the difference between revolution and evolution.

TABLE 6.2
The Great, Big and Good Ideas, and Computers That Embody Them

1945	von Neumann's Edvac (Draft) Report and IAS machines or "x"-iacs (the first computers were Manchester Mark I and Cambridge EDSAC)
1950	Commercial computer (Univac) that stimulated others (e.g., IBM).
1960s	Second generation—the "one level store" and subsequent virtual memory (Atlas)
	Minicomputers for control, switching, etc. (PDP-5 > PDP-8)
	Architecture and computer families (360)
	Multiprogramming and timesharing (B5000, IBM/360, PDP-6/10)
	Multiprocessors (1–4) for reliability and performance (Burroughs, DEC, IBM, Univac)
	Cache memory using solid-state memories (IBM/360 Model 85)
1970s	Third generation, hundreds of minicomputers using integrated circuits
	Packet switching (ARPAnet)
	First microprocessor [4004 > 8008 > 8080 $\cdots$ 80x86 (the PC)]
	Vector processor supercomputer (Cray 1)
	Fault-tolerant smC (Tandem)
	LAN-based distributed computing (at Xerox Parc)
1980s	Fourth generation—powerful CMOS microprocessors and distributed, LAN-based computing
	Hierarchy of computing facilities (VAX Homogeneous Environment)
	32-bit CMOS microprocessors for WSs using LAN distributed process (Apollo and Sun)
	Intel CMOS micros for PCs (X86s) > LAN-based computing
	Multis (small scalable mPs with 1–20 processors) (Arete, Encore, Sequent, etc.)
	RISC (HP, IBM, MIPS, and Sun)
	Scalable multiple computers (e.g., hypercubes, Transputers, and switches for smCs)
	Parallel thread execution by a multiprocessor (Alliant, Ardent, Convex, Cray)
1990s	Fifth generation . . . and the disappearance of the computer
	Size- and generation-scalable mPs (KSR)

REVOLUTIONS IN TECHNOLOGY:
THE COMPUTER AND THE INTEGRATED CIRCUIT

Figure 6.1 shows two models of progress (Gomory & Schmitt, 1988). One model is a "ladder" of scientific revolution based on important milestones in computer technology, whereas the other is a "wheel" of evolution based on continuous refinement of a basic design and process. The "rungs" of scientific revolution include the introduction of the stored-program computer (circa 1946), and the dates given are for the introduction of a particular technology into computers, not for the initial availability. For example, vacuum tubes were used in radios long before 1944. The most interesting aspect of the ladder is that it shows no computer-technology revolutions since the introduction of integrated circuits in 1967. Although optical technology (now used in communications) may eventually find its way into computers, products based on this technology are unlikely to appear during the 1990s, because there's a substantial delay between labo-

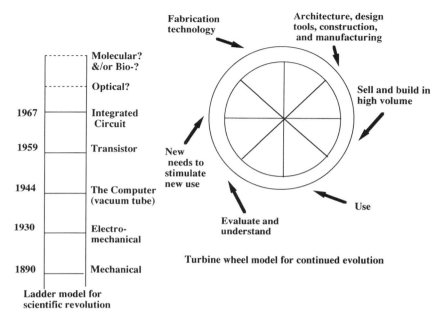

FIG. 6.1. Revolutionary (ladder) and evolutionary (wheel) models of technology progress.

ratory development and product introduction. I quantify the typical laboratory-to-product delay time like this: It takes roughly a decade (or one technology generation) from the time a significant laboratory invention occurs until it has significant use in products. Carver Mead believes major revolutions in semiconductors have occurred every 12 years: for example, the transistor (1947), integrated circuit (1959), microprocessor (1971), and silicon compiler (1984). In addition to the delay from first use to commercial exploitation, another decade may be required for wide scale assimilation. Although companies always use *revolution*[1] to describe new products or developments, evolution is a more realistic word, because progress is generally based on well-established technology and a set of design principles. In particular, circuit and memory technologies (i.e., the technologies involving the physical components that actually process and store information) are the key determinants of a computer's performance and cost, and during the past 20 years, progress in these technologies has been considerably more evolutionary than revolutionary. Unfortunately for the United States, which excels in the few revolutionary inventions, Japan excels in industrial evolution.

---

[1]A revolution should be a significant "leap" that produces an even more significant benefit.

The cycle of evolution in computer technology is driven by the interaction of many processes. New basic materials and circuits, along with advances in fabrication technology, make possible new architectures and new ways of producing the next computer. The process of selling, building in higher volumes, using, evaluating, and understanding computers raises aspirations for the next cycle of evolution. Some of these factors involve computer manufacturers, some involve users, and a few involve computer science. With the advent of increased capabilities comes the discovery of new uses and needs, which unleashes more funds to fuel the next cycle. As we enter an era of declining computer prices and profits, this cycle could undergo change because industry lacks the slack resources to search for new ideas!

THE STORED-PROGRAM COMPUTER FROM A TO Z

Virtually everyone who proposed or built an early calculator aided in the invention of the stored-program computer. Although this is not another history of the invention, it is almost safe to say that Aiken, Atanasoff, Burks, Eckert, Mauchley, von Neumann, Stibitz, Turing, and Zuse were major contributors, along with Kilburn, Williams, and Wilkes, who made the first operational computers in the United Kingdom. Turing's paper on computability planted the idea that computation was a "machine-like" process. A physical machine that could be built to compute followed. Several calculators were built in World War II to aid defense. von Neumann's name is synonymous with the stored-program concept because he drafted the first paper describing the EDVAC architecture for a working group that included Eckert and Mauchley. von Neumann also authored the paper with Burks and Goldstine (Bell & Newell, 1971) that described an architecture for a computer that was replicated at research organizations throughout the world. The economics design principle requiring compatible computers so that all sites could share and build on each other was invented just after the computer. In fact, British manufacturers made copies of the machines designed at Cambridge and Manchester Universities and the National Physical Laboratory for the software benefits.

Computers Are Universal Across a Broad Range of Functions, Applications, and Sizes

Because computers are universal finite-state machines, they can be used to simulate just about any other information-processing system functions (processing, memory, switching, control, transduction) that we understand well enough to program. They substitute for and supplement other information processors, including people. They can be used to simulate virtually anything that can be described as a procedure or collection of processes or rules (thanks to Allen). Of course, the many varieties in size and function are a result of integrated circuit evolution permitting new applications, not the computer (Fig. 6.2).

Computers Are Universal, Allowing Hierarchies of Computers to Be Built

The most important aspect of a computer is that other computers can be built on another computer in a hierarchical fashion to create more complex, higher level computers starting from basic hardware interpreter. A system of arbitrary complexity can be built in a fully layered fashion with each layer building on a lower level layer. The usual levels are micromachine—especially if microprogramming is used; hardware or instruction-set processor (ISP), but ISA (architecture) is used now; operating system; system programming language; higher level language; and an application programming language such as those used in word processors, databases, or spreadsheets.

Using this principle, a designer can make a decision about the appropriate level (e.g., hardware vs. software) to implement a given function. Paraphrasing, Perlis' "One man's constant is another man's variable"— "one person's system is another person's component." From a computer structures perspective, the hardware–software trade-off ability is the most important result of having all the levels. Frequently executed operations are placed in hardware in order to get a factor of 2–50 (depending on the operation), and we leave in software those operations that might change or that we don't understand (either because it's a new use, or an architect is uninformed). Some changes have been to place floating-point arithmetic in hardware, including vector operations, and when fast reduced instruction set computer (RISC) processors became available in the mid 1980s to move hardware functions, including memory management and infrequently executed operations, to software. One consequence is that the instruction-set architecture is covered up by the programming language . . . and usually, unless compatibility is a constraint, "speed beats elegance," although I would like to believe elegant designs are simpler, and go faster.

Computers Are Universal and One Computer Can Simulate Many Computers

A most important property of computers is first to allow computers to be multiprogrammed and hold, that is, host, a variety of independent machines so that one physical computer can do a variety of independent or related tasks. In the 1950s, the interrupt was invented to allow a machine to compute and process input/output (I/O) concurrently. In the mid 1960s multiprogramming was invented to allow multiple batch job streams with concurrent

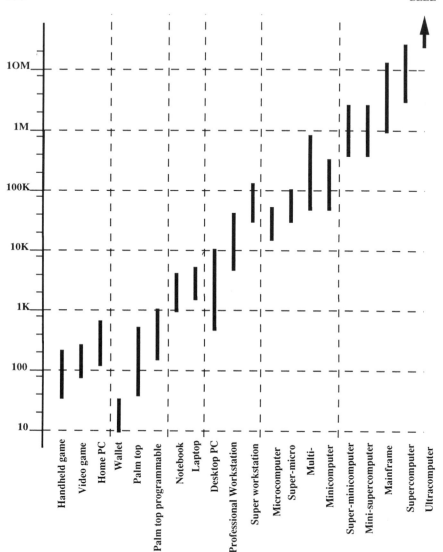

FIG. 6.2. Computer classes/prices in 1992.

I/O. Timesharing was invented to give a virtual computer to everyone who used it.

Concurrent with providing an environment that could hold and share multiple, independent programs, the principle of locality permitted programs to be located across parts of the memory hierarchy as described below. In 1960, Atlas' One-Level provided a large virtual memory using a relatively small physical memory as the first example of caching based on working sets (Denning, 1980). The paging mechanism was elegant because it also allowed programs and data to be shared among independent processes. Similarly, large addresses allows addresses to be used as name spaces.

The programming model of a single memory for multiple, large programs, including the operating system (O/S), provides the ultimate generality/flexibility because it provides a single pool of sometimes fungible resources. This motivation is critical to allowing many processes to share data and programs with one another. By the late 1980s multiple processors could operate concurrently on parallel threads of a single program, providing the first indications that fine-grain parallel processing of a single program was possible.

In 1992, massively parallel, scalable multiprocessors and multicomputers appeared with identical functionality, differing only in the underlying operations that are carried out in hardware (the multiprocessor) versus software (the multicomputer). In both cases, the end goal is a scalable multiprocessor that supports a single, multiprogrammed virtual memory environment.

Computers Are Universal and Many Distributed Computers Can Behave as One

It has always been relatively easy to interconnect computers physically, but the challenge has been to make them operate as one. This ability to aggregate computers to accomplish a common set of tasks that provide the appearance of a single, shared virtual memory computer emerged from three directions:

1. Tandem pioneered fault-tolerant computers composed of multiple computers interconnected via high-speed links where the same program is executed in two machines, and messages are sent to update the state of a program and synchronize operations. As a by-product, such a computer can be scaled over a wide range of size and be spatially distributed.

2. Distributed computing came from Xerox PARC's 1970s work and Datapoint's ARCnet. Products emerged in the early 1980s from Apollo and Sun Microsystems (Bell & McNamara, 1991) in the form of workstations. Initially computers were distributed so that each person had their own, but the trick was getting them back together in order to appear like a single timesharing system with shared files and printers, and so forth. Distributed personal computers (PCs) trailed workstations by approximately 6 years, or a half generation.

3. Scalable multicomputers using hundreds of fast, CMOS microprocessors to provide a high performance computer system were pioneered at Cal Tech and Intel, and in Europe using the Transputer. In 1992, dozens

of companies lash together microprocessors in order to achieve a wide range of scalable power from 100 Mflops to over 100 Gflops. Several thousand multicomputers were built in the 1980s for problem-specific applications. Workstations become multicomputers as the performance of individual nodes increased and could be interconnected at high data rates in the mid-1990s. Furthermore, software systems of various kinds, including compilers that automatically parallelize a program, are essential.

SEMICONDUCTOR EVOLUTION: COMPUTERS (AND MEMORIES) IN ALL SHAPES AND SIZES

While many developments have permitted the computer to evolve rapidly, the most important evolution was density increases in semiconductors and magnetics. Although improvements in these technologies have been evolutionary (i.e., conforming to the "wheel" model in Fig. 6.1), their impact on computer architecture and applications has paved the way for revolutionary changes (i.e., conforming to the "ladder" model) in those areas. At the present rates of progress in semiconductors and magnetics, the cost of hardware for computers of the type and size commonly used in 1990 will be near zero by the end of the century. Semiconductor people often make the analogy that "If cars evolved at the rate of semiconductors, today we would all be driving Rolls Royces that go a million miles an hour and cost $0.25." The difference lies entirely in the technology: Maxwell's equations governing electromagnetic radiation, which moves at the speed of light, versus Newton's laws governing the motion of objects with mass, which move at the speed of sound.

The integrated circuit was invented in 1958, the year when discrete transistors first started being used in computers. Every year from 1958 until about 1972, the number of transistors per die doubled. Starting in 1972, the number began doubling only every year and a half, or increasing at roughly 60% per year, resulting in a factor of 100 improvement each decade. Intel's founder and chairman, Gordon Moore, posited two laws based on this phenomenon:

Moore's law (1964): The density of chips doubles every year.

Moore's law (1975): The density of chips doubles every 1.5 years.

The use of memory circuits that require only one transistor per bit stored (plus some capacitance) have made bits per chip rather than transistors per chip a more interesting measure, but density has continued to quadruple every three years. This 3-year pattern is illustrated by these statistics on the number of bits per chip and the year in which each chip was introduced: 1K (1972), 4K (1975), 16K (1978), 64K (1981), 256K (1984), 1M (1987), 4M (1990), 16M (1993). This equation describes the evolution:

$$\text{Number of bits/chip} = 1K \times 2^{(t - 1972)}/1.5$$

This trend seems likely to continue until the year 2000, when extrapolation suggests that a single memory chip will store 256 million bits. In 1995 Semetech extended the forecast to 2010. The 256-million-bit figure may be slightly optimistic, however, because Meindl (1987) predicted that growth will slow down from 60% to between 20 and 35% beginning in 1992–1998. However, Meindl saw 20–35% growth persisting for another 20 years, in which case, a single die will store between 1 trillion and 100 trillion bits. The increase in density has allowed computers to operate faster while costing less, because of the following two rules:

1. The smaller everything gets, approaching the size of an electron, the faster the system behaves.
2. Miniaturized circuits produced in a batch process tend to cost very little to produce after the factory is in place.

The cost impact of the increased densities shown in Fig. 6.3 is reflected in changes in the relative cost of computing in various computer classes. For scientific computing the cost has declined over four orders of magnitude

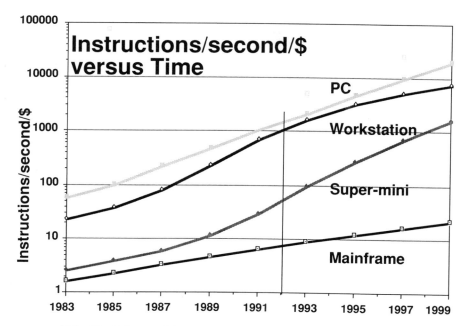

FIG. 6.3. Estimate of instructions processed per dollar versus time for various computer classes (courtesy of the Gartner Group).

during the 1950–1990 period, representing a price drop of 20% per year. In 1992, a supercomputer supplied 500–1,000 floating-point operations per second (flops) per dollar spent on the computer, whereas a workstation or scalable multicomputer provided about 5,000 flops/$. The cost per operation is likely to decline substantially more quickly over the next decade as semiconductor densities increase and commodity chips create strong competition.

Not all of the cost benefits of increased memory chip density have translated into a reduction in system cost. Some of the cost benefits have translated into larger memories, because the advances permit a given computer to have more memory for a constant price. In the 45-year period beginning in 1945, primary memories for a large computer have grown by about six orders of magnitude (2 Kbytes to 2 Gbytes), representing an increase in size at the rate of 35% per year. Figure 6.4 shows how various constant size–constant cost memories grow with time. Notice that in 2000, the memory for a current workstation (WS) or PC only occupies a fraction of a chip, and the memory portion would sell for about $10.

Processor evolution has been in response of exploiting exponential improvements in circuit/packaging technology: mainframes, minicomputers, supercomputers, and microprocessors that enabled PCs, WSs, and

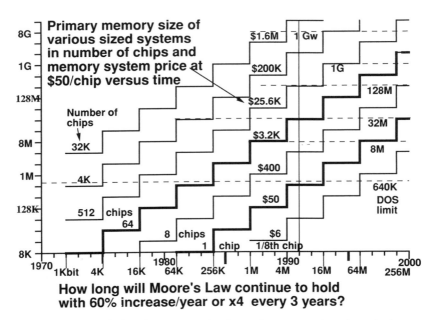

FIG. 6.4. Evolution in memory size for various constant cost–constant numbers of memory chips with time.

scalable multiprocessors. RISC microprocessors versus microprogrammed computers evolved in response to shifts in memory types, sizes, and costs.

In summary, the semiconductor density evolution has been extremely dramatic. It has spawned entire new classes of computers, new computer systems, new companies, new application opportunities, and new industries. All of the historical computer classes based on price continue to exist once established because of the need to maintain software and data in these "code museums." However, as high-performance personal computers emerge that have the power of yesteryear's mainframe or minicomputer, the number of more expensive computers will decline in a "downsizing." Most likely, this phenomena is a major cause of a continuing, worldwide recession.

TECHNOLOGY PROVIDES A HIERARCHY OF MEMORIES WITH VARYING COST AND ACCESS TIMES

Semiconductor memories are only one part of computer memory systems, which can be thought of as a hierarchy. Without the principle of locality, a hierarchy would be unnecessary. Information pertaining to a present computation is stored in fast registers, including vector registers and temporary vector registers as in Cray's architectures, that are part of the central processing unit, whereas recently referenced information is held in cache memories. Information referenced less often is stored in primary (semiconductor array) memories or in caches within the memory chips. Infrequently referenced information is stored using electromechanical technologies that record information on magnetic disks, magnetic tape, and electro-optical media. Similarly, magnetic devices use a series of cache memories for access time reduction. Although each lower level in this technological hierarchy is characterized by slower access times, the cost per bit stored is correspondingly lower.

Just as increasing transistor density has improved the storage capacity of semiconductor memory chips, increasing areal density[2] has directly affected the total information-storage capacity of disk systems. IBM's 1957 disk file, the 350 RAMAC, recorded about 100 bits along the circumference of each track, and each track was separated by 0.1 inch, giving an areal density of 1,000 bits per square inch. In early 1990, IBM announced that one of its laboratories had stored 1 billion bits in 1 square inch. This technology progression of six orders of magnitude in 33 years amounts to a density increase at a rate of over 50% per year.

Increases in areal density have led to magnetic storage systems that are not only cheaper to purchase but also cheaper to own, primarily because the

---

[2]The amount of information that can be stored per unit area.

density increases have markedly reduced floor-space requirements (which are a substantial item of expense in many environments). The 5¼- and 3½-inch drives can be mounted within a workstation, and without such high-density disks, the modern workstation environment would be impossible. In 1992, electro-optical disk technologies provide a gigabyte of disk memory at the cost of a compact audio disk, making it economically feasible for PC or workstation users to have roughly 400,000 pages of pure text or 10,000 pages of pure image data instantly available. Similarly, advances in video compression using hundreds of millions of operations per second permit VHS-quality video to be stored on a CD. In short, along with semiconductors, disks have been a necessary enabling technology for every computer class, including mainframes, minicomputers, workstations, PCs, laptops, and pocket computers.

EVOLUTION OF COMPUTERS BASED ON LOCALITY AND THREE DESIGN PRINCIPLES

The remaining ideas come from the principle of locality and three general principles of all design that apply to all systems.

The Principle of Locality

Temporal and spatial locality have been observed for much (most) computation. This means that when a datum is accessed it will be accessed again, and data that is close is likely to be accessed. Fortunately, a hierarchy of memory elements exists (described earlier) that has allowed computer architects to exploit locality through caching data in large blocks throughout the hierarchy for temporal and spatial locality.

In 1992, the key to making large, scalable, parallel computers is a belief in spatial and temporal locality, because very large systems have inherently longer processor-to-memory latencies than small, central systems. All supercomputers have a hierarchy of registers that are designed to exploit locality. Locality is the phenomenon that allowed the first one-level store computer, Atlas, to work. This led to the understanding of paging, virtual memory, and working sets that are predicated on locality. Caches exploit spatial and temporal locality automatically. Large register arrays, including vector registers, are mechanisms to exploit locality.

Replication of a Design: Performance, Reliability, and Distribution

Replication is an important design principle that allows large, man-made structures to be built efficiently from common components rather than having ad hoc designs. Replication of components provides three functions:

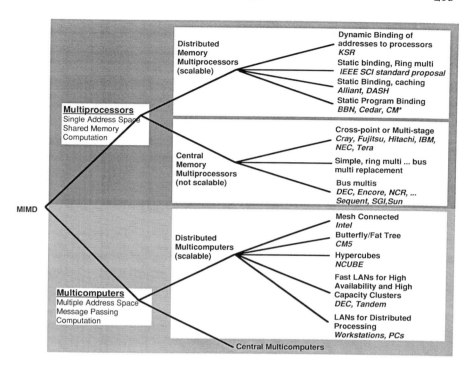

FIG. 6.5. Taxonomy of multiprocessor and multicomputer computer structures.

increased performance through parallelism, reliability through redundancy, and spatial distribution. Figure 6.5 shows a taxonomy of the alternative structures that come through replicating computers, processors, processing elements, and memories to increase parallelism spatially and temporally (pipelining). We can also look at these alternatives as transformations on the von Neumann machine (Fig. 6.6) in the search to increase performance.

Although designers have been building a large range of computers using different models, the intriguing goal has always been to have a single set of components that can be used to implement a wide range. In *Computer Structures* (Bell & Newell, 1971), Allen and I posited an alternative set of machines for the IBM System/360 that was predicated on just a few multiprocessor models. Replicatability is a form of generality, because more general components are required when a single type is needed to carry out a range of functions. Replicatability is a way of extending a design to cover a wide range of utility without specialized designs. The ultimate form of replicatability and generality is the scalable multicomputer for performance that began to emerge in the late 1980s. Scalable multicomputers for reliability and physical distribution existed for some time to a small degree

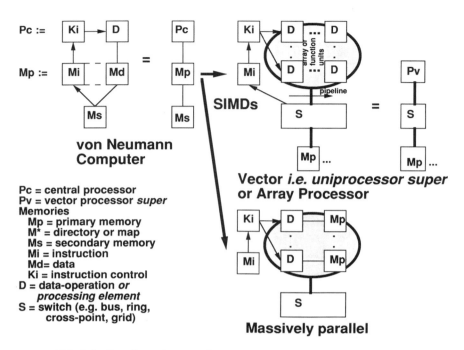

FIG. 6.6. Transformations on the von Neumann architecture to increase performance through parallelism.

at Tandem (for reliability), and as LAN connected workstation for spatial distribution.

Replicatability Within a Computer: Multiprocessors and the Opportunity for Parallelism

Multiprocessors permit a single computer to be extended to provide a completely balanced system of all resources including processing. Beginning in the mid-1960s multiprocessors evolved with several design objectives: Incremental performance increase allows the best system balance, fault tolerance, and increased performance through parallelism (Bell, 1991).

If a completely scalable computer can be built, then an arbitrary or scalable amount of processing can be provided within a given computer. The only way a scalable computer can exist is by placing the memory and processor together in exactly the same way as a collection of computers are interconnected, that is, by not having a single switch that limits performance, between the processor and memory.

The big idea of the 1990s is the scalable multiprocessor (see Fig. 6.7) that allows a single shared memory to have arbitrary processing, memory, and

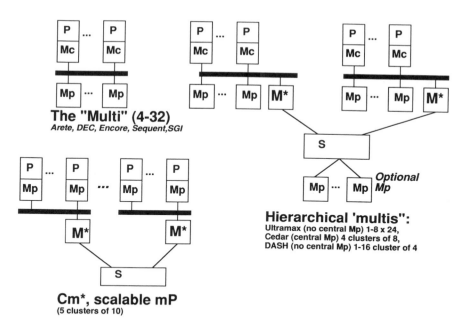

FIG. 6.7. Scalable multiprocessor structures that have limited and nearly unlimited scalability.

I/O. Carnegie Mellon University's Cm* is the first attempt to build a fully scalable multiprocessor (mP), shared-memory computer. In 1992, the first production, scalable mP was introduced by KSR, and is described later.

With scalable multiprocessors and the ability for an arbitrary number of processors to share work held in a common memory, a much larger opportunity is created: exploiting parallelism.

Replicatability of Multiple Computers, and the Problem of Making Them Operate as One

The replication and physical interconnection of multiple computers is the easy part; putting the computers together again so that they are one has always proven difficult. The degree of success depends on the objectives: reliability, physical separation with some small degree of resource sharing, or performance where all computers must behave as one.

Figure 6.8 shows that scalable multiprocessors and multicomputers interconnected by a large switch appear to be identical from a distance. Unfortunately, the difference is the amount of hardware in a multicomputer that permits it to behave as one shared-memory multiprocessor computer. Thus, the question comes back to the big idea of using software to

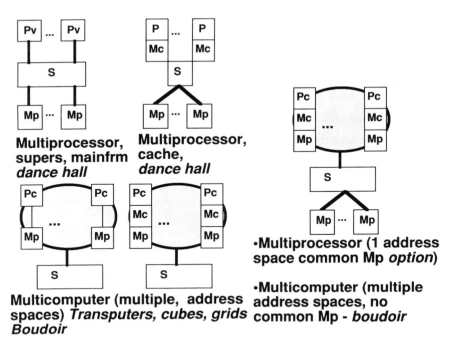

Multiprocessor, supers, mainfrm dance hall

Multiprocessor, cache, dance hall

•Multiprocessor (1 address space common Mp *option*)

•Multicomputer (multiple address spaces, no common Mp - *boudoir*

Multicomputer (multiple, address spaces) *Transputers, cubes, grids* Boudoir

FIG. 6.8. Distributed memory computers that result in either distributed shared memory (DSM) multiprocessors or multicomputer clusters.

carry out functions that hardware normally provides, including address formation and translation, data migration across the computing nodes, and the use of messages to access memory in other nodes instead of directly accessing it by name.

Economics Constrains Design

As in all systems, economics is the key part of the objective function that determine design. The market (economics) determines the form and function of computation, not elegance,[3] religion, architecture fads, and so on. Whether a computer is the "best" by economically objective measures such as performance/price or performance/time is usually irrelevant because of an organization's ability to market a product. For example, Dijkstra had nothing good to say about the System/360 announcement, yet the 360 will most likely survive by evolution longer than any other computer—except Intel's evolution of the X86 architecture from the 8080 for the PC: 8086/8088 > 80286 > 80386 > 80486 > Pentium > P6 > 64 bit architecture.

---

[3]*Elegance* is defined as having one feature that provides at least two functions.

Software Compatibility and Computer Families

Economics argue for the smallest number of machines (e.g., ISAs, O/Ss, programming languages) at each of level of the hierarchy in order to maximize user learning, build on other work, and have the greatest market. Of course, industrial forces act to increase the number of machines so that each company can differentiate itself and create monopolies. Aside from having a single computer that evolves with the addition of more address bits to access the larger memories that come with time, three innovations came about based on computer families. In 1962, SDS (now defunct) introduced three compatible minicomputers. The IBM System/360, introduced in April 1964, was the first successful family that covered a wide range of sizes (Bell & Newell, 1971). In all cases, the programming style and use evolved from a centralized, batch-processing approach. In 1975 we started the VAX project at Digital to provide a range of computers that covered a wide range of computing styles across a hierarchy of use from personal (the workstation), to distributed departmental computing, to centralized mainframe style computing in clusters that can behave as one computer.

BALANCING RESOURCES

Throughout the development of computers, a key requirement for a successful computer has been the ability to appropriately configure a computer to serve a variety of functions. This means that a given computer must be able to have an almost arbitrary amount of processing power, a memory hierarchy with a variety of sizes at each level, terminal capability including visualization, and networking to other sites. The Amdahl–Case rules of thumb were posited in the 1960s for balancing instruction speed, memory size, and I/O data rate: 1 instruction per second requires 1 byte of primary memory and 1 bit per second of I/O bandwidth. In the 1990s it's unclear whether ratios like these have meaning when a single computer is used both as a personal workstation and as a multiuser server with virtual memory. In the case of scientific computing, balancing floating-point operations per second (flops) with memory can vary from less than 1 flops/byte to 1 flops/8 bytes. Los Alamos National Laboratory estimates that for a given computer, from 5,000 to 1/15 byte of secondary memory is required per byte of primary memory for several "grand challenge" problems.

AMDAHL'S LAW

In 1967, Gene Amdahl pointed out the problem of using a large number of slow processors to do the same amount of work that a faster processor could accomplish. He looked at the problem of computation as being composed of a slow, sequential part and a part that could be accomplished in virtually zero time. The total time to do work is governed by the slow part. This applies to I/O, sequential processing, operating system overhead time—the slow part versus the fast parallel part in an mP, mC, or a fast vector operation. Today, the parallel processing dilemma is the need for a very large fraction, F, of a given program to be parallel, when using a large number of processors, N, to obtain high efficiency, $E(F,N)$:

$$E(F,N) = 1/[F + N \times (1 - F)]$$

Thus, scaling up slow processors is a losing proposition for a given fraction of parallelism. For 1,000 processors, F must be 0.999 parallel for 50% efficiency. The goal in massive parallelism is not to have the greatest number of processors, but rather providing the greatest number of usable operations in the shortest time.

COMPUTER SIZE, COMPUTER GENERATION, AND PROBLEM SCALABILITY

The perception that a computer can grow forever has always been a design goal. For example, the IBM System/360 (circa 1964) provided a 100 : 1 range, and VAX existed at a range of 1,000 : 1 over its lifetime. Ideally, one would start with a single computer and buy more components as needed to provide size scalability. Similarly, when new processor technology increased performance, one would add new generation computers in a generations-scalable fashion. Ordinary workstations provide some size and generation scalability, but are LAN-limited. Problem scalability is the ability of a problem, algorithm, or program to exist at a range of sizes so that it can be used efficiently and correctly on a given, range of scalable computers. Problem scalability, discovered in 1987, provides the economic basis for scalable computers.

GENERALITY IN DESIGN

Good design comes about in a search for generality by finding a few, simple mechanisms to accomplish a task rather than having a number of ad hoc functions that are unlikely to be related to each other. I define these designs as "elegant" because one mechanism provides multiple functions. I have enjoyed the search for generality in working on designs of general register computers, the Unibus, Ethernet, and many multiprocessors. My focus on multiprocessors as opposed to multicomputers is solely because they are elegant because they are "general" (Bell, 1991). That is, unlike multicomputers, one resource (processor, memory, or I/O channel) can be used by any process.

General registers that came about in the mid 1960s are a good example of providing one set of registers for accumulation, multiplier-quotient, indexing, stack control, and so on, rather than a collection of special registers. For performance reasons, fixed-point and floating-point registers are separated so they can be operated on independently and in parallel. The Unibus, Ethernet, and Token Rings all provide interconnection of components on a peer (general) rather than hierarchical basis. The mapping of I/O registers (state) into the memory address space used in the PDP-11, and now in all computers, is another example of generality. It is possible to go too far with generality if it costs time and space; for example, providing bit addressing and arbitrary length instruction fields has been used in unsuccessful computers.

Multiprocessors illustrate another use of generality for processing I/O including graphics and transformations and for carrying out specialized arithmetic operations. Invariably, providing more resources of a single kind (processing, memory, communication bandwidth), in a single place invariably provides a more flexible and cost-effective structure. As a taxonomist and architect, I'm interested in computers that evolve all of the design principles by extending every capability that a machine has. The following example, the last computer noted in Table 6.2, is as near the ideal of all computers that I've sought out during my three-plus decades of building computers.

THE KSR-1 SCALABLE MULTIPROCESSOR[4]

The Kendall Square Research KSR-1 is significant because it provides size (including memory and I/O) and generation-scalable smP where every node is identical; an efficient environment for both arbitrary workloads (from transaction processing to timesharing and batch) and sequential to parallel processing through a large, hardware supported address space with an unlimited number of processors; a strictly sequential consistent memory and programming model; and dynamic management of memory through hardware migration and replication of data throughout the distributed, processor-memory nodes using its Allcache mechanism.

The KSR-1 is a size- and generation-scalable, shared-memory multiprocessor computer. It is formed as a hierarchy of interconnected "ring multis."

[4]The company ceased operation in 1995 through no fault of its architecture. Distributed Shared Memory computers have been introduced by Convex and Cray Research in 1994. Several companies and various university research are aimed at building similar computers.

Scalability is achieved by connecting 32 processors to form a ring multi operating at 1 Gbyte/sec (128 million accesses per second). Interconnection bandwidth within a ring scales linearly, because every ring slot may contain a transaction. Thus, a ring has roughly the capacity of a typical cross-point switch found in a supercomputer room that interconnects eight to sixteen 100-Mbyte/sec HIPPI channels. The KSR-1 uses a two-level hierarchy to interconnect 34 rings (1,088 processors), and is therefore massive. The ring design supports an arbitrary number of levels, permitting ultracomputers costing $50–250 million to be built.

Each node is comprised of a primary cache, acting as 32 Mbytes primary memory, and a 64-bit superscalar processor with roughly the same performance as an IBM RS6000 operating at the same clock rate. The superscalar processors, containing 64 floating-point and 32 fixed-point registers of 64 bits, is designed for both scalar and vector operations. For example, 16 elements can be prefetched at one time. A processor also has a 0.5-Mbyte subcache supplying 20 million accesses per second to the processor (computational efficiency of 0.5). A processor operates at 20 MHz and is fabricated in 1.2-μm CMOS. The processor, *sans* caches, contains 3.9 million transistors in 6 types of 12 custom chips. Three-quarters of each processor consists of the search engine, responsible for migrating data to and from other nodes, for maintaining memory coherence throughout the system using distributed directories, and for ring control.

With sequential consistency, every processor returns the latest value of a written value, and results of an execution on multiple processors appear as some interleaving of operations of individual nodes when executed on a multithreaded machine. With Allcache, an address becomes a name, and this name automatically migrates throughout the system and is associated with a processor in a cache-like fashion as needed. Copies of a given cell are made by the hardware and are sent to other nodes to reduce access time. A processor can prefetch data into a local cache and poststore data for other cells. The hardware is designed to exploit the principle of locality. For example, when executing a single program on parallel data, copies of the program move dynamically and are cached in each of the operating node's primary and processor caches. Data such as elements of a matrix move to the nodes as required simply by accessing the data, and the processor has instructions that prefetch data to the processor's registers. When a processor writes to an address, all cells are updated and memory coherence is maintained. Data movement occurs in subpages of 128 bytes (16 words) of its 16-Kbyte pages.

Every known form of parallelism is supported via KSR's Mach-based operating system. Multiple users may run multiple sessions, comprising multiple applications, comprising multiple processes (each with independent address spaces), each of which may comprise multiple threads of control running simultaneously sharing a common address space. Messages passing is supported by pointer passing in the shared memory to avoid data copying and to enhance performance.

KSR also provides a commercial programming environment for transaction processing that accesses relational databases in parallel with unlimited scalability, as an alternative to multicomputers formed from multiprocessor mainframes. A 1-Knode system provides almost two orders of magnitude more processing power, primary memory, I/O bandwidth, and mass storage capacity than a multiprocessor mainframe and is completely scalable. A 1,088-node system can be configured with 15.3 terabytes of disk memory, providing 500 times the capacity of its main memory. The 32- and 320-node systems are projected to deliver over 1,000 and 10,000 transactions per second, respectively, giving it over a hundred times the throughput of a multiprocessor mainframe.

SUMMARY

Although every new computer that introduces a new idea or innovation is always described as revolutionary, such a label is almost surely marketing hype. The only two great revolutionary ideas are the computer itself, and the integrated circuit that evolves very rapidly and allows computers of all types, description, and functionality to be developed.

Three general engineering design principles have driven computer structures: general economics-based design, replication, and the search for generality.

The principle of locality is the important observation about the behavior of programs that has allowed computer inventions or big ideas to be discovered, including the memory hierarchy, the one-level store that led to the idea of a virtual memory, the cache memory, and finally scalable computers in the 1990s.

Once the computer was discovered, the big ideas that were variants on the theme of the computer included using computers for a wide range of applications, building a hierarchy of machines, and building a computer within a computer that could be shared by many programs, that is, multiprogramming and timesharing.

The building of physically distributed multicomputers created the desire to have such a collection behave as a single computer and, in 1992, to operate in parallel. In a similar fashion, building a multiprocessor computer from a common set of components created the desire to have such a collection of processors operate together on a single problem.

Thus, evolving computer structures to a collection of networked computers, each of which can have an arbitrary number of processing elements, has created two incredibly difficult problems to be solved in the 1990s:

getting these computer networks back up to the capability that existed when only a single processor controlled all the resources and behaved as an integrated system, and the opportunity for parallelism within a single virtual memory whereby all the resources can operate on a single program.

REFERENCES

Bell, C. G. (1985). Multis: A new class of multiprocessor computers. *Science, 228*, 462–467.

Bell, G. (1989). The future of high performance computers in science and engineering. *Communications of the ACM, 32*(9), 1091–1101.

Bell, G. (1991). Three decades of multiprocessors. In R. Rashid (Ed.), *CMU computer science: A 25th anniversary commemorative.* Reading, MA: ACM Press, Addison-Wesley.

Bell, G. (1992). Ultracomputers: A teraflop before its time. *Communications of the ACM, 35*(8), 27–47.

Bell, C. G., Grason, J., & Newell, A. (1972). *Designing computers and digital systems using PDP16 register transfer modules.* Maynard, MA: Digital Press.

Bell, G., & McNamara, J. (1991). *High tech ventures: The guide to entrepreneurial success.* Reading, MA: Addison-Wesley.

Bell, C. G., & Newell, A. (1971). *Computer structures: Readings and examples.* New York: McGraw-Hill.

Denning, P. J. (1980). Working sets past and present. *IEEE Transactions on Software Engineering, SE-6*(1), 64–84.

Gomory, R. E., & Schmitt, R. W. (1988). Science products. *Science, 240*, 1131–1132, 1203–1204.

Hennessy, J. L., & Patterson, D. A. (1990). *Computer architecture: A quantitative approach.* Palo Alto, CA: Morgan Kaufman.

Meindl, J. D. (1987). Chips for advanced computing. *Scientific American, 225*(10), 78–88.

Siewiorek, D., Bell, C. G., & Newell, A. (1982). *Computer structures: Principles and examples.* New York: McGraw-Hill.

DISCUSSION

Parallelism Matters

Milind Tambe
University of Southern California

Many knowledge-based systems and learning systems are built on a production-system software technology. The issue of efficiency of this technology has long been of major concern, since, a priori, matching (say) 10,000 productions against a working memory of 1000 elements 100 times a sec seems computationally intractable. Much progress has in fact been made in the underlying algorithmic and software efficiency, starting with the invention of the Rete Net technology (Forgy, 1982). However, the concerns remain critical. *We would like not 10K, but 100K or even 1M productions, and we would like 10K elements in working memory and the cycle time to be 1000 times a sec.* However, typical productions systems are only a few hundred productions, a few are in the low thousands.

This paragraph is in the words of Allen Newell. It is from a draft of a paper that we were engaged in writing in December 1991. Allen finally edited out this paragraph due to page limitations and other related concerns. But the paragraph is an important one. In particular, the emphasized sentence in the paragraph presents what could be considered as a milestone for production system implementations: the goal of achieving a million productions (or condition–action rules), 10,000 working memory elements, and a cycle time of 1,000 times a second. The cycle here refers to the recognize–act cycle, that is, the basic production system cycle used in executing tasks. Productions match working memory elements in the recognize phase of the cycle, whereas successfully matched productions fire in the act phase of the cycle, possibly changing the working memory and causing the system to execute the next recognize–act cycle.

As in other systems, the production system is a principle computational bottleneck in Soar (Tambe, 1991). Furthermore, the size of Soar's production system grows with learning—thousands of new productions can potentially be added to it, increasing the computational burden on the system. It is therefore important to explore different methods for improving production system performance.

In Chapter 6, Gordon Bell discusses scalable multiprocessors (parallel machines) and the opportunities they provide for performance improvement. Can these multiprocessors improve the performance of production systems? This is the question that I examine in this discussion. More specifically, what role can multiprocessors play in achieving the milestone outlined above? To address this question, I first review previous research in the area of using parallel machines for speeding up production systems. I then speculate on the role parallel machines are likely to play in achieving the milestone.

PARALLELISM IN PRODUCTION SYSTEMS

Research in parallel execution of production systems started in the early 1980s. At that time, production systems were seen to spend greater than 90% of their execution time in production match, that is, in the recognize phase of the recognize–act cycle. Therefore, early research in this area concentrated on exploiting parallelism in production match. Match parallelism has been the dominant topic of research in this area ever since. Hence, this chapter mostly focuses on match parallelism. However, recently researchers have shifted their focus to other sources of parallelism (Miranker, 1991). I briefly discuss these efforts near the end of this chapter.

Various research efforts were involved in the early investigation of match parallelism. Some notables among them include the production system machine (PSM) effort (Gupta, Forgy, Newell, & Wedig, 1986) (under the guidance of Allen Newell and Charles Forgy), the DADO (Miranker, 1987) and Non-Von (Hillyer & Shaw, 1986) efforts, and others (Barachini, 1991; Oflazer, 1987). These projects expected a large amount of parallelism in production match. Essentially, all the productions in the system were expected to match independently and in parallel. Furthermore, this parallelism was expected to increase with increasing number of productions— each new production could simply be matched in parallel with existing productions. However, these projects quickly discovered a surprising empirical phenomenon. Contrary to expectations, match parallelism did not increase with increasing number of productions. Basically, the total match computation per recognize–act cycle remained constant, independent of the number of productions in the system. Given this limited computation, total achievable parallelism was also limited. In fact, the total speedup from parallelism was estimated to be limited to about 10- to 20-fold (it was estimated to be double that for Soar systems).

This empirical phenomenon led to a lowering of expectations about the role parallelism was likely to play in speeding up production systems. However, a 20-fold speedup is still substantial, and therefore, implementations were developed to exploit this parallelism. The PSM effort developed implementations for commercially available shared memory machines (Gupta, Tambe, Kalp, Forgy, & Newell, 1988), which demonstrated up to 12-fold speedups on 14 processor machines. Speedups were also demonstrated on message-passing computers (Acharya, Tambe, & Gupta, 1992). Similar implementations were developed or planned by other research groups.

Unfortunately, these parallel implementations are (or were) very rarely used in practice to develop real applications. There are at least two reasons for this. First, there is continued development of highly efficient sequential match algorithms (Barachini, 1991; Tambe, 1991). This leads to an increasingly smaller proportion of execution time being spent in match (Miranker & Lofaso, 1991), reducing the real speedups available from match parallelism. Second, while uniprocessor hardware has achieved big speedups (e.g., faster workstations), parallel hardware has lagged behind (at least for machines useful for match parallelism). With slower individual processors, speedups obtained from parallel machines are not helpful.

Meanwhile, helped by the advances just outlined, uniprocessor-based production-system implementations have achieved significant speedups and have continued to move toward the milestone outlined in the previous section. Parallel implementations have lagged behind, leading to a pessimistic view about the future role of match parallelism. These faster uniprocessor implementations would actually not be of much consequence if the total match effort, and hence match parallelism, scaled with the number of productions. For instance, if the available parallelism actually scaled up to about 1,000-fold, then improved uniprocessor technology would provide very little competition.

There are, of course, some indirect benefits of the work on match parallelism. First, some algorithms (such as TREAT; Miranker, 1987) and implementations (such as ParaOPS5/CParaOPS5; Gupta et al., 1988) developed for parallel machines have turned out to be efficient and useful on uniprocessors. Second, detailed experimental measurements obtained for developing parallel implementations have turned out to be useful in designing new optimizations.

CONTRADICTIONS

Interestingly, the limited match effort per cycle can be viewed positively for learning systems like Soar: A large number of productions can be added to the system, and they will not cause an increase in the match effort per recognize–act cycle. However, data from existing learning production systems (Tambe, 1991) point in the opposite direction. It predicts an increase in the match time per recognize–act cycle with increasing number of productions. Indeed, this is part of the general utility problem in learning systems.

Thus, there are two completely contradictory views on production match: The field of parallel production systems has concluded that increasing the number of productions will not add to the match cost, whereas the field of learning systems has concluded it will. As mentioned earlier, if there is an increase in the match cost, match parallelism could play a bigger role in speeding up production systems.

Resolving this issue among others was the aim of our research effort called *large systems effort* or LSE. This was a joint project between Allen Newell, Bob Doorenbos, and myself. The goal of this project was to build large systems with thousands of productions, and investigate issues such as the one already described (Doorenbos, Tambe, & Newell, 1992; Tambe, Doorenbos, & Newell, 1992). The largest system we developed was Dispatcher-Soar. It began with 1,819 initial (unlearned) productions, and learned 10,112 new productions, bringing the total size to 11,931 productions. Over the course of the addition of 10,112 new productions, there was no increase in match cost per recognize–act cycle. However, one of our smaller systems, Path-planner-Soar, showed an increase in match cost. It began with 305 productions, learned 1,840 new productions, and showed a twofold increase in match cost per recognize–act cycle in this process.

Thus, we see one system showing no increase in match cost with the addition of 10,112 new productions, and one system showing an increase with just 1,840 productions. The other systems we developed also displayed this dichotomy in behavior, leaving open the question about whether match cost will increase with an increasing number of productions, and also the question about the possible role of match parallelism.

SUMMARY

The question I briefly examined in this chapter is, what role, if any, can parallelism play in reaching the milestone of a million productions, 10,000 working memory elements, and 1,000 cycles per second? The initial answer to this question was that parallelism would play an important role in achieving this goal. However, due to a variety of factors, this high expectation gave way to pessimism about the role of parallelism. But now we face an open question: There is a conflict of views. If in a majority of the cases the match cost increases with increasing number of learned productions, then match parallelism will play a bigger role. Otherwise, the contributions from match parallelism may be very limited.

In this brief examination, I have left out some promising directions for research on parallelism. The first direction is the possible use of task-level or application-level parallelism. This involves parallel execution of multiple recognize-act cycles. This approach is particularly beneficial for production systems that spend a large proportion of their execution time outside production match. There are some promising initial results available here (Miranker, 1991); however, much more needs to be investigated. I have also left out some new application areas for production systems, such as expert-database systems. Unlike conventional production systems, such systems allow very large working memories, and could possibly lead to very high parallelism.[1]

REFERENCES

Acharya, A., Tambe, M., & Gupta, A. (1992). Implementation of production systems on message passing computers: Simulation results and analysis. *IEEE Transactions on Parallel and Distributed Computing, 3*(4), 477–487.

Barachini, F. (1991). The evolution of PAMELA. *Expert Systems, 8*(2), 87–98.

Doorenbos, R., Tambe, M., & Newell, A. (1992). Learning 10,000 chunks: What's it like out there. *Proceedings of the National Conference on Artificial Intelligence.*

Gupta, A., Forgy, C., Newell, A., & Wedig, R. (1986). Parallel algorithms and architectures for production systems. *Proceedings of the Thirteenth International Symposium on Computer Architecture* (pp. 28–35).

Gupta, A., Tambe, M., Kalp, D., Forgy, C. L., & Newell, A. (1988). Parallel implementation of OPS5 on the Encore Multiprocessor: Results and analysis. *International Journal of Parallel Programming, 17*(2).

Hillyer, B. K., & Shaw, D. E. (1986). Execution of OPS5 production systems on a massively parallel machine. *Journal of Parallel and Distributed Processing, 3,* 236–268.

Miranker, D. P. (1987). *Treat: A new and efficient match algorithm for AI production systems.* Doctoral dissertation, Computer Science Department, Columbia University, New York.

Miranker, D. P. (1991). Guest editor's introduction [Special issue on parallel execution of rule systems]. *Journal of Parallel and Distributed Computing, 13.*

Miranker, D., & Lofaso, B. (1991). The organization and performance of a Treat-based production system compiler. *IEEE Transactions on Knowledge and Data Engineering, 3*(1), 3–11.

Oflazer, K. (1987). *Partitioning in parallel processing of production systems.* Unpublished doctoral dissertation, Computer Science Department, Carnegie Mellon University, Pittsburgh.

Tambe, M. (1991). *Eliminating combinatorics from production match.* Unpublished doctoral dissertation, School of Computer Science, Carnegie Mellon University, Pittsburgh.

Tambe, M., Doorenbos, R., & Newell, A. (1992). *The match cost of adding a new rule: A clash of views* (Tech. Rep. No. CMU-CS-92-158). Pittsburgh: Carnegie Mellon University, School of Computer Science.

---

[1]Because this chapter was written and submitted in the Fall of 1992, it does not do justice to some of the interesting recent developments in the field of parallel and efficient production systems. However, its broader conclusions still hold.

Chapter 7

Software Architectures for Shared Information Systems

Mary Shaw
Carnegie Mellon University

Software system design takes place at many levels, each with its own concerns. We learn from computer hardware design that each of these levels has its own elements and composition operators and its own notations, analysis tools, and design rules. From the 1960s through the 1980s software developers concentrated on the programming level. At this level, so-called higher level programming languages provide for the definitions of algorithms and data structures using the familiar programming language control statements, types, and procedures. Now we are turning our attention to the architectural level, in which patterns for organizing module-scale components guide software system design.

SYSTEMS INTEGRATION

Large software systems are often integrated from preexisting systems. The designer of such a system must accommodate very different—often incompatible—conceptual models, representations, and protocols in order to create a coherent synthesis. Systems integration is a problem-solving activity that entails harnessing and coordinating the power and capabilities of information technology to meet a customer's needs. It develops megasystems in which preexisting independent systems become subsystems—components that must interact with other components. Successful integration requires solution of both organizational and technical problems:

- Understanding the current organizational capabilities and processes.
- Reengineering and simplification of processes with a system view.
- Standardizing on common data languages and system architectures.
- Automation of processes and systems.

Five kinds of issues motivate companies to invest in systems integration (Computer Science and Telecommunications Board, CSTB, 1992, pp. 16–21):

- For many organizations, experiences with information technology have not lived up to expectations.
- The proliferation of information technology products and vendors has produced the need for connectivity and interoperability.
- An installed base of information technology has to accommodate new technology and new capabilities.
- Advances in technology, combined with growing appreciation of what can be accomplished with that technology, have prompted firms to search for new applications and sources of competitive advantage.
- In an increasingly global economy, firms must rely on telecommunications and information technology to manage and coordinate their operations and to stay abreast of international competitors.

Corporate mergers and reorganizations, in particular, create needs for compatibility among systems developed under different assumptions about representation and interaction. The task is difficult: It involves large, untidy problems; incomplete, imprecise, and inconsistent requirements; and "legacy" systems that must be retained rather than replaced. For systems integration to be useful, it must be globally effective within the organization. The focus of this chapter is on the enabling technologies rather than the organizational questions.

The essential enabling technologies are of several kinds (CSTB, 1992; Nilsson, Nordhagen, & Oftedal, 1990):

- Architecture: system organization; kinds of components, kinds of interactions, and patterns of overall organization; ability to evolve; consistency with available modular building blocks for hardware, software, and databases; standardization and open systems.
- Semantics: representations; conceptual consistency; semantic models; means for handing inconsistencies.
- Connectivity: mechanisms for moving data between systems and initiating action in other systems; communication platforms with flexible linkages or interfaces; network management and reliability; security.

- Interaction: granularity; user interfaces; interoperability; simplicity; underlying consistency of presentation.

The technologies for architecture are of primary interest here; to a certain extent these are inseparable from semantics.

SHARED INFORMATION SYSTEMS

One particularly significant class of large systems is responsible for collecting, manipulating, and preserving large bodies of complex information. These are *shared information systems*. Systems of this kind appear in many different domains; this chapter examines three. The earliest shared information systems consisted of separate programs for separate subtasks. Later, multiple independent processing steps were composed into larger tasks by passing data in a known, fixed format 'from one step to another. This organization is not flexible in responding to variations or discrepancies in data. Nor is it tolerant of structural modification, especially the addition of components developed under different assumptions. It is also not responsive to the needs of interactive processing, which must handle individual requests as they arrive.

Still later, often when requirements for interaction appear, new organizations allowed independent processing subsystems to interact through a shared data store. Although this organization is an improvement, it still encounters integration problems—especially when multiple data stores with different representations must be shared, when the system is distributed, when many user tasks must be served, and when the suite of processing and data subsystems changes regularly. Several newer approaches now compensate for these differences in representation and operating assumptions, but the problem is not completely solved. A common pattern, the *shared information system evolution pattern*, is evident in the application areas examined here.

DESIGN LEVELS

System design takes place at many levels. It is useful to make precise distinctions among those levels, for each level appropriately deals with different design concerns. At each level we find *components*, both primitive and composite; *rules of composition* that allow the construction of nonprimitive components, or systems; and *rules of behavior* that provide semantics for the system (Bell & Newell, 1971; Newell, 1982, 1990). Because these differ from one level to another, we also find different notations, design problems, and analysis techniques at each level. As a result, design at one level can proceed substantially autonomously of any other level. But levels are also related, in that elements at the base of each level correspond to—are implemented by—constructs of the level below.

The hierarchy of levels for computer hardware systems is familiar and appears in Fig. 7.1 (Bell & Newell, 1971, p. 3). Note first that each level deals with different content. Different kinds of structures guide design with different sets of components. Different notations, analysis techniques, and design issues accompany the differences of content matter. Note also that each level admits of substructure: Abstraction and composition take place within each level, in terms of the components and structures of that level. In addition, there is an established transformation from the primitive

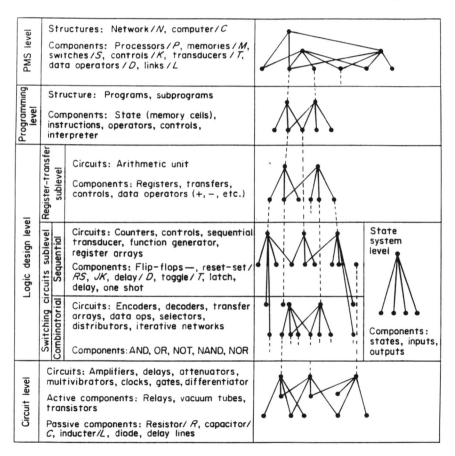

PMS level	Structures: Network / N, computer / C Components: Processors / P, memories / M, switches / S, controls / K, transducers / T, data operators / D, links / L	
Programming level	Structure: Programs, subprograms Components: State (memory cells), instructions, operators, controls, interpreter	
Logic design level — Register-transfer sublevel	Circuits: Arithmetic unit Components: Registers, transfers, controls, data operators (+, −, etc.)	
Logic design level — Switching circuits sublevel — Sequential	Circuits: Counters, controls, sequential transducer, function generator, register arrays Components: Flip-flops —, reset-set / RS, JK, delay / D, toggle / T, latch, delay, one shot	State system level
Logic design level — Switching circuits sublevel — Combinatorial	Circuits: Encoders, decoders, transfer arrays, data ops, selectors, distributors, iterative networks Components: AND, OR, NOT, NAND, NOR	Components: states, inputs, outputs
Circuit level	Circuits: Amplifiers, delays, attenuators, multivibrators, clocks, gates, differentiator Active components: Relays, vacuum tubes, transistors Passive components: Resistor/ R, capacitor/ C, inducter/ L, diode, delay lines	

FIG. 7.1. Computer hardware design levels. From Bell and Newell (1971). Reprinted by permission.

components at the bottom of each level to (probably nonprimitive) components of the level below.

Software, too, has its design levels. We can identify at least:

- *Architecture*, where the design issues involve overall association of system capability with components; components are modules, and interconnections among modules are handled in a variety of ways, all of which seem to be expressed as explicit sets of procedure calls.
- *Code*, where the design issues involve algorithms and data structures; the components are programming language primitives such as numbers, characters, pointers, and threads of control; primitive operators are the arithmetic and data manipulation primitives of the language; composition mechanisms include records, arrays, and procedures.
- *Executable*, where the design issues involve memory maps, data layouts, call stacks, and register allocations; the components are bit patterns supported by hardware; and the operations and compositions are described in machine code.

These roughly track the higher levels of hardware design. The executable and code levels for software are well understood. However, the architecture level is currently understood mostly at the level of intuition, anecdote, and folklore. It is common for a description of a software system to include a few paragraphs of text and a box-and-line diagram, but there is neither uniform syntax nor uniform semantics for interpreting the prose and the diagrams. Our concern here is in improving understanding and precision at the software architecture level. At this level the components are programs, modules, or systems; a rich collection of interchange representations and protocols connects the components, and well-known system patterns guide the compositions (Garlan & Shaw, 1993).

EXTERNAL SOFTWARE SYSTEMS

Recent work on intelligent integration of *external software systems* (ESSs) offers some hope for improving the sophistication of our integration techniques. Newell and Steier (1991) suggested that the work on agent–ESS systems may contribute to software engineering by making the power of computer software more easily accessible in the service of computational tasks. An intelligent system would learn to recognize aberrations when they arise and compensate for them, and it would adapt to new protocols and representations when the suite of available components changes.

This chapter explores what happens when independent systems become components of larger systems. It examines three examples of shared information systems:

- *Data processing*, driven primarily by the need to build business decision systems from conventional databases.
- *Software development environments*, driven primarily by the need to represent and manipulate programs and their designs.
- *Building design*, driven primarily by the need to couple independent design tools to allow for the interactions of their results in structural design.

It then shows how the software architectures of these systems changed as technology and demands on system performance changed. We close by surveying the architectural constructs used to describe the examples and examining the prospects for intelligent integration.

DATABASE INTEGRATION

Business data processing has traditionally been dominated by database management, in particular by database updates. Originally, separate databases served separate purposes, and implementation issues revolved around efficient ways to do massive coordinated periodic updates. As time passed, interactive demands required individual transactions to complete in real time. Still later, as databases proliferated and organizations merged, information proved to have value far beyond its original needs. Diversity in representations and interfaces arose, information began to appear redundantly in multiple databases, and geographic distribution added communication complexity. As this happened, the challenges shifted from individual transaction processing to integration.

Individual database systems must support transactions of predetermined types and periodic summary reports. Bad requests require a great deal of special handling. Originally the updates and summary reports were collected into batches, with database updates and reports produced during periodic batch runs. However, when interactive queries became technologically possible, the demand for interaction generated demand for online processing of both individual requests and exceptions. Reports remained on roughly the same cycles as before, so reporting became decoupled from transaction processing.

As databases became more common, information about a business became distributed among multiple databases. This offered new opportunities for the data to become inconsistent and incomplete. In addition, the representations, or schemas, for different databases were usually different; even the portion of the data shared by two databases is likely to have representations in each database. The total volume of data to handle is correspondingly larger, and it is often distributed across multiple machines. Two general strategies emerged for dealing with data diversity: unified schemas and multi-databases.

Batch Sequential

Some of the earliest large computer applications were databases. In these applications individual database operations—transactions—were collected into large batches. The application consisted of a small number of large standalone programs that performed sequential updates on flat (unstructured) files. A typical organization included:

- A massive *edit program*, which accepted transaction inputs and performed such validation as was possible without access to the database.
- A massive *transaction sort*, which got the transactions into the same order as the records on the sequential master file.
- A sequence of *update programs*, one for each master file; these huge programs actually executed the transactions by moving sequentially through the master file, matching each type of transaction to its corresponding account and updating the account records.
- A *print program* that produced periodic reports.

The steps were independent of each other; they had to run in a fixed sequence; each ran to completion, producing an output file in a new format, before the next step began. This is a *batch sequential* architecture. The organization of a typical batch sequential update system appears in Fig. 7.2 (Best, 1990, p. 29). This figure also shows the possibility of online queries (but not modifications). In this structure the files to support the

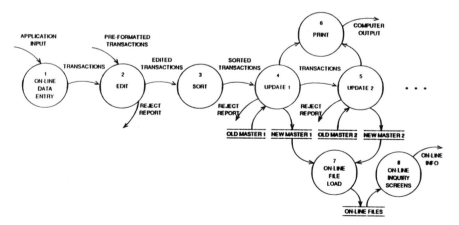

FIG. 7.2. Data flow diagram for batch databases. From *Application Architecture: Modern Large-Scale Information Processing*, by L. J. Best, 1990. Copyright © 1990 by John Wiley & Sons, Inc. Reprinted by permission of John Wiley & Sons, Inc.

queries are reloaded periodically, so recent transactions (e.g., within the past few days) are not reflected in the query responses.

Figure 7.2 is a Yourdon data flow diagram. Processes are depicted as circles, or "bubbles"; data flow (here, large files) is depicted with arrows, and data stores such as computer files are depicted with parallel lines. This notation is conventional in this application area for showing the relations among processes and data flow. Within a bubble, however, the approach changes. Figure 7.3 (Best, 1990, p. 150) shows the internal structure of an update process. There is one of these for each of the master data files, and each is responsible for handling all possible updates to that data file.

In Fig. 7.3, the boxes represent subprograms and the lines represent procedure calls. A single driver program processes all batch transactions. Each transaction has a standard set of subprograms that check the transaction request, access the required data, validate the transaction, and post the result. Thus all the program logic for each transaction is localized in a single set of subprograms. The figure indicates that the transaction-processing template is replicated so that each transaction has its own set. Note the difference even in graphical notation as the design focus shifts from the architecture to the code level.

The essential—batch sequential—parts of Fig. 7.2 are redrawn in Fig. 7.4 in a form that allows comparison to other architectures. The redrawn

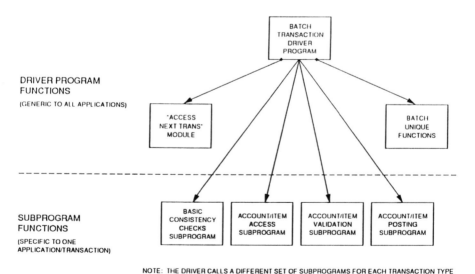

FIG. 7.3. Internal structure of batch update process. From *Application Architecture: Modern Large-Scale Information Processing*, by L. J. Best, 1990. Copyright © 1990 by John Wiley & Sons, Inc. Reprinted by permission of John Wiley & Sons, Inc.

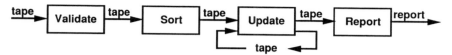

FIG. 7.4. Batch sequential database architecture.

figure emphasizes the sequence of operations to be performed and the completion of each step before the start of its successor. It suppresses the online query support and updates to multiple master files, or databases.

Simple Repository

Two trends forced a change away from batch sequential processing. First, interactive technology provided the opportunity and demand for continuous processing of online updates as well as online queries. Online queries of stale data are not very satisfactory; interaction requires incremental updates of the database, at least for online transactions (there is less urgency about transactions that arrive by slow means such as mail, because they have already incurred delays). Second, as organizations grew, the set of transactions and queries grew. Modifying a single large update program and a single large reporting program for each change to a transaction creates methodological bottlenecks. New types of processing were added often enough to discourage modification of a large update program for each new processing request. In addition, starting up large programs incurred substantial overheads at that time.

These trends led to a change in system organization. Figure 7.5 (Best, 1990, p. 81) showed a "modern"—that is, interactive—system organization. The notation is as for Fig. 7.2. This organization supports both interactive and batch processing for all transaction types; updates can occur continuously. Because these are no longer periodic operations, the system also provides for periodic operations. Here, though, the transaction database and extract database are transient buffers; the account/item database is the central permanent store. The transaction database serves to synchronize multiple updates. The extract database solves a problem created by the addition of interactive processing—namely, the loss of synchronization between the updating and reporting cycles. This figure obscures not only the difference between a significant database and a transient buffer but also the separation of transactions into separate processes.

It is possible for transaction processing in this organization to resemble batch sequential processing. However, it is useful to separate the general overhead operations from the transaction-specific operations. It may also be useful to perform multiple operations on a single account all at once. Figure 7.6 (Best, 1990, p. 158) shows the program structure for the transactions in

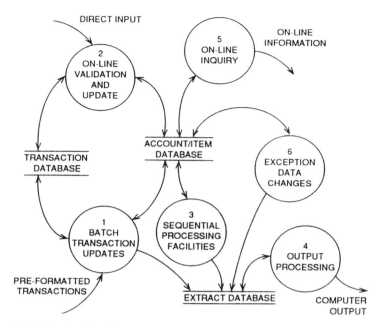

FIG. 7.5. Dataflow diagram for interactive database. From Best (1990). Reprinted by permission.

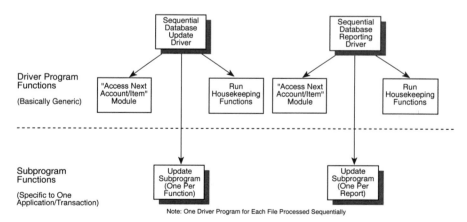

FIG. 7.6. Internal structure of interactive update process. From *Application Architecture: Modern Large-Scale Information Processing*, by L. J. Best, 1990. Copyright © 1990 by John Wiley & Sons, Inc. Reprinted by permission of John Wiley & Sons, Inc.

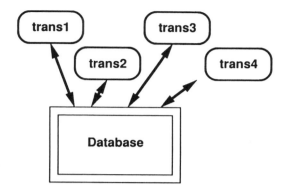

FIG. 7.7. Simple repository database architecture.

this new architecture. Because the transactions now exist individually rather than as alternatives within a single program, several of the bubbles in Fig. 7.5 actually represent sets of independent bubbles.

There is not a clean separation of architectural issues from coding issues in Figs. 7.5 and 7.6. It is not unusual to find this, because explicit attention to the architecture as a separate level of software design is relatively recent. Indeed, Figs. 7.5 and 7.6 suffer from information overload as well. The system structure is easier to understand if we first isolate the database updates. Figure 7.7 focuses narrowly on the database and its transactions. This is an instance of a fairly common architecture, a *repository*, in which shared persistent data is manipulated by independent functions each of which has essentially no permanent state. It is the core of a database system. Figure 7.8 adds two additional structures. The first is a control element that accepts the

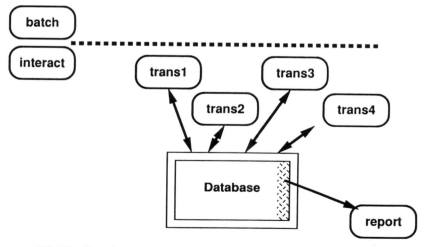

FIG. 7.8. Repository architecture for database showing control and reporting.

batch or interactive stream of transactions, synchronizes them, and selects which update or query operations to invoke, and in which order. This subsumes the transaction database of Fig. 7.5. The second is a buffer that serves the periodic reporting function. This subsumes the extract database of Fig. 7.5.

Virtual Repository

As organizations grew, databases came to serve multiple functions. Because this was usually a result of incremental growth, individual independent programs continued to be the locus of processing. In response, simple repositories gave way to databases that supported multiple views through schemas. Corporate reorganizations, mergers, and other consolidations of data forced the joint use of multiple databases. As a result, information could no longer be localized in a single database. Table 7.1 (Kim & Seo, 1991, p. 13) gives a hint of the extent of the problem through the schemas that describe books in four libraries. Note, for example, that the call number is represented in different ways in all four schemas; in this case they're all Library of Congress numbers, so the more difficult case of a mixture of Library of Congress and Dewey numbering doesn't arise. Note also the assortment of ways the publisher's name, address, and (perhaps) telephone number are represented.

Developing applications that rely on multiple diverse databases like these requires solution of two problems. First, the system must reconcile representation differences. Second, it must communicate results across distributed systems that may have not only different data representations but also different database schema representations. One approach to the unification of multiple schemas is called the federated approach. Figure 7.9 (Ahmed et al., 1991, p. 21) shows one way to approach this, relying on the well-understood technology for handling multiple views on databases. The top of this figure shows how the usual database mechanisms integrate multiple schemas into a single schema. The bottom of the figure suggests an approach to importing data from autonomous external databases: For each database, devise a schema in its native schema language that exports the desired data and a matching schema in the schema language of the importer. This separates the solutions to the two essential problems and restricts the distributed system problem to communication between matching schemas.

Figure 7.9 combines solutions to two problems. Here again, the design is clearer if the discussion and diagram separate the two sets of concerns. Figure 7.10 shows the integration of multiple databases by unified schemas. It shows a simple composition of projections. The details about whether the data paths are local or distributed and whether the local schema and import schema are distinct are suppressed at this level of abstraction; these communication

TABLE 7.1

Library Schemas in Component Databases

Library	Name Name	Attributes	General Description
CDB1: Main (Main Library)	item	(i#*, title, author-name, subject, type, language)	Library items
	lc-num	(i#*, c-letter, f-digit, s-digit, cuttering)	Library of Congress number
	publisher	(i#*, name, tel, street, city, zip, state, country)	Publishers
	lend-info	(i#*, lend-period, library-use-only, checked-out)	Lending information
	checkout-info	(i#*, id-num, hour, day, month, year)	Borrower and due date
CDB2: Engineering (Engineering Library)	items	(i#*, title, a-name, type, c-letter, f-digit, s-digit, cuttering)	Library items
	item-subject	(i#*, subject)	Subject of each item
	item-language	(id#*, language)	Language used in each item
	publisher	(i#*, p-name, str-num, str-name, city, zip, state)	Publishers
	lend-info	(i#*, lend-period, library-use-only, checked out)	Lending information
	checkout-info	(i#*, id-num, hour, day, month, year)	Borrower and due date
CDB3: City (City Public Library)	books	(i#*, lc-num, name, title, subject)	Library items
	publisher	(i#*, p-name, p-address)	Publishers
	lend-info	(i#*, l-period, reference, checked out)	Lending information
	checkout-info	(i#*, dl-num, day, month, year)	Borrower and due date
CDB4: Comm (Community College Library)	item	(i#*, lc-number, title, a-name)	Library items
	publisher-info	(i#*, p#*, name, tel)	Publishers
	publisher-add	(p#*, st-num, st-name, room-num, city, state, zip)	Publishers address
	checkout-info	(i#*, id, day, month, year)	Borrower and due date
	lc-num	(i#*, category, user-name)	Library card number

Note. Diversity of schemas for a single construct. From Kim and Seo (1991). Copyright © 1991 by IEEE. Reprinted by permission.
*Indicates key attribute.

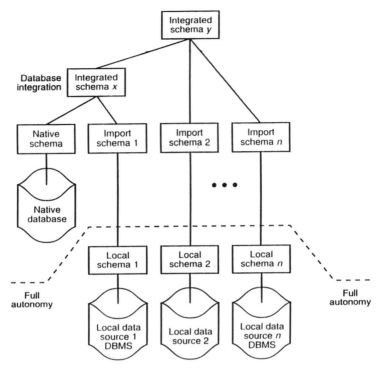

FIG. 7.9. Combining multiple distributed schemas. Copyright © 1991 by IEEE. From Ahmed et al. (1991). Reprinted by permission.

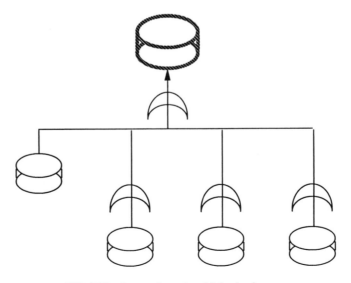

FIG. 7.10. Integration of multiple databases.

questions should be addressed in an expansion of the abstract filter design (and they may not need to be the same for all of the constituents).

Hierarchical Layers

Unified schemas allow for merger of information, but their mappings are fixed, passive, and static. The designers of the views must anticipate all future needs; the mappings simply transform the underlying data; and there are essentially no provisions for recognizing and adapting to changes in the set of available databases. In the real world, each database serves multiple users, and indeed the set of users changes regularly. The set of available databases also changes, both because the population of databases itself changes and because network connectivity changes the set that is accessible. This exacerbates the usual problems of inconsistency across a set of databases. The commercial database community has begun to respond to this problem of dynamic reconfiguration. Distributed database products organized on a client–server model are beginning to challenge traditional mainframe database management systems (Hovaness, 1992). This set of problems is also of current interest in the database research community.

Figure 7.11 (Wiederhold, 1992, p. 45) depicts one research scenario for active mediation between a constantly changing set of users and a constantly changing set of databases. Wiederhold proposed introducing active programs, called experts, to accept queries from users, recast them as queries to the available databases, and deliver appropriate responses to the users. These experts, or active mediators, localize knowledge about how to discover what databases are available and interact with them, about how to recast users' queries in useful forms, and about how to reconcile, integrate, and interpret information from multiple diverse databases.

In effect, Wiederhold's architecture uses *hierarchical layers* to separate the business of the users, the databases, and the mediators. The interaction between layers of the hierarchy will most likely be a *client–server* relation. This is not a repository because there is no enforced coherence of central shared

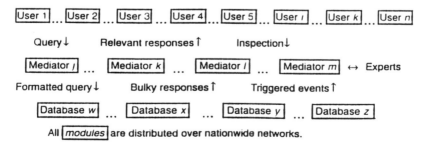

FIG. 7.11. Multidatabase with mediators. From Wiederhold (1992). Copyright © 1992 by IEEE. Reprinted by permission.

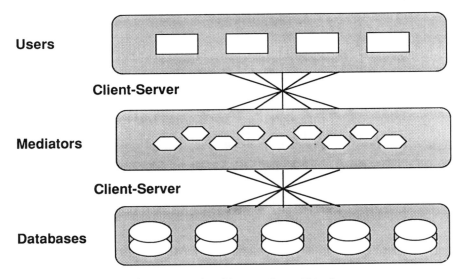

FIG. 7.12. Layered architecture for multidatabases.

data; it is not a batch sequential system (or any other form of pipeline) because the interaction with the data is incremental. Figure 7.12 recasts this in a form similar to the other examples.

Evolution of Shared Information Systems in Business Data Processing

These business data-processing applications exhibit a pattern of development driven by changing technology and changing needs. The pattern was:

- *Batch processing:* Stand-alone programs; results are passed from one to another on magtape. *Batch sequential model.*
- *Interactive processing:* Concurrent operation and faster updates preclude batching, so updates are out of synchronization with reports. *Repository model* with external control.
- *Unified schemas:* Information becomes distributed among many different databases. One virtual repository defines (passive) consistent conversion mappings to multiple databases.
- *Multi-database:* Databases have many users; passive mappings don't suffice; active agents mediate interactions. *Layered hierarchy* with client–server interaction.

In this evolution, technological progress and expanding demand drive progress. Larger memories and faster processing enable access to an ever-wider assortment of data resources in a heterogeneous, distributed world.

Our ability to exploit this remains limited by volume, complexity of mappings, the need to handle data discrepancies, and the need for sophisticated interpretation of requests for services and of available data.

INTEGRATION IN SOFTWARE DEVELOPMENT ENVIRONMENTS

Software development has relied on software tools for almost as long as data processing has relied on online databases. Initially these tools only supported the translation from source code to object code; they included compilers, linkers, and libraries. As time passed, many steps in the software development process became sufficiently routine to be partially or wholly automated, and tools now support analysis, configuration control, debugging, testing, and documentation as well. As with databases, the individual tools grew up independently. Although the integration problem has been recognized for nearly two decades (University of Toronto, 1974), individual tools still work well together only in isolated cases.

Batch Sequential

The earliest software development tools were stand-alone programs. Often their output appeared only on paper and perhaps in the form of object code on cards or paper tape. Eventually most of the tools' results were at least in some magnetic—universally readable—form, but the output of each tool was most likely in the wrong format, the wrong units, or the wrong conceptual model for other tools to use. Even today, execution profiles are customarily provided in human-readable form but are not propagated back to the compiler for optimization. Effective sharing of information was thus limited by lack of knowledge about how information was encoded in representations. As a result, manual translation of one tool's output to another tool's input format was common.

As time passed, new tools incorporated prior knowledge of related tools, and the usefulness of shared information became more evident. Scripts grew up to invoke tools in fixed orders. These scripts essentially defined batch sequential architectures.

This remains the most common style of integration for most environments. For example, in Unix both shell scripts and Make follow this paradigm. ASCII text is the universal exchange representation, but the conventions for encoding internal structure in ASCII remain idiosyncratic.

Transition From Batch Sequential to Repository

Our view of the architecture of a system can change in response to improvements in technology. The way we think about compilers illustrates this. In the 1970s, compilation was regarded as a sequential process, and the

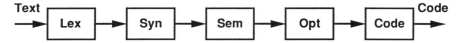

FIG. 7.13.   Traditional compiler model.

organization of a compiler was typically drawn as in Fig. 7.13. Text enters at the left end and is transformed in a variety of ways—to lexical token stream, parse tree, intermediate code—before emerging as machine code on the right. We often refer to this compilation model as a pipeline, even though it was (at least originally) closer to a batch sequential architecture in which each transformation ("pass") ran to completion before the next one started.

   In fact, even the batch sequential version of this model was not completely accurate. Most compilers created a separate symbol table during lexical analysis and used or updated it during subsequent passes. It was not part of the data that flowed from one pass to another but rather existed outside all the passes. So the system structure was more properly drawn as in Fig. 7.14.

   As time passed, compiler technology grew more sophisticated. The algorithms and representations of compilation grew more complex, and increasing attention turned to the intermediate representation of the program during compilation. Improved theoretical understanding, such as attribute grammars, accelerated this trend. The consequence was that by the mid-1980s the intermediate representation (e.g., an attributed parse tree), was the center of attention. It was created early during compilation, manipulated during the remainder, and discarded at the end. The data structure might change in detail, but it remained substantially one growing structure throughout. However, we continued (sometimes to the present) to model the compiler with sequential data flow as in Fig. 7.15.

   In fact, a more appropriate view of this structure would redirect attention from the sequence of passes to the central shared representation. When you declare that the tree is the locus of compilation information and the passes define operations on the tree, it becomes natural to redraw the architecture as in Fig. 7.16. Now the connections between passes denote control flow,

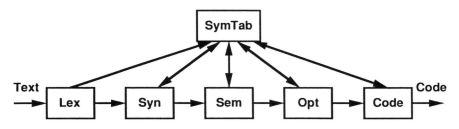

FIG. 7.14.   Traditional compiler model with symbol table.

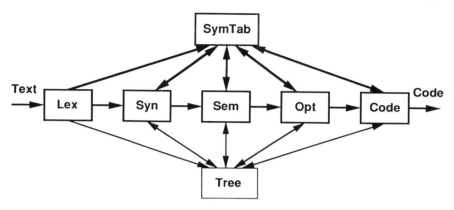

FIG. 7.15. Modern canonical compiler.

which is a more accurate depiction; the rather stronger connections between the passes and the tree/symbol table structure denote data access and manipulation. In this fashion, the architecture has become a repository, and this is indeed a more appropriate way to think about a compiler of this class.

Happily, this new view also accommodates various tools that operate on the internal representation rather than the textual form of a program; these include syntax-directed editors and various analysis tools.

Note that this repository resembles the database repository in some respects and differs in others. Like the database, the information of the compilation is localized in a central data component and operated on by a number of independent computations that interact only through the shared data. However, although the execution order of the operations in

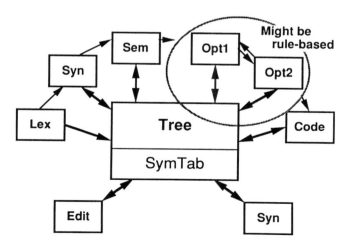

FIG. 7.16. Repository view of modern compiler.

the database was determined by the types of the incoming transactions, the execution order of the compiler is predetermined, except possibly for opportunistic optimization.

Repository

Batch sequential tools and compilers—even when organized as repositories—do not retain information from one use to another. As a result, a body of knowledge about the program is not accumulated. The need for auxiliary information about a program to supplement the various source, intermediate, and object versions became apparent, and tools started retaining information about the prior history of a program.

The repository of the compiler provided a focus for this data collection. Efficiency considerations led to incremental compilers that updated the previous version of the augmented parse tree, and some tools came to use this shared representation as well. Figure 7.17 shows some of the ways that tools could interact with a shared repository.

- *Tight coupling:* Share detailed knowledge of the common, but proprietary, representation among the tools of a single vendor.
- *Open representation:* Publish the representation so that tools can be developed by many sources. Often these tools can manipulate the data, but they are in a poor position to change the representation for their own needs.
- *Conversion boxes:* Provide filters that import or export the data in foreign representations. The tools usually lose the benefits of incremental use of the repository.

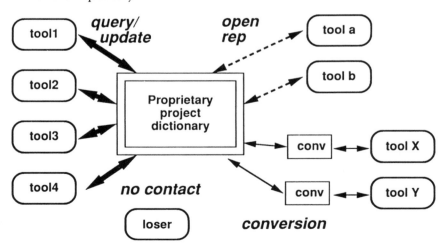

FIG. 7.17. Software tools with shared representation.

- *No contact:* Prevent a tool from using the repository, either explicitly, through excess complexity, or through frequent changes.

These alternatives have different functional, efficiency, and market implications.

Hierarchical Layers

Current work on integration emphasizes interoperability of tools, especially in distributed systems. Figure 7.18 (Chen & Norman, 1992, p. 19) shows one approach, the NIST/ECMA reference model. It resembles in some ways the layered architecture with mediators for databases, but it is more elaborate because it attempts to integrate communications and user interfaces as well as representation. It also embeds knowledge of software development processes, such as the order in which tools must be used and what situations call for certain responses.

Note, however, that whereas this model provides for integration of data, it provides communication and user interface services directly. That is, this model allows for integration of multiple representations but fixes the models for user interfaces and communication.

In one variation on the integrated-environment theme, the integration system defined a set of "events" (e.g., "module foo.c recompiled") and

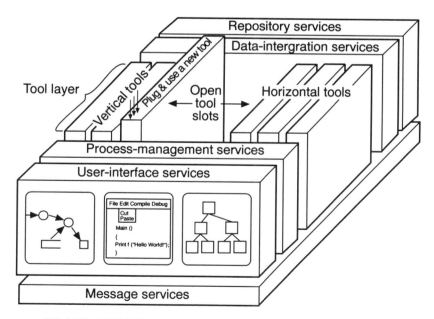

FIG. 7.18. NIST/ECMA reference model for environment integration. From Chen and Norman (1992). Copyright © 1992 by IEEE. Reprinted by permission.

provides support for tools to announce or to receive notice of the occurrence of events. This provides a means of communicating the need for action, but it does not solve the central problem of sharing information.

Evolution of Shared Information Systems in Software Development Environments

Software development has different requirements from database processing. As compared to databases, software development involves more different types of data, fewer instances of each distinct type, and slower query rates. The units of information are larger, more complex, and less discrete than in traditional databases. The lifetime of software development information, however, is not (or at least should not be) shorter than database lifetimes.

Despite the differences in application area and characteristics of the supporting data, the essential problem of collecting, storing, and retrieving shared data about an ongoing process is common to the two areas. It is therefore not surprising to find comparable evolutionary stages in their architectures.

Here the forces for evolution were:

- The advent of on-line computing, which drove the shift from batch to interactive processing for many functions.
- The concern for efficiency, which is driving a reduction in the granularity of operations, shifting from complete processing of systems to processing of modules to incremental development.
- The need for management control over the entire software development process, which is driving coverage to increase from compilation to the full life cycle.

Integration in this area is still incomplete. Data conversions are passive, and the ordering of operations remains relatively rigid. The integration systems can exploit only relatively coarse system information, such as file and date. Software development environments are under pressure to add capabilities for handling complex dependencies and selecting which tools to use. Steps toward more sophistication show up in the incorporation of metamodels to describe sharing, distribution, data merging, and security policies. The process-management services of the NIST/ECMA model are not yet well developed, and they will initially concentrate on project-level support. But integration across all kinds of information and throughout the life cycle is on the agenda, and intelligent assistance is often mentioned on the wish list.

INTEGRATION IN BUILDING DESIGN

The previous two examples come from the information technology fields. For the third example we turn to an application area, the building construction industry. This industry requires a diverse variety of expertise. Distinct responsibilities correspond to matching sets of specialized functions. Indeed, distinct subindustries support these specialties. A project generally involves a number of independent, geographically dispersed companies. The diversity of expertise and dispersion of the industry inhibit communication and limit the scope of responsibilities. Each new project creates a new coalition, so there is little accumulated shared experience and no special advantage for pairwise compatibility between companies. However, the subtasks interact in complex, sometimes nonobvious ways, and coordination among specialties (global process expertise) is itself a specialty (Terk, 1992).

In this setting it was natural for computing to evolve bottom-up. Building designers have exploited computing for many years for tasks ranging from accounting to computer-aided design. We are concerned here with the software that performs analysis for various stages of the design activity. The 1960s and 1970s saw a number of algorithmic systems directed at aiding in the performance of individual phases of the facility development. However, a large number of tasks in facility development depend on judgment, experience, and rules of thumb accumulated by experts in the domain. Such tasks cannot be performed efficiently in an algorithmic manner (Terk, 1992).

The early stages of development, involving stand-alone programs and batch-sequential compositions, are sufficiently similar to the two previous examples that it is not illuminating to review them. The first steps toward integration focused on support-supervisory systems, which provided basic services such as data management and information flow control to individual independent applications, much as software development environments did. The story picks up from the point of these early integration efforts.

Integrated environments for building design are frameworks for controlling a collection of stand-alone applications that solve part of the building design problem (Terk, 1992). They must be:

- Efficient in managing problem-solving and information exchange.
- Flexible in dealing with changes to tools.
- Graceful in reacting to changes in information and problem solving strategies.

These requirements derive from the lack of standardized problem-solving procedures; they reflect the separation into specialties and the geographical distribution of the facility development process.

Repository

Selection of tools and composition of individual results requires judgment, experience, and rules of thumb. Because of coupling between subproblems it is not algorithmic, so integrated systems require a planning function. The goal of an integrated environment is integration of data, design decisions, and knowledge. Two approaches emerged: the closely coupled Master Builder, or monolithic system, and the design environment with cooperating tools. These early efforts at integration added elementary data management and information flow control to a tool set.

The common responsibilities of a system for distributed problem solving are:

- Problem partitioning (divide into tasks for individual agents).
- Task distribution (assign tasks to agents for best performance).
- Agent control (strategy that assures tasks are performed in organized fashion).
- Agent communication (exchange of information essential when subtasks interact or conflict).

The construction community operates on divide-and-conquer problem solving with interactions among the subproblems. This is naturally a distributed approach; teams of independent subcontractors map naturally to distributed problem-solving systems with coarse-grained cooperation among specialized agents. However, the nature of the industry—its need for specialization—forces the separation into subproblems; the problems are not inherently decomposable, and the subproblems are often interdependent. This raises the control component to a position of special significance.

Terk (1992) surveyed and classified many of the integrated building design environments that were developed in the 1980s. Here's what he found:

- Data: mostly repositories: shared common representation with conversions to private representations of the tools.
- Communication: mostly shared data, some messaging.
- Tools: split between closed (tools specifically built for this system) and open (external tools can be integrated).
- Control: mostly single-level hierarchy; tools at bottom; coordination at top.
- Planning: mostly fixed partitioning of kind and processing order; scripts sometimes permit limited flexibility.

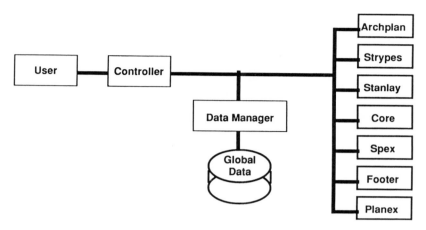

FIG. 7.19. Integrated building design environment. From Newell and Steier (1991). Reprinted by permission.

So the typical system was a repository with a sophisticated control and planning component. A fairly typical such system, IBDE (Fenves, Hendrickson, Maher, Flemming, & Schmitt, 1990), appears in Fig. 7.19. Although the depiction is not typical, the distinguished position of the global data shows clearly the repository character. The tools that populate this IBDE are:

- ARCHPLAN develops architectural plan from site, budget, geometric constraints.
- CORE lays out building service core (elevators, stairs, etc.).
- STRYPES configures the structural system (e.g., suspension, rigid frame, etc.).
- STANLAY performs preliminary structural design and approximate analysis of the structural system.
- SPEX performs preliminary design of structural components.
- FOOTER designs the foundation.
- CONSTRUCTION PLANEX generates construction schedule and estimates cost.

Intelligent Control

As integration and automation proceed, the complexity of planning and control grows to be a significant problem. Indeed, as this component grows more complex, its structure starts to dominate the repository structure of the data. The difficulty of reducing the planning to pure algorithmic form makes this application a candidate for intelligent control.

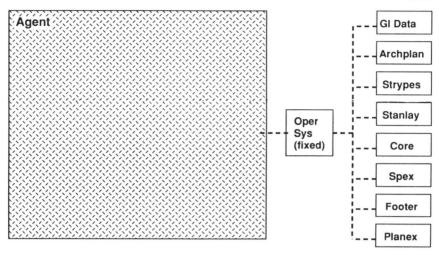

FIG. 7.20. High-level architecture for intelligent IBDE.

The Engineering Design Research Center at Carnegie Mellon University is exploring the development of intelligent agents that can learn to control external software systems, or systems intended for use with interactive human intervention. Integrated building design is one of the areas they have explored. Figure 7.21 (Newell & Steier, 1991) shows their design for an intelligent extension of the original IBDE system, Soar/IBDE. That figure is easier to understand in two stages, so Fig. 7.20 shows the relation of the intelligent agent to the external software systems before Fig. 7.21 adds the internal structure of the intelligent agent. Figure 7.20 is clearly derived from Fig. 7.19, with the global data moved to the status of just another external software system. The emphasis in Soar/IBDE was control of the interaction with the individual agents of IBDE.

From the standpoint of the designer's general position on intelligent control this organization seems reasonable, as the agent is portrayed as interacting with whatever software is provided. However, the global data play a special role in this system. Each of the seven other components must interact with the global data (or else it makes no sense to retain the global data). Also, the intelligent agent may also find that the character of interaction with the global data is special, because it was designed to serve as a repository, not to interact with humans. Future enhancements of this system will probably need to address the interactions among components as well as the components themselves.

Figure 7.21 adds the fine structure of the intelligent agent. The agent has six major components. It must be able to identify and formulate subtasks for the set of external software systems and express them in the input formats of those systems. It must receive the output and interpret it in terms of a

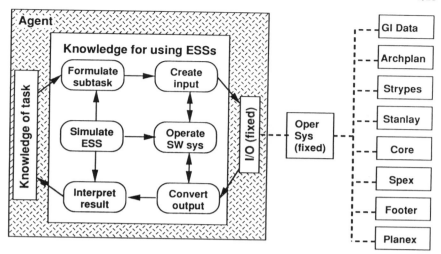

FIG. 7.21. Detailed architecture for Soar/IBDE. From Newell and Steier (1991). Reprinted by permission.

global overview of the problem. It must be able to understand the actions of the components as they work toward solution of the problem, in terms of both general knowledge of the task and specific knowledge of the capabilities of the set of external software systems.

The most significant aspect of this design is that the seven external software systems are interactive. This means that their input and output are incremental, so a component that needs to understand their operation must retain and update a history of the interaction. The task becomes vastly more complex when pointer input and graphical output are included, although this is not the case in this case.

Evolution of Shared Information Systems in Building Design

Integration in this area is less mature than in databases and software development environments. Nevertheless, the early stages of integrated building or facility environments resemble the early stages of the first two examples. The evolutionary shift to layered hierarchies seems to come when many users must select from a diverse set of tools and they need extra system structure to coordinate the effort of selecting and managing a useful subset. These systems have not reached this stage of development yet, so we don't yet have information on how that will emerge.

In this case, however, the complexity of the task makes it a prime candidate for intelligent control. This opens the question of whether intelligent control could be of assistance in the other two examples, and if so what form it will take. The single-agent model developed for Soar/IBDE

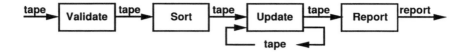

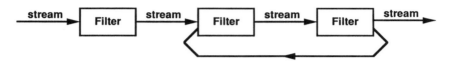

FIG. 7.22. Comparison of (top) batch sequential and (bottom) pipe/filter architectures.

is one possibility, but the enrichment of database mediators to make them capable of independent intelligent action (like knowbots) is clearly another.

ARCHITECTURAL STRUCTURES FOR SHARED INFORMATION SYSTEMS

While examining examples of software integration, we have seen a variety of general architectural patterns, or idioms for software systems. In this section we reexamine the data flow and repository idioms to see the variety that can occur within a single idiom.

Current software tools do not distinguish among different kinds of components at this level. These tools treat all modules equally, and they mostly assume that modules interact only via procedure calls and perhaps shared variables. By providing only a single model of component, they tend to blind designers to useful distinctions among modules. Moreover, by supporting only a fixed pair of low-level mechanisms for module interaction, they tend to blind designers to the rich classes of high-level interactions among components. These tools certainly provide little support for documenting design intentions in such a way that they become visible in the resulting software artifacts.

By making the richness of these structures explicit, we focus the attention of designers on the need for coherence and consistency of the system's design. Incorporating this information explicitly in a system design should provide a record that simplifies subsequent changes and increases the likelihood that later modifications will not compromise the integrity of the design. The architectural descriptions focus on design issues such as the gross structure of the system, the kinds of parts from which it is composed, and the kinds of interactions that take place.

The use of well-known patterns leads to a kind of reuse of design templates. These templates capture intuitions that are a common part of our folklore: it is now common practice to draw box-and-line diagrams that depict the architecture of a system, but no uniform meaning is yet associated with these diagrams. Many anecdotes suggest that simply providing some vocabulary to describe parts and patterns is a good first step.

By way of recapitulation, we now examine variations on two of the architectural forms that appear earlier: data flow and repositories.

Variations on Data Flow Architectures

The data flow architecture that repeatedly occurs in the evolution of shared information systems is the batch sequential pattern. However, the most familiar example of this genre is probably the Unix pipe-and-filter system. The similarity of these architectures is apparent in the diagrams used for systems of the respective classes, as indicated in Fig. 7.22. Both decompose a task into a (fixed) sequence of computations. They interact only through the data passed from one to another and share no other information. They assume that the components read and write the data as a whole—that is, the input or output contains one complete instance of the result in some standard order. There are differences, though. Batch sequential systems are

- Very coarse-grained.
- Unable to do feedback in anything resembling real time.
- Unable to exploit concurrency.
- Unlikely to proceed at an interactive pace.

On the other hand, pipe-and-filter systems are

- Fine-grained, beginning to compute as soon as they consume a few input tokens.
- Able to start producing output right away (processing is localized in the input stream).
- Able to perform feedback (though most shells can't express it).
- Often interactive.

Variations on Repositories

The other architectural pattern that figured prominently in our examples was the repository. Repositories in general are characterized by a central shared data store coupled tightly to a number of independent computations, each with its own expertise. The independent computations interact only through the shared data, and they do not retain any significant amount of private state. The variations differ chiefly in the control apparatus that controls the order in which the computations are invoked, in the access mechanisms that allow the computations access to the data, and in the granularity of the operations.

Figures 7.7 and 7.8 show a database system. Here the control is driven by the types of transactions in the input stream, the access mechanism is usually supported by a specialized programming language, and the granularity is that of a database transaction.

Figure 7.16 shows a programming-language compiler. Here control is fixed (compilation proceeds in the same order each time), the access mechanism may be full conversion of the shared data structure into an in-memory representation or direct access (when components are compiled into the same address space), and the granularity is that of a single pass of a compiler.

Figure 7.17 shows a repository that supports independent tools. Control may be determined by direct request of users, or it may in some cases be handled by an event mechanism also shared by the tools. Various access methods are available, and the granularity is that of the tool set.

One prominent repository has not appeared here; it is mentioned now for completeness—to extend the comparison of repositories. This is the blackboard architecture, most frequently used for signal-processing applications in artificial intelligence (Nii, 1986) and depicted in Fig. 7.23. Here the independent computations are various knowledge sources that can contribute to solving the problem—for example, syntactic–semantic connection, phoneme recognition, word candidate generation, and signal segmentation for speech understanding. The blackboard is a highly structured representation especially designed for the representations pertinent to the application. Control is completely opportunistic, driven by the current state of the data on the blackboard. The abstract model for access is direct visibility, as of many human experts watching each other solve a problem

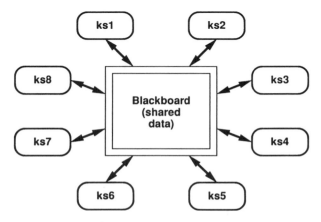

FIG. 7.23. Blackboard architecture.

at a real blackboard (understandably, implementations support this abstraction with more feasible mechanisms). The granularity is quite fine, at the level of interpreting a signal segment as a phoneme.

CONCLUSIONS

Three tasks arising in different communities deal with collecting, manipulating, and preserving shared information. In each case, changing technologies and requirements drove changes in the architectural form commonly used for the systems. We can identify that sequence as a common evolutionary pattern for shared information systems:

- Isolated applications without interaction.
- Batch sequential processing.
- Repositories for integration via shared data.
- Layered hierarchies for dynamic integration across distributed systems.

Because problems remain and new technology continues to emerge, this pattern may grow in the future, for example, to add active control by intelligent agents.

These examples show one case in which a common problem structure appears in several quite different application areas. This suggests that attempts to exploit "domain knowledge" in software design should characterize domains by their computational requirements (e.g., shared information systems) as well as by industry (e.g., data processing, software development, or facility design). In addition, the examples show that within a single domain, differences among requirements or operational settings may change the preferred architecture. Taken together, this suggests that the notion of a single domain-specific architecture serving a segment of an industry may not fully exploit our growing architectural capabilities.

The models, notations, and tools for specifying software architectures remain informal. Although even informal models are useful, research in several areas is required to make these more precise and robust:

- Complete a taxonomy of common architectural patterns.
- Define and implement better abstractions for the interactions among components; at present system descriptions are cast in terms of procedure calls no matter what the abstractions may be.
- Establish ways to encapsulate stand-alone systems and express the resulting interfaces so they can be used as subsystems; linguistically this is a closure problem.

- Continue the exploration of independent agents for integration, especially in dynamically changing distributed systems.

ACKNOWLEDGMENTS

This chapter was written in honor of Allen Newell. Although we never collaborated directly, our professional interests touched from time to time, and these encounters often shaped the subsequent path of my research. This chapter was so shaped at both ends: we discussed design levels many years ago, and I became acquainted with Soar/IBDE only in 1992. I also owe thanks to David Steier for discussions about Soar/IBDE and to David Garlan for ongoing collaboration in software architectures.

The work reported here was supported by the Carnegie Mellon University School of Computer Science and Software Engineering Institute (which is sponsored by the U.S. Department of Defense), by the a grant from Siemens Corporate Research, and by the Department of Defense Advanced Research Project Agency under grant MDA972-92-J-1002. The views and conclusions are those of the author.

REFERENCES

Ahmed, R., De Smedt, P. Du, W., Kent, W., Ketabchi, M. A., Litwin, W. A., Rafii, A., & Shan, M. C. (1991). The Pegasus heterogeneous multidatabase system. *IEEE Computer, 24*(12), 19–27.

Bell, C. G., & Newell, A. (1971). *Computer structures: Readings and examples.* New York: McGraw-Hill.

Best, L. J. (1990). *Application architecture: Modern large-scale information processing.* New York: Wiley.

Chen, M., & Norman, R. J. (1992). A framework for integrated CASE. *IEEE Software, 9*(2), 18–22.

Computer Science and Telecommunications Board. (1992). *Keeping the US computer industry competitive: Systems integration.* Washington, DC: National Academy Press.

Fenves, S. J., Hendrickson, C., Maher, M. L., Flemming, U., & Schmitt, G. (1990). An integrated software environment for building design and construction. *Computer-Aided Design, 22*(1), 27–36.

Garlan, D., & Shaw, M. (1993). An introduction to software architecture. In V. Ambriola & G. Tortora (Eds.), *Advances in software engineering and knowledge engineering* (Vol. 2, pp. 1–39). Chicago: World.

Hovaness, H. (1992). Price war: There's fierce combat ahead over the cost of client-server databases. *Corporate Computing, 1*(6), 45–46.

Kim, W., & Seo, J. (1991). Classifying schematic and data heterogeneity in multidatabase systems. *IEEE Computer, 24*(12), 12–18.

Newell, A. (1982). The knowledge level. *Artificial Intelligence, 18*(1), 87–127.

Newell, A. (1990). *Unified theories of cognition.* Harvard University Press.

Newell, A., & Steier, D. (1991). *Intelligent control of external software systems* (Tech. Rep. No. 5-55-91). Pittsburgh: Carnegie Mellon University, Engineering Design Research Center. (To appear in *AI in Engineering*)

Nii, H. P. (1986). Blackboard systems. *AI Magazine, 7*(3 & 4), 38–53, 82–107.

Nilsson, E. G., Nordhagen, E. K., & Oftedal, G. (1990). Aspects of systems integration. *Systems Integration '90, Proc. First International Conference on Systems Integration* (pp. 434–443).

Terk, M. (1992). *A problem-centered approach to creating design environments for facility development.* Unpublished doctoral dissertation, Civil Engineering Department, Carnegie Mellon University, Pittsburgh.

University of Toronto. (1974, June). *Proceedings of Workshop on the Attainment of Reliable Software.* Toronto, Canada.

Wiederhold, G. (1992). Mediators in the architecture of future information systems. *IEEE Computer, 25*(3), 38–48.

DISCUSSION

Mediating Matters:
Response to Shaw

David M. Steier
Price Waterhouse Technology Centre

Software architectures, as described in Mary Shaw's chapter, are structures that allow collections of software systems to invoke and understand each other. By definition, architectural-level control and communication mechanisms do not change over the life of the system. Yet Chapter 7 also notes that heterogeneity and evolution of software systems combine to work against any fixed mechanisms, and ultimately the integrating structure will have to adapt to accommodate the systems being integrated. Adaptation is necessary because some particular bit of knowledge, whether about the component systems or about the context of use of the total system, is just not available when the integrating structure is being created. This commentary explores the possibility that an artificial intelligent agent can mediate between the system users and the system components by searching for that missing knowledge at the time of system integration (which may even be at the time of running the components). Wiederhold used the term *mediation* to describe agents that aid in the use of heterogeneous databases, but the concept generalizes far beyond databases. It seems likely that intelligent mediators for software might enter routine use in the near future. Soar, with its capabilities for knowledge acquisition and integration, has been used as the basis for several implemented prototypes of intelligent mediators, and we briefly mention three here: Soar/IBDE, which uses several software systems to perform different aspects of a task; MDB-Soar, which uses multiple systems in the same functional way as needed to perform a task; and Soar/Mathematica, which uses a single system for a variety of functions within a task.

Given Allen Newell's characteristic foresight, it would not have surprised me if he had been the first to suggest incorporating artificial intelligence into software integration technology. But it turns out that the reason he and I began investigating this area with Soar was not some grand research question of software engineering. Rather, we were responding to a seemingly mundane complaint: We observed that it was almost never trivial to get Soar to interact with a given external software system (ESS), whether a database or a chemical process simulator. Often, the researcher settled for simulating the external software's functionality to avoid having to do the necessary systems integration. This tactic only replaced one problem with another, because extra effort was then needed to create a faithful simulation. Furthermore, the resulting Soar system was often much more inefficient than it could have been, had the required algorithmic computation just been delegated to some preexisting, preoptimized software module.

As we studied the set of instances of Soar-ESS interaction available to us, we considered how Soar itself might assist in systems integration. We soon found that what initially seemed like an internal technical problem could be viewed a research area in its own right. The focus of this area is on what general capabilities are necessary for intelligent agents to be able use external software to accomplish tasks. We enlisted the aid of several others at CMU who also found themselves building Soar systems that used ESSs, and wrote an initial report that identified a set of general agent-ESS capabilities (Newell & Steier, 1993). Figure 7.21 of Mary Shaw's chapter, taken from that report, illustrated how these capabilities interact within an intelligent mediating agent. The agent is usually invoked by a user who is trying to perform some task, although our terminology applies equally well to autonomous agents. From the total task being performed, the agent first extracts a subtask to be performed by the external system. The agent then converts the subtask, which has been formulated in its own internal representation, into input to the external systems. The agent must then invoke the external systems in the context of a heterogeneous software system environment (operating system, etc.) and monitor the execution(s) to ensure completion and record the results. The returned results must then be converted from the external representation into the internal task representation of the agent. The agent then interprets the desired information in service of the original task, which is most important if the results are not in accordance with expectations and force reconsideration of the goals. As the agent acquires experience with the external systems, the agent begins to build up an internal model of what those external systems will do under certain circumstances. Such a simulation capability can be used to detect abnormal operating conditions and to decide what subtasks can be performed.

Our research strategy in this area has been to flesh out these capabilities by creating a variety of Soar system that routinely use ESSs. Consider the Soar/IBDE example mentioned in Shaw's chapter. In its original form, IBDE consisted of seven independently developed systems, each of which specialized in some aspect of building design, ranging from architectural layout to construction scheduling, together with infrastructure that allowed the systems to communicate. IBDE allowed a user to produce a complete design by invoking the systems in the correct sequence. Soar/IBDE was built to find out if an intelligent agent who didn't know the correct sequence could learn it from experimentation. Soar/IBDE used several methods to learn this knowledge, including trial and error, means-ends analysis, and asking a user for guidance if it couldn't analyze problems on its own. Soar/IBDE therefore had to select tools, invoke them, and interpret the results, and therefore its knowledge, in terms of the generic capabilities of Fig. 1, was concentrated on formulating subtasks, operating the software systems, and interpreting results. Unfortunately, the systems integration problems involved in actually getting the software to work together forced us to work with simulated building design tools (and forced an early end to the project), but the possibility of using Soar as an intelligent planner in a heterogeneous software environment was successfully demonstrated.

An earlier part of Shaw's chapter discussed multi-database systems for integrating heterogeneous stores of data. We have also built a system, MDB-Soar, that mediates between a user and a multi-database (this work was performed by Xiaoping Li as a graduate student in the Heinz School of Public Policy and Management at CMU while advised by Professor R.

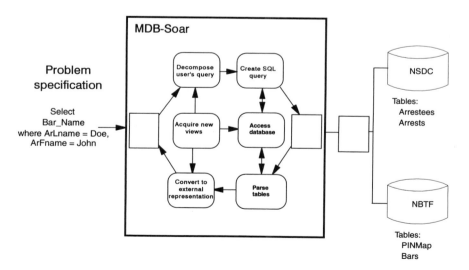

FIG. 1. MDB-Soar.

Krishnan and me). In its present form, MDB-Soar does not solve all the problems of integrating multiple databases, especially not conflicts in terms of naming, structure, and formats. What is does solve is the problem of using multiple databases to answer a query when there is no single database containing all of the relevant attributes. In this situation, MDB-Soar decomposes the query so that it can be answered efficiently by subqueries on individual databases. It uses a variant of an algorithm for finding Steiner trees to find the minimum set of tables needed to link the target attributes, and then uses knowledge of the query language SQL to generate the appropriate set of queries. One can cast the capabilities of MDB-Soar in the same form of Fig. 7.21. Figure 1 shows a situation in which a police officer wanted to know which bar John Doe had been arrested at. A mediator could decompose the query over two databases, one containing the arrest records and the other on nuisance bars. Of the six generic capabilities mentioned in Fig. 7.21, MDB-Soar supports formulate-subtask (to a limited extent), create-input, operate-software-system (although without handling errors), convert-output, and interpret-result (in a trivial way; here, the formulation of the task makes the result interpretation straightforward). Also, MDB-Soar learns as it queries the database, thus exercising a form of the simulate-ESS capability to acquire new views; it cannot, however, use this capability to influence future querying, beyond speeding up the process.

A final example focuses on a single ESS, Mathematica, as a prototypical computer algebra system, and explores the diverse set of abilities needed to use it effectively. A motivating example is a situation in which an engineer (which may be human or artificial) needs to perform a sensitivity analysis to find the dependency of system behavior with respect to some parameter, and decides to use Mathematica to perform the necessary symbolic computations. If the engineer is expert in the use of Mathematica, performance of the calculations may be trivial; however, a novice will hardly know where to start. The diverse kinds of knowledge exploited by the expert include whether the computation can be performed at all by Mathematica; how compound calculations can be split into atomic ones that can be computed directly; what Mathematica functions should be used and what arguments should be given to those functions; what expectations to set up on the results; how to interpret output as mathematical objects; how to reformulate a command in case of errors; and how to reuse previously computed results. In terms of the generic ESS capabilities then, formulate-task plans the computation, create-input converts the atomic computations in the plan into Mathematica syntax, convert-output parses the linear character sequence returned by Mathematica into mathematical objects, which interpret-result then interprets into the mathematical information necessary to complete the task. Dhiraj Pathak, a graduate student in the Robotics program at CMU, has built a mediator called Soar/Mathematica that demonstrates these capabilities in a variety of instances (Pathak & Steier, 1992).

There is clearly much work left to be done before these prototypes begin to exhibit human-scale power and flexibility in integration. But our work to date has convinced us that the use of intelligent architectures as foundations for building mediators deserves further consideration in the quest to make life easier for software users and integrators.

REFERENCES

Newell, A., & Steier, D. (1993). Intelligent control of external software systems (Tech. Rep. No. 5-55-91). *Artificial Intelligence in Engineering, 8*, 3–21.

Pathak, D. K., & Steier, D. M. (1992). *Automated performance of task-level symbolic computations in engineering design* (Tech. Rep. No. CMU-EDRC-05-61-92). Pittsburgh: Engineering Design Research Center, Carnegie Mellon University.

Chapter 8

The Human, the Computer, the Task, and Their Interaction— Analytic Models and Use-Centered Design

Stuart K. Card
Xerox Palo Alto Research Center

It is, perhaps, not well known that Allen Newell began his career with studies of human–computer interaction. Today the topic of the studies would be called "Computer Support for Cooperative Work." Typically for Newell, these studies were on a grand scale. Done at RAND and the Systems Development Corporation, the studies involved many people simultaneously engaged in cooperative work over computer links. One practical result was the SAGE air defense system. Another result was his realization with Herbert Simon that the computer could be used, rather in the manner of differential equations in physics, to reason analytically from modeled local behavior to global consequences. Newell's main interest became the technical nature of mind. His main method became applying the new insights emerging from computer science about the nature of information processing, the nature of computation, and the nature of architecture to that problem. But he started from human–computer interaction.

In later years, Newell returned to work on human–computer interaction with two main projects. On the system-building side, the ZOG system (Robertson, Newell, & Ramakrishna, 1981) investigated what could be done with a large, very fast, hypertext-linked set of frames. On the analytical side, the Applied Information Processing Psychology project at Xerox, and its later offshoots at Carnegie Mellon University (CMU), investigated whether the information-processing psychological theory that began at RAND could be developed into forms that supported the engineering of interactive human–computer systems.

So, although a bit of a sideline for Newell, studies of human–computer interaction served for him both as an inspiring task domain and as an arena to test the adequacy of theory. Human–computer interaction was also part of his view of computer science itself. He had a vision of using the analysis of human behavior to support design. In this chapter, I consider that idea—the use of analytical theories of behavior to assist in the design of computer systems. Rather than engage in the usual systematic review of the literature, I follow another method and start, as befits the occasion, from collaborative work with Newell in pursuit of this idea. Then I stand back and give a broad-brush characterization of work in human–computer interaction as the field has actually emerged today. I use this characterization to give a revised proposal for how analytical theory fits into the concern of human–computer interaction. Finally, I show how, at least in limited ways, we have been able to fulfill parts of it.

MODEL-ASSISTED DESIGN

Newell's basic premise was that computer science ought to be more symmetric relative to the human and the machine. After all, many topics in computer science, such as programming languages or operating systems, imply systems that work with people on the one side and machines on the other. On the people side, one might think there would be studies of the composability, error characteristics, and understandability of programming languages. On the machine side, there would be studies of techniques for parsing and compiling, distributed computing, theory of computation, and the like. In fact, computer science had been very asymmetrical, with almost all effort going into the machine side. Newell's belief was that more work was due on the human side.

An opportunity to act on this belief came in 1970, when Xerox opened a research laboratory in Palo Alto and Newell became one of its early consultants. In 1971, he proposed forming an applied psychological research unit as part of the laboratory (Newell, 1971). His basic goal for this unit was the use of information-processing psychology for real tasks. His argument was that the human side of computer science involved closed symbolic tasks, ones close enough to then-existing theory as to hold promise: programming, coding, debugging, and system design. These were tasks that would have some payoff if pursued successfully.

By 1974, Newell had managed to get such a unit going with Tom Moran and me as the workers. But the goals, responding to perceived Xerox needs, were transformed. Instead of concentrating on computer science tasks themselves, such as programming, the emphasis was to be on the use of computers and their interfaces to end users. The goal was to work toward the sort of supporting science that was routine in engineering, but unusual in psychology. And that involved analyzing a situation to make predictions about its characteristics as an aid to design. Specifically, the goals were (1) a theory of the user in the context of office work; (2) calculation of behavioral parameters from analysis of the situation (task analysis, approximation, and calculation); (3) contributions across the spectrum (from evaluation to generation of new design concepts); and (4) integration into design practice (Card, Moran, & Newell, 1977).

Although evaluation was important, the real payoff was clearly in design. Design is where the action is. The goal was to get some theory that could actually be used in design practice. In style, the aim might be described as a sort of civil engineering of the user, that is, methods that combine theory when possible with the pragmatics and data of the situation, which is often not practically knowable in precise detail.

The Model Human Processor

The main results of this effort were reported in a book, *The Psychology of Human–Computer Interaction* (Card, Moran, & Newell, 1983). This book had two main pieces of theory. One of these, the Model Human Processor, was an attempt to summarize the psychology of the day in a way that would allow simple calculations. Part of the impetus was the calculations Herb Simon used to make at Carnegie Mellon psychology department colloquia, in which he would try (to the speaker's consternation and the graduate students' amusement) to compute the speaker's results before the speaker could present them. We wanted to be able to do at least as well as Simon did.

The technique was to summarize the mind in terms of processors, memories, and switches (as Siewiorek, Bell, & Newell, 1981, had done for complex computer systems in their book *Computing Structures*). In the Model Human Processor, the mind is modeled as if there were three processors and four memories. The three parallel processors are the cognitive processor, a perceptual processor (really, a set of processors for each sensation), and a motor processor. Each of these has a characteristic cycle time τ derived from experiments in the psychological literature. Likewise, four memories are modeled: acoustic and iconic image stores, working memory, and long-term memory. Each of these memories is characterized by a number of parameters: a half-life decay constant δ, a capacity μ, and a class of representations κ. In addition, there are a few other useful parameters, such as saccadic eye movement time. All the parameters are summarized in Fig. 8.1. The idea was to model in this approximate way enough of the factors that govern behavior that a wide variety of simple predictions could be computed off the model.

In the psychological literature, there are both remarkable agreement on approximate values of some of these parameters and tenacious variation

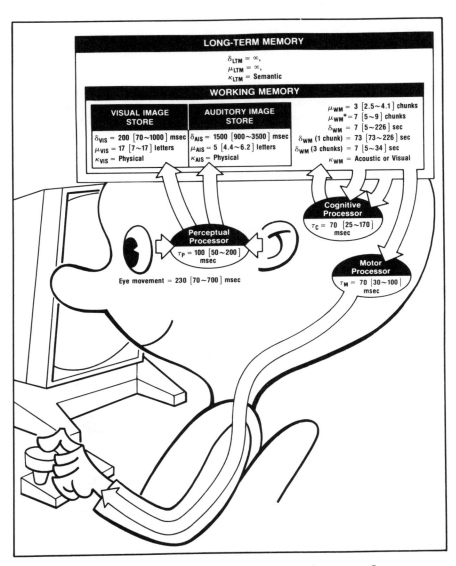

FIG. 8.1. The Model Human Processor—memories and processors. Sensory information flows into Working Memory through the Perceptual Processor. Working Memory consists of activated chunks in Long-Term Memory. The basic principle of operation of the Model Human Processor is the Recognize–Act Cycle. The Motor Processor is set in motion through activation of chunks in Working Memory. From Card, Moran, and Newell (1983, p. 26). Reprinted by permission.

due to different definitions, measurement techniques, subjects, and interactions. To handle both the constancy and the variation, each parameter of the Model Human Processor is characterized by a minimum credible value, a maximum credible value, and a typical value. For many useful purposes, the fact that there is some disagreement about one of these parameters does not matter because a particular conclusion is unaffected by which value within the credible range is used for the parameter. For example, no matter what cycle time is chosen for the motor processor, we could still conclude that someone could not type at 600 words/min, because the fingers just could not be moved that fast. (Of course, such a thing might be conceivable if a way could be invented that did not demand the usual number of typing movements.)

The constants of Fig. 8.1 are supplemented by a set of "Principles of Operation," empirical relations from the literature. These are given in Table 8.1.

From the Model Human Processor a number of simple predictions related to design tasks can be calculated. For example:

Problem: How fast can a user repetitively push with one finger a key on the typewriter keyboard? How fast can he push two keys using alternate hands?

Solution: In the case of a repeated keystroke, the finger must first be cocked back, then brought forward. Each half of the stroke, according to the Model Human Processor, will take $\tau_M = 70$ ms and the whole will take $\tau_M + \tau_M = 140$ ms. In the case of keystrokes between alternate hands, it should be possible for one hand to stroke in parallel while the other is cocking if the strokes are coordinated, so in these cases strokes could follow each other within 70 ms.

Although simple, this example contains the essence of what we wished to achieve. There is a design subproblem—determining an upper bound on typing speed. There is a theory—the Model Human Processor—that can be deployed in the service of getting insight. There is often an artifact that is either being evaluated or designed.

In fact, something close to this very calculation was employed in an actual engineering investment decision in Xerox. An engineer claimed to have invented a technique through which typewriters could be designed that allowed a user to type 600 words/min and wanted money to fund a project. A more elaborate variant of the preceding calculation showed that this could not possibly be the case, even under generous assumptions. Without the calculation, funding might have been approved, eventually wasting hundreds of thousands of dollars. With the model, it took about an hour to reject, with comfort, this intuitively appealing, but ultimately hopeless, idea.

TABLE 8.1

Model Human Processor Principles of Operation

P0. *Recognize–act cycle of the cognitive processor.* On each cycle of the cognitive processor, the contents of working memory initiate actions associatively linked to them in long-term memory; these actions in turn modify the contents of working memory.

P1. *Variable perceptual processor rate principle.* The perceptual processor cycle time τ_P varies inversely with stimulus intensity.

P2. *Encoding specificity principle.* Specific encoding operations performed on what is perceived determine what is stored, and what is stored determines what retrieval cues are effective in providing access to what is stored.

P3. *Discrimination principle.* The difficulty of memory retrieval is determined by the candidates that exist in the memory, relative to the retrieval clues.

P4. *Variable cognitive processor rate principle.* The cognitive processor cycle time τ_C is shorter when greater effort is induced by increased task demands or information loads; it also diminishes with practice.

P5. *Fitts' law.* The time T_{pos} to move the hand to a target of size W which lies a distance D away is given by:
$$T_{pos} = I_M \log_2(D/W + 0.5) \text{ where } I_M = \log_2(D/W + 0.5)$$

P6. *Power law of practice.* The time T_n to perform a task on the nth trial follows a power law:
$$T_n = T_1 N^{-\alpha}, \text{ where } \alpha = 0.4 \ [0.2-0.6]$$

P7. *Uncertainty principle.* Decision time T increases with uncertainty about the judgment of decision to be made:
$$T = I_C H$$
where H is the information-theoretic entropy of the decision and $I_C = 150$ [0–157] ms/bit. For n equally probably alternatives (called Hick's law):
$$H = \log_2(N + 1)$$
For n alternatives with different probabilities p_i of occurrence:
$$H = S_i P_i \log_2(1/p_i + 1)$$

P8. *Rationality principle.* A person acts so as to attain goals through rational action, given the structure of the task and inputs of information and bounded by limitations on that person's knowledge and processing ability:
$$Goals + task + operators + inputs + knowledge + processing\ limits \rightarrow behavior$$

P9. *Problem space principle.* The rational activity in which people engage to solve a problem can be described in terms of (1) a set of states of knowledge, (2) operators for changing one state into another, (3) constraints on applying operators, and (4) control knowledge for deciding which operator to apply next.

A more amusing example of the Model Human Processor comes from one of the principles in Table 8.1, the Principle of Encoding Specificity. This principle states that specific encoding operations performed on what is perceived determine what is stored, and what is stored determines what retrieval cues are effective in providing access to what is stored. Because I was always mislaying Newell's phone number, I encoded it into an example illustrating the fact that more information can be remembered by recoding it into a form that requires fewer chunks:

Binary digits: 010000100001001101100110 1000
Grouped binary digits: 0100-0010-0001-0011-0110-0110-1000
Hexadecimal digits: 4-2-1-3-6-6-8

The example had originally been written in terms of octal digits, but in proof Newell caught the error that 8 is not an octal digit without ever realizing that he was looking at his own phone number, thus providing a perfect example of the Principle of Encoding Specificity.

GOMS

The other group of theories were the GOMS family of models of routine cognitive skill. Many tasks people do with computers are overlearned and in stable environments—text editing, for example. Under these routine cognitive skill conditions, we can do a rational analysis of the things some-one does in terms of Goals, Operations, Methods, and Selection rules (GOMS) among the methods. For example, a simple high-level analysis of an editing task was analyzed as:

GOAL: EDIT-MANUSCRIPT
   GOAL: EDIT-UNIT-TASK   • *repeat until no more tasks*
     GOAL: ACQUIRE-UNIT-TASK   • *if not remembered*
     GET-NEXT-PAGE   • *if at end of page*
      GET-NEXT-TASK   • *if an edit task found*
     GOAL: EXECUTE-UNIT-TASK
      GOAL- LOCATE-LINE   • *if task not on line*
       [select: USE-QS-METHOD
        USE-LF-METHOD]
      GOAL: MODIFY-TEXT
       [select USE-S-COMMAND
        USE-M-COMMAND]

From the analysis, an approximate time could be calculated for the tasks, or the reason why a task takes so long could be computed, or the set of possible methods and their trade-offs could be explored. Simplified versions of this analysis were proposed according to whether one knew only how many unit tasks were required or whether one could actually know the keystrokes involved. Over the years, variants have been proposed that refine this analysis: Cognitive Complexity Analysis (Bouvair, Kieras, & Polson, 1990), which attempts to predict transfer of learning; CPM-GOMS (Gray, John, & Atwood, in press), which attempts to take into account the limited parallelism possible in human behavior; and Howe and Young's

(1991) system, which uses semantic concept representations from Task Action Grammar to predict learnability of task-action mappings. Some variants have attempted to make the method more robust and of industrial strength: NGOMSL (Kieras, 1988) aims at making the rules better defined; SANe (Westfalische Wilhelms Universitat Munster, 1993) provides a computer-based method that is used in Europe for designing cars. As an example, Corker, Davis, Papazian, and Pew (1986) used a variant on the GOMS idea to provide a task analysis dynamically responsive to changes in terrain for a helicopter simulation, from which this code is extracted:

```
POP-UP-AND-SCAN
  POP-UP-FOR-SCAN
    [in-parallel-do:
      LOOK-FOR
      POP-UP]
    STABILIZE-CRAFT
  HOVER-AND-SCAN
    [in-parallel-do:
      HOVER
      SCAN]
```

So this is the idea of an engineering-oriented analytic theory of behavior: gradually building up a corpus of theory and analytical technique that could assist in design for interactive computer systems in just exactly the same way that other kinds of theory assist in design for other engineering and design disciplines. As any engineer knows, this means being able to handle the pragmatics of important gaps in theoretical coverage, of important uncertainties in the analysis, of shifting specifications and goals. Engineering is essentially the application of knowledge derived from scientific analysis to problems of design. It is not the only way of doing design, and engineering is not the only thing an engineer does in doing design. Engineering methods attempt to improve on pure cut-and-try for meeting a specified performance with a limited resource. But intuitive methods, cut-and-try testing, and other techniques must be used to fill in for gaps in available theory-based methods and to validate the application of those methods. This point has not been well understood in the psychological and anthropological communities. Even with very strong theories based on chemistry and physics, an engineering or design discipline needs pragmatic and craft methods to fill in the gaps, to validate designs, and to validate whether the designs scale up to practical levels.

Newell would say analytical theory for model-assisted design was exactly the program we were still carrying out. And so would I. But in trying to carry out this program, the interaction of theory with design is more subtle than it might first appear. In the years since the publication of *Human–Computer Interaction*, a field of study emerged around human interaction with computers. I would now like to give a characterization of this field, partly as a way of showing where Newell's desire of a computer science that gives more symmetrical attention to the machine and the human has reached and partly to in order to pursue the idea of model-assisted design into a wider context.

HUMAN–COMPUTER INTERACTION[1]

As it turned out, the rapid growth in computer use in society meant that the field of human–computer interaction was shaped by the confluence of developments in several disciplines. Actually, there have been several thrusts of study around the interaction of people and machines: industrial engineering, human factors, ergonomics, man–machine symbiosis, cybernetics, man–machine systems, and cognitive engineering—each of these with a particular way of carving up the intellectual territory. Human–computer interaction is a confluence of lines of development within these other areas, particularized to computers, and strongly influenced by the rapid growth of computer technology and the rapid expansion in society of the numbers these machines, particularly the personal computer.

Although it is difficult to give a definitive description of what emerged, because different things happened from different points of view, it is possible to give a sense of the field by pragmatically defining it and by listing what its (teachable) results might be.

A Definition of Human–Computer Interaction

To my knowledge, the term *human–computer interaction* was first used as the title of our book (Card et al., 1983). There is no currently agreed upon definition of the range of topics which form the area of human–computer interaction. But for practical purposes, a proposed practical working definition adopted by the ACM SIGCHI Committee on Curriculum Development (1992) is as follows:

> Human–computer interaction is a discipline concerned with the design, evaluation and implementation of interactive computing systems for human use and with the study of major phenomena surrounding them.

[1]This description draws heavily on work done as a member of the ACM SIGCHI Curriculum Development Committee (1992), in collaboration with the other committee members (T. Hewett, R. Baecker, T. Carey, J. Gasen, M. Mantei, G. Perlman, G. Strong, & W. Verplank) and is a modified version of the description given there. I am indebted to Allen Newell for extensive discussion through several drafts.

From a computer science perspective, the focus is on *interaction* and specifically on interaction between one or more *humans* and one or more computational *machines*. The classical situation that comes to mind is a person using an interactive graphics program on a workstation. But it is clear that varying what is meant by *interaction, human,* and *machine* leads to a rich space of possible topics, some of which, although we might not wish to exclude them as part of human–computer interaction, we would, nevertheless, wish to identify as peripheral to its focus. Other topics we would wish to identify as more central.

Take the notion of *machine.* Instead of workstations, computers may be in the form of embedded computational machines, such as parts of spacecraft cockpits or microwave ovens. Because the techniques for designing these interfaces bear so much relationship to the techniques for designing workstation interfaces, they can be profitably treated together. But if we weaken the computational and *interaction* aspects more and treat the design of machines that are mechanical and passive, such as the design of a hammer, we are clearly on the margins, and generally the relationships between humans and hammers would not be considered part of human–computer interaction. Such relationships clearly would be part of general human factors, which studies the human aspects of all designed devices, but not the mechanism of these devices. Human–computer interaction, by contrast, studies both the mechanism side and the human side, but of a narrower class of devices.

Or consider what is meant by the notion *human.* If we allow the human to be a group of humans or an organization, we may consider interfaces of distributed systems, computer-aided communications between humans, or the nature of the work being cooperatively performed by means of the system. These are all generally regarded as important topics central within the sphere of human–computer interaction studies. If we go further down this path to consider job design from the point of view of the nature of the work and the nature of human satisfaction, then computers will only occasionally occur (when they are useful for these ends or when they interfere with these ends) and human–computer interaction (HCI) is only one supporting area among others.

There are other disciplinary points of view that would place the focus of HCI differently than does computer science, just as the focus for a definition of the databases area would be different from a computer science versus a business perspective. HCI is emerging as a specialty concern within several disciplines, each with different emphases: computer science (application design and engineering of human interfaces), psychology (the application of theories of cognitive processes and the empirical analysis of user behavior), sociology and anthropology (interactions between technology, work, and organization), and industrial design (interactive products).

From a computer science perspective, other disciplines serve as supporting disciplines, much as physics serves as a supporting discipline for civil engineering, or as mechanical engineering serves as a supporting discipline for robotics. A lesson learned repeatedly by engineering disciplines is that design problems have a context, and that the overly narrow optimization of one part of a design can be rendered invalid by the broader context of the problem. Even from a direct computer science perspective, therefore, it is advantageous to frame the problem of human–computer interaction broadly enough so as to help students (and practitioners) avoid the classic pitfall of design divorced from the context of the problem.

To give a further rough characterization of human–computer interaction as a field, we can list some of its special concerns.

- The joint performance of tasks by humans and machines.
- The structure of communication between human and machine.
- Human capabilities to use machines (including the learnability of interfaces).
- Algorithms and programming of the interface itself.
- Engineering concerns that arise in designing and building interfaces.
- The process of specification, design, and implementation of interfaces, and design trade-offs.

Human–computer interaction thus has science, engineering, and design aspects.

Regardless of the definition chosen, HCI is clearly to be included as a part of computer science. If, for example, one adopts Newell, Perlis, and Simon's (1967) classic definition of computer science as "the study of computers and the major phenomena that surround them," then the interaction of people and computers and the uses of computers are certainly parts of these phenomena. If, on the other hand, we take the recent Association for Computing Machinery (ACM; Denning et al., 1988) report's definition as "the systematic study of algorithmic processes that describe and transform information: their theory, analysis, design, efficiency, implementation, and application," then those algorithmic processes clearly include computers in interaction with humans. The algorithms of computer graphics, for example, are just those algorithms that give certain experiences to the perceptual apparatus of the human. The design of many modern computer applications inescapably requires the design of some component of the system that interacts with a user. Moreover, this component typically represents more than half a system's lines of code. It is intrinsically necessary to understand how to decide on the functionality a system will have, how to bring this out to the user, how to build the system, and how to test the design.

Because human–computer interaction studies a human and a machine in communication, it draws from supporting knowledge on both the machine and the human side. On the machine side, techniques in computer graphics, operating systems, programming languages, and development environments are relevant. On the human side, communications theory, graphic and industrial design disciplines, linguistics, social sciences, cognitive psychology, and human performance are relevant. And, of course, engineering and design methods are relevant.

An Inventory of Human–Computer Interaction Results

Another way to define an area is to list its results, and a particular way of doing this is to ask what is known that is worth teaching. Putting these together allows us to see the general shape of the field, even if there may be some disagreement on the details. The following inventory of teachable results in HCI is offered in this spirit. Relevant topics from other disciplines are included if they bear directly on the subject matter.

The inventory was constructed by generating a list of results and topics from course syllabi, the literature, and personal knowledge. Topics included had to be sufficiently mature that they were treated in the literature and teachable. Thus the inventory does not include topics on the research edge. For convenience, the results have been arranged into 18 groups (Fig. 8.2). These derive from a consideration of five interrelated aspects of human–computer interaction: (1) reflections on the nature of human–computer interaction, (2) the use and context of computers, (3) human characteristics, (4) computer system and interface architecture, and (5) the design process. The groups are expanded into a detailed inventory in the Appendix.

Figure 8.2 is meant to suggest the interrelationships among these topics: Interaction between humans and computational devices can be considered from several viewpoints (1). Computer systems exist within a larger social, organizational, and work milieu (2.1). Within this context there are applications for which we wish to employ computer systems (2.2). But the process of putting computers to work means that the human, technical, and work aspects of the application situation must be brought into fit with each other through human learning, system tailorability, or other strategies (2.3).

In addition to the use and social context of computers, on the human side, we must also take into account the human information processing (3.1), communication (3.2), and physical (3.3) characteristics of users.

On the computer side, a variety of technologies have been developed for supporting interaction with humans: Input devices and their drivers (4.1) and recognition algorithms (4.2) connect the human and the machine. Output devices (4.3) and the associated rendering algorithms from

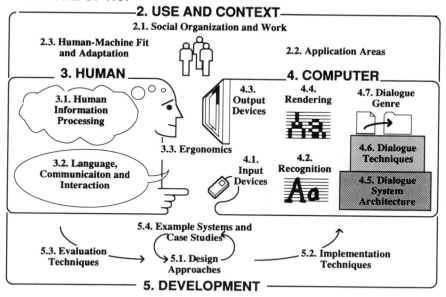

1. NATURE OF HCI
2. USE AND CONTEXT
2.1. Social Organization and Work

2.3. Human-Machine Fit and Adaptation

2.2. Application Areas

3. HUMAN
3.1. Human Information Processing

4.3. Output Devices

4.4. Rendering

4.7. Dialogue Genre

4. COMPUTER

3.3. Ergonomics

3.2. Language, Communicaiton and Interaction

4.1. Input Devices

4.2. Recognition

4.6. Dialogue Techniques

4.5. Dialogue System Architecture

5.4. Example Systems and Case Studies

5.3. Evaluation Techniques

5.1. Design Approaches

5.2. Implementation Techniques

5. DEVELOPMENT

FIG. 8.2. Major topic areas of human–computer interaction. Revised version of Fig. 1 in ACM (1992, p. 16). Original figure drawn by William Verplank.

computer graphics (4.4) connect the machine with the human. These are used in a number of techniques for organizing a dialogue (4.6). Dialogues are used in turn to implement larger design elements, such as the metaphor of the interface (4.5). Complex dialogues lead into considerations of the systems architecture necessary to support such features as interconnectable application programs, real-time response, network communications, and multitasking of dialogue objects (4.7).

Finally, there is the process of design itself (5.1), techniques and tools (5.2), techniques for evaluation (5.3), and a number of classic designs for study (5.4).

The inventory itself is given in the Appendix and shows that there is an accumulation of results on the design, evaluation, and implementation of interactive computer systems and on the phenomena surrounding them. The Appendix summarizes more than a hundred topic groups. Many dialogue techniques have been developed. Many input/output devices have been developed. Many methods have been invented for evaluating system usability.

The success of early computing devices caused the concerns of the field to broaden to encompass how these machines fit the physical and cognitive attributes of humans, how easy they are to use, and how easy they are to

1. NATURE OF HCI

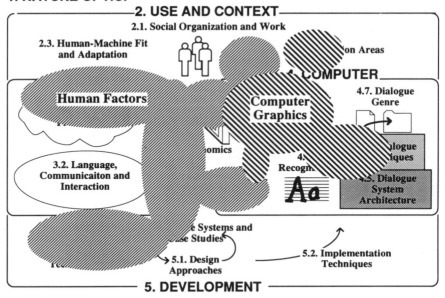

FIG. 8.3. Content of HCI covered by related disciplines.

learn. From there the field has further broadened to address how these machines fit the social and organizational contexts within which they are used, how they effect organizational productivity, how they affect the power relationships within organizations, and how they change the way in which organizations themselves are formed. Future concerns can be expected to consider even broader concerns such as the effect of such machines on culture and fundamental social institutions like the school and the library (e.g., see Nunberg, 1993).

This then is the present shape of the study of human–computer interaction. It shares concerns with other human and systems disciplines and we can see these from (Fig. 8.3). For example, the content of human factors is concentrated on the boundaries between the human and the machine, whereas HCI extends into the machine components (but for a narrower class of machines). Interactive computer graphics is concentrated on the machine side, largely in the rendering area, but also somewhat in the input device area, whereas HCI's interest has more concentration on the human side (and the interest in computer graphics algorithms is shallower). But there certainly are beginning to be results and the results are beginning to fit into a coherent pattern. Although computer science remains asymmetrical as a discipline, and perhaps reasonably so, there is beginning to be more balance.

USE-CENTERED DESIGN

Let us now return to our original question of model-assisted design. Our inventory of the topics of HCI shows that there are many areas in which models might be of assistance in design. We list a few:

- Models of work processes or other contexts of use (task analysis)
- "Reference models" of the computer system components and operations
- Interaction models of the human–machine communication process
- Design user conceptual models (how the designer intends the user to think about the system)
- Empirical user conceptual models (how users actually think about the system)
- Human performance models

Whether the insights derived from models actually can be used in design of interactive systems is another question. There are at least two issues. First, there is a question of practice, which is an issue in all design and engineering professions. Rouse and Cody (1988) concluded:

> Designers spend most of their time in an insular environment bounded by project co-workers and personal experience. Their information requirements span an enormous range, some of which can be satisfied only from project sources and others which can be satisfied in a variety of ways. Designers satisfy those requirements that can be met in more than one way by accessing sources with the least overhead in terms of their effort. These sources are social contact with co-workers and definitely not formally printed materials. (Rouse & Cody, 1988; see also Rouse & Cody, 1989)

Even if good analytical techniques are developed, one should expect them not to be instantly adopted.

More fundamental to the intellectual substance of the discipline is whether analytic methods actually can deliver value and insight into practical designs. Again, this is a question for the supporting sciences of all engineering professions. Some theoretical computer science and theoretical operations research, for example, has been criticized for not being relevant to practical situations. In a study of vision and cognition models for use in designing helicopter cockpits by the National Research Council (Elkind, Card, Hochberg, & Huey, 1990), we found mixed results. Engineering uses often require broad coverage of phenomena, whereas scientific models are often aimed at uncovering the mechanisms behind narrow phenomena. Models were often inadequate because of lack of content validity, idealizations that did not match their use, inability to be integrated with other models, lack of formalization, or lack of use experience (Card, 1989a). All models require idealizations, dropping out details that will have little effect on outcome so that the analysis of the important characteristics is tractable. But which details can be dropped out may depend on the use to which they will be put:

> System design and analysis have special needs and require basic theoretical work on models that are aimed at supporting this kind of design and analysis. These requirements differ substantially from those that often motivate traditional academic research on models of human performance. The system design context is a powerful vehicle for exposing shortcomings in models and linkages and, as a result, imposes a valuable discipline on research and development of such models. (Elkind et al., 1990, p. 307)

Nevertheless, there were design activities and situations that could be assisted by models.

In order to understand better the potential use of models in design activities, I would like to look for a moment at the context of use of such models and, more specifically, at the nature of invention and technology development.

Technology Evolution and the Systems Research Paradigm

A simple, but rather naive, view of the way in which technology evolves is from scientific theory to empirical test to application. In fact, the relationship between science and technology is a good deal more complex. Technology has its own engine of development and is not a simple consequence of the application of new science. Historically, many different patterns can be found (Ziman, 1976), ranging from the stated simple view, to the case where technology develops without much help from science at all (e.g., the bicycle), to reverse cases where technology projects lead and stimulate scientific advance.

Hughes (1983), in a study of the history of invention in the electronic power industry, defined several stages of invention. One of these is of particular interest—the problem identification phase. The inventors studied by Hughes often sought to identify a demand or function to be performed on the one hand and a resource on the other (Fig. 8.4). Then they would try to develop new technology that used the resource efficiently to meet the demand precisely. If the demand is stipulated and the search is for technology to fill it, then the invention is *demand pull*. If the technology is stipulated and the search is for a demand, then it is *technology push*. Both exist and can lead to successful systems.

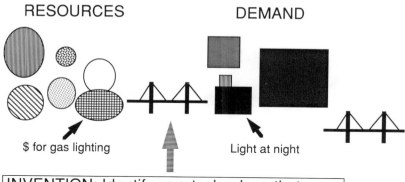

FIG. 8.4. Invention as technology that bridges the gap between resources and demand.

The inventor identified a problem by looking for what Hughes calls a *reverse salient*, a weakness in the technology. He then tried to identify a *critical problem*, that is, a problem to be solved that would correct the reverse salient. For Edison, the reverse salient was usually economic, the critical problem usually technical, thus linking the parameters of invention success to some of those for innovation success.

What is important to realize is that the process of bringing out an innovation may focus on either of these activities: searching for a new function ("application" in the computer industry) that utilizes a technology, or searching for a technology that is a good fit to a defined problem.

Each attempt at innovation, in retrospect, has some aspect that can be improved. Either the demand can be satisfied better or the resource can be used more efficiently or a new demand can be identified. The result is the familiar cycle of technology improvements. This is true for even such a lowly invention as the paper clip (Petroski, 1992). Figure 8.5 shows in graphical form the result of such a process for interactive systems.

One consequence is that instead of the theory-confirmation-application progression often assumed in science, we get another progression in technology. An idealized version of this progression is what might be called the system research paradigm[2] (Fig. 8.6). First there is one, then a few, scattered versions of some system. These give an existence proof that some-

---

[2]This way of putting the aims of systems research was originally Rick Beach's idea, and the current form developed out of our conversations.

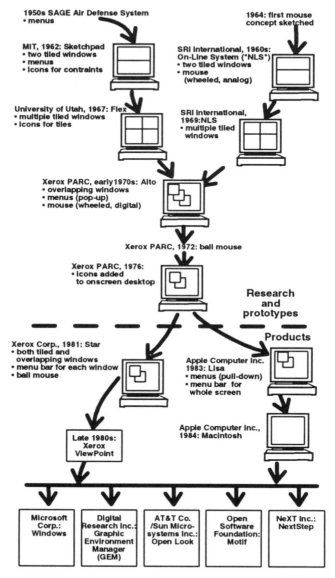

FIG. 8.5. Food chain of ideas for the graphical user interface. The diagram illustrates the chain of improvements by which technology develops. From Perry and Voelcker (1989). Reprinted by permission.

thing can be done, and they form the initial chain of improvements. Many technologies just stay in this mode, in a chain of such improvements (e.g., paper clips). But it is often possible through systematic investigation to characterize regions of the design space through models and theories. This brings new insight into the design process and gives intellectual substance. In a third stage, these theories are used to build new systems, thus confirming or infirming notions of what works. The goal is a final stage in which it is possible to articulate a set of principles that can be used to build a system that will perform in a manner specified at design time.

The system researcher's goal, as opposed to the system developer's goal, is to carry forward these stages. Of course, real technology development is much messier. Technology may proceed for a long time in Stage 1 by purely incremental improvements. Or advances in Stage 2 may inspire a set of Stage 1 explorations. The confusing part to get straight is that in technology what look like applications to a scientist may precede the theory (and indeed may be the basis of its induction) and that technology may also progress even in the absence of theories.

Most interactive computer systems belong to the first stage, but as the discipline of building interactive systems develops, we would expect knowledge of how to build some systems to progress to other stages. In fact, advancing to higher stages is what we mean by maturing the discipline. That is the point of system research. One thing we seek from theories that will support design is the ability to help in this second phase of Fig. 8.6, to characterize the design or the situation in such a way as to assist directly or indirectly. Such characterization and the exploitation of characterization is what we mean by *model-assisted design*.

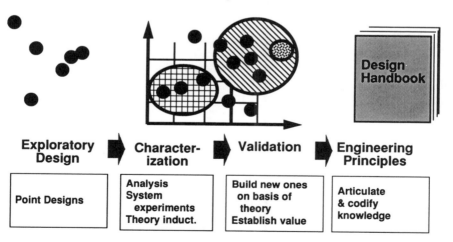

Exploratory Design	Character-ization	Validation	Engineering Principles
Point Designs	Analysis System experiments Theory induct.	Build new ones on basis of theory Establish value	Articulate & codify knowledge

FIG. 8.6. Systems research paradigm. Idealized view of a progressive set of goals in systems research and technology development.

Use-Centered Design

Newell began with the notion of a behavioral theory robust enough that it could support the design of interactive systems. Here I want to give a revised statement of this idea from the design side. This time, instead of stating the idea in terms of the characteristics of the theory to be developed, I want to state it in terms of an idealized design methodology.

As we have seen, the fundamental proposition in invention is finding some technology that will use a resource efficiently to meet a demand precisely. Understanding the demand or use is therefore of fundamental importance. Each time in the computing industry a major new use has been identified and technology applied to it, major expansions of the industry have occurred. One need think only of text editing for the PC, spreadsheets for the Apple II, desktop publishing for the Macintosh.

Therefore, of the entities in Fig. 8.2, the most fundamental in interactive systems is not the system, nor even the human, but the use to which a system will be put. The human has something he or she wants to do in some context. The computer's role is as a mediator of this use (Fig. 8.7). Such a consideration leads us not to a *user-centered design* (Norman & Draper, 1986), but to a *use-centered design* approach.

In the use-centered approach, design proceeds ideally from an understanding of the essence of the use to matching the characteristics of the user. There are basically five things to do. From a design point of view there is (1) understand the use and its context, (2) create a computing system that embodies a compact abstraction of the task, and (3) create a user illusion

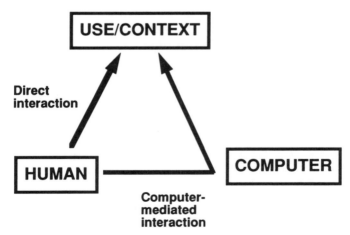

FIG. 8.7. Basic HCI design problem. The use of an interactive system is fundamental. The problem is to design a computer system that mediates between the characteristics of the use and the capabilities of the human.

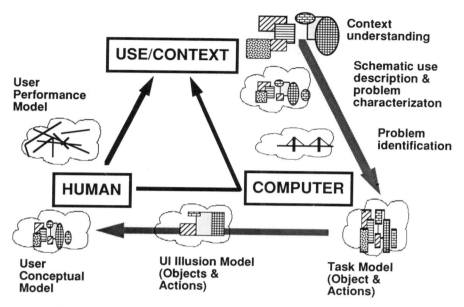

FIG. 8.8. Model-assisted design. Design proceeds out from an understanding of the use by building up a series of abstractions or models, or using such models that already exist.

that fits over the application abstraction and fits the capabilities of the user. From an implementation point of view there is (4) mature the prototype and (5) evaluate the result. Each of these can be assisted by models (Fig. 8.8).

It is easiest to think of the use-centered methodology not as a set of processes to do, but as mileposts to achieve (see Table 8.2):

Understand the Use and Its Context. Use mileposts:

1. Naturalistic study of use and context
2. Schematization of use
3. Problem characterization
4. Critical problem identification

Essentially (Table 8.2), the job is to understand where value can be added. A potential use and its context have to be identified in a way that "what-if" questions can be asked. The idea is to start from the richest possible description of the potential use and its context and then to proceed through a set of abstraction exercises that give insight.

TABLE 8.2
Design Mileposts

Milepost	Description
Use Mileposts	
1. Naturalistic description of use and context	Naturalistic descriptions that explicate interrelationships and context
2. Schematization of use	Empirically based abstractions
3. Problem characterization	Identification of key factors and parameters of variation; analytical theory that lays bare the hidden structure
4. Critical problem identification	Identification of solvable problem that will lead to high payoff
Artifact Mileposts	
1. Solution as idea	Inspiration for invention, expressed notebook drawing, napkin, seminar, or hallway coversation
2. Application model	Internal clockworks model of the application
3. Interaction model	Internal clockworks model of the user–machine communication
4. User's design conceptual model	Model of the application as intended to be seen from the user
5. Wizard can use	Demonstration of feasibility
6. Friends of wizard can use	Demonstration of surmounting the grubby details
7. People who don't even know the wizard can use	Demonstration of robustness
8. Application programmer interface	Documented and rationalized
9. Replicable	Demonstration that same technique can reliably be applied again with the same good result
Evaluation Mileposts	
1. Is artifact usable?	Users can actually put to use (including opening box and setting up)
2. Performance characterization	Determinants and limits of performance identified
3. Is the artifact useful?	Daily use
4. Has the artifact solved a problem in a useful domain?	Propagation of system to larger groups of users
4. Is the artifact commercially applicable?	Product program
5. Is the artifact commercially successful?	Sales

Naturalistic, descriptive study of the use and its context can be through interviews, observation, or perhaps direct participation. The point is to get a broad, contextualized understanding of the problem and for work contexts the work practice. Schematization of use can be through scenarios or other techniques. The purpose here is to abstract from the particulars of specific observation to get concrete typical cases against which to run designs and ideas. Problem characterization tries to identify key factors and underlying invisible structure, to penetrate below the surface to underlying structure. Theories and models can be of great help here. Finally, critical problem identification is the identification of a likely solvable technical problem that will add value to the situation.

Derive a Task Machine That Embeds a Compact Abstraction of the Task.

Artifact mileposts:

1. Solution as idea
2. Application model

An application gets its power by having the ability to perform a large number of tasks through the combinatorial mixing of a small number of components. A principal task in designing an application is to invent, derived from an analysis of the use, a set of abstractions cast, for example, as objects and actions that can be combined to allow the user to accomplish a relatively large number of tasks while learning a relatively small number of things. Of course, another principal task is to manage the complexity of implementation.

We start with the germ of an idea related to the critical problem. The application model is the abstract clockworks, the application algebra that gives combinatorial power. The models may be expressed in terms of the abstract objects in the system and the actions possible on these objects or in some other way. Attempts at such models are sometimes referred to as *reference models*.

Design the User Illusion.

Artifact mileposts:

3. Interaction model
4. User's design conceptual model

After the task machine is somewhat known, then the task is to design the *user illusion*, the set of objects and interactions associated with communicating with the machine. Just as the task machine had to be abstracted and reduced to a combinatorial model, so too the user illusion needs to be reduced to a small number of elements.

The interaction model is about the communication paradigm with the user. The user's design conceptual model is the way the designer intends the system to be thought of from the user's point of view. Designing these may utilize performance models as a resource.

Mature the Prototype.

Artifact mileposts:

5. Wizard can use (feasibility).
6. Friends of wizard can use (can surmount the grubby details).
7. People who don't even know wizard can use (robustness).
8. Application programmer interface.
9. Solution can be replicated.

These other mileposts trace the maturity of the system through its ability to work and be used in contexts increasingly remote from its builders and increasingly closer to the intended context of use. Mileposts 5–7 are the scale Ed McCreight introduced at the Xerox Palo Alto Research Center (PARC) for describing experimental systems. Milepost 8 is a documented rationalized version of the system. Milepost 9 indicates that the ideas are sturdy enough that they are not dependent on the particulars of people or specific pieces of code.

Evaluate the Result.

Evaluation mileposts:

1. Is the artifact usable?
2. Performance characterization.
3. Is the artifact useful?
4. Has the artifact solved a problem in an important domain?
5. Is the artifact commercially applicable?
6. Is the artifact commercially successful?

Finally, there are some mileposts about whether the overall goals are actually being achieved: Many techniques have been developed for usability testing and the identification of problems. Performance characterization is something a little different. The idea is to figure out what sort of performance to expect and what the limiting factors are and over what sorts of ranges. Again, this is a use of human performance models.

Casting what needs to be done in terms of mileposts instead of processes is to emphasize that what we seek is results, not methods for their own sake. There's more than one way to skin a design. Successful systems *can* be done by skipping mileposts. This is equivalent to asserting, for example, that one already understands the use. In return for the time gained by so doing, however, the result is at increased risk.

The methods of HCI, such as "cognitive walkthrough," can be seen as essentially techniques to assess the state of a design or figure out how to progress to the next level (Card, in press). Models and theories are only some of the methods for attacking the mileposts. Methods in HCI can be arranged along essentially three dimensions (see Fig. 8.9): The first dimension is the distinction between *analytic methods* and *synthetic methods.* The same milepost can sometimes be achieved either with analytic methods (e.g., interviews) or by synthetic methods (composing artifacts and trying them out on users) or with a combination. The second dimension is the amount of *idealization of context* involved. At the one extreme are methods such as field interviews and user observation in which there is little idealization of context. The methods are aimed at the direct external setting in which a system will actually be used. These methods attempt to tap the richly textured, contextualized information that comes from the natural setting without any intermediate abstraction or encoding. A less expensive, but more idealized and less ecologically valid, alternative to dealing directly with an external cost, is the use of the self or local group as a context. At the other extreme is a constructed, artificial context, in which the context is idealized by underlying parameters of variation in order to make inference easier and formal experiments. The third dimension is the *idealization of representation.* At one end are methods, such as building prototypes for self use or field interviews, that do not use a representational articulation of the design, the situation, or the behavior. At the other end are methods that have a notational representation, such as *analytic calculations.* In between are methods that have some sort of informal representation, such as the use of scenarios to represent a situation.

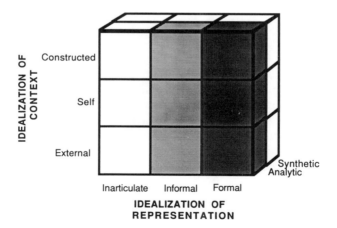

FIG. 8.9. Space of methods for user interface design. Based on Card (in press). Shaded boxes represent the subset of methods referred to in model-assisted design.

Essentially, these three dimensions of methods—analytic versus synthetic, idealization of context, and idealization of representation—represent trade-offs among three pragmatic variables: (1) power, (2) richness, and (3) cost (see Fig. 8.6). Methods oriented toward the external context and the methods with inarticulate representation have access to the full, richly textured experience of users and situations. But the analysis that can be done with these is limited. As the representation of the situation moves toward a more idealized context or toward more formal representations, these methods employ abstractions that selectively omit information. These abstractions introduce possibilities for error in understanding a situation. In return, they enable the use of more powerful operations on the representation.

Model-assisted design uses methods from the shaded region of Fig. 8.9 together with nonmodeling methods. Actually, the situation is more complex than Fig. 8.9 suggests. Formal theories may often establish a set of facts about the world that were previously unclear. These can then be used in completely empirical methods. For example, Fitts' law establishes that pointing time is almost independent of whether the target is a picture or a word. This fact can be used to set up pointing device tests without ever directly invoking Fitts' law. Such facts can pass as tacit assumptions into practice.

EXAMPLES OF MODEL-ASSISTED DESIGN

I have given this sketch of the use-centered research paradigm as a way of discussing the idea of using analytic models to assist the design of interactive systems and of showing the relationship between analytical knowledge and design. I now want to show instances where we have been able to use this idea to achieve practical results in the design of novel systems.

Pointing Devices

The Mouse.   The first example is of devices for pointing to locations on a computer screen. Schematically, we can put the problem as in Fig. 8.10. The problem is to point at objects on the screen. The challenge is how to characterize the performance of competing pointing devices. A useful part of such a characterization is to identify the functions and their parameters that govern their pointing time. The theory is Fitts' law, a human performance model. The artifact is the mouse.

The time to point to a target with a mouse (Fig. 8.11) was discovered to be governed by Fitts' law (Card, English, & Burr, 1978) (see Fig. 8.12), the same law governing this action when done by the hand. According to one version of Fitts' law, the time to point using a mouse to a target of width W when it is distance D away is given by

$$\text{Movement time} = K + I_M \log_2(D/W + 0.5) \tag{1}$$

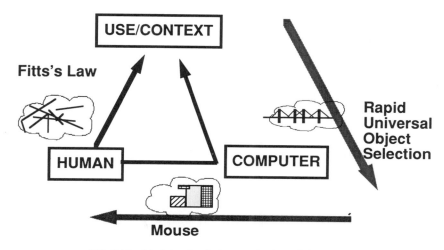

FIG. 8.10. Model-assisted characterization of the mouse.

Furthermore, the constant I_M of proportionality is approximately the same as for the hand. This means that the limitation in pointing speed is not in the mouse, but in the eye–hand coordination system and that, furthermore, the mouse is nearly optimal, so it is unlikely that a new pointing device would be introduced that outperforms it.

Here we have a case where an analytic theory is used to characterize a device, which leads to a design choice. The results are practical. They were

FIG. 8.11. Mouse.

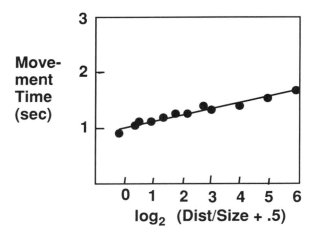

FIG. 8.12.   Fitts' law characterization of the mouse.

used to overcome opposition and finally to introduce the mouse commercially on the Xerox Star. They were also used by Apple in deciding to introduce the mouse on the Lisa.

Head Mouse.   But we can take the analysis further. The problem is again pointing to an object on the screen (Fig. 8.13). The theory is again Fitts' law. But the device is an alternative to the mouse, the head mouse.

The head mouse is a set of three ultrasonic receivers placed around the head (see Fig. 8.14). An ultrasonic source placed atop the CRT display puts

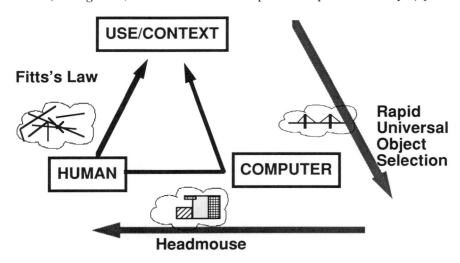

FIG. 8.13.   Model-assisted evaluation of the head mouse.

FIG. 8.14. Head mouse.

out ultrasonic pulses. By turning his or her head, the user changes the relative time at which the receivers detect the sound and this is used to move a cursor. We can use our analysis to show the head mouse is unlikely to be a successful device (Card, Mackinlay, & Robertson, 1991) for general pointing.

The same basic theory that shows how the mouse is an optimal control device also shows us where in the design space to look for devices that might beat the mouse. Basically, this is a matter of looking for muscle groups of high bandwidth to attach to input transducers. Figure 8.15(a) shows the time to do four important selection tasks with the mouse: (1) selecting a period, (2) selecting a character, (3) selecting a word, or (4) selecting a paragraph.

Selecting a word is reasonably easy. Most people feel subjectively that selecting a character is a hard task, but not too hard. Let us use the task of pointing to a character with the mouse as the *easiest hard task* (other tasks, such as pointing to a period are even harder). Because hard pointing tasks take more time than easy pointing tasks (by Fitts' law), let us say that any task that takes more *time* than pointing to a character with the mouse is a hard task. Similarly, we take the *time* it takes to point to a word as

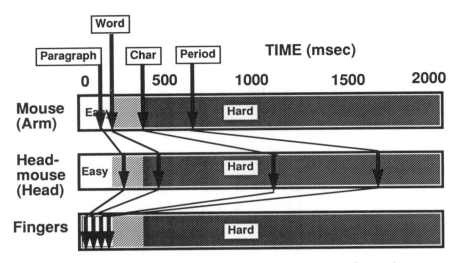

FIG. 8.15. Use of Fitts' law and bandwidth of muscle group to characterize pointing tasks as easy or hard.

defining the *hardest easy task* (other tasks, such as pointing to a paragraph, are even easier).

A head mouse depends on the neck muscles; these seem to have a bandwidth about half of those of the hand (Radwin, Vanderheiden, & Lin, 1990). We would therefore expect our four benchmark tasks to be shifted as in Fig. 8.15(b): that is, almost all of the tasks are shifted to become hard tasks.

The problem is that an excellent transducer has been applied to a set of muscles with too low a bandwidth. Without the analysis, one might just as easily think that the problem was that users just had many more hours of learning with the mouse. In fact, this was claimed by a colleague who thereupon set out to spend a day using only the head mouse in order to acquire the hours of practice necessary prove his point. Of course, he was wrong. As predicted, he couldn't improve much and then had to suffer with a stiff neck through lectures about why his experiment was doomed in principle, an application of analytic models even more pleasurable than the original prediction.

Again, we have an analytic theory being deployed in a practical design context, this time to diagnose the fatal defect of a design.

Finger Mice. Now let us turn the tables and consider the use of an analytic model to generate a new design instead of merely evaluating existing ones. The problem is a pointing device that beats the mouse (Fig. 8.16). The theory is Fitts' law. The artifact is a new family of "finger mice."

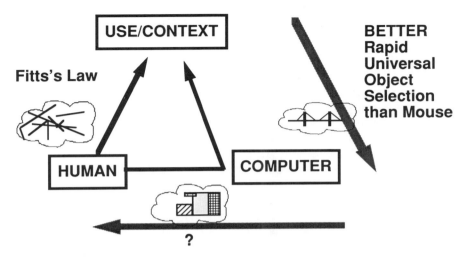

FIG. 8.16. Model-assisted search for a device that improves on the mouse.

The theory suggests how it would be possible to make a pointing device that should be able to beat the mouse—just attach the transducer to muscles with higher bandwidth, thus favorably changing the constant I_M in Equation 1. Langoff's (1973) published data on the bandwidth of the fingers (see Fig. 8.17) suggests that the fingers might be the proper set of muscles. According to Fig 8.15(c), which projects Langoff's data through Fig. 8.1 onto editing tasks, if the fingers could be harnessed, it might be possible to shift most of our benchmark tasks into the easy region. The invention

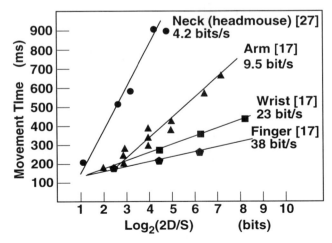

FIG. 8.17. Langoff's characterization of muscle bandwidth. From Langoff (1973, p. 145). Adapted by permission.

of a nonmechanical optoelectronic transducer for Xerox mice by Lyon (1981) meant that the large case was no longer required to house the transducer. This meant that the case could be reshaped to mate the transducer with the higher-bandwidth finger muscles. Figure 8.18 gives the essential idea. The pencil represents a shape that could be grasped with the fingers. The eraser suggests the housing to hold the transducer.

This idea was pursued as part of the product design for the Xerox 6085 system. Figure 8.19 shows a family of designs done collaboratively with Bill Moggridge and Danny De Iuliis at ID TWO (Card & De Iuliis, 1984). These designs map the basic idea into three points along a trade-off curve between technology risk and performance in order to give the trade-off manager a set of choices. One design (not shown) was a mouse modified so as to maximize the amount of finger control. This was the most conservative design, calculated to have low risk in engineering and manufacturing. The design in Fig. 8.19(a) is more adventurous and achieves more finger control by recasting the shape of the mouse to be a puck. Figure 8.19(b) is an articulated pen-like device designed to maximize finger–device transfer.

FIG. 8.18. Essential idea for high-performance mouse.

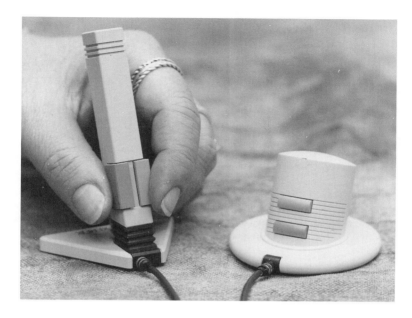

FIG. 8.19. Finger mice—high-performance input devices produced by model-based design.

Each of the devices is designed to retain a major advantage of the mouse—that it can be grasped while looking elsewhere (whereas grasping an ordinary pen is a complex grasp).

Again, analytic models helped lead to a practical result. Here the analytic theory let us reconceptualize the design space so as to make it easier to find the sweet spot. The models, of course, do not automatically produce the design. They are tools for thought, resources that the designer can use in the same way that structural calculations are resources that the architect can use in design.

Unfortunately, the product manager chose not to go for a mouse replacement. Even though it is a decade later, some of these ideas are still open to pursue.

3D Point-of-Interest Movement. Now let us consider yet another use of analytic theory for design. The problem is how to move the camera or point of view in three-dimensional (3D) user interfaces very rapidly, but without overshooting the target (Fig. 8.20). What makes this difficult is that the user must somehow control 6 (or if we count velocities, 12) degrees of freedom. Current solutions involve the use of special input devices, such as the SpaceBall or the Bat or DataGloves. The theory is again Fitts' law,

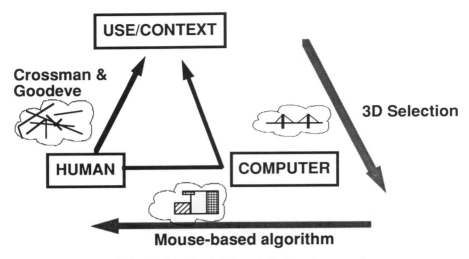

FIG. 8.20.   Model-assisted design of 3D viewpoint controller.

this time one of the derivations of it. The artifact is the "point of interest" movement algorithm.

In this case we take inspiration from one of the methods used to derive Fitts' law. There are many such derivations; one of the most provocative comes from Crossman and Goodeve (1963).[3] Suppose a person wishes to move his hand D cm to reach a D-cm-wide target (Fig. 8.21). The movement of the hand, according to this derivation, can be considered to consist of a series of microcorrections at about 240-ms intervals, each with a certain accuracy of about 7%. The series of corrections continues until the hand is within the target. Thus smaller targets require more time to select, and, in fact, the logarithmic relation of Equation 1 is obtained.

We invert this reasoning to produce the *point-of-interest movement* technique (Mackinlay, Card, & Robertson, 1991). The mouse is used to select a point on a 3D object with the cursor. The indicated point on this object serves as a target, controlling subsequent motion. The user presses a button to indicate motion toward this target. On each animation cycle, the point of view is moved a fixed percentage of the way toward the target (Fig. 8.22). This has the effect of having the user approach the target logarithmically. The user approaches the target at very high speeds when the target is distant, but very low speeds when the target is very close. As a consequence, just as in the case of mouse movement, user perceptual error is kept constant. Although it uses only the mouse, this scheme produces very rapid movement to the target without ever colliding with it.

---

[3]This derivation does not actually fit all the known empirical facts, but it is a useful enough approximation for our purposes.

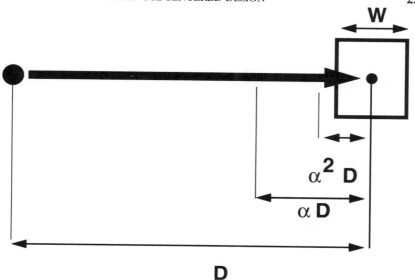

FIG. 8.21. Crossman and Goodeve (1963) derivation of Fitts' law.

In this case, the analytic theory gives us a mechanism, an invisible underlying structure to the behavior. The understanding of this mechanism then inspires the design of the new technique. In fact, contrary to the main direction of the industry, the theory allowed us to identify a technique that does not require a special 3D input device. While empirical comparisons do not yet exist in the literature, the new technique is believed to be faster for moving to a target than techniques using special devices.

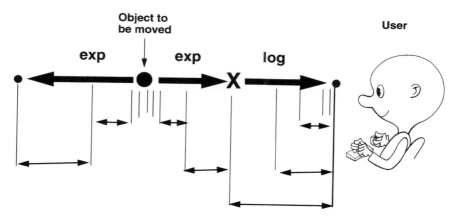

FIG. 8.22. Reverse application of Crossman and Goodeve (1963) derivation to 3D viewpoint movement design.

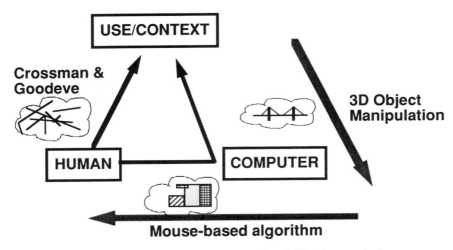

FIG. 8.23.   Model-assisted design of mouse-based 3D object manipulator.

3D Object Movement.   Finally, we can extend these results even further, to invent a new technique for moving 3D objects in space using only a mouse. The problem (Fig. 8.23) is to move objects around in a simulated 3D space. The theory is again the Crossman and Goodeve derivation of Fitts' law. The artifact is a mouse-based algorithm for moving objects in 3D space.

We divide the problem into two parts. One part is moving the object around on a plane perpendicular to the line of sight (Fig. 8.24), and the other part is moving the object in a direction perpendicular to the line of sight. To move the object in the plane perpendicular to the screen, we just map this movement onto the regular two-dimensional (2D) movement of the mouse. The user selects the object by holding down a button, causing visual feedback about which object has been selected and causing a plane to be drawn on the screen perpendicular to the line of sight. This plane indicates the mapping of mouse movements into the 3D world.

To move the object in a direction perpendicular to the screen, we map the movement onto a new version of the point-of-interest (POI) viewpoint movement technique (Fig. 8.25), which, it will be remembered, is a version of the Crossman and Goodeve Fitts' law derivation. To move the object away, the user presses another button (the same one for POI viewpoint movement) causing the object to accelerate at constant rate, that is, to move away at exponentially increasing velocity. Another button causes to object to move toward the user at exponentially increasing velocity until it gets within a certain distance, after which the object approaches the user at logarithmic speed, just as in the POI movement. The result is to allow the user to grasp and manipulate objects over very great ranges, to do it rapidly, and to do it without using special devices, using only a mouse.

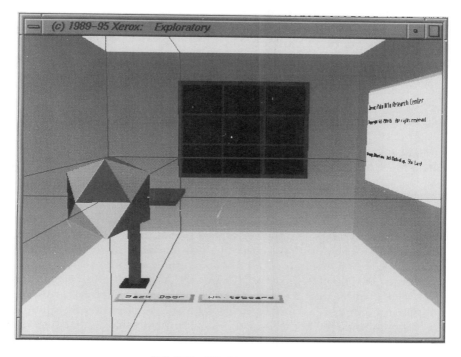

FIG. 8.24. 3D object movement.

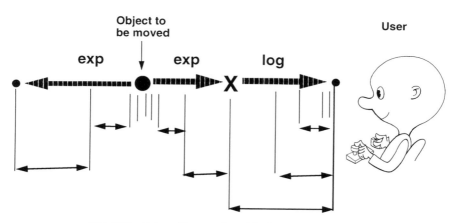

FIG. 8.25. Point of interest logarithmic object movement.

We have now gone through five cycles of reuse of a single set of theoretical ideas, first to characterize system components, then to invent new, practical, nonobvious interaction techniques. Once the basic theory was in hand, these new techniques could be invented much more rapidly than would have been the case had we depended on simple rapid prototyping trial and error. The use of theory has been across the board from evaluation to design. Contrary to the common belief that using models or theories is more expensive in time than empirical cut-and-try techniques, the models appear to have made design and evaluation much more rapid because they provided tools for thought that structured the design space and because they connected the current design effort to a literature of other knowledge.

Virtual Workspaces

We now turn to another sort of analytic model. This time the problem is that window systems require too much overhead (Fig. 8.26). The theory will be a characterization of window use called the "window working set theory." The artifact that we will design is called Rooms, a multiple-workspace paradigm.

Rooms. Central to current techniques for user interface design is the notion of a "window." Windows allow the user to interact with multiple sources of information at the same time, as if he or she had a set of dynamic

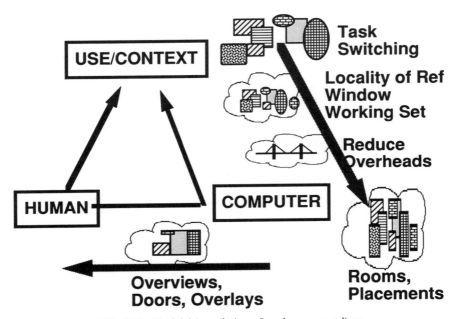

FIG. 8.26. Model-driven design of workspace paradigm.

pieces of paper. Just as in the case of multiple pieces of paper, the user uses windows as a form of external memory. A fundamental limitation on a person's ability to do any kind of intellectual task is his or her ability to access information, especially information that is in active play in the task itself. Windows allow multiple independent pieces of information from different applications to exist opportunistically at the same time and also, by being overlappable, allow the user to keep track of more information than fits on the screen at one time.

The problem with windows is that they can demand a lot of shuffling and scrolling. Users complain about seeing a restricted "keyhole view" of their information. Sometimes window systems have been accepted, especially on large-screen workstations; other times users have rejected them, especially on small-screen personal computers.

The screen of the display is a resource with very definite constraints (Henderson & Card, 1986). Regardless of how advantageous it might be to display more to the human, there is only so much space. If the screen is small and the windows are numerous, the user may spend most of his or her time shuffling the windows rather than getting anything done.

The situation is reminiscent of the design of demand paging algorithms for the virtual memory algorithms of operating systems (Denning, 1970). Programs running on a computing system often have virtual memory much larger than the physical memory available for the program, particularly when they run in a multiple programming environment. During some interval of time, only a portion of the pages of the program's virtual memory is actually referenced. This set of pages is called the program's working set. If the number of pages in the program's working set is not greater than the number of pages actually available for the program to run, the program will run efficiently. If, however, the working set is larger, then the program will spend most of its time reading and writing pages back and forth from main memory to some secondary memory device, a condition known as thrashing.

We can define an analogous concept of a *window working set* (Card, Pavel, & Farrell 1985). During a short period of time, the user desires access to a set of windows, the window working set. If the window working set can fit on the screen, then the task can be accomplished. But if it cannot, then a nonlinear transformation of behavior is likely to occur. The user will spend a larger and larger portion of his or her time in window overhead activities— bringing windows to the top, expanding and shrinking icons, scrolling. If the window working set size is large enough relative to the display size, overhead activities will dominate. The nonobvious characteristic of user behavior with windows is that overhead activities can get suddenly worse as the ratio between the window working set size and the available display space increases. There is a sort of "phase change" between these two situations. Thus the experience of users using windows on 20-in workstations may be dramatically different than the experience of users on PCs with 14-in displays.

Empirically, window references do seem to exhibit the property of locality of reference as shown by Fig. 8.27, from which we could project "swapping curves" like Fig. 8.28. The problem is made worse by the fact that users as they work seem to engage in extensive task switching (Bannon, Cypher, Greenspan, & Monty, 1983; Card & Henderson, 1987). This loads the screen up with many windows.

Task switching and the window working set notions give us a characterization of the window problem. They also suggest an improvement on window systems by utilizing the statistics of window reference in the same way that virtual memory systems utilize the locality of reference statistics for memory: Some virtual memory operating systems improve performance by using a preloading policy. If a set of memory locations can be identified that have higher probability of being referenced, given that a certain location has been referenced, then those memory locations can be swapped in ahead of time instead of being faulted in one-by-one as needed.

The Rooms™ window manager is a version of this scheme (Fig. 8.29). The user is encouraged to organize his or her windows in screens called *rooms* according to tasks, such as working on a project or reading the mail. Doors provide a method for the user to change from one room to another in a single button click. Changing rooms rapidly and automatically puts away one set of windows and displays another set. Windows can be in more than one room at the same time.

In this case, we started out with observations of user behavior. These observations were then characterized by the window working set theory. This theory revealed part of the hidden structure underlying the use. The

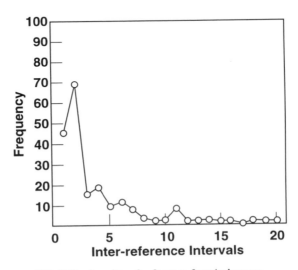

FIG. 8.27. Locality of reference for window use.

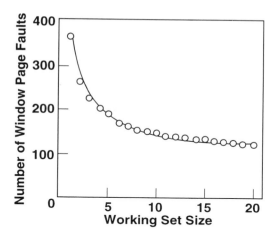

FIG. 8.28. Dependence of window faulting on size of window.

problem with window system is revealed as a nonlinear resource contention. This resource contention escalates suddenly as the resource becomes overloaded. The theoretical characterization suggests solutions that are analogies to solutions in another domain, namely, the preloading policy in virtual memory operating systems. The resulting design is a system, Rooms, widely imitated in the market.

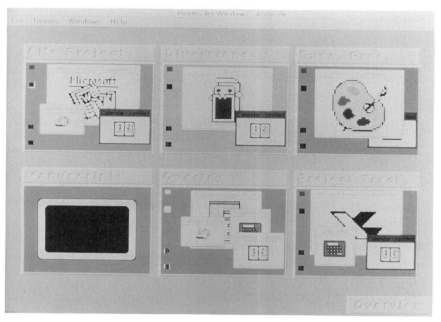

FIG. 8.29. Overview in the PC version of the Rooms[TM] multiple workspace manager.

3D Rooms. In organizing 3D workspaces, the same basic argument prevails. How can we assist a user working on large tasks with large amounts of information? The problem is the 3D analog of the desktop problem (Fig. 8.26), except that this time there is no established paradigm equivalent to the 2D desktop. We are to invent the paradigm. The theory is the window working set. The artifact is 3D Rooms.

Figure 8.30 shows the result of applying this technique to a 3D workspace. The figure shows the overview, from which all of the rooms in the workspace can be viewed. The user can traverse between rooms via *doors* or can zoom back to the overview and enter individual rooms from there. Unlike the 2D version of Rooms, the user has an arbitrary position and orientation in the room, can move in 3D, and can move objects in 3D. For these purposes, the point-of-interest flier and the object manipulation described before are used.

In this case, again we are able to reuse theoretical ideas in another context and even combine several of these designs together. Because of the abstraction of our characterization, it is possible to make numerous variants of the basic idea.

Information Visualization

We have discussed the use of analytic models to evaluate designs, to help generate designs, and to characterize a context of use. Now we use an

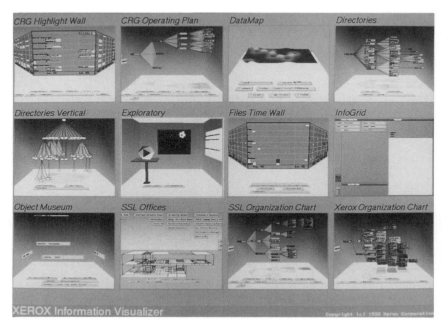

FIG. 8.30. Overview in Information Visualizer version of 3D Rooms.

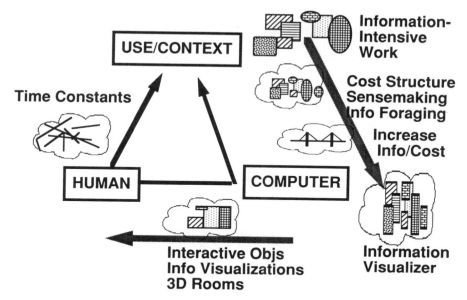

FIG. 8.31. Model-based analysis for the information visualizer.

approximate analysis of the task environment to guide experimental programming explorations of a new user interface paradigm. In this case we are in the first stage of Fig. 8.6. The problem is the access of information for information-intensive tasks (Fig. 8.31). The artifact is the Information Visualizer. The analysis is to characterize information access in terms of the cost structure of operations on information.

The information retrieval problem is usually defined more or less as follows: There exists a set of documents of various types and a person who has an interest in the information in some of them. Those documents that contain information of interest are *relevant*, others not. The problem is to find all and only the relevant documents. There are two standard figures of merit for comparing and evaluating retrieval systems: *Recall* is the percentage of all the relevant documents found, and *precision* is the percentage of the documents found that are relevant.

This formulation has been useful in the past for comparing different approaches, but new possibilities are opened up if we take a larger context into account. From a user's point of view, document retrieval and other forms of information retrieval are almost always part of some larger process of information use (Card, 1989b; Card, Robertson, & Mackinlay, 1991). Examples are sense-making (building up an interpretation of understanding of information), design (building an artifact), decision-making (building up a decision and its rationale), and response tasks (finding information to respond to a query). In each of these cases:

1. Information in the form of documents (and in less tangible forms, such as remembered knowledge or conversation) is used to produce more information, often in the form of documents, or to act directly.
2. The new information produced is usually at a higher level of organization relative to some purpose.

Framing the problem in this way suggests that what is really needed, from the viewpoint of the user, is not so much information retrieval itself but rather devices for the amplification of information-intensive work.

A key part of the analysis is to observe that information has a cost structure. Information on a (reasonably clean) desk has a lower cost of access than information in the file cabinet, which has lower cost than information in the library. Most information systems organize files in cost hierarchies, reflecting the fact that the need for information is not uniform but reflects statistics such as locality of reference, as we saw for the rooms system. The Information Visualizer system (Card et al., 1991) takes the point of view that the retrieval of information is really just the rearrangement of the cost structure of information. This is called the *information workspace* concept (Fig. 8.32). Information is retrieved into a workspace, where it is available at low cost to the user for use in his task.

The Information Visualizer project pursued four main thrusts to reducing the average cost of information access: First, the workspace is made physically larger, by use of the Rooms technique (Fig. 8.29). Second, the workspace is

Information Workspace Concept

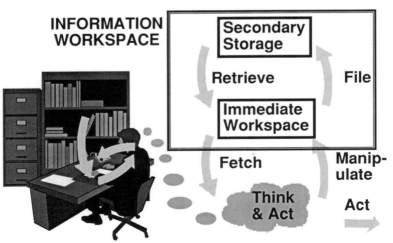

FIG. 8.32. The information workspace concept.

made more dense through use of animation and 3D. For example, the point-of-interest flier (already described) allows us to zoom in quickly on a small figure. Various models are used to set the initial design of the dynamics of the system. For example, the 100-ms constant from the Model Human Processor tells us that if it takes more than 100 ms to draw the screen, the illusion of animation will degenerate (it may actually start to degenerate before this, depending on details of the display), so there is a *governor* in the Information Visualizer that monitors drawing time and reduces rendering quality if the drawing rate becomes too slow. Using animated transitions allows the user to maintain object constancy; if the transitions are too rapid, users are confused by the transition. On the other hand, if the transition is longer than about 1 sec, the user becomes impatient. Thus the 1-sec rule (sometimes called the "uh-huh constant" in psycholinguistics) is used to pace user–system communication dialog rates.

Third, agents are used to offload work from the user. Currently, these agents are quite simple. Search agents do specialized searches, analysis agents do automatic clustering of information, and presentation agents do tailored presentations. Fourth, information visualizations are used to recode abstract information into visual structures that allow the user to quickly assimilate large amounts of information (Fig. 8.33).

In this case, an approximate theory is used to organize an experimental system approach. The experimental system is used to drive the exploration into greater depth. This system has been built (Robertson, Card, & Mackinlay, 1993). The analysis so far has allowed us to get to an architecture for this paradigm.

In the foregoing, we have illustrated a number of ways in which models can assist design to practical result: to characterize the performance of a device or other artifact, to detect and explain a fatal design choice, to generate novel designs, to reveal invisible limiting mechanisms, to give us abstractions that are the basis of the reuse of ideas across situations, to allow us to accumulate the experience from superficially different designs, or to organize an experimental system exploratory program.

CONCLUSION

Allen Newell's main interest was in the technical nature of mind. His assumption was that any good theory of the mind would have practical applications and furthermore that real applications are a testing ground (and a breeding ground) for the theory. He was particularly interested in the use of analytical theories for the design of interactive systems in the tradition of the use of other scientific theories in engineering endeavors. He thought such theories could be of use in helping to build up results on the human side of computer science.

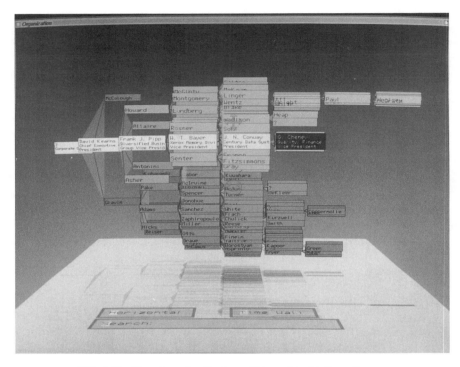

FIG. 8.33. Cone-tree visualization of hierarchical information.

The last 20 years has in fact seen a growth of work on the human side of computer science. This has led to the fledgling subdiscipline of human–computer interaction. Presently there exists a set of research results together with relevant results assimilated from supporting disciplines. The field is awaiting a codification of these results. It is not certain whether this will develop into a single field or whether it will split into a set of specialties of various disciplines. Whatever happens, human–computer interaction in some form seems almost certain to become a part of computer science. This is because over half of the code for interactive systems is concerned with interacting with the user, and computer science is being partially driven by the search for new applications and uses of computers. Furthermore, new techniques for user interfaces, such as computational video and computer graphics, are probably the largest consumer-increased computational capability.

It is natural that as experience with techniques for interacting with computers progresses and as computers become even more embedded in daily life, studies of human–computer interaction will mature by developing a set of abstractions and models that express increased understanding of the ways in which people and computers communicate. Of course, there will also be the codification of empirical methods and probably a set of approaches imported from the design and creative disciplines. This is just to say there will be artistic and engineering aspects to the design of interactive computing systems just as there are for architecture or cinema.

In the foregoing, I have tried to argue that it is, in fact, possible to make progress on the technical side of human–computer interaction, to formulate and get practical results from model-assisted design. In addition to the premium on theories that can be applied predictively to a new situation, as Newell stressed, I have also argued that it is helpful to take into account the requirements of technology development. To this end, I have tried to formulate an idealized methodology for design, model-assisted use-centered design. Then I have given examples of the use of this method to assist in the production of new and practical designs. These methods have had the practical results expected for any engineering research: new product introductions, imitations in the marketplace, and patents based on the models.

Model-assisted design is not the dominant mode for pursuing human–computer interaction today. It probably never will be, just as model-assisted design is not the dominant mode in many design disciplines. Successful theories tend to get embedded in tools or in work practices and so to become invisible in application. Most designs are just derivations of existing designs for new problems. But a field cannot intellectually mature without a process of abstraction, analysis, and codification. Moreover, even at the early stages, a little understanding can be thoroughly profitable. It is this process of abstraction, analysis, and codification, the gradual accumulation of methods and understanding resulting in the power to design, that was Newell's goal. As Newell himself put it:

All science is in the technique—all else is commentary.

APPENDIX: INVENTORY OF TEACHABLE TOPICS IN HCI

1. Nature of human–computer interaction

   - Points of view (e.g., HCI as communication, agent paradigm, tool paradigm, work-centered point of view, human/system/tasks division)
   - Objectives (e.g., productivity, user empowerment)
   - History and intellectual roots

2. Use and context of computers

   2.1. Social organization and work

      - Point of view (e.g., industrial engineering, operations research, Rasmussen's cognitive engineering, Aarhus, Hewitt's open systems)

- Models of human activity (e.g., opportunistic planning, open procedures)
- Models of small groups, organizations
- Models of work, work flow, cooperative activity, office work
- Sociotechnical systems, human organizations as adaptive open systems, mutual impact of computer systems on work and vice versa, computer systems for group tasks, case studies
- Quality of work life and job satisfaction

2.2. Application areas
- Characterization of application areas (e.g., individual vs. group, paced vs. unpaced)
- Document-oriented interfaces: text editing, document formatting, illustrators, spreadsheets, hypertext
- Communications-oriented interfaces: electronic mail, computer conferencing, telephone and voice messaging systems
- Design environments: programming environments, CAD/CAM
- Online tutorial systems and help systems
- Multimedia information kiosks
- Continuous control systems: process control systems, virtual reality systems, simulators, cockpits, video games

2.3. Human–machine fit and adaptation
- Alternate techniques for achieving fit
- Nature of adaptive systems, adaptations of human systems that cancel reliability improvements, the nature of error in adaptive redundant systems, empirical findings on user improvisation with routine systems, determinants of successful systems introduction,
- System selection: theories of system adoption
- System adaptation: customization and tailorability techniques
- User selection: compatibilities of user and system characteristics
- User adaptation: ease of learning, training methods (e.g., online tutorials), relation to system design
- User guidance: help techniques, documentation, error-handling techniques

3. Human characteristics

3.1. Human cognitive organization
- Models of cognitive architecture: symbol–system models, connectionist models, engineering models
- Phenomena and theories of memory
- Phenomena and theories of perception
- Phenomena and theories of motor skills

- Phenomena and theories of attention and vigilance
- Phenomena and theories of problem solving
- Phenomena and theories of learning and skill acquisition
- Phenomena and theories of motivation
- Users' conceptual models
- Models of human action
- Human diversity including handicapped populations

3.2. Language, communication, and interaction

- Aspects of language: syntax, semantics, pragmatics
- Formal models of language
- Pragmatic phenomena of conversational interaction (e.g., turn-taking, repair)
- Speech phenomena
- Specialized languages (e.g., graphical interaction, query, command, production systems, editors)
- Interaction reuse (e.g., history lists)

3.3. Ergonomics

- Anthropometrics in relation to workspace design
- Arrangement of displays and controls, link analysis
- Human cognitive and sensory limits
- Sensory characteristics of CRT and other display technologies, legibility, display design
- Control design
- Fatigue and health issues
- Furniture and lighting design
- Design for disabilities

4. Computer system and interface architecture

4.1. Input devices

- Survey, mechanics of particular devices, performance characteristics (human and system), devices for the handicapped, handwriting and gestures, speech input, exotic devices, characteristics, virtual devices

4.2. Recognition

- Methods for signal noise filtering
- Handprint and handwriting recognition methods (e.g., the Ledeen recognizer, the Rubine recognizer); gesture recognition methods
- Neural net recognizers, backpropagation, feature-based recognition
- Video feature recognition (e.g., pan and zoom detection), face identification, object detection
- Barcodes, glyphs, and other recognition-oriented displays

4.3. Output devices

- Survey, mechanics of particular devices, vector devices, raster devices, frame buffers and image stores, canvases, event handling, performance characteristics, devices for the handicapped, sound and speech output, 3D displays, exotic devices, characteristics, virtual devices

4.4. Rendering

- Geometry in 2- and 3-space, linear transformations
- Graphics primitives and attributes: bitmap and voxel representations, raster-op, 2D primitives, text primitives, polygon representation, 3D primitives, quadtrees and octtrees, device independent images, page definition languages
- Solid modeling, splines, surface modeling, hidden surface removal, animation, rendering algorithms, lighting models
- Color representation, color maps, color ranges of devices

4.5. System architecture

- Layers model of the architecture of dialogues and windowing systems, dialogue system reference models
- Screen imaging models (e.g., RasterOp, Postscript)
- Window manager models (e.g., shared address space, client–server), analysis of major window systems (e.g., X, New Wave, Macintosh)
- Models of application-to-dialogue manager connection
- Look and feel
- Standardization and interoperability

4.6. Dialogue architecture

(a) Dialogue inputs

- Types of input purposes (e.g., selection, discrete parameter specification, continuous control)
- Input techniques: keyboard techniques (e.g., commands, menus), mouse-based techniques (e.g., picking, rubber-band lines), pen-based techniques (e.g., character recognition, gesture), voice-based techniques

(b) Dialogue outputs

- Types of output purposes
- Output techniques (e.g., scrolling display, windows, animation, sprites, fish-eye displays)
- Screen layout issues (e.g., focus, clutter, visual logic)

(c) Dialogue interaction techniques

- Dialogue type and techniques (e.g., alphanumeric techniques, form filling, menu selection, icons and direct manipulation, generic functions, natural language)

- Navigation and orientation in dialogues, error management
- Multimedia and nongraphical dialogues: speech input, speech output, voice mail, video mail, active documents, videodisk, CD-ROM
- Agents and AI techniques
- Multiperson dialogues

(d) Dialogue issues
- Real-time response issues
- Manual control theory
- Supervisory control, automatic systems, embedded systems
- Standards
- Look and feel, copyright

4.7. Dialogue genre

- Interaction metaphors (e.g., tool metaphor, agent metaphor)
- Content metaphors (e.g., desktop metaphor, paper document metaphor)
- Persona, personality, point of view
- Workspace models
- Transition management (e.g., fades, pans)
- Relevant techniques from other media (e.g., film, theater)
- Style and aesthetics

5. Development process

5.1. Approaches to design

- Industrial design basics
- Alternative system development processes (e.g., waterfall model, participatory design), life cycle model, choice of method under time/resource constraint
- Task analysis techniques (e.g., field studies, analytical methods), task allocation, market analysis
- Design specification techniques
- Design analysis techniques (e.g., objects and actions)
- Industrial design basics
- Design case studies and empirical analyses of design

5.2. Implementation techniques and tools

- Relationships between design, implementation, and testing
- Independence and reusability, application independence, device independence
- Prototyping techniques (e.g., storyboarding, video, "Wizard of Oz," HyperCard, rapid prototype implementations)
- Dialogue toolkits (e.g., MacAp, NextStep, UIMSs, HyperCard)

- Object-oriented methods
- Data representation and algorithms

5.3. Evaluation techniques

- Productivity
- Figures of merit (e.g., time, errors, learnability, design for guessing, preference, etc.)
- Usability testing techniques, linking testing to specifications
- Formal evaluations techniques, field observation methods, participant observers, interview techniques, questionnaire design, psychometric methods, sample bias, video protocols, system logging, experiment design, methods from psychological and sociological evaluation fields, subject ethics

5.4. Example systems and case studies

(a) Command-oriented

- OS/360 JCL (batch-oriented command style, baseline for seeing later improvements)
- PC DOS (command style interface learned by millions)
- Airline check-in system (time pressure, ambiguous input, distributed system)

(b) Graphics-oriented

- Xerox Star (icon-window interface, generic commands)
- Apple Macintosh (similar interface over many applications)
- HyperCard (frame-based system)

(c) Frame-oriented

- Promis (rapid response to large set of frames, touch-panel oriented)
- ZOG (user-tailorable, rapid-response system, large number of frames, first commercial frame-based system)
- HyperCard (graphically oriented frame-oriented system with user programming language, first mass market frame-oriented system)

(d) User-defined combinatorics

- UNIX operating system (strong combinatoric architecture paired with weak human factors)
- Emacs (language-oriented, large combinatoric command set)
- VisiCalc (home-run application with strong conceptual model that succeeded despite weak human factors)
- DBaseIII (simple, but successful, user applications generator)

(e) Interfaces for untrained, walk-up users

- Olympic Message System (practical use of user testing under time pressure)
- Nintendo Super Mario Brothers (learnable without a manual by grade-school children)

REFERENCES

ACM Special Interest Group on Computer-Human Interaction Curriculum Development Group. (1992). *ACM SIGCHI curricula for human–computer interaction.* New York: ACM.

Bannon, L., Cypher, A., Greenspan, S., & Monty, M. L. (1983, December). Evaluation and analysis of users' activity organization. *Proceedings of the CHI '83 ACM Conference on Human Factors in Software, Boston* (pp. 54–57). New York: ACM Press.

Bouvair, S., Kieras, D. E., & Polson, P. G. (1990). The acquisition and performance of text-editing skill: A cognitive complexity analysis. *Human Computer Interaction, 5*(1), 1–48.

Card, S. K. (1989a). Theory-driven design research. In G. R. McMillan, D. Beevis, E. Salas, M. H. Strub, R. Sutton, & L. van Breda (Eds.), *Applications of human performance models to system design* (pp. 501–509). New York: Plenum Press.

Card, S. K. (1989b, September). Information workspaces. *Proceedings of Friend21 International Symposium on Next Generation Human Interface Technologies*, Tokyo, Japan (pp. 5-A-1–5-A-8). Tokyo: Institute for Personalized Information Environment.

Card, S. K. (in press). Pioneers and Settlers: Methods used in successful user interface design. In C. Lewis & P. Polson (Eds.), *Success cases in HCI*. San Francisco: Morgan-Kaufmann.

Card, S. K., & De Iuliis, D. (1984). *Finger manipulable, sliding pointing device for human-computer interaction* (Invention Proposal IP/840816). Palo Alto, CA: Xerox Palo Alto Research Center.

Card, S. K., English, W. K., & Burr, B. J. (1978). Evaluation of mouse, rate-controlled isometric joystick, step keys, and text keys for text selection on a CRT. *Ergonomics, 21*, 601–613.

Card, S. K., & Henderson, D. A., Jr. (1987). A multiple, virtual-workspace interface to support user task switching. In J. M. Carroll & P. P. Tanner (Eds.), *Proceedings of HCI+GI*, Toronto, April 5–9 (pp. 53–59). New York: ACM.

Card, S. K., Mackinlay, J. M., & Robertson, G. G. (1991). A morphological analysis of the design space of input devices. *ACM Transactions on Information Systems, 9*(2), 99–122.

Card, S. K., Moran, T. P., & Newell, A. (1977). *Applied information processing psychology for Xerox office information systems* (AIP Memo 99). Palo Alto, CA: Xerox Palo Alto Research Center.

Card, S. K., Moran, T. P., & Newell, A. (1983). *The psychology of human–computer interaction.* Hillsdale, NJ: Lawrence Erlbaum Associates.

Card, S. K., Pavel, M., & Farrell, J. E. (1985). Window-based computer dialogues. *Human-computer interaction—Interact '84* (pp. 239–243). Amsterdam: North Holland.

Card, S. K., Robertson, G. G., & Mackinlay, J. D. (1991). The Information Visualizer: An information workspace. In *Proceedings of CHI '91, ACM Conference on Human Factors in Software Development* (pp. 181–188).

Corker, K., Davis, L., Papazian, B., & Pew, R. (1986). *Development of an advanced task analysis methodology and demonstration for Army-NASA aircrew/aircraft integration* (Tech. Rep. No. 6124). Cambridge, MA: Bolt Beranek and Newman, Inc.

Crossman, E. R. F. W., & Goodeve, P. J. (1963, July). *Feedback control of hand movements and Fitts' law.* Paper presented at a meeting of the Experimental Psychology Society, Oxford.

Denning, P. J. (1970). Virtual memory. *Computing Surveys, 2*(3), 153–189.

Denning, P. J., et al. (1988). *Report on the ACM task force on the core of computer science* (Order No. 201880). New York: ACM Press.

Elkind, J. I., Card, S. K., Hochberg, J., & Huey, B. M. (1990). *Human performance models for computer-aided engineering.* Boston: Academic Press.

Gray, W., John, B. E., & Atwood, M. E. (1993). Project Ernestine: Validating a GOMS Analysis for predicting and explaining real-world task performance. *Human-Computer Interaction, 8,* 237–309.

Henderson, D. A., Jr., & Card, S. K. (1986). Rooms: The use of multiple virtual workspaces to reduce space contention in a window-based graphical user interface. *ACM Transactions on Graphics, 5*(3), 211–243.

Howe, A., & Young, R. M. (1991). Predicting the learnability of task-action mappings. *Proceedings of ACM CHI '91 Conference on Human Factors in Computing Systems* (pp. 113–118).

Hughes, T. P. (1983). *Networks of power, electrification in western society, 1880–1930.* Baltimore, MD: Johns Hopkins University Press.

Kieras, D. (1988). Towards a practical GOMS model methodology for user interface design. In M. Helander (Ed.), *Handbook of human–computer interaction* (pp. 135–157). New York: North-Holland.

Langoff, G. D. (1973). *Human motor performance in precise microscopic work.* Unpublished doctoral dissertation, University of Michigan.

Lyon, R. F. (1981). *The optical mouse and an architectural methodology for smart digital sensors* (Tech. Rep. No. VLSI-81-1). Palo Alto, CA: Xerox Palo Alto Research Center.

Mackinlay, J. D., Card, S. K., & Robertson, G. G. (1991). Rapid, controlled movement through a virtual 3D workspace. *Computer Graphics, 24*(4, August), 1971–1976.

Newell, A. (1971). *Notes on a proposal for a psychological research unit* (AIP Memo No. 1). Palo Alto, CA: Xerox Palo Alto Research Center.

Newell, A., Perlis, A., & Simon, H. (1967). What is computer science? *Science, 157,* 1373–1374.

Norman, D. A., & Draper, S. W. (Eds.). (1986). *User centered system design: New perspectives on human-computer interaction.* Hillsdale, NJ: Lawrence Erlbaum Associates.

Nunberg, G. (1993). The places of books in the age of electronic reproduction. *Representations, 42*(Spring), 13–37.

Perry, T. S., & Voelcker, J. (1989, September). Of mice and menus: Designing the user-friendly interface. *IEEE Spectrum,* 46–51.

Petroski, H. (1992). The evolution of artifacts. *American Scientist, 80*(5), 416–420.

Radwin, R. G., Vanderheiden, G. C., & Lin, M. (1990). A method for evaluating head-controlled computer input devices using Fitts' law. *Human Factors, 32*(4), 423–438.

Robertson, G. G., Card, S. K., & Mackinlay, J. D.(1993). Information visualization using 3D interactive animation. *Communications of the ACM, 36*(4), 56–71.

Robertson, G., Newell, A., & Ramakrishna, K. (1981). The ZOG approach to man-machine communication. *International Journal of Man-Machine Studies, 14*(4, May), 461–488.

Rouse, W. B., & Cody, W. J. (1988). On the design of man-machine systems: Principles, practices, and prospects. *Automatica, 24.*

Rouse, W. B., & Cody, W. J. (1989). Designers' criteria for choosing human performance models. In G. R. McMillan, D. Beeris, E. Salas, M. H. Strub, R. Sutton, & L. Van Breda (Eds.), *Application of human performance models to system design* (pp. 7–14). New York: Plenum.

Siewiorek, D., Bell, G., & Newell, A. (1981). *Computer structures.* New York: McGraw-Hill.

Westfalische Wilhelms Universitat Munster. (1993). *SANe.* Demonstration, InterCHI 93, Amsterdam.

Ziman, J. (1976). *The force of knowledge.* Cambridge: Cambridge University Press.

DISCUSSION

Task Matters

Bonnie E. John
Carnegie Mellon University

Allen Newell believed there was a symbiotic relationship between theory and application. In particular, a good theory of the human mind would "help us in arranging [the human–computer] interface so it is easy, efficient, error-free—even enjoyable" (Card, Moran, & Newell, 1983, p. 1). In return, "applied investigations vitalize the basic science; they reveal new phenomena and set forth clearly what it is that needs explanation" (Card et al., 1983, p. 14). In Chapter 8, Stuart Card gave us many examples on one side of this relationship, that is, how theories of human performance can be applied to the design of computer systems. He showed us how theories can be used to evaluate artifacts and design ideas, how they can generate novel ideas, give us abstractions to help accumulate design experience, and help organize exploratory systems development. In this chapter, I take us around the full cycle of the symbiotic relationship several times, from application to theory, from theory to application, with human–computer interaction (HCI) in computer system design as the application and Soar as the theory of human performance.

Before we begin our circular journey, we should examine the choice of HCI as an application area. When looking to cultivate a theory/application relationship, the task matters. That is, many application tasks will fit into such a relationship, but different tasks will provide different opportunities for the theory to contribute to the world and different feedback to expand the horizons of the theory. With Newell's goal of understanding the mechanisms of intelligence, HCI is by no means the only task that would have

313

a productive relationship with Soar. However, it does have some properties that make it a good choice.

To illustrate those properties, consider Fig. 1, which shows the cycle of activities people perform when they are doing HCI tasks. People get information visually and aurally from the computer or other external sources, process that information in some way, and respond with an action that affects the world, often by inputting information to the computer, all the while keeping within real-time demands, learning, and making errors. Models of human performance on tasks described by this cycle must be complete—that is, they must include a theory of each of the relevant activities. Even if a model finesses some aspect of the behavior (e.g., perception, motor action, or learning) or ignores the commission and detection of errors or the passage of real time, the human performance data

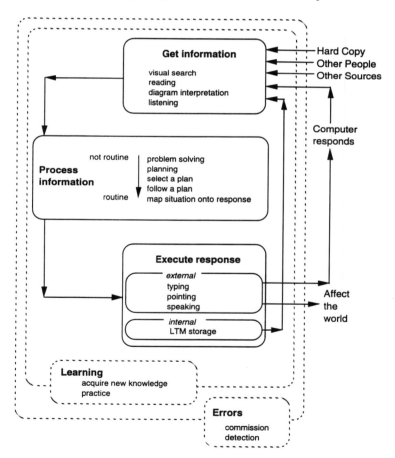

FIG. 1. Activities involved in many HCI tasks.

are there as a reminder of opportunities for the theories to be extended or refined. Thus, HCI tasks force complete models of performance (although they may be quite approximate in spots), force consonance with human capabilities, and force real-time demands on theories of the mind. On the other side of the theory/application relationship, HCI problems are rampant in the world, and pragmatically useful theory-based solutions to those problems would be joyfully welcomed. Newell also encouraged the pursuit of other applied problems with Soar, some of which are discussed in other chapters of this volume. For instance, building Soar-based autonomous agents can be pragmatically important and can force models to deal with completeness, uncertainty, and real time but not necessarily consonance with human capabilities. Natural language comprehension can have important applications in information retrieval or filtering and it forces models to deal with real time and human capabilities, but (as it is studied today by most linguists) not an extended cycle of activity. Newell thought education was an interesting application for testing Soar, but never pursued that option in depth apart from computer-assisted education (often considered a form of HCI). As Card told us, HCI captured Newell's attention early in his career and provided a rich enough arena to hold his attention for decades.

Having identified HCI as an application symbiote of a theory of mind, we can trace some cyclical contributions from application to theory and back again. We start with HCI influences on the Soar architecture, move to Soar's modeling of specific HCI tasks and what those tasks forced the Soar theory to confront, and end with the influences of an HCI formalism, GOMS, on mechanisms in Soar and how those Soar mechanisms in turn pose questions back to GOMS (Fig. 2).

THE INFLUENCE OF HCI ON THE SOAR ARCHITECTURE

In *Unified Theories of Cognition* (Newell, 1990), Newell described the Model Human Processor (MHP; Card et al., 1983; also Fig. 8.1, in this volume) as a harbinger of unified theories of cognition and, by implication, of Soar.

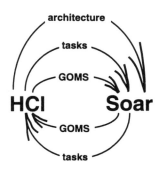

FIG. 2. The symbiotic cycle between HCI and Soar.

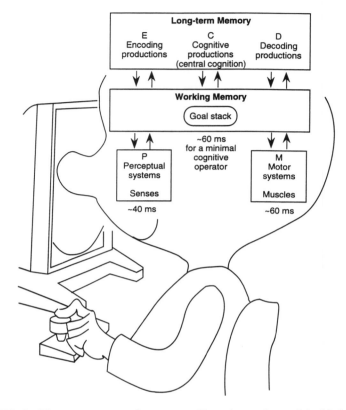

FIG. 3. The components and constants of Soar. An amalgam of the Model Human Processor (Fig. 2.1, Card, Moran & Newell, 1983), the total cognitive system (Fig. 4.15, Newell, 1990), and the stipulated time constants for Soar (Fig. 5.6, Newell, 1990).

Card told us that one goal of the MHP was to allow calculations of human performance in HCI tasks at least as good as Herb Simon's colloquium estimates. To this end, the MHP provided a component structure, processor cycle times, and the means to combine them to make quantitative estimates of performance. This proved so useful both pragmatically for HCI design and as a test of cognitive theory that Soar also uses a similar structure and similar cycle times to make such calculations (Fig. 3).

SOAR MODELS OF HCI TASKS

In recent years, the Soar architecture has been the basis for several research projects in HCI. Because Soar is embodied in a programming language, it is more practical for exploring more extensive and complex tasks than the

MHP allowed with its reliance on hand calculations. Because Soar encompasses both problem solving and learning, it significantly extends the tasks that can be modeled beyond the capabilities of the more shallow and less mechanistic MHP. Among others, HCI tasks modeled in Soar include the use of a browser for finding information in a programming environment (Peck & John, 1992), the video game playing of a 9-year-old (John & Vera, 1992), students' learning in an educational microworld (Conati & Lehman, 1993), the communications and checklist maintenance of the NASA Test Director (John, Remington, & Steier, 1991), the use of an automated teller machine (Vera, Lewis, & Lerch, 1993; Wharton, 1994), and problem solving in an operating system (Rieman, Lewis, Young, & Polson, 1994). In addition to providing insight into the details of specific tasks, models such as these have helped provide explicit, operational definitions of key usability concepts (e.g., consistency in an interface; Rieman et al., 1994).

In addition to these traditional cognitive models that contain the knowledge of how to perform specific tasks, Soar is the basis for an alternative use of cognitive models in HCI called programmable user models (PUMs). PUMs can be considered "generic learners" and the HCI designer "teaches" the PUM how to use a proposed interface. If it is easy to teach the PUM to use an interface, then it will be easy to teach people to use that interface. Thus, PUMs provide a method for assessing the learnability of an interface (Young, Green & Simon, 1989).

Unlike a robust model like Fitts' Law, for which Card demonstrated several roles in the design of input devices, Soar models have not yet reached the stage where they can be applied reliably or efficiently to real-world HCI design problems. However, their potential for prediction and explanation of learning and problem solving holds the promise of expanded use of analytic models in HCI design in the future.

On the return trip in the symbiotic cycle, these HCI models have pushed the envelope of Soar's theory and capabilities. As just one example, consider the task of the NASA Test Director (NTD). The NTD's task is to keep track of the thousands of tests that must be performed on the Space Shuttle before it can launch. To do this, he communicates with the 200 members of the launch team and manipulates what amounts to a 3,000-page checklist. This task requires visual search, natural-language comprehension and generation, and specialized task knowledge. The effort to model the real-time behavior of the NTD using Soar was the first to test the rhetoric of a unified theory of cognition: that independently developed models of different human capabilities should be easily integrated in the service of tasks that use those capabilities. NTD-Soar combined independently developed models of visual search (Weismeyer, 1992) and natural-language comprehension (Lehman, Lewis, & Newell, 1991; Lewis, 1993) with task knowledge. This HCI model defined the problems of such integration and proposed solutions (Nelson, Lehman, & John, 1994), significantly advancing the Soar community's understanding of how to integrate independently developed models. For instance, models of a single task often rely on an impasse situation where no operators for that task are applicable. However, models of complex tasks that combine several subtasks requiring different capabilities rarely run out of things to do in this way; rather, they must learn to interrupt lower priority subtasks in favor of higher priority subtasks to complete the total task successfully. This dictates a different impasse and problem-space design than was foreseen by any of the single-task models but that can now be used by single-task models in preparation for future integration.

GOMS AND SOAR

Another fruit of Newell's HCI work with Stuart Card and Tom Moran was the GOMS family of models Card discussed in Chapter 8. This family of models has been used to predict expert behavior with a large variety of HCI applications: text editors (Bovair, Kieras, & Polson, 1990; Card et al., 1983; Polson & Kieras, 1985), graphic editors (Ziegler, Hoppe, & Fahnrich, 1986), spreadsheets (Lerch, Mantei, & Olson, 1987), digital oscilloscopes (Lee, Polson, & Bailey, 1989), video games (John, Vera, & Newell, 1994), telephone operator workstations (Gray, John, & Atwood, 1993; Nielsen & Phillips, 1993) map digitizing (Haunold & Kuhn, 1994), ergonomic CAD (computer-assisted design) systems (Gong & Kieras, 1994), and a pilot's flight management computer (Irving, Polson, & Irving, 1994). Because this modeling technique stems from the same information-processing approach as Soar, we should be able to map the constructs of GOMS to the constructs of Soar, thereby allowing Soar to replicate the successes of GOMS.

The components of a GOMS analysis are the user's goals, the operators (perceptual, cognitive or motor acts) afforded by the computer system to accomplish those goals, frequently used series of operators and subgoals called methods, and, if there are several methods to accomplish a single goal, selection rules to choose between them. Card et al. (1983) demonstrated an iterative-deepening approach to defining goals and operators: That is, the analyst first defines high-level functional goals and coarse operators that accomplish those goals. Depending on the requirements of the design situation, the analyst can then split these coarse operators into their component parts, transforming the coarse operators into goals and defining methods to accomplish these goals comprised of a sequence of smaller operators.

Given this procedure for conducting a GOMS analysis, the obvious mapping between GOMS components and the constructs of Soar are that

FIG. 4. Partial instantiation of a
GOMS analysis of a 9-year-old playing Super Mario Bros. 3™.

```
GOAL: PLAY-GAME
.   GOAL: SEARCH-IN-BLOCK
.   .   GOAL: HIT-FROM-BOTTOM
.   .   .   PRESS-RIGHT-BUTTON
.   .   .   PRESS-A-BUTTON
.   GOAL: ATTACK-ENEMY
.   .   GOAL: JUMP-ON
.   .   .   PRESS-RIGHT-BUTTON
.   .   .   PRESS-A-BUTTON
```

GOMS goals map to Soar operators that are implemented in their own problem spaces, and GOMS operators map to the lowest level Soar operators. GOMS methods are simply subgoals in a goal hierarchy and map to Soar operators that are implemented in lower level problem spaces. Finally, GOMS selection rules are Soar productions that contain search-control knowledge.

As an example of this straightforward mapping of GOMS to Soar, consider the GOMS model of a 9-year-old playing the Nintendo of America, Inc., game Super Mario Bros. 3™ in Fig. 4. If you implement each goal in the GOMS analysis as a nonprimitive operator in a Soar model, and allow each such operator to impasse and be implemented in a lower problem space, Soar's problem-space structure and prechunked behavior mirror the GOMS analysis (Fig. 5).

This mapping seems straightforward and natural for Soar; it seems that we are listening to the architecture and doing what it suggests. However, if we listen more closely, we find that there is a severe problem with this implementation of GOMS in Soar. GOMS has been characterized as a formalism for describing the goal hierarchy of experts. As such, it has had success at predicting the routine performance of experts, as opposed to novices who have to search or problem-solve to accomplish a task. But Fig. 5 shows the structure and behavior of a Soar model that has not yet learned how to perform this task. It has a lack of knowledge in an upper problem space and impasses to find the necessary information. Soar will learn from the resolution of the impasse and store the results in a chunk. This chunk will then be available in the same situation where the impasse occurred the next time through the game, and the Soar model will no longer need to impasse. Hence, the postlearning behavior will be as shown in Fig. 6. This postlearning model claims that our 9-year-old would simply decide to play the game and proceed to press all the buttons at the right time with his fingers connected directly to his eyes, without any thought at all. Although informal observations of 9-year-olds may lend support to this prediction, more precise measurements of their response times reveal that there do seem to be some thought processes intervening between the perceptual and motor processes.

This and several other HCI tasks being modeled in Soar seemed to reach the same problem at the approximately the same time. This problem has led to a serious rethinking of the representation of goal hierarchies in Soar and the interaction between learning and input/output. The Soar community is actively researching these interesting questions, exploring a design space of modeling idioms unarticulated before the problems were brought to the fore with HCI tasks (Howes & Young, 1992).

As much as implementing GOMS has influenced research in Soar, this exploration in Soar confronts GOMS and the HCI community with several questions. The most poignant questions the role of goal hierarchies in expert behavior. GOMS models have always been most successful at pre-

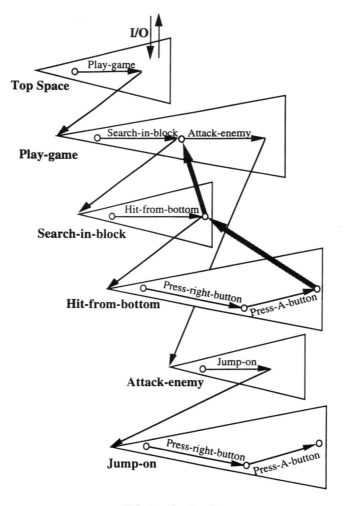

FIG. 5. *(Continued)*

```
G:  G1
P:  P1 (top-space)
S:  S1
O:  O1 (play-game)
==>  G:  G2
     P:  P2 (play-game)
     S:  S2
     O:  O2 (search-in-block)
     ==>  G:  G3
          P:  P3 (search-in-block)
          S:  S3
          O:  O3 (hit-from-bottom)
          ==>  G:  G4
               P:  P4 (hit-from-bottom)
               S:  S1
               O:  O4 (press-right-button)
*******************Right-Button Pressed
               O:  O5 (press-A-button)
*******************A-Button Pressed
     O:  O2 (attack-enemy)
     ==>  G:  G3
          P:  P3 (attack-enemy)
          S:  S3
          O:  O3 (jump-on)
          ==>  G:  G4
               P:  P4 (jump-on)
               S:  S1
               O:  O4 (press-right-button)
*******************Right-Button Pressed
               O:  O5 (press-A-button)
*******************A-Button Pressed
```

FIG. 5. (a) Problem-space diagram of the straight-forward mapping of the GOMS model in Fig. 4 to Soar. (b) This trace of the Soar model depicted in Fig. 5a matches the goal structure of the GOMS model. (Lines marked by *** indicate that a motor action has been taken in the external environment, outside of central cognition.

dicting the behavior of experts and thus the components of a GOMS model, the goal hierarchy in particular, have come to be associated with the knowledge that experts possess and the processes they go through. However, there has been a quiet, almost unarticulated controversy within the GOMS community that is made clear by the Soar explorations. Card et al. (1983) originally found no additional predictive power in including time for goal manipulation so they omitted it as superfluous. However, other versions of GOMS assign time to explicit goal manipulation in their predictions of task performance (Bovair et al., 1990). Likewise, some of the Soar modeling techniques currently being explored encode the goal hierarchies with deliberate acts, adding time for each level in the goal hierarchy, and others provide the goal hierarchy for novice behavior but it chunks away with practice and is no longer evident in expert behavior. At present, there is no empirical evidence to unequivocally support or

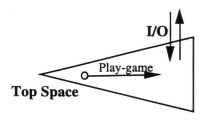

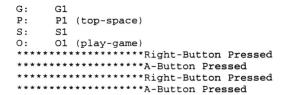

```
G:      G1
P:      P1 (top-space)
S:      S1
O:      O1 (play-game)
******************Right-Button Pressed
******************A-Button Pressed
******************Right-Button Pressed
*****************A-Button Pressed
```

FIG. 6. Problem-space diagram and the post-chunking Soar trace for the straight-forward mapping of the GOMS model in Fig. 4 to Soar. The post-chunking trace does not retain the goal/subgoal hierarchy and produces super-human behavior, predicting that there will be no processing in central cognition once the game is started, only perception and motor actions outside of central cognition. (Lines marked by *** indicate that a motor action has been taken in the external environment, outside of central cognition.) Super Mario Bros. 3 is a registered trademark of Nintendo of America, Inc.

refute either of these hypotheses or the several others in between. In this contribution of theory to application, Soar not only clarifies a long-standing but unarticulated difference between GOMS modeling practices, but provides a mechanism for exploring the space of possibilities.

And so it goes. The symbiotic cycle continues toward Newell's goal of understanding of the human mind, producing interesting questions for both theory and applications and useful side effects for HCI as it spirals forward.

REFERENCES

Bovair, S., Kieras, D. E., & Polson, P. G. (1990). The acquisition and performance of text-editing skill: A cognitive complexity analysis. *Human–Computer Interaction, 5*(1), 1–48.

Card, S. K., Moran, T. P., & Newell, A. (1983). *The psychology of human-computer interaction.* Hillsdale, NJ: Lawrence Erlbaum Associates.

Conati, C., & Lehman, J. F. (1993). Toward a model of student education in microworlds. *Proceedings of the Fifteenth Annual Conference of the Cognitive Science Society* (pp. 353–358), Boulder, CO.

Gong, R., & Kieras, D. (1994). A validation of the GOMS methodology in the development of a specialized, commercial software application. *Proceedings of the CHI'94 Conference on*

Human Factors in Computing Systems (pp. 351–357). New York: Association for Computing Machinery.

Gray, W. D., John, B. E., & Atwood, M. E. (1993). Project Ernestine: Validating a GOMS analysis for predicting and explaining real-world task performance. *Human-Computer Interaction, 8,* 237–309.

Haunold, P., & Kuhn, W. (1994). A keystroke level analysis of a graphics application: Manual map digitizing. *Proceedings of the CHI'94 Conference on Human Factors in Computing Systems* (pp. 337–343). New York: Association for Computing Machinery.

Howes, A., & Young, R. M. (1992, October). *Organizing goals in Soar: Articulating the design space.* Paper presented at the Eleventh Soar Workshop, Carnegie Mellon University, Pittsburgh.

Irving, S., Polson, P., & Irving, J. E. (1994). A GOMS analysis of the advanced automated cockpit. *Proceedings of the CHI'94 Conference on Human Factors in Computing Systems* (pp. 344–350). New York: Association for Computing Machinery.

John, B. E., Remington, R. W., & Steier, D. M. (1991). *An analysis of space shuttle countdown activities: Preliminaries to a computational model of the NASA test director* (Tech. Rep. No. CMU-CS-91-138). Pittsburgh: Carnegie Mellon University, School of Computer Science.

John, B. E., & Vera, A. H. (1992). A GOMS analysis for a graphic, machine-paced, highly interactive task. *Proceedings of the CHI'92 Conference on Human Factors in Computing Systems* (pp. 251–258). New York: Association for Computing Machinery.

John, B. E., Vera, A. H., & Newell, A. (1994). Toward real-time GOMS: A model of expert behavior in a highly interactive task. *Behavior and Information Technology, 13,* 4.

Lee, A. Y., Polson, P. G., & Bailey, W. A. (1989). Learning and transfer of measurement tasks. *Proceedings of the CHI'89 Conference on Human Factors in Computing Systems* (pp. 115–120). New York: Association for Computing Machinery.

Lehman, J. F., Lewis, R. L., & Newell, A. (1991). *Natural language comprehension in Soar: Spring 1991* (Tech. Rep. No. CMU-CS-91-117). Pittsburgh: Carnegie Mellon University, School of Computer Science.

Lerch, F. J., Mantei, M. M., & Olson, J. R. (1989). Translating ideas into action: Cognitive analysis of errors in spreadsheet formulas. *Proceedings of the CHI'89 Conference on Human Factors in Computing Systems* (pp. 121–126). New York: Association for Computing Machinery.

Lewis, R. L. (1993). *An architecturally-based theory of human sentence comprehension* (Tech. Rep. No. CMU-CS-93-226). Pittsburgh: Carnegie Mellon University, School of Computer Science.

Nelson, G. H., Lehman, J. F., & John, B. E. (1994). Integrating cognitive capabilities in a real-time task. *Proceedings of the Sixteenth Annual Conference of the Cognitive Science Society* (pp. 658–663), Atlanta, GA.

Newell, A. (1990). *Unified theories of cognition.* Cambridge, MA: Harvard University Press.

Nielsen, J., & Phillips, V. L. (1993). Estimating the relative usability of two interfaces: Heuristic, formal, and empirical methods compared. *Proceedings of INTERCHI, 1993* (pp. 214–221). New York: Association for Computing Machinery.

Peck, V. A., & John, B. E. (1992). Browser-Soar: A cognitive model of a highly interactive task. *Proceedings of the CHI'92 Conference on Human Factors in Computing Systems* (pp. 165–172). New York: Association for Computing Machinery.

Polson, P. G., & Kieras, D. E. (1985). A quantitative model of learning and performance of text-editing knowledge. *Proceedings of the CHI'85 Conference on Human Factors in Computing Systems* (pp. 207–212). New York: Association for Computing Machinery.

Rieman, J., Lewis, C., Young, R. M., & Polson, P. G. (1994). "Why is a raven like a writing desk?" Lessons in interface consistency and analogical reasoning from two cognitive architectures. *Proceedings of the CHI'94 Conference on Human Factors in Computing Systems* (pp. 438–444). New York: Association for Computing Machinery.

Vera, A. H., Lewis, R. L., & Lerch, F. J. (1993). Situated decision-making and recognition-based learning: Applying symbolic theories to interactive tasks. *Proceedings of Fifteenth Annual Conference of the Cognitive Science Society* (pp. 84–95), Boulder, CO.

Wharton, C. (1994). *A comparison study of Soar and the construction-integration model.* Unpublished doctoral dissertation, University of Colorado, Boulder.

Wiesmeyer, M. D. (1992). *An operator-based model of human covert visual attention.* Unpublished doctoral dissertation, University of Michigan, Ann Arbor.

Young, R. M., Green, T. R. G., & Simon, T. (1989). Programmable user models for predictive evaluation of interface designs. *Proceedings of CHI'89 Conference on Human Factors in Computer Systems* (pp. 15–19). New York: Association for Computing Machinery.

Ziegler, J. E., Hoppe, H. U., & Fahnrich, K. P. (1986). Learning and transfer for text and graphics with a direct manipulation interface. *Proceedings of CHI'86 Human Factors in Computing Systems* (pp. 72–77). New York: Association for Computing Machinery.

Chapter 9

Scientific Discovery Processes in Children, Adults, and Machines

David Klahr
Carnegie Mellon University

Allen Newell's primary research goals were so fundamental, and his accomplishments so prodigious, that two fields—cognitive psychology and artificial intelligence (AI)—trace their ancestry to his pioneering work with Herbert Simon in the late 1950s. Newell and Simon started investigating the nature of intelligence by using very simple domains: closed-form games and puzzles. Forty years later, their successes are indicated by the fact that we are able to use the current versions of the methodologies and theories that they invented to investigate the cognitive processes that support scientific discovery: a domain that represents one of the pinnacles of human intelligence. The early tensions and mutual interactions between psychological approaches and artificial intelligence approaches remain in the studies of scientific discovery: In psychology, the research goal is to determine just how people manage to do science, whereas in AI the goal is to build systems that can make discoveries. This work has produced an accumulating body of evidence that there can really be a "science of science." As a result, the old view of scientific discovery—that it is mystical, ineffable, transcendent, unknowable—is giving way to both a descriptive and a synthetic science of discovery. The descriptive side is mainly from cognitive psychology, and the synthetic side is mainly from machine learning. Early interest in the psychology of science can be traced to Bruner, Goodnow, and Austin (1956), Wason (1960), and Simon (1966, 1973), among others. The state of the art as of a dozen years ago is summarized in Tweney, Doherty, and Mynatt (1981). The more recent resurgence of interest in the "cognitive science of science" can be attributed to Simon and his colleagues (Cheng & Simon, 1992; Kulkarni & Simon, 1988; Langley, Simon, Bradshaw, & Zytkow, 1987; Qin & Simon, 1990; Valdez-Perez, Simon, & Murphy, 1992). But psychologists were not the first, nor the only, scientists to argue for the ultimate knowability of the process of scientific discovery. More than 50 years ago, Einstein wrote: "The whole of science is nothing more than a refinement of every day thinking" (Physics & reality, 1936, reprinted in Einstein, 1950, p. 59). He also wrote, "The scientific way of forming concepts differs from that which we use in our daily life, not basically, but merely in the more precise definition of concepts and conclusions; more painstaking and systematic choice of experimental material, and greater logical economy" ("The common language of science," 1941, reprinted in Einstein, 1950, p. 98).

So the basic premise—that scientific thinking involves some of the same processes used by ordinary folks—is not new. What *is* new is what we have learned in recent years about the psychological process underlying scientific discovery: the "precise definitions," "systematic choices," and "logical economy" of which Einstein speaks. These are the processes that empower scientific discovery, and that is what I address in this chapter.

There are five parts to this chapter: In the first part, I describe a framework for characterizing the discovery process. Next, I describe the psychological processes used by adults and children when they are engaged in scientific discovery. I summarize the results of empirical studies in my lab, as well as a few studies by others who have also been looking at developmental differences in scientific discovery processes. In the third part of the chapter, I say a bit about machine discovery systems. These systems continue the two-faceted approach that manifested itself in the earliest days of artificial intelligence. Some are computational models of human discovery processes, whereas others are a species of machine learning systems designed to support scientific discovery by machines. In the fourth section I attempt to characterize different approaches within cognitive science to understanding discovery, and finally, in the fifth part, I talk about the frontiers of this research.

SCIENTIFIC DISCOVERY AS DUAL SEARCH

Our research is based on the idea that scientific discovery is a type of problem solving in which there are two problem spaces: a space of hypotheses and a space of experiments. Both of these problem spaces require heuristics for constraining search. This dual search notion is an extension of Simon and Lea's (1974) generalized rule inducer. In our model, hypotheses correspond to GRI's rules, and experiments correspond to instances. In order to further specify this very general characterization, Kevin Dunbar and I proposed a framework that we called SDDS, for "scientific discovery as dual search." The

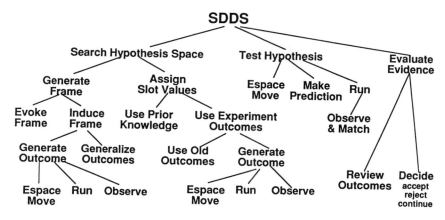

FIG. 9.1. SDDS framework.

SDDS framework (Fig. 9.1) depicts the relationship among the component processes that coordinate the dual search (Klahr & Dunbar, 1988).

The three top-level components control the entire process: First, you have to Search the Hypothesis Space, then you have to Test that Hypothesis, and then you have to Evaluate the Evidence in order to decide whether the cumulative evidence—as well as other considerations—warrants acceptance, rejection, or continued consideration of the current hypothesis. That is a pretty conventional view of the discovery process. Now let's descend a level, and look more carefully at how hypotheses are generated.

There are two subcomponents for Search Hypothesis Space. One component generates the broad scope for the hypotheses, and the second component refines it and further specifies it. Because we use Minsky's "frame" notion, for representing hypotheses, we show this as first Generating a Frame and then Assigning Slot Values.

Where do these initial frames and their associated slot values come from? We propose two different types of sources for new hypotheses. One source is prior knowledge stored in memory, and the other source is the external world. The two different sources are evoked in both Generate Frame and in Assign Slot Values.

Generate Frame has two subcomponents corresponding to the two ways that a frame may be generated.

Evoke Frame is a search of memory for information that could be used to construct a frame. Prior knowledge plays an important role here. In cognitive psychology, several mechanisms have been proposed to account for the way in which initial hypotheses are generated. These include memory search, analogical mapping, remindings, and view instantiation (Dunbar & Schunn, 1990; Gentner, 1983; Gick & Holyoak, 1983; Klahr & Dunbar, 1988; Ross, 1984; Shrager, 1987). Each of these mechanisms emphasizes a different aspect of the way in which search in the hypothesis space is initiated. Although the SDDS framework doesn't have anything to add to these views, there is an important distinction between this form of frame generation and the other process under the Generate Frame node: Induce Frame.

Induce Frame generates a new frame by induction over a series of outcomes (Holland, Holyoak, Nisbett, & Thagard, 1986). It includes two subprocesses: The first Generates an Outcome, and the second Generalizes over the results of that (and other) outcomes to produce a frame.

This first process is of particular interest, for it calls for an experiment to be run (via E-Space Move). But this is an odd sort of experiment: It is not testing any hypothesis, because we don't have one yet. We are still in the part of the model that is searching for a hypothesis.

By including E-Space Move in this portion of the framework, we acknowledge the importance of running so-called "experiments" in the absence of a clear theory. This corresponds to pretheoretical observations and measurements of how one thing affects another with no clear-cut theory. This is not the conventionally assigned role for experimentation, but we all know how important it is.

Notice also that the E-Space Move occurs in two additional parts of the framework: not only in the service of inducing a frame, but also under Assign Slot Values, when the theory has been partially specified, and one is seeking a bit more constraint on the theory. E-Space Move also occurs under Test Hypothesis in its "traditional role" in the evaluation of fully specified hypotheses. By calling this a "move" in a "space" we emphasize the fact that the decision about what kind of data to collect, or what kind of observation to make in a problem-solving task that requires constrained search in a very large space.

If we move back up to the distinction between Generate Frame and Assign Slot Values, we can see that the two processes correspond to major and minor moves in the hypothesis space. Generate Frame involves the creation of a new hypothesis that may involve entirely new structural relations among its elements, whereas Assign Slot Values takes the structure— the frame, that is—as given, and refines some of its unresolved elements.

Once again, the location of E-Space Move reflects the fact that much of the experimentation that takes place within a paradigm is not of the grand hypothesis testing type, but rather the more data-driven attempt to induce a new theory, or to refine an existing theory by discovering a better set of slot values.

Let me summarize the main points of our theoretical orientation. Scientific discovery is comprised of three main components:

1. *Searching the hypothesis space.* The process of generating new hypotheses is a type of problem solving in which the initial state consists of some

knowledge about a domain, and the goal state is a hypothesis that can account for some or all of that knowledge in a more concise or universal form. Once generated, hypotheses are evaluated for their initial plausibility. Expertise plays a role here, as subjects' familiarity with a domain tends to give them strong biases about what is plausible in the domain. Plausibility, in turn, affects the order in which hypotheses are evaluated: Highly likely hypotheses tend to be tested before unlikely hypotheses (Klayman & Ha, 1987; Wason, 1968). Furthermore, subjects may adopt different experimental strategies for evaluating plausible and implausible hypotheses.

2. *Searching the experiment space.* One of the most important constraints on this search is the need to produce experiments that will yield interpretable outcomes. For human discovery systems, this requires domain-general knowledge about one's own information-processing limitations, as well as domain-specific knowledge about the pragmatic constraints of the particular discovery context. As we will see, there are important developmental differences in people's ability to constrain search in the experiment space.

3. *Evaluating evidence.* In contrast to the binary feedback provided to subjects in the typical psychology experiment, real-world evidence evaluation is not very straightforward. Relevant features must first be extracted, potential noise must be suppressed or corrected, and the resulting internal representation must be compared with earlier predictions. When people are reasoning about real world context, their prior knowledge imposes strong theoretical biases. These biases influence not only the initial strength with which hypotheses are held—and hence the amount of disconfirming evidence necessary to refute them—but also the features in the evidence that will be attended to and encoded.

Each of these three components is a potential source of developmental change, and most psychologists have studied them in isolation. But such decomposition begs the very question of interest: the coordination of search in two spaces. We wanted to try a different approach. We wanted to study discovery behavior in situations that required coordinated search in both the experiment space and the hypothesis space. In order to do this, we set up laboratory situations that were designed to place subjects in various parts of this framework and then looked at how they managed the dual search process.

LABORATORY INVESTIGATIONS OF SCIENTIFIC REASONING

Given this goal of studying scientific reasoning in the psychology lab, and given our additional goal of addressing some developmental questions, and inspired by earlier work with Jeff Shrager (Shrager & Klahr, 1986) we decided to study scientific discovery by using the device shown in Fig. 9.2a.

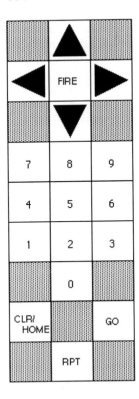

FIG. 9.2. BigTrak keypad.

We used a computer-controlled toy robot tank called BigTrak. It is a battery-operated programmable self-contained vehicle, about 2 ft long. The functions on the BigTrak keypad interface are depicted in Fig. 9.2. The basic execution cycle involves first clearing the memory with the CLR key and then entering a series of up to 16 instructions, each consisting of a function key (the command) and a one- or two-digit number (the argument). The five command keys are ↑, move forward; ↓, move backward; ←, rotate left; →, rotate right; and FIRE. When the GO key is pressed, BigTrak executes the program. For example, suppose you pressed the following series of keys:

$$\text{CLR } ↑5 ← 7 ↑ 3 → 15 \text{ FIRE } 2 ↓ 8 \text{ GO}$$

When the GO key was pressed, BigTrak would move forward 5 ft, rotate counterclockwise 42 degrees (corresponding to 7 minutes on an ordinary clock face), move forward 3 ft, rotate clockwise 90 degrees, fire (its "laser cannon") twice, and back up 8 ft.

Procedure

Our procedure had three phases. In the first, subjects were introduced to BigTrak and instructed on the use of each basic command. Subjects were instructed in how to generate verbal protocols. During this phase, the RPT key was not visible. Subjects were trained to criterion on how to write a series of commands to accomplish a specified maneuver. The end of this phase corresponded to a scientist having a basic amount of knowledge about a domain.

In the second phase, subjects were shown the RPT key. They were told that it required a numeric parameter (N), and that there could be only one RPT N in a program. They were told that their task was to find out how RPT worked by writing programs and observing the results. This corresponded to a new problem in the domain: an unresolved question in an otherwise familiar context.

Finally, in the third phase, subjects could formulate hypotheses about RPT and run experiments to test those hypotheses. This required decisions about hypotheses and decisions about experiments. Subjects were never told whether or not they had discovered how RPT worked. They had to decide when to terminate search.

The task has several properties that make it appropriate for studying scientific discovery in the laboratory:

1. Prior knowledge can influence initial hypotheses as well as the strength with which subjects hold them.
2. Subjects have to design and evaluate their own experiments.
3. The mapping between experimental outcomes and hypotheses is nontrivial.
4. We do not tell subjects whether or not they have discovered a true hypothesis. That is for them to decide.
5. The task is interesting and challenging for a wide range of ages.

Hypothetical Behavior

What would you do, if faced with this problem? What kind of scientific reasoning would *you* use, if asked to figure out how the RPT key worked? Figure 9.3 shows a hypothetical sequence of hypotheses, predictions, and experimental outcomes.

Hypothesis x (Hx) says that when you put in a RPT and a number, the whole program repeats that many times. That turns out to be a very popular hypothesis. Many subjects start out with this one, or something very similar to it.

Your first BigTrak Experiments

Hx: RPT N repeats the entire program N times.
Hy: RPT N repeats the Nth step once.

E1: ↑ 1 RPT 1

Hx prediction: ↑ 2
Hy prediction: ↑ 2
BT's behavior: ↑ 2

E2: ↑ 1 FIRE 2 ↓ 1 RPT 2

Hx prediction: ↑ 1 FIRE 2 ↓ 1 ↑1 FIRE 2 ↓ 1
Hy prediction: ↑ 1 FIRE 2 ↓ 1 FIRE 2
BT's behavior: ↑ 1 FIRE 2 ↓ 1 FIRE 2 ↓ 1

FIG. 9.3. Hypothetical behavior in BigTrak task.

Hypothesis y (Hy) is a little odd: it says that RPT N takes the Nth step in the program and repeats it one more time. That is not a very popular hypothesis. Very few subjects start out with it.

What about experiments? What kind of program would you write in order to test your hypotheses? Suppose you want to start simple, just to see what might happen. So you write Experiment 1: (↑1 RPT 1). Although this is a simple and easy to observe experiment, it is not very informative, because if Hx is right, BigTrak will go forward two times, but it will do the same thing if Hy is right. So this experiment can't discriminate between the two hypotheses. (This experiment might not be a total loss if BigTrak did something inconsistent with both hypotheses, but it doesn't.)

How about Experiment 2: ↑ 1 FIRE 2 ↓ 1 RPT 2.

Now the two hypotheses make distinctive predictions:

Hx predicts ↑ 1 FIRE 2 ↓ 1 ↑ 1 FIRE 2 ↓ 1.

Hy predicts ↑ 1 FIRE 2 ↓ 1 FIRE 2.

So Experiment 2 is critical with respect to the two hypotheses. It also has some nice properties; it is pretty short, so you can keep track of what is going on, and it has easily distinguishable components, so each piece of behavior is highly informative.

So you enter the program shown in E2, and you run it. BigTrak goes like this:

$\uparrow$ 1 FIRE 2 $\downarrow$ 1 FIRE 2 $\downarrow$ 1

Which is not what either theory predicted.

Now you have to look carefully at the behavior, and, if you are very discerning, you notice that it repeated the last two steps. You also notice that you used a 2 as the value of N. If you are really on the ball here, you hypothesize that RPT N repeats the last N instructions one time. And that's the way the original BigTrak really worked.

So now you have discovered how RPT works: It repeats the last N instructions one time. And you did it with only three hypotheses and two experiments.

Performance: Adults Versus Children

How did our subjects do? In one of our studies (Dunbar & Klahr, 1989) we used two groups of subjects: Carnegie Mellon University (CMU) undergraduates, and children between the ages of 8 and 11 years. Table 9.1 shows the overall results. Recall that the RPT key takes the N instructions preceding the RPT instruction and it repeats that sequence one more time. It's a pretty nonintuitive function, and it was not easy to discover.

Children's success rate was very low. Only 2 of 22 children were successful, although 12 of the unsuccessful children were sure they had discovered the correct rule, and they terminated their experiments quite satisfied with their discovery. In contrast, nearly all of the adults discovered the correct rule. But it was not a trivial task for them. In fact, with respect to average time, number of hypotheses, and number of experiments, the adults were not very different from the children. The explanation for these vastly different success rates must lie at a deeper level. We need to look more closely at the nature of the hypothesis space and the experiment space.

Table 9.2 lists the more common hypotheses that subjects proposed in order of decreasing popularity or plausibility. Recall that the correct rule is number 5: Repeat the last N steps once. On the right side of the table

TABLE 9.1
Overall Performance of Children and Adults on BigTrak Task

	Adults	Children
Solvers	19 of 20	2 of 22
Mean time	20 min	20 min
Number of hypotheses	4.6	3.3
Number of programs	18	13

TABLE 9.2
Common Hypotheses (in Decreasing Order of Popularity or Plausibility)

RPT N tells BigTrak to:	Role of N
Repeat the entire program N times.	Counter
Repeat the last step N times.	Counter
Repeat the subsequent steps N times.	Counter
Repeat the entire program once.	nil
Repeat the last N steps once.	Selector
Repeat the Nth step once.	Selector
Repeat the first N steps once.	Selector
Repeat the entire program $f(N)$ times.	Counter

hypotheses are classified according to the role that they assign to the parameter that goes with the RPT command, shown here as "the role of N." In hypotheses 1, 2, 3, and 8, N counts the number of repetitions. We call these Counter hypotheses. In hypotheses 5, 6, and 7, N determines which segment of the program will be selected to be repeated again. We call these Selector hypotheses. This distinction, between Counters and Selectors, turns out to be a very useful distinction in our subsequent experiments. Search in the BigTrak hypothesis space can involve local search among Counters or among Selectors, or it can involve more far-ranging search between counter frames and selector frames.

What about the BigTrak experiment space? How can we characterize it? By one reckoning, it is enormous: For example, there are over 5^{15} distinct programs that subjects could write. However we have found that we can adequately characterize the experiment space in terms of just two parameters. The first is λ—the length of the program preceding the RPT. The second is the value of N—the argument that RPT takes. Because both parameters must be less than or equal to 15, there are 225 "cells" in the λ-N space. The regions and their general properties are depicted in Fig. 9.4.

We have divided the E-space into three regions, according to their general informativeness with respect to alternative hypotheses. Rather than go into details, I'll just remind you about the earlier example in which some experiments were very poor at distinguishing among competing theories, whereas others were very effective. The most important thing to note is that region 2 is particularly informative. This is where the program length is greater than the value of N.

This analysis of the H-space and the E-space revealed a couple of interesting things about how subjects went about this task. We found that there were two distinct types of subjects, with fundamentally different strategies. We distinguished between the two groups on the basis of how much information they had when they changed from a counter frame to a selector frame. If they made the switch without having seen the result of a region

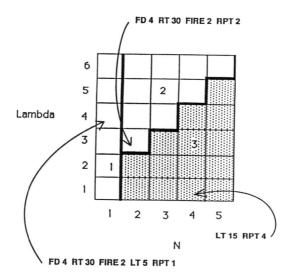

FIG. 9.4. BigTrak experiment space.

Region 1: Poor discriminating power.

Region 2: Maximally discriminates among all of the common hypotheses. Can distinguish selectors from counters, and *which* selector or counter.

Region 3: Confusing for selector rules, because N gets truncated to λ and a sequence of experiments that varies N has no effect.

2 experiment, then we called them "Theorists," because they could not have based their decision on conclusive experimental evidence. On the other hand, if they made the switch from Counters to Selectors only after running region 2 experiments, then we called them "Experimenters." (By the way, this analysis only makes sense for the adults, because so few children proposed selectors.)

The two kinds of strategies were accompanied by other differences (shown in Table 9.3). Experimenters took twice as long to discover how RPT worked; they explored much more of the experiment space, and they conducted many more experiments without any active hypothesis. That is, they spent a lot of time down in the lower left-hand region of the SDDS framework, as they ran experiments in order to generate a data pattern over which they could induce a frame.

TABLE 9.3
Performance Differences Between Theorists
and Experimenters on BigTrak Task

	Theorists	*Experimenters*
Defining property	State selector frame without sufficient evidence	State selector frame only after sufficient evidence
Time (min)	11	25
Total experiments	9.3	18.4
Experiments without hypotheses	0.8	6.1
Comments about experiment space	5.9	0.9
E-space cells used	5.7	9.9

This tendency to suspend the hypotheses testing mode while attempting to discover some kind of regularity in the data suggested to us that we needed to find out a lot more about how subjects searched the experiment space, and about how different goals might influence that search. We also began to look at developmental differences in some of the key components of the SDDS model. As a developmentalist, I was particularly interested in addressing two long-standing disputes over the developmental course of scientific reasoning skills:

1. The *domain-specific* or *domain-general* debate asks whether there are any general, domain-independent rules used in scientific reasoning, or whether all developmental improvements can be attributed to domain-specific acquisitions. Of course, the question is not limited to scientific reasoning skills: it pervades all of cognitive development. It is analogous to the distinction in AI between *weak methods* and *knowledge-rich* approaches. Like most of the dichotomies in psychology, this one should not be over-emphasized, because it is not a clear-cut distinction. But developmentalists devote a lot of energy to arguing about it, so I wanted to address it in my work.

2. The *child-as-scientist* debate asks whether or not it makes sense to describe the young child as a scientist. Some folks say, "yes, of course," and others say, "obviously not." Unfortunately, one can find empirical support for each position. On the one hand, results of formal studies, as well as abundant everyday experience, provide evidence that trained scientists, and even untrained adults, commonly outperform children on a variety of scientific reasoning tasks (Kuhn, 1989). On the other hand, the empirical literature on scientific reasoning shows that adults demonstrate systematic and serious flaws in their reasoning, whereas young children are capable of surprisingly competent reasoning about hypotheses testing and experimentation (Brewer & Samarapungavan, 1991; Schauble, 1990; Vosniadou & Brewer, 1992).

It is clear that a one-bit answer to either of these questions will be inadequate. The questions have to be addressed in more depth. We decided to recast the questions in terms of the components of the SDDS framework. In particular, we decided to use the BigTrak paradigm in such a way that we could focus on developmental differences in the heuristics used to constrain search in the experiment space.

The BT Microworld

For this study we moved from the original BigTrak toy to a computer microworld called BT. The toy tank became an animated "rocket ship" icon, and the BigTrak keypad became a screen display activated by pointing and clicking with a mouse (see Klahr, Fay, & Dunbar, 1993, for details). We explored the effect of domain-specific knowledge by manipulating the plausibility of hypotheses. Our goal was to investigate the extent to which prior knowledge—as manifested in hypothesis plausibility—influenced how people designed experiments and how they interpreted the results of those experiments.

Procedure. The study had three phases. The first and third phases were the same as in the previous study. Subjects learned about all the normal keys and were trained to criterion on getting BT to move around the screen. In the second phase, the RPT key was introduced as before. Subjects were told that their task was to find out how RPT worked by writing at least three programs and observing the results. But then we changed the procedure a bit, by suggesting one way that RPT might work. The experimenter said: "One way that RPT might work is:" and then we stated one of four hypotheses listed next. Then we told subjects to write at least three programs to see if the repeat key really did work the way we had suggested, or some other way. The entire session lasted approximately 45 minutes.

Throughout the study, we used only four rules for BT. The two popular, or plausible hypotheses were the two Counters:

A: Repeat the entire program N times.
B: Repeat the last step N times.

In contrast, there were two hypotheses that subjects were unlikely to propose. These are the two Selectors:

C: Repeat the Nth step once.
D: Repeat the last N steps once.

TABLE 9.4
Design of BT Experiment:
Specific Hypotheses for Each Given–Actual Condition

Given Hypothesis	*Actual Rule*	
	Counter	*Selector*
Counter	B: Repeat last step N times. ↓ A: Repeat entire program N times. THEORY REFINEMENT	A: Repeat entire program N times. ↓ D: Repeat the last N steps once. THEORY REPLACEMENT
Selector	D: Repeat the last step N steps once. ↓ A: Repeat entire program N times. THEORY REPLACEMENT	C: Repeat step N once. ↓ D: Repeat the last N steps once. THEORY REFINEMENT

Design. The design is shown in Table 9.4. We provided each subject with an initial hypothesis about how RPT might work. The Given hypothesis was always wrong. BT was always set to work according to some rule other than the Given rule. We called that the Actual rule. Both the Given and Actual could be either plausible (i.e., a Counter) or implausible (i.e., a Selector). In Counter → Counter and Selector → Selector conditions, the Given hypothesis was only "somewhat" wrong, in that it was from the same frame as the way that RPT actually worked. In Counter → Selector and Selector → Counter conditions, the Given was "very" wrong, in that it came from a different frame than the Actual rule. The subjects' task in the former situation corresponded to theory refinement, whereas in the latter situation it corresponded to theory replacement.

Subjects

We used four different groups of subjects, Carnegie Mellon (CM) undergraduates, Community College (CC) students, "sixth" graders (a mixed class of fifth to seventh graders, mean age 11 years), and third graders (mean age 9 years). CMs were mainly science or engineering majors, whereas the CCs had little training in mathematics or physical sciences. Children came primarily from academic and professional families. Most of the third graders had about 6 months of LOGO instruction. Note that CCs had less programming experience than the third graders.

Results. The proportion correct for each group in each condition is shown in Fig. 9.5. As we expected, domain-specific knowledge—manifested in expectations about what "repeat" might mean in this context—played an important role. Regardless of what the Given hypothesis was, subjects found it easier to discover Counters (81%) than Selectors (35%).

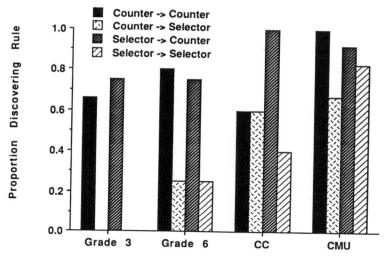

FIG. 9.5. Percentage correct.

There was also a main effect for group: The correct rule was discovered by 83% of the CMs, 65% of the CCs, 53% of the sixth graders, and 33% of the third graders. This group effect is attributable to the Actual = Selector conditions, in which 56% of the adults but only 13% of the children were successful. In fact, none of the third graders discovered Selectors. For Counters, adults and children were not as different in their success rates (88% vs. 75%).

What about subjects' reactions to the Given hypothesis? Recall that we presented subjects with either plausible or implausible hypotheses in order to determine the extent to which search in the hypothesis space was influenced by plausibility. This is one of the points at which domain-specific knowledge (which determines plausibility) might affect domain-general knowledge about experimental strategies.

Prior to running the first experiment, subjects were asked to predict what would happen. Their predictions indicated the extent to which they understood and accepted the Given hypotheses. Each subject's response to the Given hypothesis was assigned to one of three categories: I, Accept the Given hypotheses; II, accept the Given, but also propose an alternative; III, reject the Given, and propose an alternative. The number of subjects in each category is shown in Table 9.5 as a function of grade level and type of Given hypothesis. In both conditions, the adults always accepted the Given hypothesis, either on its own (category I), or in conjunction with an alternative that they proposed (category II). Adults never rejected the Given hypothesis. In contrast, no third grader and only two sixth graders ever proposed an alternative to compare to the Given (category II). Instead, children consid-

TABLE 9.5
Subjects' Responses to the Given Hypothesis

	Adults		Children	
Response to Given Hypothesis	Counter	Selector	Counter	Selector
Accept Given	.70	.60	.71	.33
Accept Given and propose alternative	.30	.40	.06	.06
Reject given; propose alternative	0	0	.23	.61

ered only one hypothesis at a time. When given Counters, they mainly accepted them, but when given Selectors, they mainly rejected them and proposed an alternative, which was usually a Counter of their own design.

This propensity to consider multiple versus single hypotheses affected the type of experimental goals set by the subjects. These goals, in turn, were used to impose constraints on search in the experiment space. We looked at these goals more closely by analyzing (a) what subjects said about experiments and (b) the features of the experiments that they actually wrote. Subjects' verbal protocols contain many statements indicating both explicit understanding of the experiment space dimensions, as well as what might be called a general notion of "good instrumentation": designing interpretable programs containing easily identifiable markers. Subjects made explicit statements about both kinds of knowledge. Here are some typical adult statements:

1. "I don't want to have two of the same move in there yet, I might not be able to tell if it was repeating the first one or if it was doing the next part of my sequence."
2. "I'm going to use a series of commands that will . . . that are easily distinguished from one another, and won't run it off the screen."
3. "So I'm going to pick two [commands] that are the direct opposite of each other, to see if they don't really have to be direct opposites but I'm just going to write a program that consists of two steps, that I could see easily."

Sixth graders were somewhat less articulate, but still showed a concern for both experiment space dimensions and program interpretability. In contrast, third graders rarely made such comments. The proportion of subjects making such comments is shown in the top row of Table 9.6.

At a finer level of detail, good instrumentation was assessed by the extent to which subjects observed three pragmatic constraints: (a) using standard units of rotation, such as 15 or 30 "minutes" (90 and 180 degrees), for rotate commands; (b) using small numeric arguments (values <5) on move commands, so that the actions of BT are not distorted by having it hit the

TABLE 9.6
Proportion of Self-Generated Constraints

Constraint	Student Group			
	CMU	CC	Sixth	Third
Explicit λ-N comments	.83	.60	.53	.20
Standard turn units	.92	.95	.71	.53
Small arguments	.92	.85	.65	.47
Proportion of programs in small[a] E-space region	.50	.63	.26	.31

[a] $4 \times 3 = 5\%$ of 15×15.

boundaries of the screen; and (c) using distinct commands in a program where possible. Programs constrained in these ways produce behavior that is easier to observe, encode, and remember. For both turns and moves, there was a strong effect of grade level.

Another interesting difference between the children and the adults was the way in which adults limited their search to a small "corner" of the experiment space. We looked at the section of the E-space with λ between 1 and 4, and N between 1 and 3. This corresponds to only 5% of the full E-space. But we discovered that over half of the adults' experiments occurred within this small area. On the other hand, children's experiments were much more scattered throughout the space.

Overall, Table 9.6 shows us that both what subjects said and what they did produced different patterns for the different groups: Older subjects—even those with weak technical backgrounds—were better able than children to constrain their search in the experiment space and to design interpretable experiments.

What were subjects trying to do here? What were their experimental goals? How can we infer these goals from the kinds of experiments they ran? We reasoned as follows: If the experimental goal is to identify which of the program steps are repeated for Selector hypotheses, or to discriminate between Selectors and Counters, then subjects should write programs having more than N steps (i.e., with $\lambda > N$). (In programs where λ is several steps greater than N, it is easy to distinguish among repeats of all steps, first step, last step, and N steps.) On the other hand, if the goal is to demonstrate the effect of a Counter, then subjects should use larger values of N and (for pragmatic reasons) relatively short programs (i.e., programs with $\lambda \leq N$). This all works out to a prediction about the conditions under which λ should be greater than N. Figure 9.6 shows the proportion of subjects in each condition whose first programs had $\lambda > N$. Responses of both of the adult groups and the sixth graders were consistent with the normative account I just gave. Third graders showed the opposite pattern.

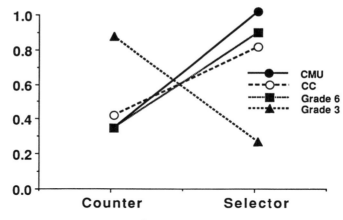

FIG. 9.6. λ-N on first experiment.

Heuristics for Constraining Search in the Experiment Space

These analyses reveal a distinctive pattern of results that differentiate the different groups. Our interpretation of these patterns is that they result from a set of domain-general heuristics that allow some subjects to constrain their search in the experiment space. These heuristics are differentially available to children and adults. Based on these and other analyses, we have proposed the following four heuristics:

E1. *Focus on one dimension of an experiment or hypothesis.* An incremental, conservative approach has been found to be effective in both concept attainment and hypothesis testing. This heuristic suggests that in moving from one experiment to the next or one hypothesis to the next one should decide upon the most important features of each and focus on just those features. Here, the CM adults stood apart from the other three groups. They were much more likely than any of the three other groups to make conservative moves—that is, to minimize differences in program content between one program and the next.

E2. *Use the plausibility of a hypothesis to choose experimental strategy.* In this study, we found that both children and adults varied their approach to confirmation and disconfirmation according to the plausibility of the currently held hypothesis. When hypotheses were plausible, subjects at all levels tended to set an experimental goal of demonstrating key features of the given hypothesis, rather than conducting experiments that could discriminate between rival hypotheses.

For implausible hypotheses, adults and young children used different strategies. Adults' response to implausibility was to propose hypotheses from frames other than the Given frame, and to conduct experiments that could discriminate between them. Our youngest children's response was to propose a hypothesis from a different, but plausible, frame and then to ignore the initial, and implausible, hypothesis while attempting to demonstrate the correctness of the plausible one. Third graders were particularly susceptible to this strategy.

E3. *Maintain observability.* As BT moves along the screen it leaves no permanent record of its behavior. Subjects must remember what BT actually did. Thus, one way to implement this heuristic is to write short programs. Adults almost always used it, whereas the youngest children often wrote programs that were very difficult to encode. This heuristic depends on knowledge of one's own information-processing limitations as well as a knowledge of the device. Our finding that the third graders often failed to maintain observability may be a manifestation, in the realm of experimental design, of more general findings about the development of self-awareness of cognitive limitations.

E4. *Design experiments giving characteristic results.* This heuristic maximizes the interpretability of experimental outcomes. Physicians look for "markers" for diseases, and physicists design experiments in which suspected particles will leave "signatures." In the BT domain, this heuristic is instantiated as "use many distinct commands." On average, about half of all programs in each group did not contain any repeated commands. However, because third graders were more likely to use long programs, they were more likely to use repeated commands, which reduced the possibility of generating characteristic behavior.

Kulkarni and Simon (1988) proposed another heuristic called *Exploit surprising results.* They built it into in their computational model of Hans Krebs' discovery of how amino acids work in the kidney. In the BT domain, it is manifested when subjects replace their current goal—such as trying to determine the number of times something gets repeated—with a new goal of determining why an unexpected program segment was repeated. This appears to be a very useful way to constrain search in the experiment space, but in our own studies the evidence for its use is not strong. The data supported it in one of our adult studies, but not in subsequent ones.

Although I have described five heuristics for constraining search in the experiment space, I have not said anything about how they get invoked, or how their inherent contradictions are handled. For example, E1 calls for conservative moves, whereas exploiting surprise calls for bold pursuit of a surprising result. Adults not only used these heuristics effectively, but also they were able to deal with these inherent contradictions. In contrast, children either failed to use some of these heuristics at all, or else they tended to let one of them dominate. We still have a lot to learn about how this heuristic conflict is resolved.

Heuristics for Modifying Hypotheses

These rules help to constrain search in the E-space. But experiments are supposed to be related to hypotheses, and subjects are supposed to use the results of experiments to modify their hypotheses. How do they do it? How should they do it? The overwhelming evidence, from our own research and from many other labs, is that people seem to follow the following heuristic for dealing with disconfirming evidence: "Don't give up the ship!" On the cover of the announcement of the *Mind Matters* symposium, the organizers included a remarkable quotation from Allen Newell:

> Working with theories is not like skeet shooting, where theories are lofted up and BANG, they are shot down with a falsification bullet, and that's the end of that theory. Theories are more like graduate students, once admitted you try hard to avoid flunking them out, it being much better for them and for the world if they can become long-term contributors to society. (Newell, 1990)

The statement says as much about Newell the mentor and teacher as Newell the scientist, but I confine my remarks to the scientific claim in the statement. It bears on a part of the discovery process that remains quite undeveloped, in the SDDS framework as well as in machine discovery systems. Just how do people evaluate evidence that bears on their theory? One thing is clear from our studies and those in other labs: Newell's statement is correct with one modification. Although most people like to treat other people's theories like clay pigeons, they do treat their own theories like their own graduate students. They nurture them, tolerate their failings, and strive mightily to improve them rather than abandon them. How do they manage do this while maintaining scientific respectability?

Some people have proposed a Bayesian framework for understanding the process of evidence interpretation and theory revision (Cheeseman, 1990), but such approaches do not attempt to get at the underlying psychological processes. The problem is that when you are faced with the canonical equation for revising your priors, you still have to estimate a series of conditional probabilities. How do you decide how likely the current evidence is, given that one or another hypothesis is true or false?

Chinn and Brewer (1992) noted that most scientific discovery and theory revision systems assume that when empirical data conflict with the current theory, it is the theory that must be changed. In contrast, they argue, psychologists who study how people treat anomalous data have long recognized that people are pretty good at discounting some anomalies, some of the time. Chinn and Brewer go on to propose a taxonomy for the different ways that humans react to anomalous data. I have summarized their taxonomy in Table 9.7.

TABLE 9.7
Psychological Responses to Anomalous Data

Response to Anomalous Data About Theory A	Accept Data as Valid?	Explain Why Data Accepted?	Change Theory in Any Way?
Ignore data	No	—	—
Reject data	No	Yes	No
Exclude data from domain of theory	Maybe	Yes	No
Hold data in abeyance	Yes	No	No
Reinterpret data and retain A	Yes	Yes	No
Reinterpret data and tinker:			
A → A′	Yes	Yes	Minor
Accept data and change:			
A → B	Yes	Yes	Yes

Note. From Chinn and Brewer (1992). Adapted by permission.

The taxonomy includes seven kinds of responses to anomalies, which differ along three dimensions: (a) whether or not the anomalous data are accepted as valid, (b) whether or not the scientist explains how that judgment (i.e., to accept or reject the data) was made, and (c) whether or not the theory is changed as a result of the anomalous data. The normative, "skeet shooting" response is shown in category 7, but the table makes it clear that it is far from the only possible response. Category 2 is particularly interesting because it is frequently used when the scientist claims that an experimental error has occurred. Suppose you know that there is some probability of false positives or false negatives in your experimental outcomes. How does that affect the way you interpret the outcomes that do or don't agree with your predictions? We have been extending earlier work by Gorman (in press) on this question by presenting subjects with errorful feedback that includes both false positives and false negatives, in order to find out more about how subjects deal with such error (Penner, 1993).

Category 4 is also interesting: Here the scientist accepts the anomaly as valid, that is, not irrelevant to the domain, and not a fluke of experimental procedure. However, it is not yet clear what to do about it, other than to hope to come back to it at some point. This category has some of the properties of Kulkarni's and Simon's heuristic to exploit surprising results, for during that exploration, the scientist usually holds on to the current theory, but still peruses more information that may bear on it.

Category 4 also is characteristic of a strategy that another one of my graduate students, Chris Schunn (Schunn & Klahr, 1992), found in a more complex version of BT. He found that when subjects were attempting to discover a complex but decomposable rule, they would take an unexpected result and defer pursuing it for a while. He calls it the *put upon stack heuristic* (PUSH). Now PUSH and "Exploit surprises" are quite incompatible with one another, and at this point we do not know the conditions under which one or the other will dominate. Nor do we know which of these responses is favored by children. This remains a promising area for further research.

Young Children as Good Scientists

It is tempting to conclude—from the results of our studies with BT—that children simply don't understand the underlying logic of scientific reasoning. But consider the results of a recent study by Sodian, Zaitchik, and Carey (1991). They gave first and second graders a problem concerning a mouse in a house, and asked them to distinguish between conclusive and inconclusive experiments to find out something about the mouse. The story went something like this:

1. A mouse has been eating stuff in the kitchen at night.
2. It is either a big mouse or a little mouse.
3. We have a food box with a little hole, just wide enough for a little mouse, but too narrow for a big mouse.
4. We have another food box with a big hole, wide enough for either mouse.

Then the children were asked two questions (in counterbalanced order):

The Find Out question: Suppose we want to find out which mouse it is? Which box should we put out?

The Feed question: Suppose we want to be sure that the mouse gets the food. Which box should we put out?

For the Find Out question, the correct response is put out the box with the little hole: If the food is gone, then the mouse that took it must be small. If it is not gone, then the big mouse couldn't get to it. For the Feed question, the correct answer is to put out the box with the big door.

The majority of the first graders and most of the second graders gave the correct answer to both the Find Out question and the Feed question. Thus, the children demonstrated the ability to discriminate between testing a hypothesis and getting an effect. But notice: There were only two hypotheses, they were mutually exclusive and exhaustive, and the children did not have to search for them. Same thing for experiments. Under such conditions, even first-grade children show an ability to distinguish theory from evidence.

So: When do children think "scientifically"? I believe that our analysis, when combined with the related work from other laboratories, of the kind I just described, clarifies the conditions under which children's domain-general reasoning skills are adequate to successfully coordinate search for hypotheses and experiments. Even first-grade children can exhibit an understanding of some basic components of the logic of scientific reasoning if at least these three conditions are satisfied:

1. Hypotheses must be easily accessible (such as the highly plausible Counters in our study) or few in number (as in the two-alternative situations used in Carey's lab).
2. The experimental alternatives must also be few in number so that E-space search demands are minimized (also as in the mouse experiments).
3. The domain must provide feedback relevant to discriminating among plausible hypotheses (as in region 2 experiments in BT studies).

In situations lacking any of these constraints, children will appear to be very poor scientists. Notice that this is not just another consequence of children's inadequate encoding or mnemonic skills. On the contrary, in our BT studies, when experimental outcomes were consistent with children's expectations, they were correctly encoded, even though they were much longer than those incorrectly encoded, but discrepant from children's expectations. Instead, the adult superiority appears to derive from a set of domain-general skills that go beyond the logic of confirmation and disconfirmation and deal with the coordination of search in two spaces.

MACHINES AS DISCOVERY SYSTEMS

So far I have talked about two of the three types of discovery systems mentioned in my title. Now I turn to the third type: machine discovery systems. As in many of the domains that have been approached by both the AI community and the cognitive psychology community, the strengths of one approach are the weaknesses of the other. The great advantage in studying humans is that they are obviously capable of making discoveries. All the great discoveries in the world are made by humans, and just about nothing of any importance has yet been discovered by a machine. In contrast, the advantage of focusing on machine discovery systems is that we know everything there is to know about how they work, because we built them, whereas we still have a lot to learn about human discovery systems (both old and young).

If you look at the existing machine discovery systems in terms of the SDDS model (Fig. 9.1), you find systems that address one or another parts of the overall process, but nothing that really takes on the entire framework (see Cheng, 1992). For example, Thagard (1989) constructed a system that models the way in which a body of evidence is evaluated in terms of currently competing theories. His system focused almost entirely on the Evaluate Evidence process.

But where do hypotheses come from? SDDS proposes two sources. One source, Search H-Space, relies heavily on analogy (see Shrager & Langley, 1990). For example, both Shrager's (1987) "view application" process and Falkenhainer's (1990) Phineas system attempt to reason about novel situations in terms of analogies and partial matches to prior knowledge structures. Both of these systems, then, correspond to the Evoke Frame node in SDDS. The other source of new hypotheses is via induction. In many cases they are induced from regularities in empirical data. This process, which corresponds to SDDS's Induce Frame node, is the domain of the original Bacon series, as well as more recent systems such as Nordhausen and Langley's (1990) IDA system. But it does not address problems of search in the experiment space. In contrast, both Kulkarni (1989) and Rajamoney (1990) have proposed systems that propose experiments to discriminate among candidate hypotheses. Each of these systems corresponds to the "conventional" use of experimentation that is represented in SDDS by the E-space search in the service of Test Hypothesis. And so on. I could continue this exercise, but the message is clear. There are machine discovery systems that focus on segments of the overall process shown in Fig. 9.1, but the UTD—the unified theory of discovery—is not with us yet.

DISCOVERING DISCOVERY PROCESSES

Now I move up a level, from a description of how machines or humans do scientific discovery, to a characterization of the discovery processes used in the field. My analysis is based on two premises. The first premise is that the SDDS framework is applicable to any form of scientific discovery. The second premise is that people engaged in research on discovery processes are themselves engaged in scientific discovery: They are attempting to discover the discovery process. From these two premises, it follows that we can use the dual space concept to characterize our own endeavors.

I believe that most of the effort in the creation of computational models of discovery takes place in the Generate Frame part of Hypothesis Space Search. That is, the process of constructing such systems can be viewed as an attempt to evoke frames in the space of hypotheses stated as running programs. These hypotheses are instantiated as discovery systems, but they are only weakly constrained by empirical evidence from human performance. In general, this work is highly analytic: It is based on a normative analysis of what ought to be the case, with the assumptions derived from intuition or logic, rather than from induction over a rich database.

What about psychological studies of scientific reasoning of the type that I described today? I think that this work is mainly comprised of search in the space of experiments; moreover, this E-space search is not usually in the service of hypothesis testing, but rather it is mainly at the level of either evoking frames or filling slot values. Most of the effort in my own work has been focused on empirical studies about the nature of human thinking in situations that approximate "real" scientific discovery. So I would put most of the work from my lab, as well as many of the other psychological studies on discovery processes, in the regions where we have E-space search in the service of evoking or refining hypotheses.

Although these two approaches, the H-space and the E-space searches, start from quite different points, use different search processes, and use different criteria to evaluate their progress, I think that they are converging on the same general discoveries about the discovery process. Indeed, that is what one would hope for, for our basic premise is that search in the two spaces should converge toward discovery. In this case, the entity doing the dual search is the field at large, rather than a single scientist, but I see convergence, nevertheless.

DISCOVERY FRONTIERS

One of the many remarkable things about Allen Newell that always impressed me was how cheerfully he could list all the current inadequacies and flaws in his current position on a topic. I think he could do that because he had the conviction that, for all its flaws, his game was the best game in town.

In Allen Newell's view, the current limitations of the field simply presented yet another challenge, and he was always able to put a positive spin on them. In fact, he ended his book with a chapter that listed things that Soar had not done. But did he call the chapter "weaknesses and limitations"? Not at all. He called it "Along the Frontiers." I like that title: Not only does it imply discoveries yet to be made, but it also captures some of Allen Newell's enthusiastic optimism. How exciting to be on a frontier! So in this concluding section, I make a few comments about directions in which I believe that research on scientific reasoning should be extended.

More Space

The SDDS framework emphasizes two primary spaces, but it is clear that scientific discovery takes place in several other spaces:

• The *instrumentation* space has been alluded to in my earlier discussions of how subjects decide about how to insert markers in their programs, but in the real scientific context, it is clearly a complex and fundamental space in its own right. From high-energy physics to cognitive neuroscience, advances in instrumentation are at the cutting edge of the science. Machine discovery systems do not worry about this much: They assume that the data are there, waiting to be analyzed by the discovery system, or else they postulate an idealized set of experiments to generate such data.

• The *representation* space has also received short shrift in my account, although its role is also crucial. Cheng and Simon (1992) argued that "law induction, and scientific discovery more generally, requires the right representation for success," and they compared the relative difficulty of mathematical and diagrammatic representations in Gallileo's research. Finding the right representation is crucial, and finding it requires constrained search in a large space of possibilities.

• By *communication* space, I mean the set of choices that scientists must make about how to package, disseminate, promote, and defend their science, as well as what to read, whom to listen to, what meetings to attend. In many cases, these considerations, of audience, of intended impact, of how to tie one's work to the existing body of knowledge, have far-reaching impact on the kind of core science that one does (see Bazerman, 1988, for a discussion of how publication options impacted Newton's seminal work on light refraction).

These three do not exhaust the space of spaces. Indeed, in a commentary on our SDDS model Newell (1989) proposed several others for the BigTrak world and he went on to link these multiple spaces to the "architectural features of the foothills (of rationality)."

> With Soar, we have finally found out how to have multiple problem spaces. Not one or two problems spaces, but problem spaces all the way down. Furthermore, this is driven by the architecture—scratch an impasse, get another problem space. The proliferation of spaces may be modulatable ever so slightly by deliberation, but not much. Thus, the multiple problem-space character of a task is not a strategy choice for an intelligent agent or even a task characteristic. Multiple problem spaces are a feature of the foothills, created by the nature of the cognitive architecture. (p. 432)

Complexity and Knowledge

Some machine discovery systems deal with enormously complex "real world" domains. However, much of the work on discovery—both the construction of machine discovery systems and the psychological studies of discovery—is in highly simplified domains. The BigTrak is a pale shadow of the complexity of domains in which real scientific discovery occurs. Therefore, the question remains about the extent to which our results would scale up when we move to domains in which either prior knowledge or inherent complexity of the domain is increased.

We have been perusing this by looking at people's reasoning and experimental strategies in domains where they have strong intuitions and biases about how the physical world works. For example, David Penner and I (Penner & Klahr, 1993) have been studying how people generate experiments in order to determine the factors that affect the rate at which objects sink in water. In a related study in the domain of biology, Kevin Dunbar (1993a) created a computer-based microworld that captured several important features surrounding the discovery of the mechanisms of genetic control.

In addition to adding more knowledge, we need to add more complexity. At present, most discovery tasks studied in the psychology laboratory do not require subjects to decompose a complex phenomenon into its components in order to investigate them in isolation. However, as I mentioned earlier, in Chris Schunn's complex microworld we sometimes do see such a decomposition of a complex theory into its components, an independent investigation of each component, and then an assembly and integration of the components into a comprehensive model. This behavior does not reveal itself in simpler discovery experiments because it is not necessary.

But the most ambitious extension of the dual-search framework is an ongoing study by Kevin Dunbar, who decided to move far beyond the microworld tasks into the real world of world-class scientists working in their labs (Dunbar, 1993b, 1995). Dunbar spent a year making daily observations in four different labs working in the area of molecular biology. He is using the SDDS framework to structure his observations and interpretations of what is happening in an ongoing, collaborative and cutting edge scientific endeavor. And, of course, he will use these observations to further elaborate the framework itself.

This is a very exciting undertaking, as it simultaneously moves along most of the fronts listed here. Not only does it involve multiple spaces, and more knowledge, but it will also address issues of social context and motivation, which you can see further down on the list of frontier issues.

Social Context

Clearly, the social context provides a rich source of knowledge and constraint in scientific discovery. Cooperation is important. So is competition. Sociologists and historians focus almost entirely on processes outside the individual that shape scientific discovery (Bijker, Hughes, & Pinch, 1987), but they are silent on the cognitive processes that are involved in this social exchange. Cognitive psychologists are just beginning to investigate the role of collaboration in scientific reasoning. But we have a long way to go.

Motivation

In our own work, we found a curious phenomenon: When we suggest hypotheses to subjects they are much less likely to believe them, and much more willing to reject them, than when they generated the very same hypotheses themselves. The motivation to prove the other person wrong and to prove oneself right is very strong.

Much of the best work in machine discovery is based on the historical record of the great scientists making the great discoveries. But we have been very selective in extracting information from those historical accounts. Such accounts are often filled with statements about excitement, astonishment, disappointment, envy, doubt, despair. Are these descriptions of emotional and motivation states irrelevant to understanding science? I doubt it.

Learning

Why does it take so long to train a scientist? Is it all due to the slow learning rate of humans and the huge amount of content knowledge and specific techniques necessary to work in a field? Why don't we start earlier then? Is it because we can't? That is, because the kind of domain-general search constraints are simply not available to young children? That is what the results reported here today imply, but we have a lot more work to do before we really understand the nature of these cognitive limitations.

Development

All of the discoveries I have been talking about so far are discoveries about things "out there": discoveries about devices, or about the planets, or about the kidney. What about discovery "in here"? When my colleague Bob Siegler (Siegler & Shipley, 1995) talks about discovery, he is talking about how children discover new strategies in doing arithmetic, or solving problems, or playing games. To what extent is what we have learned about discovery processes in the first sense relevant to discovery processes in the second sense? Is self-awareness of one's own discovery processes a useful skill for the scientist who is attempting to discover something about the world? Do the same heuristics and search constraints apply? It is clear that search in a large space faces those who would discover more about discovery, and our challenge is to see whether we can effectively constrain that search as we seek to discover discovery systems.

ACKNOWLEDGMENTS

Sections of this chapter are based on research done in collaboration with Kevin Dunbar and Anne L. Fay, and supported by grants from the National Institute of Child Health and Human Development (R01-HD25211) and the A. W. Mellon Foundation.

REFERENCES

Bazerman, C. (1988). *Shaping written knowledge: The genre and activity of the experimental article in science.* Madison: University of Wisconsin Press.

Bijker, W. E., Hughes, T. P., & Pinch, T. (1987). *The social construction of technological systems: New directions in the sociology and history of technology.* Cambridge, MA: MIT Press.

Brewer, W. F., & Samarapungavan, A. (1991). Child theories versus scientific theories: Differences in reasoning or differences in knowledge? In R. R. Hoffman & D. S. Palermo (Eds.), *Cognition and the symbolic processes: Applied and ecological perspectives* (pp. 209–232). Hillsdale, NJ: Lawrence Erlbaum Associates.

Bruner, J. S., Goodnow, J. J., & Austin, G. A. (1956). *A study of thinking.* New York: Science Editions.

Cheeseman, P. (1990). On finding the most probable model. In J. Shrager & P. Langley (Eds.), *Computational models of scientific discovery and theory formation* (pp. 73–95). San Mateo, CA: Morgan Kaufman.

Cheng, P. C.-H. (1992). Approaches, models and issues in computational scientific discovery. In M. T. Keane & K. Gilhooly (Eds.), *Advances in the psychology of thinking* (pp. 203–236). Hempstead, Herefordshire: Harvester-Wheatsheaf.

Cheng, P. C.-H., & Simon, H. A. (1992). The right representation for discovery: Finding the conservation of momentum. *Machine Learning: Proceedings of the Ninth International Workshop* (ML92) (pp. 62–71). San Mateo, CA: Morgan Kaufmann.

Chinn, C. A., & Brewer, W. F. (1992). Psychological responses to anomalous data. *Proceedings of the Fourteenth Annual Conference of the Cognitive Science Society* (pp. 165–170). Hillsdale, NJ: Lawrence Erlbaum Associates.

Dunbar, K. (1993a). Concept discovery in a scientific domain. *Cognitive Science, 17*(3), 397–434.

Dunbar, K. (1993b). In vivo cognition: Knowledge representation and change in real-world scientific laboratories. *Proceedings of the 60th Meeting of the Society for Research in Child Development.* New Orleans.

Dunbar, K. (1995). How scientists really reason: Scientific reasoning in real-world laboratories. In R. J. Sternberg & J. Davidson (Eds.), *Mechanisms of insight.* Cambridge, MA: MIT Press.

Dunbar, K., & Klahr, D. (1989). Developmental differences in scientific discovery. In D. Klahr & K. Kotovsky (Eds.), *Complex information processing: The impact of Herbert A. Simon* (pp. 109–143). Hillsdale, NJ: Lawrence Erlbaum Associates.

Dunbar, K., & Schunn, C. D. (1990). The temporal nature of scientific discovery: The roles of priming and analogy. *Proceedings of the Twelfth Annual Conference of the Cognitive Science Society* (pp. 93–100). Hillsdale, NJ: Lawrence Erlbaum Associates.

Einstein, A. (1950). *Out of my later years.* New York: Philosophical Library.

Falkenhainer, B. (1990). A unified approach to explanation and theory formation. In J. Shrager & P. Langley (Eds.), *Computational models of scientific discovery and theory formation* (pp. 157–196). San Mateo, CA: Morgan Kaufman.

Gentner, D. (1983). Structure-mapping: A theoretical framework for analogy. *Cognitive Science, 7,* 155–170.

Gick, M. L., & Holyoak, K. J. (1983). Schema induction and analogic transfer. *Cognitive Psychology, 7,* 1–38.

Gorman, M. E. (1992). Experimental simulations in falsification. In M. T. Keane & K. Gilhooly (Eds.), *Advances in the psychology of thinking* (pp. 147–176). Hempstead, Herefordshire: Harvester-Wheatsheaf.

Holland, J., Holyoak, K., Nisbett, R. E., & Thagard, P. (1986). *Induction: Processes of inference, learning, and discovery.* Cambridge, MA: MIT Press.

Kaplan, C. A., & Simon, H. A. (1990). In search of insight. *Cognitive Psychology, 22,* 374–419.

Klahr, D., & Dunbar, K. (1988). Dual space search during scientific reasoning. *Cognitive Psychology, 12,* 1–55.

Klahr, D., Fay, A., & Dunbar, K. (1993). Heuristics for scientific experimentation: A developmental study. *Cognitive Psychology, 25*(1), 111–146.

Klayman, J., & Ha, Y. (1987). Confirmation, disconfirmation and information in hypothesis testing. *Psychological Review, 94,* 211–228.

Kuhn, D. (1989). Children and adults as intuitive scientists. *Psychological Review, 96,* 674–689.

Kulkarni, D. (1989). *The processes of scientific research: The strategy of experimentation.* Unpublished doctoral dissertation, School of Computer Science, Carnegie Mellon University, Pittsburgh.

Kulkarni, D., & Simon, H. A. (1988). The processes of scientific discovery: The strategy of experimentation. *Cognitive Science, 12,* 139–175.

Langley, P., Simon, H. A., Bradshaw, G. L., & Zytkow, J. M. (1987). *Scientific discovery: Computational explorations of the creative processes.* Cambridge, MA: MIT Press.

Newell, A. (1989). Putting it all together. In D. Klahr & K. Kotovsky (Eds.), *Complex information processing: The impact of Herbert A. Simon* (pp. 399–440). Hillsdale, NJ: Lawrence Erlbaum Associates.

Newell, A. (1990). *Unified theories of cognition.* Cambridge, MA: Harvard University Press.

Nordhausen, B., & Langley, P. (1990). An integrated approach to empirical discovery. In J. Shrager & P. Langley (Eds.), *Computational models of scientific discovery and theory formation* (pp. 97–128). San Mateo, CA: Morgan Kaufman.

Penner, D. (1993). *Scientific reasoning in the presence of data errors.* Unpublished doctoral dissertation, Department of Psychology, Carnegie Mellon University, Pittsburgh.

Penner, D., & Klahr, D. (1993). *The interaction of domain-specific knowledge and domain-general discovery strategies: A study with sinking objects.* Working paper, Department of Psychology, Carnegie Mellon University, Pittsburgh.

Qin, Y., & Simon, H. A. (1990). Imagery and problem solving. *Proceedings of the Twelfth Annual Conference of the Cognitive Science Society* (pp. 646–653). Hillsdale, NJ: Lawrence Erlbaum Associates.

Rajamoney, S. (1990). A computational approach to theory revision. In J. Shrager & P. Langley (Eds.), *Computational models of scientific discovery and theory formation* (pp. 225–253). San Mateo, CA: Morgan Kaufman.

Ross, B. H. (1984). Remindings and their effects in learning a cognitive skill. *Cognitive Psychology, 16,* 371–416.

Schauble, L. (1990). Belief revision in children: The role of prior knowledge and strategies for generating evidence. *Journal of Experimental Child Psychology, 49,* 31–57.

Schunn, C. D., & Klahr, D. (1992). Complexity management in a discovery task. *Proceedings of the Fourteenth Annual Conference of the Cognitive Science Society* (pp. 900–905). Cambridge, MA: MIT Press.

Shrager, J. (1987). Theory change via view application in instructionless learning. *Machine Learning, 2,* 247–276.

Shrager, J., & Klahr, D. (1986). Instructionless learning about a complex device. *International Journal of Man-Machine Studies, 25,* 153–189.

Shrager, J., & Langley, P. (Eds.). (1990). *Computational models of scientific discovery and theory formation.* San Mateo, CA: Morgan Kaufman.

Siegler, R. S., & Shipley, C. (1995). Variation, selection, and cognitive change. In T. Simon & G. Halford (Eds.), *Developing cognitive competence: New approaches to process modeling* (pp. 31–76). Hillsdale, NJ: Lawrence Erlbaum Associates.

Simon, H. A. (1966). Scientific discovery and the psychology of problem solving. In R. Colodny (Ed.), *Mind and cosmos* (pp. 22–39). Pittsburgh: University of Pittsburgh Press.

Simon, H. A. (1973). Does scientific discovery have a logic? *Philosophy of Science, 40,* 471–480.

Simon, H. A., & Lea, G. (1974). Problem solving and rule induction: A unified view. In L. Gregg (Ed.), *Knowledge and cognition* (pp. 105–128). Hillsdale, NJ: Lawrence Erlbaum Associates.

Sodian, B., Zaitchik, D., & Carey, S. (1991). Young children's differentiation of hypothetical beliefs from evidence. *Child Development, 62,* 753–766.

Thagard, P. (1989). Explanatory coherence. *Behavioral and Brain Sciences, 12,* 435–502.

Tweney, R. D., Doherty, M. E., & Mynatt, C. R. (Eds.). (1981). *On scientific thinking.* New York: Columbia University Press.

Valdes-Perez, R. E., Simon, H. A., & Murphy, R. F. (1992, July). Discovery of pathways in science. *Proceedings of the Machine Discovery Workshop, International Conference on Machine Learning* (pp. 51–57). Abendeen, Scotland.

Vosniadou, S., & Brewer, W. F. (1992). Mental models of the earth: A study of conceptual change in childhood. *Cognitive Psychology, 24,* 535–585.

Wason, P. C. (1960). On the failure to eliminate hypotheses in a conceptual task. *Quarterly Journal of Experimental Psychology, 12,* 129–140.

Wason, P. C. (1968). Reasoning about a rule. *Quarterly Journal of Experimental Psychology, 20,* 273–281.

DISCUSSION

Development Matters

Tony Simon
Georgia Institute of Technology

Soar is a computational architecture for the realization of intelligent, behaving agents. It is also a theory of the human cognitive system. As is characteristic of both such entities, it exhibits self-modification. Thus, over time, Soar's behavior changes as a function of its knowledge state and the interaction of the tasks it undertakes, the processing that arises, and the learning that is a consequence. Because of these characteristics, the Soar project is populated by a group of scientists who are unusual in that they continually ask themselves questions such as "Where did this particular competence come from?" or "How did this piece of knowledge come to be constructed?" Those same features mean that Soar can act as a vehicle for the direct study of mechanisms of human cognitive development, an enterprise that involves the investigation of essentially identical questions.

In this discussion I use some general issues that arose during the symposium and some specific issues raised by David Klahr to argue the importance of cognitive-developmental research to an enterprise like the Soar project. I suggest that developmental issues present a number of challenges. Answering these will both strengthen the psychological accuracy of Soar as a theory of the human cognitive architecture and enable us to make progress toward explaining an essential aspect of cognition: where competencies come from and how they change as a function of experience.

DEVELOPMENTAL ISSUES

A number of chapters in this volume, and discussions during the symposium brought up issues explicitly concerning development. The reason is that in honoring the work of Allen Newell, the symposium took Soar as its central focus and many questions were asked about the nature of that architecture for intelligent behavior. Whenever we analyze such an architecture we are addressing questions about which aspects of the cognitive system are innate (in human terms) and which others, by implication, arise from learning the results of processing task-specific representations. Furthermore, to characterize cognitive change as primarily domain-specific learning means that Soar becomes a vehicle for empirically investigating the hypothesis that learning and development are not distinct processes. This view says that what are usually referred to as developmental transitions can be accounted for with an architecture that has only one simple learning mechanism. Thus it should be apparent that development matters greatly, for it is a central concern when working with a self-modifying theory of human cognition.

Adopting a unified view of intelligent behavior means that even where one is not directly concerned with human cognition, analyzing an architecture like Soar raises issues that have resonance to the developmental psychologist. John Laird's characterization of the Soar architecture evoked a question about whether it should be taken as an equally accurate model of children's and adult's cognitive system or whether any modifications would be necessary in order to account for the less mature cognitive state. Zenon Pylyshyn and Rick Lewis addressed the issue of which aspects of the cognitive system, particularly in relation to language, are modular and how learning and change may affect our conceptions of modularity. Richard Young debated Marcel Just and Pat Carpenter's view of the source of processing limitations in the human cognitive system and how these might change over time with effects such as aging as well as learning. Even in the context of machine learning, Tom Mitchell and Paul Rosenbloom discussed which are the sufficient learning mechanisms that the architecture should be endowed with such that all learning tasks across any agent's life span can be carried out. Due to the special characteristics of a system like Soar, this can be validly viewed as a question about the innate competencies of the human cognitive machinery.

DOMAIN-GENERAL CHANGE

David Klahr's presentation, among other things, described developmental differences in discovery and scientific thinking. He characterized discovery as a form of problem solving where there are two kinds of search: one among hypotheses and the other among experiments that can either generate or evaluate hypotheses. Although the research of Klahr and his colleagues has shown that differences in domain-specific knowledge between children and adults affect their performance in discovery tasks, by far the biggest separation of the age groups is in terms of domain-general knowledge. These differences emerge in the form of heuristics that can be used to guide search, especially with respect to designing and running experiments that will lead to the creation of accurate hypotheses about the domain. In short, children rarely demonstrate knowledge or use of the heuristics that are seen in adults when they solve discovery problems.

So, if the major developmental transition in scientific thinking is in terms of the formation of domain-general heuristics, we need to ask how to explain this kind of development from the perspective of Soar. It has already been clearly demonstrated that chunking in Soar is sufficient to account for domain-specific change in a wide variety of tasks covering a broad time scale of cognitive activity (Lewis et al., 1990). For example, chunking in Soar has been used to model transitions ranging from the power law of practice in the Siebel 1,023-choice reaction task (Newell, 1990) to the development of number conservation in children (Simon, Newell, & Klahr, 1991; Simon & Klahr, 1995). Our first challenge, then, is to ask what account follows from Soar with regard to the construction of domain-general heuristics.

The answer is simple to state at an abstract level. Like all other learning in Soar, the construction of this kind of knowledge will be the result of chunking that arises from impasses in task processing. In other words, the scientist's task is to determine which tasks Soar would have to engage in while solving discovery problems. The goal is to produce processing that causes the knowledge that implements the heuristics to be constructed. At first glance this answer can seem like obfuscation. However, it must be remembered that Soar is a theory of the cognitive architecture and not of any given task. It provides the mechanisms by which new knowledge can be created. These mechanisms are independent of the knowledge, tasks, and goals of the system at any point in time. The action is in the problem solving, which is where representations are processed, and the role of chunking is to record some of those as results. Specifying the right representations is the job of the theorist. Despite the often dizzying complexity of discovering the right specifications (as David Klahr's chapter describes), Soar heavily constrains the search by providing a fixed architecture and learning mechanism. Among the many alternative accounts that could be created to account for a particular set of data, many are simply ruled out by inconsistency with the way Soar works. In other words, not all solutions can be implemented in Soar, and very few that can will continue to create representations that support meaningful behavior when transformed by chunking.

SOAR AND DEVELOPMENT

When considering Soar as a theory of the human cognitive architecture it is necessary to apply those same constraints of architecture and learning to the basic competencies of the system. A central goal of Soar research bears repeating here. All representations that Soar processes, except for those which are part of the architecture, should arise from chunking. However, there are bodies of knowledge that exist as part of all Soar models that have not arisen from Soar's own processing. One ever-present body of knowledge and one competence that may become ubiquitous serve as illustrations here.

For as long as Soar has had universal subgoaling, it has employed a set of knowledge defined in what are called the *default rules*. Without deliberate excision, these rules are loaded whenever Soar is started up and they come into play to control the processing in impasse resolution whenever specific task knowledge is not retrieved. As such they almost have the status of architectural knowledge but they are not part of the architecture. This *pseudo-architectural* knowledge is the best example of domain-general heuristics that there is to be found in Soar. However, the default rules were not constructed by chunking; they were written and provided by programmers. Yet this is precisely the kind of knowledge shown by David Klahr to develop and change over the life span, thereby greatly influencing the analytical thinking abilities of the human problem solver. Would these default rules be the same if Soar had built them?

Another example concerns the natural language capability that currently exists in Soar as what we might term *supra-architectural* knowledge. In other words, it exists as descriptions of the knowledge required for natural language comprehension, implemented in the problem spaces of a system called NL-Soar (Lehman, Lewis, & Newell, in press). Such knowledge might one day become part of Soar's architecture. The developers of NL-Soar are well aware that to complete the Soar account of human language use, they will need to account for language generation as well as comprehension. However, they also must be prepared to account for acquisition of the knowledge that is the basis of their theory.

As it stands, Soar is a model of young-adult cognition. The regularities used as a foundation for the construction of the architecture and many of the subsequent cognitive models were observed in the performance of college-age subjects for the most part. Thus, our second challenge is to answer the question, "Is Soar a legal state in the space of cognitive architectures?" Soar in its current state is constituted as a clearly defined set of structures and processes that stands as a model of human cognition. However, in reaching that state it is not clear that the initial state or the operators were specified correctly. Neither is it clear that the correct sequence of operators were applied, and finally, few in the field are certain how to clearly define the goal state of a fully specified theory of the human cognitive architecture. In other words, since Soar did not develop to its current state via self-modification, questions must remain about the details of its specifications.

Although it is unrealistic to require Soar to have grown from a version only capable of human infant competence, it seems clear that accounting for the entire transition from infancy to old age is probably the most stringent test for a candidate architecture of cognition. Such a task poses some very difficult but important questions for a cognitive theory. I elaborate by providing just a couple of illustrative examples.

One question that can be asked about the cognitive architecture is whether some aspects of it change over the life span. The time scale of human action that Allen Newell presented in *Unified Theories of Cognition* (1990) derived from earlier work on the model human processor (Card, Moran, & Newell, 1983) research primarily carried out on young adult subjects. The developmental literature shows that children and old people process information more slowly, and possibly even in qualitatively different ways than do young adults (e.g., Kail & Salthouse, 1994). The bases of these differences are only just beginning to be understood, and it is unclear how much of each effect is accounted for directly by changes in the architecture and how much is a function of changes in knowledge. Nevertheless, the question of whether the architecture for a "Kiddie-Soar"[1] or a "Granny-Soar" needs to be qualitatively and/or quantitatively different from the current instantiation must be considered.

The second example relates to an emerging view in developmental psychology of the human infant as a problem solver faced with a huge inductive task of constructing his or her own version of reality. The infant is provided with some innate knowledge of its world which helps to bias the induction by favoring the construction of certain kinds of representations and knowledge (e.g., Carey & Gelman, 1991). Such a view presents two challenges to Soar research. One is to determine what kinds of innate knowledge, if any, should exist in the architecture. The other is to ensure the "infant" architecture is provided with the kind of inductive capabilities that can use that knowledge to create our recognizable adult version, given appropriate experiences.

To conclude, I want to stress that these are challenges rather than shortcomings. In Soar we have a vehicle for direct experimentation on the nature of the human cognitive architecture and the mechanisms for its self-modification over the life span. We can ask of it the kinds of questions I have outlined and listen to the architecture for guidance. Not to do so would be to miss the main chance in constructing a unified theory of cognition.

---

[1]This idea is based on the notion of a "Kiddie-MHP" posited by David Klahr (1992) in considering whether specifications of cognitive architectures require distinct versions to account for children's cognition.

That is the chance to explain how the human mind develops the ability to exhibit the rich diversity of competencies that people display.

ACKNOWLEDGMENTS

I thank Mimi Recker and Dorrit Billman for helpful and challenging comments on a draft of this chapter.

REFERENCES

Card, S., Moran, T. P., & Newell, A. (1983). *The psychology of human–computer interaction.* Hillsdale, NJ: Lawrence Erlbaum Associates.

Carey, S., & Gelman, R. (1991). *The epigenesis of mind: Essays on biology and cognition.* Hillsdale, NJ: Lawrence Erlbaum Associates.

Kail, R., & Salthouse, T. A. (1994). Processing speed as a mental capacity. *Acta Psychologica, 86,* 199–225.

Klahr, D. (1992). Information processing approaches to cognitive development. In M. H. Bornstein & M. E. Lamb (Eds.), *Developmental psychology: An advanced textbook* (3rd ed., pp. 273–336). Hillsdale, NJ: Lawrence Erlbaum Associates.

Lehman, J. F., Lewis, R. L., & Newell, A. (in press). NL-Soar: Architectural influences of language comprehension. In Z. Pylyshyn (Ed.), *Cognitive architecture.* Norwood, NJ: Ablex.

Lewis, R. L., Huffman, S. B., John, B. E., Laird, J. E., Lehman, J. F., Newell, A., Rosenbloom, P. S., Simon, T., & Tessler, S. G. (1990, Spring). Soar as a unified theory of cognition: Spring 1990. *Proceedings of the Twelfth Annual Conference of the Cognitive Science Society* (pp. 1035–1042). Hillsdale, NJ: Lawrence Erlbaum Associates.

Newell, A. (1990). *Unified theories of cognition.* Cambridge, MA: Harvard University Press.

Simon, T. J., & Klahr, D. (1995). A computational theory of children's learning about number conservation. In T. J. Simon & G. S. Halford (Eds.), *Developing cognitive competence: New approaches to process modeling* (pp. 315–354). Hillsdale, NJ: Lawrence Erlbaum Associates.

Simon, T., Newell, A., & Klahr, D. (1991). A computational account of children's learning about number conservation. In D. Fisher, M. Pazzani, & P. Langley (Eds.), *Concept formation: Knowledge & experience in unsupervised learning* (pp. 423–462). San Mateo, CA: Morgan Kaufmann.

Chapter 10

The Process of Deduction

Philip N. Johnson-Laird
Princeton University

From his early work on the "logic theorist" (e.g., Newell, Shaw, & Simon, 1963) to one of his last papers (Polk & Newell, 1995), the process of deduction was never far from Allen Newell's thoughts. The aim of this chapter is to examine the topic, touching where relevant on Newell's ideas, and seeking above all to establish a common cause with them. This cause is that deductive reasoning is a semantic process—one that depends on the meaning of premises and its use in the construction of mental models (Johnson-Laird, 1983)—rather than a syntactic process in which the logical forms of premises are manipulated by mental embodiments of formal rules of inference.

The chapter begins with an incidental observation about the errors that reasoners make in trying to prove formal theorems in Boolean algebra—an observation that points in the direction of semantics. It then considers deductions with a sensible everyday content that depend on the Boolean connectives *and*, *or*, and *if*. It shows that the experimental evidence counts against theories of reasoning based on formal rules of inference, and it argues instead that logically untrained individuals reason by using their knowledge of the meaning of premises to construct mental models of the relevant situation. It turns next to simple deductions based on quantifiers, dealing first with inferences in which only a single quantifier occurs, and then with syllogisms, that is, pairs of premises that both contain a quantifier. Newell himself proposed several theories of syllogistic reasoning, and as a precursor to the description of the first of them, this chapter explains the two main diagrammatic methods for syllogistic reasoning, Euler circles and Venn diagrams. It describes the author's own model-based theory of syllogisms, which accounts for the phenomena in terms of the "figure" of the syllogism (the arrangement of its terms) and its models. Newell once considered that the "atmosphere" hypothesis might explain how reasoners generate putative conclusions to syllogisms—that is, they are biased toward using the same quantifiers as those that occur in the premises. He later abandoned this idea, and the present chapter shows that he was right to do so. It uses the model theory to dispel the atmosphere hypothesis. It also shows how general knowledge can enter directly into the process of deduction, contrary to theories based on formal rules of inference. The final section of this chapter takes up Newell's last views about syllogistic reasoning and the work of his student, Thad Polk, on VR, a theory of verbal reasoning that gives an excellent account of individual differences. This theory postulates that reasoning is a purely verbal process, and that even though it depends on the construction of models there may be no need to invoke a search for alternative models. This chapter attempts to rebut both of these ideas. What is ultimately important, however, is Newell's prescience in arguing for a semantic process of deduction.

SEMANTIC FACTORS IN FORMAL PROOFS

The Logic Theory Machine was a computer program that proved theorems in the propositional calculus in a way that resembled the proofs constructed by human reasoners (see Newell et al., 1963). Many years ago it prompted an unpublished study of the author's that examined how mathematicians prove theorems in Boolean algebra—the algebra of *not, and*, and *or*. They had to prove equivalences using a very parsimonious set of axioms, which are stated in Table 10.1.

The difficulty of proving a theorem tends to depend on the length of the required derivation, that is, the number of formal steps it requires (see Newell & Simon, 1972). Other factors, however, are likely to affect performance, and one purpose of the experiment was to determine whether "detours" affected the difficulty of a proof. Thus, suppose that a long expression has to be derived from a short expression; then the obvious step is to increase the number of symbols in the short expression. The task will be relatively easy if such a step is correct, and relatively hard if it is incorrect. Consider, for example, the following Boolean equivalence:

$$a \ \& \ T = (a \ \& \ a) \ \text{or} \ F$$

where "a" is a variable denoting a proposition, "&" denotes conjunction, "or" denotes an inclusive disjunction, "T" denotes a true proposition, and

TABLE 10.1
Eight Axioms for Boolean Algebra, Where "a" and "b"
Are Variables Denoting Propositions, "&" Denotes Conjunction,
"or" Denotes Inclusive Disjunction, "T" Denotes a True Proposition,
and "F" Denotes a False Proposition

1	(a & b)	= (b & a)
1'	(a or b)	= (b or a)
2	a & (b or c)	= (a & b) or (a & c)
2'	a or (b & c)	= (a or b) & (a or c)
3	(a & T)	= a
3'	(a or F)	= a
4	(a & not-a)	= F
4'	(a or not-a)	= T

Note. In Boolean algebra, the *dual* of an expression is obtained by substituting "&" for "or," and "T" for "F," and vice versa. The axioms are arranged in four pairs, where each member of a pair is the dual of the other member of the pair. The only rule of inference is the usual rule of substitution: Any uniform substitution of one expression for another can be made within any expression.

"F" denotes a false proposition. If you work from the left-hand side, then sooner or later you will have to increase the number of symbols that it contains. Hence, an obvious step is to expand the T according to axiom 4'. But if you are working from the right-hand side, then the obvious step is one that decreases the number of symbols. In this case, however, the correct initial step is to increase the number of symbols by expanding F. Thus, the proof proceeds as follows:

(a & a) or F	[right-hand side of the equivalence]
(a & a) or (a & not-a)	[by axiom 4]
a & (a or not-a)	[by axiom 2]
a & T	[by axiom 4']

The problem should therefore be easy when working from its left-hand side, but it calls for a detour when working from its right-hand side. To test this prediction, each subject attempted to prove the problem and its dual, a or F = (a or a) & T, working from the short side in one case and the long side in the other case.

The detour did indeed make the theorem harder to prove: Without it, 70% of the subjects proved the theorem; with it, only 28% of the subjects proved the theorem. In retrospect, however, an incidental observation now seems more important than the effect of detours. Even though the instructions stressed that each step in a proof must be based on an axiom and the subjects were mathematics majors, they did not merely fail to prove theorems in the allotted time; over a third of them made downright errors. These errors were almost always semantically plausible (88% of the errors), although not, in fact, sanctioned by an axiom. Here are some typical examples:

(1)　　　a & a
　∴　　a
(2)　　　a
　∴　　a or a
(3)　　　(a & a) or F
　∴　　a

An obvious interpretation of this phenomenon is that the mathematicians' semantic intuitions were guiding the process of proof and sometimes led them to take a step that was not warranted by any single axiom in the set. These intuitions, which were almost invariably correct, could not be suppressed and played an important role in the process of thought. But if mathematicians trying to reason about abstract premises in a purely formal way are guided by semantic intuitions, then logically untrained individuals trying to reason about meaningful matters might similarly be engaged in a semantic process. Let us examine this idea with everyday deductions corresponding to Boolean proofs.

DEDUCTION WITH PROPOSITIONAL CONNECTIVES

Many deductions in daily life depend on the connectives *not, if, and,* and *or,* for example:

> The turbine should be rotating fast enough to generate emergency electricity, or else the experiment should not continue.
> The turbine is not rotating fast enough to generate emergency electricity.
> ∴　The experiment should not continue.

Such deductions have been formalized by logicians in the propositional calculus (which closely relates to Boolean algebra), and most psychologists who have thought about the matter assume that there is a mental logic corresponding to this calculus, made up of formal rules of inference such as those presented in Table 10.2 (see, e.g., Braine, 1978; Macnamara, 1986; Osherson, 1975; Rips, 1983, 1994; Smith, Langston, & Nisbett, 1992). In such a "natural deduction" system, there are rules for introducing and for eliminating each of the connectives. The semantics for the propositional calculus is often formulated using the familiar apparatus of truth tables. Table 10.3, for example, states the truth table for inclusive disjunction.

TABLE 10.2
Some Typical Formal Rules of Inference Postulated
as Part of Mental Logic by Many Psychologists

Rules That Eliminate Connectives	Rules That Introduce Connectives
p & q ∴ p	p q ∴ p & q
p or q not-p ∴ q	p ∴ p or q
if p then q p ∴ q	p ⊢ q ∴ if p then q

Note. "⊢" signifies that q can be derived from hypothesizing p.

Although Osherson (1974–1976) raised the possibility of a semantically based psychological theory of deduction, he pointed out that the difficulty of a deduction failed to correlate with the number of rows in its truth table. The disjunctive inference just given concerns two atomic propositions, and its truth table has four rows. In general, a deduction based on n atomic propositions calls for a truth table with 2^n rows. Yet the mere addition of an atomic proposition does not necessarily make a deduction more difficult. The following example is unlikely to be twice as difficult as the previous one, although it calls for a truth table containing eight rows:

> The turbine should be rotating fast enough to generate emergency electricity, or else the experiment should not continue and the engineer in charge should be notified.
>
> The turbine is not rotating fast enough to generate emergency electricity.
>
> ∴ The experiment should not continue and the engineer in charge should be notified.

TABLE 10.3
Truth Table for Inclusive Disjunction

p	q	p or q, or both
T	T	T
T	F	T
F	T	T
F	F	F

Note. Each row represents a possible assignment of truth values to the propositions denoted by p and q. The first row in the table shows that case where p is true and q is true; in this case, the inclusive disjunction, p or q or both, is also true. As the table shows, the disjunction is false if, and only if, both p and q are false.

For some years, the semantic approach to propositional reasoning remained at this apparent impasse. Eventually, Ruth Byrne and the author found a way around and formulated an alternative semantic theory based on mental models (Johnson-Laird & Byrne, 1991). The theory postulates that reasoners construct models of the states of affairs described by premises, that is, they represent situations, not the truth values of different contingencies. Hence, given the inclusive disjunction:

There is a circle or there is a triangle, or both.

They construct the following three alternative mental models:

[O]

        [Δ]

[O]   [Δ]

where each line represents a separate model. Such models correspond only to those rows in the truth table that are true. The square brackets indicate that the relevant items—circles and triangles—have been exhaustively represented in the present set of models (i.e., a triangle cannot be added to the second model, and a circle cannot be added to the third model).

In systems based on formal rules, inference calls for a search for the derivation of a conclusion, where each step in the derivation is warranted by a rule of inference. One problem for these accounts is to explain the particular conclusions that human reasoners tend to draw, because, logically speaking, an infinite number of different conclusions can be correctly derived from any set of premises. Hence, given the premises,

There is a circle or there is a triangle, or both.

There is not a circle.

the following conclusions can all be proved using the rules in Table 10.2:

There is a triangle.

There is a triangle and there is not a circle.

If there is not a circle, then there is not a circle and there is a triangle.

If there is not a circle, then there is not a circle and there is a triangle and there is not a circle.

. . . and so on.

Nearly everyone, however, is likely to draw the first or second of these conclusions; the remaining conclusions are too trivial to be worth inferring.

Yet it is by no means trivial to guide a formal rule system so that it reaches only sensible conclusions.

Human reasoners appear to draw conclusions that make explicit what is not overtly stated by any premise, and they seek to do so in ways that are verbally parsimonious. In the model theory of propositional reasoning, the basic method of inference is to combine the models corresponding to different premises and to describe the resulting set of models as parsimoniously as possible. The principle of combination corresponds to the semantics of conjunction: Each of the models in the set corresponding to the previous premises is combined with each of the models of the current premise, but no model can be combined with a model containing the negation of one of its constituents (i.e., the result is the "null" model akin to the empty set). Redundant items are similarly dropped from the resulting set of models. Consider, for instance, the premises:

There is a circle or there is a triangle, or both.

There is not a circle.

As we have seen, the first of these premises yields the models:

[O]
       [Δ]
[O]   [Δ]

The second premise yields a single model:

[¬ O]

where "¬" represents negation. The second model is inconsistent with any model containing a circle, and so it eliminates two of the models of the disjunction. The final result is accordingly:

[¬ O]   [Δ]

If we omit the description of the categorical premise, which can be taken for granted, this model yields the conclusion:

There is a triangle.

which makes explicit a state of affairs that is not asserted by any single premise.

The model theory may seem to be a simple notational variant of the formal rule theories. But, in fact, the model theory makes predictions that cannot be derived from any existing rule theories. Granted the limited processing capacity of working memory, the model theory predicts that the greater the number of models to be constructed in making a deduction, the harder the task should be. It should take longer and be more prone to error. Hence, the theory predicts that deductions based on inclusive disjunctions, such as "There is a circle or there is a triangle, or both" should be harder than deductions based on exclusive disjunctions, such as "There is a circle or there is a triangle, but not both." Inclusive disjunctions call for three models (see earlier discussion), but exclusive disjunctions call for only two models:

[O]
　　　　[Δ]

Our experimental results corroborate this prediction (Johnson-Laird & Byrne, 1991; Johnson-Laird, Byrne, & Schaeken, 1992). Yet formal-rule theories have no way of making it: They allow that one rule may be harder to use than another, but they are forced to assess the differences post hoc because they have no machinery for predicting them a priori.

One point remains to be made about the model theory of propositional reasoning. The theory postulates that disjunctions are initially represented with only their positive instances made explicit (e.g., "There is a circle or else there is a triangle" has a model of the case where there is a circle, and a model of the case where there is a triangle). Reasoners should bear in mind that in the first case there isn't a triangle, and in the second case there isn't a circle, but this information is not explicitly represented. Similarly, conditionals are initially represented with only their positive cases made explicit. For example, the conditional:

If there is a circle, then there is a triangle

is initially represented by an explicit model of the case where there is a circle and a triangle, but a wholly implicit model of the other possibilities, as represented by the ellipsis:

O   Δ
　. . .

Reasoners again ought to bear in mind that circles cannot occur in the possibilities represented by the ellipsis, but they are likely to forget this information as the load on working memory increases.

One unexpected consequence of these assumptions is that the theory predicts the existence of illusory inferences with conclusions that are compelling but egregious errors (Johnson-Laird & Savary, 1995). For example, given the following exclusive disjunction about a particular hand of cards:

> If there is a king in the hand then there is an ace in the hand, or else if there isn't a king in the hand then there is an ace in the hand.

reasoners should construct only the following two explicit models:

> king   ace
> ¬king   ace

Hence, they should conclude that an ace is in the hand. In fact, it is impossible for an ace to be in the hand. Granted an exclusive disjunction of two conditionals, one of them must be true and the other must be false—it is the latter that will tend to be overlooked. If the first conditional is false, then there is a king but no ace in the hand; if the second conditional is false, then there is no king and no ace. Either way, there is no ace, and so it is impossible for this card to be in the hand. We have found a variety of illusory inferences based on different connectives: what they have in common is that they arise from interactions between the wholly or partially implicit models that reasoners are apt to use (Johnson-Laird & Savary, 1995).

REASONING WITH SINGLE QUANTIFIERS

A mental model of the simplest sort corresponds to a class of situations, and there will be infinitely many possible members of the class (see Barwise, 1993). This point becomes clear if we turn from propositional reasoning to reasoning based on individuals and a single quantifier. Consider, for example, the following problem from an unpublished study carried out in collaboration with Patrizia Tabossi of the University of Bologna:

> Ann is not in the same place as Tom.
> Tom is in the same place as all the students.
> ∴ Ann is not in the same place as any of the students.

The first premise calls for a simple model, which can be denoted by the following diagram:

> | Ann | Tom |

in which the vertical lines demarcate separate places. The model represents nothing about the relative locations of the two places, and so it is com-

patible with infinitely many different possibilities. The information from
the second premise can be added to the model by assuming a small arbitrary
number of students and by representing them exhaustively, as shown by
the square brackets:

    | Ann | Tom [student] [student] [student] |

The model supports the conclusion:

    Ann is not in the same place as any of the students.

No alternative model of the premises refutes this conclusion, and so it is
valid.

The subjects in the experiment had to evaluate a variety of inferences
by responding "yes" or "no" depending on whether or not the conclusion
was valid. We compared one-model problems such as the one above with
multiple-model problems, such as:

    Ann is in the same place as Tom.
    Tom is not in the same place as some of the students.

These premises yield an initial model of the sort:

    | Ann Tom | student student student |

which is consistent with the conclusion:

    Ann is not in the same place as any of the students.

But this conclusion is refuted by the model:

    | Ann Tom student | student student student |

The two models together support the conclusion:

    Ann is not in the same place as some of the students.

As a control condition, the experiment also included multiple-model
problems that did not yield a valid conclusion interrelating the two terms
occurring in the different premises. On half the trials with each of the
problems with valid conclusions, the correct response was "yes," and on
half the trials the correct response was "no" because the presented conclusion did not follow validly.

The model theory predicts that the one-model problems should be easier than the multiple-model problems with valid conclusions. This prediction was confirmed: The subjects made 91% correct "yes" responses to the one-model problems, but only 73% correct "yes" responses to the multiple-model problems with valid conclusions. Similarly, there was a reliable difference in the mean latencies of these responses: 9.1 sec for the one-model problems, but 11.1 sec for the multiple-model problems with valid conclusions. The results accordingly confirmed the model theory's predictions about difficulty: More models lead to more errors and longer latencies. One of the model theory's other main predictions concerns the nature of the erroneous conclusions that reasoners are likely to draw, but in order to examine this prediction, we need to consider more difficult deductions, such as syllogisms, for which Allen Newell proposed several theories during his career.

SYLLOGISMS AND THE ATMOSPHERE HYPOTHESIS

Syllogisms were first formalized by Aristotle. They are based on two premises that each contain a single quantifier, for example:

> Some actuaries are businessmen.
> All businessmen are conformists.
> ∴ Some actuaries are conformists.

Traditionally, the premises and conclusions are in one of four "moods":

All X are Y.   (abbreviated as A)
Some X are Y.   (abbreviated as I)
No X are Y.   (abbreviated as E)
Some X are not Y.   (abbreviated as O)

For a valid deduction, the two premises must contain a term in common (the so-called middle term) and the terms in the premises can be in one of four possible arrangements (or "figures"):

A-B   B-A   A-B   B-A
B-C   C-B   C-B   B-C

Thus, the example just given is in the first of these figures.

A persistent view about syllogisms is that logically untrained individuals do not really reason with them at all, but instead are prey to a variety of superficial biases. The atmosphere hypothesis, which was first proposed over

50 years ago, is the classical version of this doctrine (Woodworth & Sells, 1935). But it continues to attract adherents to this day (e.g., M. Levine, personal communication; Wetherick & Gilhooly, 1990), including at one time Allen Newell himself (Polk & Newell, 1988). According to the atmosphere hypothesis, human reasoners make errors because they are biased by the superficial form of the premises. In a succinct formulation due to Begg and Denny (1969), whenever at least one premise is particular, that is, contains the quantifier "some," reasoners are biased toward a particular conclusion; otherwise, they are biased toward a universal conclusion. Similarly, whenever at least one premise is negative, reasoners are biased toward a negative conclusion; otherwise, they are biased toward an affirmative conclusion. Revlis (1975) showed that an algorithm for syllogistic inference could be based on these principles, and recent theorists have followed suit. Wetherick and Gilhooly (1990) adopted a simplified version of the atmosphere hypothesis. They argued that some subjects are sometimes able to reason deductively—as did Woodworth and Sells (1935)—but that some merely select a conclusion that matches the mood of a premise. Marvin Levine (personal communication) has explored a similar idea, although he allows that reasoners may become confused and in consequence decide that nothing follows from the premises. Both Madruga (1984) and Polk and Newell (1988) argued that the atmosphere of the premises suggests a candidate conclusion, which model-based reasoning may modify or reject. In fact, the atmosphere hypothesis is probably wrong, but before replacing it by the model theory, it is necessary to outline various diagrammatic methods of syllogistic reasoning, which are precursors to this theory.

EULER CIRCLES AND VENN DIAGRAMS

Euler circles are a traditional informal method for syllogistic reasoning. They were invented by Leibniz but owe their fame to Euler, who used them to teach elementary logic to a princess (Kneale & Kneale, 1962, pp. 337, 349). Each premise is represented by a set of diagrams in which sets are denoted by diagrams. For example, a premise of the form

All A are B.

is represented by two diagrams. In one, a circle representing A is properly included within a circle representing B to indicate that the set A is properly included within the set B; in the other diagram, the two circles are coextensive to indicate that the two sets, A and B, are coextensive. An assertion of the form

Some A are B.

in its logical sense (at least some A are B) calls for four distinct diagrams, respectively denoting that the set A overlaps with the set B, A is properly included within B, B is properly included within A, and the two sets are coextensive. Wason and Johnson-Laird (1972) informally adopted an Eulerian account of syllogistic reasoning, but Erickson (1974) developed a full-fledged theory.

The great drawback of Euler circles both as a psychological theory and as a pedagogical technique is that even the simplest of deductions need a large number of diagrams. The syllogism:

> Some A are B.
> All B are C.
> ∴ Some A are C.

is the easiest of all syllogisms (see, e.g., Johnson-Laird & Bara, 1984). Yet it calls for 16 different Euler diagrams, and there is no simple procedure for checking that all of them have been constructed. Erickson (1974) avoided this problem by stipulating in one version of this theory that no more than four diagrams are ever constructed, but this assumption sacrifices logical competence—the ability to get the right answer for the right reasons—for psychological plausibility.

A superior diagrammatic method was devised by the Reverend John Venn (Kneale & Kneale, 1962, p. 420). The three sets, A, B, and C, are represented in a single diagram by three overlapping circles, and each premise is interpreted by shading out those areas it indicates are empty and adding plus signs to those areas that it indicates are not empty. The method is closely related to one based on truth tables, which we will consider in detail because it underlies Newell's first theory of syllogistic reasoning (Newell, 1980).

Suppose that a syllogism concerns the following three sets of individuals: actuaries, businessmen, and conformists. There are eight possible subsets, which are laid out here:

Actuaries	Businessmen	Conformists
+	+	+
+	+	−
+	−	+
+	−	−
−	+	+
−	+	−
−	−	+
−	−	−

The first row, for instance, corresponds to the subset of individuals who are actuaries, businessmen, and conformists; the second row corresponds to the subset of individuals who are actuaries, businessmen, but not conformists; and so on. The premise,

Some actuaries are businessmen,

means that at least one subset containing both actuaries and businessmen has some members, and so it can be represented by indicating that the first or second row, or both, are not empty:

Actuaries	Businessmen	Conformists	First Premise
+	+	+	+ or
+	+	−	+
+	−	+	
+	−	−	
−	+	+	
−	+	−	
−	−	+	
−	−	−	

The premise,

All businessmen are conformists,

means that any subset containing businessmen who are not conformists is empty. This premise accordingly rules out the second and the sixth row in the table:

Actuaries	Businessmen	Conformists	Both Premises
+	+	+	+
+	+	−	−
+	−	+	
+	−	−	
−	+	+	
−	+	−	−
−	−	+	
−	−	−	

Individuals corresponding to the first row in the table therefore definitely exist, and so one can conclude:

Some actuaries are conformists.

The reader will note that subsets corresponding to the third, fourth, fifth, and seventh rows may or may not have members, and so there are $2^4 = 16$ possible Euler diagrams for these premises. The subset corresponding to the eighth row may or may not exist, but this subset has no Eulerian representation because it corresponds to individuals who are not actuaries, businessmen, or conformists.

Newell's (1980) theory of syllogistic reasoning closely resembles this tabular method. It represents a premise of the form

All A are B

by the string of symbols

pos a b c, pos a b −c,

where "pos" corresponds to possibly, and a minus sign indicates the complement of a set. Thus, the subset a b c may have members, or the subset a b −c may have members, or both. Newell devised rules for manipulating such strings in a way that is similar to the tabular method. The main problem with this theory is that it offers no account of the relative difficulty of different syllogisms or of the erroneous conclusions that human reasoners tend to draw—precisely those errors that originally led to the atmosphere hypothesis.

THE MODEL THEORY OF SYLLOGISTIC REASONING

The mental model theory was initially developed to account for syllogistic reasoning (Johnson-Laird, 1975). The theory of syllogisms, however, has undergone a series of progressive modifications (Johnson-Laird & Bara, 1984; Johnson-Laird & Steedman, 1978). What is described here is the account in Johnson-Laird and Byrne (1991), slightly updated in the light of a recent computer implementation by the author. The theory postulates four main stages: the initial interpretation of premises, the combination of these interpretations into a single model, the formulation of a conclusion, and the search for alternative models that might refute the conclusion.

The initial interpretation of a premise represents a set of individuals by a small arbitrary number of mental tokens. The theory accordingly postulates the following initial models for the four sorts of premise

All the A are B: [a]   b
                    [a]   b
                    · · ·

where each line represents a separate individual in the same model, and the ellipsis represent an implicit individual, that is, one with no initially explicit properties. Readers familiar with the previous version of the theory (Johnson-Laird & Bara, 1984) will note that we have abandoned the use of tokens representing optional individuals in favor of the use of "exhaustive" representations using square brackets: [a] indicates that the a's are exhausted, that is, they cannot occur in fleshing out the implicit individual. This modification brings the theory into line with the account above of conditionals.

Some of the A are B: a   b
                         a
                               b
                         . . .

None of the A is a B: [a]
                         [a]
                                 [b]
                                 [b]
                         . . .

Because the b's are exhausted, it follows at once that the a's can be explicitly represented as not-b's:

                         [a]   ¬b
                         [a]   ¬b
                                [b]
                                [b]
                          . . .

Some of the A are not B: a   ¬b
                              a   ¬b
                                    b
                                    b
                              . . .

The interpretation of premises in this last mood has always been problematical, but the present proposal seems to be the most plausible psychologically. The initial model supports the converse conclusion

Some of the B are not A

and many people make this erroneous inference. This conclusion can be refuted by an alternative model:

$$
\begin{array}{cc}
\text{a} & \neg\text{b} \\
\text{a} & \neg\text{b} \\
\text{a} & \text{b} \\
\text{a} & \text{b}
\end{array}
$$

The principles for forming an integrated model that combines the interpretations of the two premises are straightforward. First, following Johnson-Laird and Bara (1984), two operations may be used in order to bring the tokens corresponding to the middle terms into contiguity: (a) reversing the order of the two models before they are combined, and (b) swapping around the order of the items in a model (cf. Hunter, 1957). These operations account for various effects of figure, and they apply according to the figure of the premises in the following way:

Figure	A-B	
	B-C:	No operations needed.
Figure	B-A	
	C-B:	Reverse the order of the two models.
Figure	A-B	
	C-B:	Swap around the order of elements in the second model, or reverse the order of the two models and then swap around the order of elements in the A-B model.
Figure	B-A	
	B-C:	Swap around the order of elements in the first model, or reverse the order of the two models and then swap round the order of elements in the B-C model.

The operation for combining models is simple: Ensure that the models of the two premises contain the same number of tokens corresponding to the middle term, and then join these individuals one-to-one. For example, the premises

Some of the aviators are boarders.

All of the boarders are churchgoers.

yield the following respective models:

aviator   boarder
aviator   boarder
      . . .

and:

```
[boarder]      churchgoer
[boarder]      churchgoer
        . . .
```

Both models have the same number of tokens of the middle term, boarder, and so they can be directly combined:

```
aviator      [[boarder]      churchgoer]

aviator      [[boarder]      churchgoer]
        . . .
```

Likewise, for the premises

None of the aviators is a boarder.

All of the boarders are churchgoers.

the initial combined model is:

```
[aviator]      ¬boarder
[aviator]      ¬boarder
        [boarder]      churchgoer
        [boarder]      churchgoer
        . . .
```

Conclusions are formulated by describing the relation between the tokens representing the two end terms, that is, the two terms that occur in separate premises. If there are no negative tokens in a model, then the description is affirmative: If each end token, x, occurs in an individual that also contains the other end token, y, then the conclusion is:

All the X are Y.

Otherwise, if at least one end token, x, occurs in an individual that also contains the other end token, y, then the conclusion is:

Some of the X are Y.

And if this condition fails, then there is no valid conclusion to be drawn. If there is a negative token in a model, then the conclusion is negative: If the end tokens, x and y, do not occur in the same individual, and at least one of these two sets is exhaustively represented, then the conclusion is:

None of the X is a Y.

Otherwise, if at least one individual is an x but not a y, then the conclusion is:

Some of the X are not Y.

And if this condition fails, then there is no valid conclusion to be drawn.

The theory postulates that human reasoners attempt to search for alternative models that will falsify putative conclusions. The evidence, as we shall see, implies that they have no simple or certain algorithm for making such searches. Indeed, little is known about how they attempt to make searches beyond the fact that the task is difficult and likely to defeat them. The computer program implementing the theory accordingly draws conclusions from the initial model of the premises, scanning the model first in one direction and then the other; it then uses three sorts of operation to search for alternative models—breaking individuals into two, adding new individuals to the model, or joining two separate individuals into one. The operations may not be psychologically realistic; they are designed merely to ensure that the program's search is complete. For an affirmative conclusion, if there is an individual containing both end tokens, a and c, and the middle term, b, which is not exhausted, the first operation breaks this individual into two separate individuals:

    a   b   c

becomes:

    a   b
         b   c

Otherwise, if an end term is not exhausted, the second operation adds further such end terms to the model, one at a time unless more are needed to falsify a conclusion. For example, given the initial model

    [a]   [b]   c
    [a]   [b]   c
           . . .

and the conclusion

    All the C are A,

the operation of adding c's yields a new model that refutes the conclusion:

```
[a]    [b]    c
[a]    [b]    c
              c
. . .
```

For a negative conclusion, if an individual corresponds to one exhausted end term but not the other, then the third operation moves the individual and joins it to one corresponding to the other end term. Such moves are made one at a time unless more are needed to falsify a conclusion. For example, the initial model:

```
[a]    ¬b
[a]    ¬b
       [b]    ¬c
       [b]    ¬c
              [c]
              [c]
```

yields the conclusion:

None of the A is a C.

This conclusion is refuted by two joins:

```
[a]    ¬b     [c]
[a]    ¬b     [c]
       [b]    ¬c
       [b]    ¬c
```

Otherwise, if there is a nonexhausted end term, add further instances of it to the model one at a time unless more tokens are needed to falsify a conclusion. For example, the initial model

```
[a]    ¬b
[a]    ¬b
       [b]    c
       [b]
              c
```

supports the conclusion:

None of the A is a C.

This conclusion is refuted by adding a token:

```
[a]     ¬b     c
[a]     ¬b
        [b]    c
        [b]
               c
```

The model theory establishes a close relation between conditionals, such as "If a person is an aviator then he or she is a boarder," and universally quantified assertions, such as "All the aviators are boarders." The initial model of the quantified assertion is:

```
[aviator]     boarder
[aviator]     boarder
      . . .
```

Like the initial model of the conditional, it can be fleshed out in two distinct ways:

```
[aviator]      [boarder]
[aviator]      [boarder]
[¬aviator]     [¬boarder]
```

and

```
[aviator]      [boarder]
[aviator]      [boarder]
[¬aviator]     [boarder]
[¬aviator]     [¬boarder]
```

The first model corresponds to the class of situations in which the two sets are coextensive, and the second model corresponds to the class of situations in which the set of aviators is properly included with the set of boarders. The two ways of fleshing out the initial model accordingly correspond to the two alternative Euler diagrams for the premise. Indeed, as Stenning and Oberlander (1992) showed, it is possible to reconstruct the model theory in terms of Euler circles. One point of the model theory, however, is that logically untrained individuals are not aware of the different logical interpretations of quantified assertions or conditionals. They are also unlikely to be aware of either Euler circles or Venn diagrams unless they have encountered the "new math." The advantage of working with the initial mental model is that it obviates the combinatorial explosion that occurs with Euler circles. In addition, the model theory generalizes to multiply-quantified assertions, such as "All of the philosophers have read some of the books," which cannot even be represented in Euler circles or Venn diagrams.

THE CAUSES OF DIFFICULTY IN SYLLOGISTIC REASONING

The model theory makes three main predictions about deductive reasoning. First, as we have seen, it predicts that the greater the number of models that have to be constructed to make a deduction, the harder the task will be. Second, it predicts that erroneous conclusions should be consistent rather than inconsistent with the premises. This is a simple objective prediction because it can be checked even in the absence of a theory specifying the different models of the premises. Such errors arise because reasoners construct some of the possible models of the premises, but overlook others. Hence, the conclusion will be possibly true, that is, merely consistent with the premises, rather than necessarily true. Third, the theory predicts that general knowledge can influence the process of reasoning. Reasoners construct a putative conclusion on the basis of their initial model of the premises. If this conclusion fits their beliefs, they may be satisfied and accordingly fail to search scrupulously for alternative models. But, if the conclusion is incompatible with their beliefs, they will be dissatisfied and accordingly search more assiduously for an alternative model. The theory therefore provides a mechanism for inferential satisficing (cf. Simon, 1959)—a tendency that is well attested by the sort of cognitive errors that occur in daily life, for example, the operators at Three Mile Island inferred that overheating at a relief valve was caused by a leak, and they overlooked the possibility that the valve was stuck open. We examine evidence for each of the three predictions in turn.

Syllogisms differ strikingly in their difficulty. Some are so easy that even 7-year-old children can draw their own correct conclusions to them (Bara, Bucciarelli, & Johnson-Laird, 1995). Others are so difficult that few adults can do reliably better than chance with them. Why is there this enormous range in difficulty among such an apparently homogeneous set of problems? According to the model theory, the two decisive factors are the number of models and the figure of the premises. The difficulty of forming an initial integrated model should increase over the four figures (according to the account outlined earlier), with a concomitant increase in responses of the form, "there is no valid conclusion." The evidence bears out this prediction (Johnson-Laird & Bara, 1984). It also bears out the existence of a response bias based on figure. If the order of terms in a conclusion depends on the order in which items are entered in the integrated model, then A-B, B-C premises should tend to elicit A-C conclusions whereas B-A,

C-B premises should tend to elicit C-A conclusions. Certain syllogisms, however, have valid conclusions that run contrary to these response biases, and they are accordingly very difficult indeed. For example, the premises

None of the aviators is a boarder.

All of the boarders are churchgoers.

yield the model:

[aviator]	¬boarder	
[aviator]	¬boarder	
	[boarder]	churchgoer
	[boarder]	churchgoer
. . .		

and this model supports the conclusion:

None of the aviators is a churchgoer (65%),

or its converse, which is contrary to the figural bias:

None of the churchgoers is an aviator (15%).

The percentages of subjects drawing each conclusion come from the results of four correlated experiments (see Johnson-Laird & Byrne, 1991). These conclusions can be refuted by the alternative models:

[aviator]	¬boarder	churchgoer
[aviator]	¬boarder	
	[boarder]	churchgoer
	[boarder]	churchgoer
. . .		

and:

[aviator]	¬boarder	churchgoer
[aviator]	¬boarder	churchgoer
	[boarder]	churchgoer
	[boarder]	churchgoer
. . .		

A reasoner who drew the first of the conclusions above is now likely to respond, scanning the models from aviators to churchgoers:

No valid conclusion (17%).

But if the models are scanned from churchgoers to aviators, that is, contrary to the figural bias, the valid conclusion can be drawn:

Some of the churchgoers are not aviators (2%).

The figural bias undoubtedly contributes to the difficulty of certain syllogisms. Its proper interpretation, however, is a matter of controversy. The model theory explains the bias in terms of the order in which information enters the models of the premises. Johnson-Laird and Bara (1984) raised the possibility that the bias had a grammatical origin: in the A-B, B-C figure, the only end-term to occur in the subject of a premise is A; and in the B-A, C-B figure, the only end-term to occur in the subject of a premise is C. Hence, a bias to maintain the subject of a premise as the subject of a conclusion would create the observed bias in conclusions. These authors abandoned this hypothesis in the light of their findings about the ease of forming models across the four figures: the increasing proportion of "no valid conclusion" responses suggested that subjects were having an increasing difficulty in building an initial model. This phenomenon fits the working memory explanation, but not the grammatical hypothesis. Recently, however, the grammatical hypothesis has been independently advanced by Wetherick and Gilhooly (1990). In an unpublished study, Victoria Shaw and the author have obtained evidence that counts against it, using multiply quantified premises of the form:

All of the aviators and all of the boarders are in the same place.

All of the boarders and all of the churchgoers are in the same place.

The subjects' task was to state what conclusion, if any, followed from the premises. All three terms occur in the grammatical subject of a premise and so grammatical status makes no prediction about any resulting response bias. But, as the working memory hypothesis predicts, the subjects were biased toward conclusions either of the form:

All of the aviators and all of the churchgoers are in the same place.

or of the form:

All the aviators are in the same place as all the churchgoers.

rather than toward conclusions in which the terms occurred in the opposite order.

Of the 64 logically possible forms of syllogistic premise, 10 yield one-model problems, 17 yield multiple-model problems with a valid conclusion, and 37 yield multiple-model problems with no valid conclusion interrelat-

TABLE 10.4
Percentages of Correct Responses Drawn by Adults, Adolescents,
and Children to Syllogisms of All 64 Sorts

	One-Model Syllogisms	Multiple-Model Syllogisms with a Valid Conclusion	Multiple-Model Syllogisms with No Valid Conclusion
Adults (over 21 years)	83	30	33
Adolescents (14–15 years)	74	22	16
Children (9–10 years)	66	11	7

Note. From Bara, Bucciarelli, and Johnson-Laird (1995). Reprinted with permission.

ing the end terms. Table 10.4 presents the percentages of correct conclusions to these three sorts of syllogism, drawn respectively by adults, adolescents, and children, in a recent study by Bara et al. (1995). As the table shows, there is a large difference in difficulty between one-model syllogisms and multiple-model syllogisms with valid conclusions: Only one out of the 60 subjects failed to conform to this difference.

In summary, the cause of difficulty in syllogistic reasoning appears to be the figure of the premises, which can adversely affect the construction of a model and the formulation of the correct conclusion, and the need to construct multiple models of the premises, that is, to search for and to find alternative models that falsify the conclusions based on the initial models of the premises.

DISPELLING ATMOSPHERE: THE REAL CAUSE OF ERRONEOUS CONCLUSIONS

A common sort of error in syllogistic reasoning is exemplified by arguing from the premises:

All the athletes are bakers.
Some of the bakers are chemists.

to the conclusion:

Some of the athletes are chemists.

Errors of this sort fit the various versions of the atmosphere hypothesis (see the earlier account): there is a particular premise, that is, one containing "some," so there is a bias toward a particular conclusion. The model theory, however, provides an alternative explanation for the error, which according to its account arises, not from a superficial and irrational linguistic process, but from a genuine attempt to reason. The initial model of the premises is as follows:

```
[[athlete]    baker]    chemist
[[athlete]    baker]
                        chemist
        . . .
```

and it supports the conclusion:

Some of the athletes are chemists.

This conclusion is refuted by the alternative model formed by breaking the first individual in the model into two:

```
[athlete]    baker
             baker    chemist
[athlete]    baker
                      chemist
        . . .
```

Reasoners who fail to construct this alternative model will draw the erroneous conclusion. It is a striking fact that the initial model for each of the multiple-model problems yields a conclusion that matches the mood of one of the premises. Hence, the model theory also explains the tendency for erroneous conclusions to match the "atmosphere" of the premises. But which account is correct—the atmosphere hypothesis or the model theory?

There are three phenomena that count in favor of the model theory and decisively against the atmosphere hypothesis. The first phenomenon is that if subjects were guided solely by the atmosphere of the premises, then they would never respond "no valid conclusion." In fact, they do make this response, and they do so reliably better than chance for premises that do not yield a valid conclusion interrelating the end terms (Johnson-Laird & Bara, 1984). The model theory allows that subjects may succeed in constructing an alternative model of the premises, and that the resulting set of models fails to support any valid conclusion interrelating the end terms. No version of the atmosphere hypothesis offers a principled account of "no valid conclusion" responses.

The second phenomenon concerns those conclusions that match the mood of one of the premises. In those cases where the premises yield only one model, such conclusions are valid; in other cases, the syllogism may support more than one model yet still yield a conclusion that matches the mood of a premise. For example, premises of the form

All the A are B.

Some of the C are not B.

yield the initial model:

```
[a]       b
[a]       b
          ¬b    c
          ¬b    c
          . . .
```

which supports the conclusion:

Some of the A are not C

or its converse:

Some of the C are not A.

The further model:

```
[a]       b     c
[a]       b     c
          ¬b    c
          ¬b    c
          . . .
```

refutes the first conclusion, so subjects who have initially drawn it should now respond "no valid conclusion," but the model still supports the second conclusion, which is valid. According to the atmosphere hypothesis, the two sorts of conclusion—those for one model and those for multiple models—should occur with comparable frequencies. They both derive from the same "matching" process. According to the model theory, however, the one-model matching conclusions should occur more often than the multiple-model matching conclusions, because the latter should tend sometimes to be refuted as shown in the previous example. The data bear out this prediction. The percentages of matching conclusions from four correlated experiments were as follows: The one-model problems yielded 76% matching conclusions, whereas the multiple-model problems yielded only 39% matching conclusions (see Johnson-Laird & Byrne, 1991, Table 6.1).

The third phenomenon arose in a study of "only" as a quantifier (Johnson-Laird & Byrne, 1989). According to the model theory, an assertion such as

Only the boarders are aviators

brings to mind two distinct sorts of individuals: boarders who are aviators, and nonboarders who are not aviators. It thus has the following sort of initial model:

boarder   [aviator]
boarder   [aviator]
[¬boarder]   ¬aviator
[¬boarder]   ¬aviator
        . . .

The assertion thus has the same truth conditions as:

All the aviators are boarders

but this fact is not immediately obvious because the model of the latter assertion is:

[aviator]   boarder
[aviator]   boarder
        . . .

Yet both models can be fleshed out explicitly to capture either that aviators are properly included in the set of boarders or that the two sets are coextensive. Because the initial model based on "only" is more complex than the initial model based on "all," the theory predicts that reasoning should generally be harder with "only" than with "all." The results confirmed this prediction in an experiment comparing syllogisms in which both premises contained "all" with equivalent syllogisms in which both premises contained "only." The subjects drew 46% correct conclusions to the "all" syllogisms with a mean latency of 6.5 sec, but only 26% correct conclusions to the "only" syllogisms with a mean latency of 8.0 sec (both differences were reliable).

A further experiment showed that one-model syllogisms based on "only" were reliably easier than multiple-model syllogisms based on "only." Moreover, this experiment even failed to confirm the atmosphere effect itself. When both premises contained "only," such as:

Only the artists are beekeepers.
Only the beekeepers are chemists.

most subjects preferred to draw conclusions based on "all": All the chemists are artists. Overall, when both premises were based on "only" there were

45% conclusions based on "all" and just 16% of conclusions based on "only." When just one premise was based on "only" the percentage of conclusions based on "only" fell to 2%. These findings count decisively against any hypothesis that purports to explain syllogistic reasoning in terms of the superficial matching of quantifiers in the premises. The results are predictable, however, in terms of the model theory: The greater complexity of the semantics of "only" deters subjects from using it. Although Polk and Newell (1988) dallied with the atmosphere hypothesis as a means for generating initial conclusions, the latest version of their theory abandons the idea in favor of a semantic process for generating conclusions (Polk & Newell, 1995). A bad atmosphere has been finally dispelled: The hypothesis is more accurate as an account of its own origins than as an explanation of syllogistic reasoning.

HOW KNOWLEDGE INFLUENCES THE PROCESS OF REASONING

If reasoning were the syntactical manipulation of logical structures according to formal rules of inference, then general knowledge could not affect the process of reasoning. It might influence the interpretation of premises; it might lead to the incorporation of additional premises or to the suppression of given premises. But once the premises had been interpreted and their logical form mentally represented, knowledge could play no role because the process would be purely formal, that is, a syntactic manipulation of uninterpreted structures. If reasoning is a semantic process based on the construction of models, then in contrast knowledge can influence the process. Jane Oakhill, Alan Garnham, and the author have obtained evidence in favor of this prediction from studies of syllogistic reasoning (e.g. Oakhill, Johnson-Laird, & Garnham, 1989). Given the following sort of premises:

All the Frenchmen are gourmets.

Some of the gourmets are wine-drinkers.

the majority of our subjects (72%) drew the conclusion:

Some of the Frenchmen are wine-drinkers.

But given the following sort of premises:

All the Frenchmen are gourmets.

Some of the gourmets are Italians.

only a few of our subjects (8%) drew the equivalent conclusion:

Some of the Frenchmen are Italians.

No subject saw both of these problems, but they each saw a set of problems in which the initial conclusion predicted by the model theory was highly believable—as rated by an independent panel of judges—and a set of problems in which the initial putative conclusion was rated as highly unbelievable. The results bore out the pattern illustrated here.

What seems to have occurred can be elucidated by the model theory. In the case of the first example, the theory predicts that reasoners will construct the following sort of initial model:

```
[[Frenchman] gourmet]    wine-drinker
[[Frenchman] gourmet]
                         wine-drinker

           . . .
```

which yields the conclusion: Some of the Frenchmen are wine-drinkers. This conclusion is highly believable, and so the subjects satisfice—they fail to search for alternative models of the premises that might refute it. In the case of the second example, the theory predicts that reasoners will construct the same sort of initial model:

```
[[Frenchman] gourmet]    Italian
[[Frenchman] gourmet]
                         Italian

           . . .
```

which yields the conclusion: Some of the Frenchmen are Italians. This conclusion is highly unbelievable, so the subjects search for an alternative model. They may succeed in constructing the model:

```
[Frenchman]    gourmet
[Frenchman]    gourmet
               gourmet    Italian
               gourmet
                          Italian

           . . .
```

If so, they will respond that there is no valid conclusion. The initial conclusion is invalid in both cases, but plausible only in the first case. It is hard to see how a theory based on formal rules of inference could even generate the initial invalid conclusion, let alone account for the effects of believability.

WHY REASONING IS UNLIKELY TO BE A PURELY VERBAL PROCESS

Polk and Newell returned to the topic of syllogistic reasoning in one of Newell's final papers (see Polk & Newell, 1995). They proposed a revised theory, which they implemented in a computer program, VR (for verbal reasoning), and, using a remarkable program that Polk devised for fitting multiparameter theories to data, they showed that this theory provides an excellent account of individual differences in syllogistic reasoning. VR has parameters for dealing with individual differences in the initial interpretation of premises, the formulation of conclusions, and the search for alternative models. For example, one setting of the parameter governing the interpretation of "all" premises yields the coextensive interpretation, and another setting yields the proper inclusion interpretation. Although much is in common between VR and the model theory outlined in this chapter, there are two main points of divergence. First, VR postulates that reasoning is a purely verbal process in which a model is constructed from verbal premises, a conclusion is constructed, if possible, by describing the model, and, depending on the setting of a parameter, an attempt is made to construct an alternative model. In contrast, the model theory postulates that reasoning can be based on models that are constructed nonverbally on the basis of, say, perception or imagination. Second, in VR, a response of the form "there's no valid conclusion" arises solely from the failure to construct a model yielding a conclusion that meets the criteria for acceptable conclusions—that is, the conclusion must interrelate the two end terms. In contrast, the model theory postulates that "no valid conclusion" responses can arise either from the failure to construct a model or from the construction of alternative models that fail to support any common relation between the end terms. The latter possibility is critical if reasoners are to make this response for the right reasons. However, the best fit of VR to individual protocols is obtained without using the option to search for alternative models. Polk and Newell (1995) therefore suggested that the author may have overemphasized the importance of the search for counterexamples. The aim of this final section of the chapter is to defend the model theory: Deductive reasoning is not necessarily a purely verbal process, and logically untrained individuals can and do search for alternative models of premises.

There is nothing intrinsically verbal about Polk and Newell's theory: Perception could give rise to the sorts of model that they envisage, and the notion that individuals can reason about what they perceive goes back to Aristotle. A skeptic might argue that perception yields representations with a propositional format equivalent to those for verbal premises (see, e.g., Palmer, 1975, and Pylyshyn, 1973, for claims of this sort). Yet, as we shall see, a case can be made for a distinct form of perceptual model. This case arises from research in collaboration with Malcolm Bauer on the use of diagrams in deduction (see Bauer & Johnson-Laird, 1993).

The deductive task was a so-called *double disjunction*, for example,

Jane is in Atlanta or Raphael is in Tacoma, or both.

Jane is in Atlanta or Paul is in Philadelphia, or both.

What follows?

The premises yield the following five models:

```
[a]    [t]    [p]
[a]    [t]
[a]           [p]
[a]
       [t]    [p]
```

where "a" denotes Jane in Atlanta, "t" denotes Raphael in Tacoma, "p" denotes Paul in Philadelphia, and each line denotes an alternative model. Hence, the premises validly imply the conclusion:

Jane is in Atlanta, or Raphael is in Tacoma and Paul is in Philadelphia.

A previous study using verbal premises confirmed the model theory's predictions (Johnson-Laird et al., 1992): Exclusive disjunctions are easier than inclusive disjunctions, and "affirmative" problems where the individual common to both premises is in the same city are easier than "negative" problems where the individual common to both premise is in different cities, as in

Jane is in Atlanta or Raphael is in Tacoma, or both.

Jane is in Seattle or Paul is in Philadelphia, or both.

What follows?

The most obvious phenomenon, however, was that double disjunctions are difficult. Could they, perhaps, be made easier by diagrams?

In an initial experiment, Bauer and Johnson-Laird (1993) compared verbal problems with diagrammatic problems. One group of subjects read double disjunctive premises, and another group of subjects worked purely from diagrams. The diagrams represented people by lozenge shapes and cities by oval shapes—each labeled with the appropriate name. Hence, Jane is in Atlanta was represented by a lozenge labeled 'Jane' lying within an ellipse labeled 'Atlanta'. A premise consisted of two such shapes joined together by lines that met at a small box, and, as the subjects were told, an empty box represented inclusive disjunction, and a box containing a cross represented exclusive disjunction. The experiment replicated the greater ease of exclusive disjunctions over inclusive disjunctions, and the greater ease of affirmative problems over negative problems. But diagrams had no effect on performance: Overall, there were 28% correct conclusions to the diagrammatic problems and 32% correct conclusions to the verbal problems.

In retrospect, the weakness of the diagrams was that they failed to make explicit the alternative possibilities inherent in the disjunctions. Hence, in a subsequent experiment, we tried to correct this problem by using diagrams analogous to those for electrical circuits. Figure 10.1 shows a diagram presenting a problem about people and places. For a certain event to occur there has to be a completed path from one side of the diagram to the other, and a path can be completed by inserting shapes corresponding

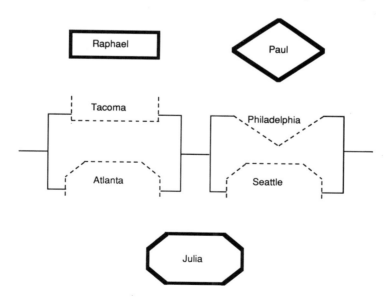

The event is occuring.
What follows?

FIG. 10.1. Diagram representing a double disjunctive problem (negative inclusive) about people and places.

to people into gaps corresponding to places. The diagram thus makes explicit that Jane can be in Atlanta or Seattle: A simple mental manipulation of the shape representing Jane allows it to fit into the gap representing Atlanta or the gap representing Seattle. The experiment tested four groups of subjects: One group had diagrammatic problems such as the one shown in Fig. 10.1, one group had similar diagrams of electrical circuits with switches wired in parallel, one group had verbal problems about people and places, and one group had verbal problems about electrical circuits.

There was a striking effect of diagrams: Overall, there were 78% correct conclusions drawn by the subjects in the diagrammatic groups as opposed to only 46% correct conclusions drawn by the subjects in the verbal groups. (There was no reliable difference between the switch domain and the people and places domain.) Similarly, the subjects in the diagrammatic groups drew their correct conclusions reliably faster (a mean latency of 99 sec) than the subjects in the verbal groups (a mean latency of 135 sec). These two measures also confirmed that exclusive disjunctions are easier than exclusive disjunctions, and that affirmative problems are easier than negative problems. The majority of the erroneous conclusions were, once again, consistent with the premises rather than inconsistent with them, thus bearing out the claim that the subjects had considered only some of the possible models of the premises.

Appropriate diagrams can help individuals to reason: They draw more correct conclusions, and they are faster to do so. This result casts doubt on the hypothesis that diagrams yield propositional representations equivalent to those for verbal problems: If they had done so, then it is hard to see why the diagrams would have improved reasoning over the verbal conditions. Reasoners attempt to construct mental models of the situations corresponding to premises, and evidently they find it easier to do so when the information in the premises is presented in diagrams that make the various alternatives explicit. The route from diagrams to the visualization of a set of mental models is more efficient than the route from verbal premises to a set of mental models. Reasoning need not be a purely verbal process.

Human beings are rational in principle, but err in practice (Johnson-Laird & Byrne, 1991). The process of deduction depends on the principle of semantic validity: An argument is good only if there are no counterexamples to it, that is, its conclusion must be true given that its premises are true. This principle is tacitly embodied in the system's search for alternative models of the premises. Logically naive individuals may be unable to articulate the principle, yet it is apparent in their ability to perform reliably better than chance with premises that do not yield valid conclusions interrelating end terms—as our studies of spatial and temporal deduction, one-quantifier deductions, syllogisms, and multiply-quantified deductions all have shown. Subjects generally perform well with such problems, so one can conclude that for the most part they are making the right response for the right reasons: They have discovered that the premises support alternative models that refute putative conclusions. Likewise, in these domains, subjects are able to draw valid conclusions to multiple-model problems that support them. They are slowed down and they are not as accurate as with one-model problems, yet their performance is better than chance. This pattern of results also bears out the claim that correct performance depends on the search for alternative models. As the diagram experiments show, the search takes longer and is less likely to be successful as the number of possible models increases. In short, the success of Polk and Newell's (1995) program in accounting for individual differences without such a search must be taken in the context of the rest of their theory, which is restricted to syllogistic reasoning—it tells us nothing in absolute terms about such searches. Thus, if VR contained different parameters with different values, it is entirely possible that a search for counterexamples would improve its fit to the data. An urgent task is to examine a parameterized version of the present theory based on models to determine how well it accounts for individual protocols.

CONCLUSION

Allen Newell's major achievement in the study of deduction was his development of a model-theoretic approach to the domain. A mental model, as he maintained, was a state in a problem space. He argued that it was not necessarily a visual image—indeed, its structure and format were not necessarily available to introspection. He accordingly had no qualms about introducing hybrid models that contained "propositional annotations" (see Newell, 1990, Section 7.2.2), such as an annotation representing negation. Once again, his intuitions have been corroborated by experimental data—it is difficult to explain the contrast between "all" and "only" without postulating that "only" calls for an annotation representing negation. Newell's last thoughts about deduction derive from his commitment to Soar. One future task for which this architecture seems most fitting is to explain how naive performance based on models can ultimately lead to the discovery of formal rules of inference, that is, to explain how reflection on relations in meaning between premises and conclusions can be transmuted into formal logic on the one hand, and into psychological theories of reasoning on the other hand.

REFERENCES

Bara, B., Bucciarelli, M., & Johnson-Laird, P. N. (1995). The development of syllogistic reasoning. *American Journal of Psychology, 108*, 157–193.

Barwise, J. (1993). Everyday reasoning and logical inference. *Behavioral and Brain Sciences, 16*, 337–338. [Commentary on Johnson-Laird and Byrne, 1991.]

Bauer, M. I., & Johnson-Laird, P. N. (1992). How diagrams can improve reasoning. *Psychological Science, 4,* 372–378.

Begg, I., & Denny, J. (1969). Empirical reconciliation of atmosphere and conversion interpretations of syllogistic reasoning. *Journal of Experimental Psychology, 81,* 351–354.

Braine, M. D. S. (1978). On the relation between the natural logic of reasoning and standard logic. *Psychological Review, 85,* 1–21.

Erickson, J. R. (1974). A set analysis theory of behaviour in formal syllogistic reasoning tasks. *Loyola Symposium on Cognition* (pp. 305–329). Hillsdale, NJ: Lawrence Erlbaum Associates.

Hunter, I. M. L. (1957). The solving of three term series problems. *British Journal of Psychology, 48,* 286–298.

Johnson-Laird, P. N. (1975). Models of deduction. In R. J. Falmagne (Ed.), *Reasoning: Representation and process in children and adults.* Hillsdale, NJ: Lawrence Erlbaum Associates.

Johnson-Laird, P. N. (1983). *Mental models: Towards a cognitive science of language, inference and consciousness.* Cambridge: Cambridge University Press.

Johnson-Laird, P. N., & Bara, B. (1984). Syllogistic inference. *Cognition, 16,* 1–61.

Johnson-Laird, P. N., & Byrne, R. M. J. (1989). Only reasoning. *Journal of Memory and Language, 28,* 313–330.

Johnson-Laird, P. N., & Byrne, R. M. J. (1991). *Deduction.* Hillsdale, NJ: Lawrence Erlbaum Associates.

Johnson-Laird, P. N., Byrne, R. M. J., & Schaeken, W. (1992). Propositional reasoning by model. *Psychological Review, 99,* 418–439.

Johnson-Laird, P. N., & Savary, F. (1995). How to make the impossible seem probable. In J. D. Moore & J. F. Lehman (Eds.), *Proceedings of the Seventeenth Annual Conference of the Cognitive Science Society* (pp. 381–384). Mahwah, NJ: Lawrence Erlbaum Associates.

Johnson-Laird, P. N., & Steedman, M. (1978). The psychology of syllogisms. *Cognitive Psychology, 10,* 64–99.

Kneale, W., & Kneale, M. (1962). *The development of logic.* Oxford: Clarendon Press.

Macnamara, J. (1986). *A border dispute: The place of logic in psychology.* Cambridge, MA: Bradford Books, MIT Press.

Madruga, J. A. G. (1984). Procesos de error en el razonamiento silogistico: doble procesamiento y estrategia de verificacion por. In M. Carretero & J. A. G. Madruga (Eds.), *Lecturas de psicologia del pensamiento.* Madrid: Alianza.

Newell, A. (1980). Reasoning, problem solving and decision processes: the problem space as a fundamental category. In R. Nickerson (Ed.), *Attention and performance* (Vol. VIII). Hillsdale, NJ: Lawrence Erlbaum Associates.

Newell, A. (1990). *Unified theories of cognition.* Cambridge, MA: Harvard University Press.

Newell, A., Shaw, J. C., & Simon, H. A. (1963). Empirical explorations with the Logic Theory Machine. In E. Feigenbaum & J. Feldman (Eds.), *Computers and thought.* New York: McGraw-Hill.

Newell, A., & Simon, H. A. (1972). *Human Problem Solving.* Englewood Cliffs, NJ: Prentice-Hall.

Oakhill, J. V., Johnson-Laird, P. N., & Garnham, A. (1989). Believability and syllogistic reasoning. *Cognition, 31,* 117–140.

Osherson, D. (1974–1976). *Logical abilities in children,* Vols. 1–4. Hillsdale, NJ: Lawrence Erlbaum Associates.

Osherson, D. (1975). Logic and models of logical thinking. In R. J. Falmagne (Ed.), *Reasoning: Representation and process in children and adults.* Hillsdale, NJ: Lawrence Erlbaum Associates.

Palmer, S. E. (1975). Visual perception and world knowledge: notes on a model of sensory-cognitive interaction. In D. A. Norman, D. E. Rumelhart, & the LNR Research Group (Eds.), *Explorations in cognition.* San Francisco: Freeman.

Polk, T. A., & Newell, A. (1988). Modeling human syllogistic reasoning in Soar. *Tenth Annual Conference of the Cognitive Science Society* (pp. 181–187). Hillsdale, NJ: Lawrence Erlbaum Associates.

Polk, T. A., & Newell, A. (1995). A verbal reasoning theory for categorical syllogisms. *Psychological Review, 102*, 533–566.

Pylyshyn, Z. (1973). What the mind's eye tells the mind's brain: A critique of mental imagery. *Psychological Bulletin, 80*, 1–24.

Revlis, R. (1975). Two models of syllogistic reasoning: Feature selection and conversion. *Journal of Verbal Learning and Verbal Behavior, 14*, 180–195.

Rips, L. J. (1983). Cognitive processes in propositional reasoning. *Psychological Review, 90*, 38–71.

Rips, L. J. (1994). *The Psychology of Proof.* Cambridge, MA: MIT Press.

Simon, H. A. (1959). Theories of decision making in economics and behavioral science. *American Economic Review, 49*, 253–283.

Smith, E. E., Langston, C., & Nisbett, R. E. (1992). The case for rules in reasoning. *Cognitive Science, 16*, 1–40.

Stenning, K., & Oberlander, J. (1992). *A cognitive theory of graphical and linguistic reasoning: Logic and implementation* (Tech. Rep. Res. Paper 20). University of Edinburgh, Human Communication Research Centre.

Wason, P. C., & Johnson-Laird, P. N. (1972). *Psychology of reasoning: Structure and content.* Cambridge, MA: Harvard University Press.

Wetherick, N., & Gilhooly, K. (1990). The figural effect in syllogistic reasoning. In K. Gilhooly, M. T. G. Keane, R. Logie, & G. Erdos (Eds.), *Lines of thought: Reflections on the psychology of thinking* (Vol. 1). London: Wiley.

Woodworth, R. S., & Sells, S. B. (1935). An atmosphere effect in formal syllogistic reasoning. *Journal of Experimental Psychology. 18*, 451–460.

DISCUSSION

Reasoning Matters:
Mental Models and Soar

Thad Polk
University of Pennsylvania

The traditional view of deductive reasoning holds that people reason syntactically, by applying formal rules of inference. Mental model theory (Johnson-Laird, 1983; Johnson-Laird & Byrne, 1991) provides a semantic alternative—subjects reason by constructing a mental model of what the premises are about (*comprehension*), generating conclusions based on that model (*description*), and searching for alternative models that falsify their putative conclusions (*validation*). In addition to its intuitive appeal, model theory has accumulated a significant amount of empirical evidence in its favor. Indeed, Johnson-Laird and Byrne (1991) recently showed that model theory can be used to make accurate predictions about human performance on the entire range of standard tasks that have been used to study deductive reasoning in humans.

One of the first questions Allen Newell always asked when he encountered a successful theory was how (or whether) that theory could be naturally incorporated into Soar. In the case of model theory, he thought the answer was obvious—the states in Soar's problem spaces should be mental models. As my first project in graduate school, he gave me the task of demonstrating the feasibility of that idea by implementing Johnson-Laird's theory in Soar and reproducing his results. With a few minor exceptions, that project turned out to be very straightforward. By using mental models as our state representation and *comprehend*, *describe*, and *validate* as our problem space operators, we were able to replicate within Soar the accurate predictions derived from model theory.

Although our original goal was just to show that model theory could be naturally incorporated into Soar, this exercise actually led to a novel insight into the nature of reasoning itself. It did so by forcing us to address a *genesis question*—How could the knowledge represented in the Soar system arise? In Soar, this question usually takes the more specific form, "How could the productions arise by chunking?" It was in trying to answer this question that we came to view reasoning from a different perspective.

Consider asking how the three main processes in model theory—comprehension, description, and validation—could arise. Because comprehension and description are standard linguistic processes, they presumably arise via language acquisition. Of course, the details of this acquisition are a topic of considerable research and debate, but the fact that such an acquisition process exists is not controversial. What about validation, the process of constructing an alternative model of a set of premises in order to falsify a putative conclusion? The main application of such a process is presumably deductive reasoning (which requires that conclusions necessarily follow), so it is unlikely that it would arise through language acquisition. It seems more likely that validation is a cognitive strategy that is acquired through extensive practice or explicit training on deductive tasks. According to this view, validation is an underdeveloped process in untrained subjects and is less central to deduction than are comprehension and description.

Perhaps this suggestion seems like a minor variant of the basic model theory. After all, I am still assuming the use of mental models as well as two of the three basic processes assumed in model theory. But emphasizing linguistic processes rather than validation suggests a very different way of characterizing deductive reasoning than has previously been proposed. According to previous accounts, people make deductions by applying some built-in reasoning-specific process (the application of formal rules or the search for alternative models). The linguistic processes of encoding the problem and decoding the result are simply transduction operations. I would propose instead that linguistic processes are at the very heart of making the deductions themselves, at least for untrained subjects. I refer to such behavior as *verbal reasoning*.

In order to investigate this hypothesis, Allen and I built a computational model of syllogistic reasoning called VR (for verbal reasoner). VR's basic control structure is shown in Fig. 1. The details of VR are beyond the scope of this paper (see Polk, 1992, or Polk & Newell, 1995), but it should be clear from the figure that linguistic processes (especially reencoding), rather than reasoning-specific processes, are at the heart of its behavior.

VR accurately predicts all the standard regularities of syllogistic reasoning as well as the behavior of individual subjects. Figure 2 demonstrates both. The left of the figure shows human data (collected by Inder, 1987, Johnson-Laird & Bara, 1984, and Johnson-Laird & Steedman, 1978) as well

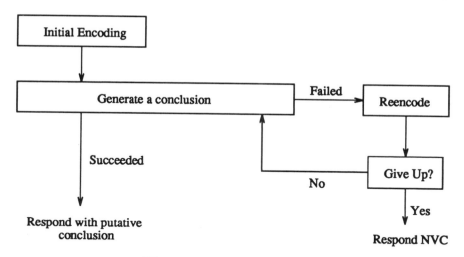

FIG. 1.   The control structure of VR.

as VR's predictions and what would be expected by chance alone. Both
VR and the human subjects exhibit a difficulty effect (they only solve
between 50% and 60% of the tasks correctly) and validity effect (their
performance is much better than chance) as well as producing significantly
more responses in keeping with the so-called atmosphere, conversion, and
figural effects than would be expected at random. VR also predicts a belief
bias and elaboration effect, but these are not shown in the figure (see
Polk, 1992, and Polk & Newell, 1995). In addition to accounting for aggregate data, VR predicts the behavior of individual subjects with great
accuracy (Fig. 2, right). Not surprisingly, its predictions are more accurate

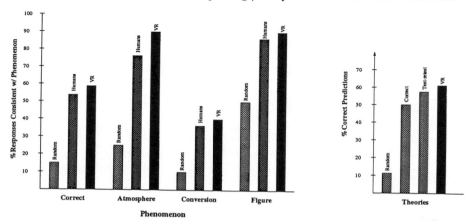

FIG. 2.   VR's predictions of regularities and individual data.

than a theory that always chooses the correct response or a random theory. But what is much more impressive is that its predictions actually rival the test–retest reliability of the subjects themselves. VR is the first theory to make such accurate, detailed predictions about syllogistic reasoning.

A natural question is whether adding a validation process would improve the predictions. If validation really is at the heart of deduction, then one might expect the fits to improve significantly if VR were augmented with such a strategy. Figure 3 presents such an analysis. Using subjects from six experiments (again from Johnson-Laird and colleagues as well as Inder) we compared VR's predictions (a) without validation, against three different validation strategies: (b) if an alternative model is found that falsifies the putative conclusion, respond "no valid conclusion," (c) if such a model is found, then produce a response based on that model, and (d) repeatedly validate until no alternative model can be found. The top rows show the fits without validation (a), while the bottom rows show the fits using whichever validation strategy best fit the subject (b, c, d). Better fits are indicated with boxes, and fits that differ by more than 5% are indicated by heavy boxes. In only 15 out of 103 cases was the fit affected by more than 5%, and in 14 of those 15 cases it was the fit *without* validation that was better. So in only one case out of 103 subjects was the fit with validation more than 5% better than the fit without. This analysis suggests that validation is an extraneous assumption for VR.

It is worth making explicit a few points about verbal reasoning that sometimes cause confusion. First, the claim is not that all reasoning is verbal.

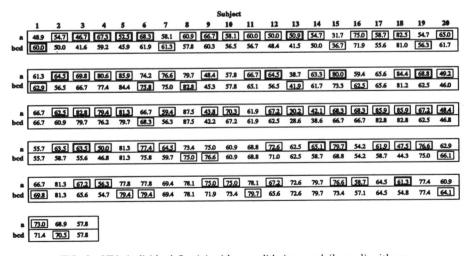

FIG. 3. VR's individual fits (a) without validation, and (b, c, d) with any of three validation strategies. Better fits are indicated by boxes. Heavy boxes indicate fits that differ by more than 5%.

The subjects must have no logical training (so they will not have acquired strategies such as validation), the problem must be verbal (e.g., diagrams can presumably be processed by nonlinguistic mechanisms), and the knowledge used to solve the problem must be inherent in the problem itself (so other knowledge does not come into play). Most deductive reasoning experiments have satisfied these constraints, but the task need not be deductive. Second, it is the *processes* in verbal reasoning that are verbal, not the representation (which is a mental model). Hence, it is misleading to categorize verbal reasoning with theories that propose that the representation itself is linguistic (e.g., Clark, 1969). Finally, although verbal reasoning claims that linguistic, rather than reasoning-specific, processes are central to deduction in untrained subjects, this does not imply that humans are inherently irrational or lack the competence to make valid inferences. VR does have the ability to recognize counterexamples (through its encoding processes); it just fails to appreciate the need to generate counterexamples or it lacks the skills to do so (although this skill could probably be acquired with practice by exploiting the ability to construct models and recognize counterexamples). According to VR then, untrained subjects have the competence to make valid inferences (based on their ability to construct models and appreciate counterexamples), but they fail to do so in practice because they do not systematically generate counterexamples.

Mental model theory represented a major advance in our understanding of human deduction and so it was important to demonstrate that it could be naturally incorporated into Soar. It came as a pleasant surprise when this exercise led to the novel idea of verbal reasoning—a view that now has substantial empirical support. This result is a good example of how a unified theory of cognition like Soar can facilitate progress in cognitive science, sometimes in very unexpected ways. As Allen so aptly put it, "there are more things in an architecture, Horatio, than are dreamt of in your theorizing" (Newell, 1990, p. 306).

REFERENCES

Clark, H. H. (1969). Linguistic processes in deductive reasoning. *Psychological Review, 76*(4), 387–404.

Inder, R. (1987). *The computer simulation of syllogism solving using restricted mental models.* Unpublished doctoral dissertation, University of Edinburgh.

Johnson-Laird, P. N. (1983). *Mental models: Towards a cognitive science of language, inference, and consciousness.* Cambridge, MA: Cambridge University Press.

Johnson-Laird, P. N., & Bara, B. G. (1984). Syllogistic inference. *Cognition, 16,* 1–61.

Johnson-Laird, P. N., & Byrne, R. M. J. (1991). *Deduction.* Hillsdale, NJ: Lawrence Erlbaum Associates.

Johnson-Laird, P. N., & Steedman, M. (1978). The psychology of syllogisms. *Cognitive Psychology, 10,* 64–99.

Newell, A. (1990). *Unified theories of cognition*. Cambridge, MA: Harvard University Press.

Polk, T. A. (1992). *Verbal reasoning* (Tech. Rep. No. CMU-CS-92-178). Pittsburgh: Carnegie Mellon University.

Polk, T. A., & Newell, A. (1995). Deduction as verbal reasoning. *Psychological Review, 102*(3), 533–566.

Chapter 11

The Patterned Matter
That Is Mind

Herbert A. Simon
Carnegie Mellon University

The implicit function of the final chapter of a volume like this one is to sum up what has gone before, but I am not going to try to perform that function. The symposium was organized to honor Allen Newell, who, to the deep sorrow of all of us, did not live to attend it. In reporting a substantial number of examples of good science, we have already, in the symposium and ensuing volume, honored him in the way that would have meant the most to him. I too wish to honor Al by discussing science.

Some of the preceding chapters reported particular pieces of research and their implications. Others discussed basic issues relating to mind and those theories of mind that take the form of computer simulations. Although Al Newell believed that most scientific talk should report specific research—that science is in the details—he himself occasionally yielded to the temptations of philosophy and methodology, and gave a number of memorable talks about foundations, the most notable being his William James Lectures (Newell, 1990).

I take shelter behind his example to discuss an issue that is fundamental to the entire information-processing paradigm within which we all work. In particular, I wish to review the status of the physical symbol system hypothesis, which underlies both Soar and the other architectures (including connectionist architectures) that have aimed at building precise and testable theories of cognition.

The nature of symbols became an important topic in the first conversations that Al and I had, 40 years ago, when we were seeking to understand the information-processing behavior of members of the crew of an Air Force early warning station. The nature of symbols became crucial when, with Cliff Shaw, we searched for the means to build our first AI system, the Logic Theorist, and found those means in list-processing languages (Newell, Shaw, & Simon, 1957). The topic took on new importance when we began to perceive that list processing was not merely a programming convenience but an integral part of the psychological theories we were constructing. We formulated our views on symbols most explicitly in the physical symbol system hypothesis that was set forth in our Turing Award lecture (Newell & Simon, 1976).

But a question as fundamental as this one does not long remain dormant, and Allen Newell subsequently addressed it several more times: in his paper on physical symbol systems (Newell, 1980) and most recently in *Unified Theories of Cognition* (Newell, 1990). Both of us had occasion to think further about it again during the last months of Allen's life, when Alonso Vera and I (Vera & Simon, 1993) were preparing an analysis of the relation of the physical symbol system hypothesis to the new viewpoints of situated action, but those conversations were never completed.

This chapter represents an additional step, inspired in no small measure by what Allen had to say about symbols in *Unified Theories*. Because we never had the opportunity to discuss this extension, I cannot certify that he would agree with it, but it is wholly consistent with what went before.

WHAT IS A SYMBOL?

Dictionary definitions of *symbol* do not reflect accurately the way in which the term has been used throughout the history of information processing psychology. As it is the latter usage I wish to discuss, I do not take time to review the alternative meanings that can be found in the dictionary.

Patterns Defined

I start with the term *pattern*. By pattern, I mean an arrangement of some elements selected out of a population of possible arrangements. Thus, a particular arrangement of holes in an old-fashioned IBM card is a pattern. So is the arrangement of ice particles in a snowflake. So is the arrangement of color and lines in wallpaper. These examples may suggest both the ubiquity of patterns and the diversity of their kinds. The components of patterns may be discrete, but need not be. A continuous sine wave is a pattern.

It should be evident (e.g., from the wallpaper and sine wave examples) that there is nothing peculiarly linguistic about patterns, although all languages use patterns to represent such entities as letters, phonemes, words, sentences, and so on. A pattern in the form of an iris or a fish, or the pattern consisting of the forms, shapes, and arrangement of head, antennae, legs, thorax, and wing covers that enables one to recognize a beetle as *Calosoma scrutator* need have nothing to do with language, as the latter term is commonly understood, even though ideographic languages may incorporate patterns like these in their structures. Patterns of the kinds called *schemas* and those called *diagrams*, both of which we have occasion to consider here, are obviously nonlinguistic in character.

The nonequivalence of systems of patterns with language is a point I emphasize more than once, for some critics of the physical symbol system hypothesis have supposed, erroneously, that the symbols (hence patterns) to which that hypothesis refers are linguistic, or have some special relation to systems called languages and to the particular forms of reasoning with languages called *logics*. I argue that, on the contrary, languages, including natural languages, formal (logical) languages, and computer languages, form only a special class of symbol systems.

Patterns may have other patterns as components, down to some level of primitive patterns, or elements. What constitutes a primitive will vary from system to system. For example, a pattern in the form of a square may consist of four lines, oriented and connected in an appropriate way. Alternatively, it may consist of an array of pixels in a raster. In the first representation, the lines and their relations are the primitives, and in the second, the pixels. Physicists once took protons and electrons as the primitives of the patterns of matter. Now they are inclined to view quarks, or even strings, as the appropriate primitives. Notice that the composition of patterns at one level into those at the next level above involves not only the lower level patterns but some set of relations among them.

With pairs of patterns we associate a test of *equivalence*. Two patterns drawn from the population are the same if they pass the test, and are different otherwise. Different tests of equivalence may be defined for the same population of patterns. For example, in the population of letters in the Roman alphabet, r and R may be the same by one test, but different by a stricter test.

The patterns we are interested in are physical—that is, they are made of something, or, as in the case of the IBM cards, consist of the absence of something. The pattern is a figure against a ground, or the ground can become a pattern, viewed against the figure.

Given two populations of patterns, we may be able to define an *isomorphism* (or a homeomorphism) from one to the other. In going from a pattern in population A to its isomorph in population B, we say that we are coding, or recoding, or *encoding* the pattern from A to B. I use these three terms interchangeably.

Symbols Defined

We are now ready to define symbols. *Symbols* are patterns that denote something. In English, the pattern "star" denotes a celestial object of a certain kind. Thus, denotation is a mapping of patterns onto their meanings. The things denoted by symbols may be concrete or abstract objects or relations among objects in the world outside. They may also be other symbols or symbol structures, that is, patterns (stored, perhaps, in a human head or a computer memory).

If m is a pattern in population M, and n its isomorph in N under some encoding, and if n denotes an entity, or thing, E, then m also denotes E. Thus, denoting is transitive, so that it may be propagated through a sequence of encodings. If the encoding is an isomorphism, no information is lost in the transformation, If it is a many–one transformation, information will in general be lost. In real systems the isomorphisms and homeomorphisms may be only approximate—noisy. In this case also, information will be lost in the transformation. Human translators, especially those who have occasion to translate poetry, have long been aware that natural languages are only approximately isomorphic. The same is true of other systems of patterns: Two such systems are seldom exact isomorphs.

DENOTATION AND RECOGNITION

To determine whether a particular entity, E, is denoted by the pattern P, we associate with a class to which E belongs a test, T, that can be applied to patterns. If and only if the test can be applied to P and P passes the test, E belongs to the class of entities denoted by P.

The test need not be applied to P directly, but to an isomorph or homeomorph of P, P', obtained from P by a sequence of one or more recodings. For example, when a pattern of light is recorded on the retina, a succession of perceptual processes will extract a variety of features from it. This set of features (we can think of it as a bit vector) is—according to many theories of perception—the pattern, P', to which the test is applied. If the entity, E, that produced the retinal pattern was a cat, and if the test, Tc, is one that recognizes the features that will be coded from such retinal patterns, then P' will be adjudged by Tc to denote a cat.

As this example shows, the test of whether a particular pattern denotes a particular kind of entity may be composite, consisting of a number, large or small, of component tests. It may also admit a partial and/or a redundant match. That is, the composite test, T, may not require that all of the constituent features be present, or if present, that all pass their tests. Hence, a test may contain many more potential components than would be essential to identify E uniquely. Finally, there may be alternative tests for the same symbol, so that if an item is viewed from different angles or under different conditions it may be assigned the same denotation. If there are many ways to skin a cat, there are also many ways of recognizing one.

The act of applying tests to determine what symbol denotes E is called *recognition*. The result of recognizing E is to gain access to this symbol. In human perception, the recognition process places the symbol in short-term memory, where other processes can now act on it. Notice that the same entity may be denoted by many different symbols. E may be recognized as a cat, as a mammal, as a marmalade cat, as a brown creature, or mis-recognized as a fox. What tests are applied in the recognition process may depend on context, and the outcome of the tests may depend on what features were extracted from the particular pattern that formed on the retina.

As George Miller remarked in Chapter 4, when a pattern satisfies several different tests, hence denotes several different patterns, we call it *polysemic*—it has several meanings. When context fails to choose among these meanings, we call it *ambiguous*.

Recognition involves the recoding of the pattern initially sensed to extract from it more or less *invariant features* that are then tested to discriminate it from other classes of patterns. The letter C, for example, might be recognized by extracting from it the invariant features that it contains a curved line but no straight line or closed curve. Sorting these features down a discrimination net can distinguish it from other letters, thereby recognizing it.

A more complex example might be the recognition by a driver that the car is approaching a curve having a certain radius of curvature. If this particular visual feature can be extracted by recoding from the retinal image or a succession of images, then we see how the symbol *curve(r)* can serve as a condition in a production whose action is to cause the driver to turn the wheel by an amount appropriate to the radius: curve(r) → turn(f(r)). An encoding of an environmental invariant of this kind is sometimes called an *affordance*. In fact, precisely this kind of capability is incorporated in the visual recognition system of the driverless vehicle, NAVLAB.

How easy or hard it is for a symbol system to recognize patterns by extracting invariants from them depends on what kinds of regularities exist in the outside world, and what capabilities the system has for feature extraction. (For an early exposition of this approach to perception, see Gibson, 1950.) We can assume that evolution has brought about some degree of compatibility between the regularities in the sensed world and the kinds of invariant features that living systems can extract. Invariants associated with the kinematics and dynamics of rigid objects are especially good candidates for such evolutionary matching.

Symbols as Pointers: P-Symbols

One use of symbols—the use that Allen Newell emphasized in *Unified Theories of Cognition* (1990, pp. 72–80)—is to serve as pointers to information without themselves containing the information to which they point. Thus, the symbol "chair" in the index to an encyclopedia or in the heading of an article points to information about chairs. By using the page reference associated with the index entry, we gain access to that information. The word *chair* itself tells us nothing about chairs, what they look like, what they are made of, or how they are used, whereas the encyclopedia article may tell us all of those things and more.

We may regard the symbol "chair" in this situation as an encoding of the entity, but an encoding that does not preserve information. Yet the symbol, associated with the address, serves as a pointer that allows us to recover the information.

Newell made the very important point that in processing information with some end in view, the potentially relevant information may be enormous in quantity, so that we can attend to it only piece by piece, a small part at a time. Then pointers, by giving us *access* to the information in very condensed form (at the expense of not providing it directly), allow us to retain contact with very large contexts and to bring in any particular component of a context whenever it becomes relevant to our processing.

This function of symbols would be unimportant if we had an infinite parallel computer (called Jehova?) that could assemble and operate simultaneously upon whole contexts of arbitrary size. Because real-world computers can embrace, at a given moment, only very modest quantities of information, the ability to handle pointers to information as well as the information itself is crucial to their effectiveness. We broaden context by stretching computation over longer intervals of time, moving from one subcontext to the next, and we retain coherence by using pointers, which I call *P-symbols*, as surrogates for the information pointed to.

A dictionary provides a very trivial illustration of this fundamental point. When we look up a word in the dictionary to find its meaning, we may discover that we do not know the meanings of all of the words in the definition. We can then use these words as pointers (P-symbols) to access their definitions, which give those meanings.

A different kind of example is a description of an object in terms of its parts, each part, in turn, being described by *its* parts, and so on. Thus, an automobile consists of chassis, body, engine, wheels, and so on. But the engine consists of an engine block, cylinders, and so on. Cylinders consist of. . . . Each term in such a hierarchic scheme serves a double purpose: It provides information about the thing of which it is a part, and it is a pointer to information about its parts.

We must now examine in more detail this dual character of symbols (or symbol structures): their capacity to contain information, and their role as "mere" pointers.

Symbols as Encodings of Information: I-Symbols

Fundamental to any use of symbols is that they are patterns, hence belong to populations, or sets, whose members can be distinguished one from another. In information-theoretic terms, this means that symbols contain information, its quantity in bits equal to the logarithm of the number of sets that can be discriminated. Because symbols can be informative, they can be used in two fundamentally different ways: (a) as we have already seen, they may be used as pointers, to access information; (b) they may themselves be designed to "contain" the information. Letters of a conventional alphabet, like the Roman, are employed in the former way. Genuinely ideographic symbols (as Chinese characters are supposed to be, but mostly aren't) are employed in the latter way. To distinguish them from P-symbols, I refer to information-containing symbols as *I-symbols*.

Of course an I-symbol can also function (but inefficiently) as a P-symbol. In using symbols as pointers, they must be encoded efficiently, so that large contexts (or pointers to them) can be squeezed into small spaces, with a consequent loss of information. Apart from its use in preventing and detecting errors, redundancy is unnecessary and unwanted in P-symbols.

By contrast, in using symbols as carriers of information, their size and complexity must be commensurate with the information they contain. Thus, the word *cat*, a P-symbol, is written as a sequence of three letters, each of about five bits, or a total of fifteen bits. On the other hand the picture of a cat in a book on mammals, an I-symbol, may contain hundreds or thousands of bits of information.

Now consider the act of recognition, when the object recognized is a cat. The result of that act is to encode a complex retinal image (an I-symbol denoting the visible cat) into a pointer in short-term memory, which, though containing only a small number of bits of information, is free from ambiguity. (If, for example, we think a human being might learn to discriminate among a billion things, probably an overestimate, each P-symbol would need to contain about 30 bits of information, and hence could be encoded as a sequence of about six Roman letters.)

But this concise pointer, in turn, gives us access to all the things we know about cats (have stored in memory about them). That knowledge may enable us not only to reproduce (at least approximately) all of the information in the retinal image that triggered the recognition, but a great deal more: what we know about the varieties of cats, what cats eat, how they behave, and so on. This knowledge is also stored in a pattern: an I-symbol structure or schema of some sort, but a very baroque one, not at all concise. This pattern may be highly diffuse and widely distributed throughout memory, many of its components being themselves pointers to other patterns.

Described in this way, the recognition process has a certain air of paradox about it. We encode retinal images into small (30-bit?) P-symbols in order to gain access to memory stores, which are I-symbols, containing information that may be orders of magnitude greater than the initiating images. How can the small pointer contain enough information to discriminate between different memory stores: between cats and dogs, say?

The paradox vanishes when we consider that the actual things one finds in the world (so-called "natural kinds") are far fewer than the potential things (Simon, 1991). Our pointers (P-symbols) need only be numerous enough to name all the things we wish to consider. The symbol structures in memory that describe these things (I-symbols) must be sufficiently large to distinguish them from other *potential* things. Let me try to clarify this statement, which might otherwise appear to be slightly mysterious, or even mystical.

Consider any thing we might want to talk about: cat, dog, black raven, white shoe, or whatnot. We envision encoding anything we might learn about it in a bit vector, an I-symbol, each bit denoting the presence or absence of some feature. The overwhelming majority of possible bit vectors would describe nonexisting objects, objects that are not found, as unicorns are, even in mythology, We would only have in memory bit vectors for objects that actually existed, or that, although hypothetical or even mythical, had some kind of intellectual interest. To point to them, we would need only as many P-symbols as there were such objects, not nearly as many as there are possible bit vectors. Hence the numbers of bits in the *names* of the I-symbols (i.e., in the P-symbols) would be very small compared with the numbers of bits in the I-symbols themselves.

This rarity of I-symbols that need to be stored can be interpreted as reflecting the great redundancy of the world. If we begin with a set of primitive predicates and their arguments, then most compounds built randomly out of these predicates describe nothing of interest in or about the world. Hence, we can encode the predicates that are of interest into a much smaller number of efficiently coded (nonredundant) names, P-symbols. But each of the structures (I-symbols) pointed to by one of the P-symbols might be arbitrarily large, its size depending on the amount of knowledge we have about the thing in question—usually far more than the amount needed to identify or recognize it.

We need not limit ourselves to maximally efficient P-symbols and informationally comprehensive I-symbols. We can also use intermediate representations that are compact enough to be useful as pointers, yet contain some information about the things pointed to. Noun phrases are examples of such composite structures. "Black cat" may be used as a pointer to information about cats of that kind, but it also provides a little information about the thing pointed to: namely, that it is a subcategory of cat, and, in particular, the subcategory of cats that are black in color.

PHYSICAL SYMBOL SYSTEMS

Having said what symbols and symbol structures are, and their two principal functions in symbol systems, it is time to turn to physical symbol systems themselves. Here we are on familiar ground.

A *physical* symbol system is a system, realized in some physical structure, that is capable of storing patterns—hence symbols—and performing certain operations on them. These operations, as usually enumerated, include inputing patterns, outputing them, compounding them into relational structures, retaining and erasing them, and comparing them for equivalence (and branching on the basis of the outcome of the comparison). Because the operations work on patterns of any kind, we might speak of "physical pattern systems," but as the phrase "physical symbol systems" is well entrenched, we may as well retain it.

Among the important operations for our purposes are tests that determine whether one symbol (pattern structure) denotes another, and processes that recode symbol structures from one representation to another. We have already mentioned the particular class of tests that recognize patterns in the sense organs and thereby retrieve the P-symbols that denote the external stimuli responsible for producing the sensory patterns: for example, the tests that recognize C's and cats and curves when they are visible.

Two classes of physical symbol systems of special interest in our world today are electronic computers and human nervous systems. To understand the operation of each and the relation between them, it is helpful to define a simple taxonomy of the symbol structures one finds in them. I begin with computers. (This taxonomy is based on one worked out with Alonso Vera in our analyses of situated action in Vera and Simon, 1993.)

A Taxonomy of Symbols: Computers

The computer programs that we find written on pieces of paper are themselves examples of symbol structures. We call these *structures of category 1*. They are linguistic in character, although the languages they are written in are artificial. Humans can read them, extract their meanings, and even interpret them as theories (of the behavior of a computer or a person).

Computers themselves output (write) and input (read) strings of patterns, which are usually intended (by the user and perhaps by the computer) to denote something, hence which are symbol structures. We call these inputs and outputs *symbol structures of category 2C.* (Some structures of category 2C may also belong to category 1, for computers may print out their own programs. Regarded as outputs, they belong to category 2C; interpreted as programs [theories] they belong to category 1.)

Within computers we find patterns of electromagnetism—varying greatly in nature with the computer hardware. From a physical standpoint, the machines of almost each decade since the invention of the computer use totally different physical means to represent and process patterns, yet their capabilities for symbol processing (apart from speed and memory size) are almost identical. The most obvious evidence for this equivalence is that virtually every computer, at least among those built since the mid-1950s, can execute the same programs written in Fortran or Lisp, producing the same outputs. This equivalence is achieved by an automatic encoding, by compiler or interpreter, of the symbols of the higher level language into symbols of the machine language.

The patterns in the computer that represent programs are symbol structures whose denotations are the symbol-processing actions they cause the computer to perform. The pattern interpretable as "add" causes numbers to be added. We should think of it as "Add!" If we think of programs as linguistic structures, that is, as sequences of sentences, we should view them as written in the imperative, not the declarative, mode. We will call stored programs *symbol structures of category 3Ca.*

The remaining patterns in the computer, except those in its input and output organs, are referred to as data structures. They may be language-like in structure and organization, or they may not. We will call them *symbol structures of category 3Cb.*

The patterns in the input and output organs we put in a separate category, which we call *category 3Cc.* On the input side, these are the patterns (symbols) that record information received by the sensors, hence denote "directly" the sensed external objects. On the output side, these are the patterns (symbols) that cause motor actions, hence denote those external actions. I assign them to a separate category, not because they are different from other symbol structures (they aren't) but because, in mapping between the internal and external worlds, they provide the system with a real-world semantics.

I might mention in passing that if Searle had provided his notorious Chinese room with sensory and motor organs, it, too, could have had a semantics and learned to understand Chinese—instead of translating it mechanically, without understanding. Searle's Chinese room proved nothing about the ability of machines to understand; it was simply the wrong room. Hermetically sealed from the world, it could not learn the denotations of words in *any* language.

All meanings, that is, denotations, of the symbols inside the computer derive directly or indirectly from the patterns created by external objects on the sensors and the effects upon external objects of the motor organs, in interaction, of course, with the operations of the structures of category 3Ca.

Notice that the boundary between category 2C and category 3Cc symbols is at the "skin" of the computer. Category 2C symbols, both input and output, are external to the computer: they are the external signals that impinge on it(input), or that, having been emitted by it (output), impinge on the environment. The category 2C inputs create category 3Cc symbols inside the computer; the category 2C outputs are created by internal symbols of category 3Cc that are transmitted to the output ports.

Because the input and output channels of computers are commonly electronic, there may be little or no recoding of symbols at the skin, in distinction to the human case. In this respect the passage from outside to inside and inside to outside may be less complex and eventful than it is for human beings and other animals. But with robots, even this difference vanishes. The robot must have means to convert impinging light rays into electrical signals compatible with the computer's internal language, and signals into actions that control motor elements acting on the real world.

A Taxonomy of Symbols: Humans

Thus far we have considered only symbols in computers. When we move from them to human beings we must be a bit more speculative, for we do not have the same freedom to open the "box" as we do with machines. To remove this difficulty, we follow the procedure that is customary in science: We postulate how the things are that we cannot observe directly; we make as many predictions of observables as our postulates permit; and we then test these predictions. If the predictions are generally correct, we have earned the right to call our postulates a theory until such time as new conflicting data are observed, or another theory comes along that does a better job than ours of predicting the facts.

The physical symbol system hypothesis asserts that intelligent behavior is produced in the brain in basically the same way that it is in computers. That is to say, it postulates that the brain is a physical symbol system, and that approximate isomorphisms can be created between its patterns and the processes that alter them, on the one hand, and the corresponding patterns and processes in an appropriately programmed computer, on the other. The full theory consists of the symbol system hypothesis together with the computer program (a category 1 structure) that achieves the postulated simulation.

Of course, the isomorphism will hold only down to some level of detail; below that level, the components of computers will be quite different from neurons and neuronal circuits. Different versions of the theory may operate at different levels of aggregation.

In particular, we postulate here two categories of symbol structures in the human system. *Category 2H*, input and output, corresponds to category 2C in the computer, whereas *category 3H*, divided into 3Ha, 3Hb and 3Hc, corresponds to category 3C (3Ca, 3Cb and 3Cc, respectively) in the computer. The category 2C symbols, insofar as the simulation is veridical, will be identical with the human category 2H symbols. Category 3H symbols, on the other hand, must be realized by neuronal structures, quite different from the physical implementation of the symbol structures in the computer.

In particular, the patterns on the retina, in the inner ear and in other sensory organs are category 3Hc symbol structures. On the output side, the patterns of nerve action that stimulate the muscles are also category 3Hc structures. We emphasize that these patterns, both sensory and motor, satisfy our definition of symbol structures. The patterns in the sensory organs denote the objects from which the stimuli emanate, and their relations; the patterns on the motor side denote the actions they cause. They both have "meanings," which are transmitted to or from the brain, respectively.

The symbol system hypothesis places only rather general constraints on the way in which symbolic structures and processes are realized in the brain by neurons. As these constraints, especially the temporal ones, are discussed at some length in *Unified Theories*, especially Chapter 3, I need not repeat that discussion here. In the present state of our experimental knowledge the question of "what is the engram" has not received a very clear answer. As far as the evidence goes, we may well conceive of symbol structures as having the form of Hebbian cell assemblies, but there are many other possibilities—many ways in which innumerable complex patterns might be stored in the brain and fairly rapidly accessed and modified.

ARE THERE PATTERNS THAT ARE NOT SYMBOLS?

The term *pattern* is extremely broad. In its simplest form, we think of a pattern as some kind of spatial arrangement of elements (e.g., dots or lines or areas), usually more or less contiguous and localized. But we need not limit the concept in this way. What is crucial to a pattern is that there be some way of distinguishing (at least approximately) elements that belong to it from elements that do not, and of applying tests that can discriminate it (at some level of reliability) from different patterns.

We can think of the totality of English-speaking persons distributed around the world as forming a pattern. There are some areas of high density of its elements (e.g., North America, the British Isles, Australia), and there is a scatter of elements almost everywhere else, disbursed among clusters of speakers of other languages. There is a simple test of whether a person belongs to the English-speaking pattern or some other, and this same test discriminates among the various patterns, so that we can find areas that are predominately English-speaking, predominately French-speaking, and so on. We would call patterns of this sort *distributed* rather than *localized*.

The location of patterns within the brain has been a major preoccupation of neurophysiology, first with the aid of evidence from brain-damaged patients, and more recently with the aid of various brain-scanning procedures. Animal studies, where deliberate excisions can be made, have also been an important source of evidence. The picture is very mixed. There is evidence both for considerable localization and for participation of multiple brain locations in a single function.

But our experience with computers teaches us that, for many purposes, localization is rather unimportant. What is important is not where things are, but what things are connected to what other things. And with linear structures like wires and neurons, proximity is not a necessary condition for connection (although distance may slow down transmission). Hence, we can not discriminate between patterns that serve as symbols and those that do not on the basis of whether or not they are localized. The definitional criterion is whether they denote or not.

There has been much discussion of whether connectionist systems are or are not symbolic. In a connectionist system that has learned to discriminate the letters of the English alphabet, a so-called "hidden layer" composed of many unitary elements (nodes) may be capable of denoting all of the letters in the alphabet, without particular nodes in that layer corresponding to particular letters (see the lower half of Fig. 11.1). Thus, one pattern of activation of the nodes would denote an "A" (and would activate a node in the output layer that would serve as the P-symbol for "A"); another pattern of activation of the same nodes would denote a "B," and so on. The fact that human eyes are not able to recognize (at least not without training) these distinct patterns of activation in the hidden layers does not impede their power of denotation, and hence does not make them less symbolic. The hidden layer in a connectionist system is not different from the bank of lights on a Broadway sign that with one pattern of illumination forms the word "luminous" and with another pattern, using the same lights, forms "election."

In a serial symbolic system, also, letters are recognized by detecting the presence of a variety of features in them, and the memory storage of the set of these features can be wholly distributed even if the detection of each feature is itself localized. Detection of one set of (distributed) features leads to recognition of a particular letter; detection of another set leads to recognition of a different letter. And if recognition is accomplished, as in the program Elementary Perceiver and Memorizer (EPAM; Feigenbaum & Simon, 1984), by sorting through a discrimination net, different letters share features, and hence also share portions of the net, the degree of sharing varying with the degree of similarity in appearance of the letters.

In the upper half of Fig. 11.1, we depict a simplified EPAM net for sorting letters, where A and T, for example, share the features "horizontal

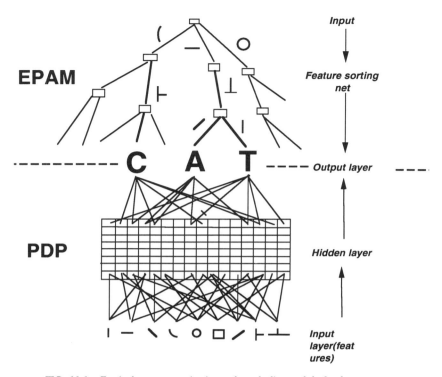

FIG. 11.1. Equivalent connectionist and symbolic models for letter recognition: EPAM (top-down) and PDP (bottom-up). Each recognizes the word *cat* by means of the features possessed by the letters of the word.

straight line" and "vertical axis of symmetry," which are used to sort them through the first two nodes. They are separated at the third node, the A possessing a diagonal line, the T a vertical one. Hence the usual dichotomy between distributed and localized memories does not at all distinguish between connectionist systems and classical symbolic systems.

In a fashion quite similar to EPAM, and depicted in the lower half of Fig. 11.1, the typical organization that leads to the letter-recognition process in a connectionist system also begins with a set of patterns, each corresponding to a (localized) letter feature. The different patterns of activation in the hidden layer are produced by activation of different combinations of letter features—hence constitute a recoding of the latter. The patterns in the hidden layer are recoded to activate the separate nodes (symbols) that denote the letters.

What makes this system seem "nonsymbolic" to some is that the individual components of the hidden layer are not dedicated to forming components of specific letters. At one time they participate in signaling one letter, and at another time, another. But the same may be said, as we have just seen, of the test nodes in the EPAM net or the pixels on a computer screen or a printing device. There is nothing about the physical symbol system hypothesis that requires a particular component to serve exclusively as part of a specific pattern; it may participate in many patterns, just as the letter C participates in many words.

Another feature sometimes regarded as specific to connectionist recognition schemes is that a particular letter does not correspond to a precise pattern of activation; correspondence need be only approximate. Different letters "compete," by mutual inhibition, to appropriate the various patterns of activation, similarity of pattern being the decision criterion. Thus, more than one pattern of activation may be encoded as the same letter, and the system can proceed smoothly across the boundary that separates the encodings of one letter from those of another. This continuity allows the system to accommodate approximate correctness, incomplete information, and noise.

Although these are potentially desirable characteristics of such a system, they do not make it less symbolic. Moreover, this same flexibility is achieved in a system like EPAM by incorporating in it the kind of redundant recognition paths described earlier.

Finally, we might at first doubt whether we should regard the patterns of stimulation of sensory organs as symbols. Two questions might be raised. First, a strip of metal on a thermostat senses the air temperature and, when appropriate, activates the furnace. Shall we say that the bend in the metal is a symbol denoting the air temperature? It certainly satisfies our definition of symbol, although it does not satisfy the definitions of those who hold that the symbol system must possess an "intention" or understanding of the meaning (denotation) of the symbol. I do not find any particular convenience in the latter convention, or any inconvenience in the simpler one. We should retain our right to define words in ways that will contribute parsimony to our science, and the broader and simpler definition seems to do that: Symbols are patterns that denote.

The same objection has been raised to the idea (implicit in our definition) that the image in a mirror could be a symbol of the object that produced the reflected light. I would reply to the objection in the same way.

Another objection is almost the opposite of this one: The successive encodings from an object in the environment, through the light rays, the retinal image, and the successive recodings of that image until the object is recognized, are far too complex and variable, it is argued, to permit the patterns at the various stages along the path (and in particular, the retinal image) to be regarded as symbols. Many different objects, casting highly varied patterns on the retina, may end up identified as cats (sometimes even erroneously). Those who find it objectionable to call this a symbolic process sometimes, after christening the relation between source and final encoding an affordance, abandon all attempts to find a mechanism to account for it.

Again, the objection has no sound basis. The real question is not whether it is convenient to call such a process symbolic; it is whether we can create artificial systems able to carry it out with anything like the success of the human or, more generally, the mammalian eye or ear. This is the challenge of computer vision (and speech recognition), and up to the present time the challenge has been met only to a limited degree. In our earlier driving example, with the relatively straightforward method that was shown there for extracting the relevant invariants, we illustrated how affordances can be extracted in simple cases. There is no reason to elevate difficulty in analyzing and simulating a complex system into a philosophical impossibility.

In the case of speech recognition, for instance, steady progress has shown us how a remarkably diverse collection of speech sounds can be encoded appropriately as a particular phoneme of a natural language. Both serial symbolic techniques and connectionist and other parallel techniques have contributed to that goal.

Whether we are speaking of "classical" symbol systems or connectionist systems, the process for recognizing external stimuli represents a whole sequence of often complex recodings, beginning with a pattern of stimulation received by the sensory organs (I-symbol) and ending with access to a pointer (P-symbol) and an associated schema (I-symbol) that contains information about the external stimulus. Thus, the retinal pattern may be recoded by a set of feature extractors, and the features (which are also I-symbols) presented to a discrimination net for sorting down to the recognized P-symbol and its associated I-symbol. In this process, learning may take place: new information may be added to the I-symbol and the discrimination net may be elaborated.

To conclude, it seems inconvenient and undesirable to alter the definition of symbol on the grounds that some encodings are far simpler, and some far more complex, than others.

LEARNING PATTERNS

A major task of an intelligent symbol system is to acquire symbols to denote the objects and concepts with which it has to deal. Philosophy of science makes a distinction between terms that represent the direct objects of perception (*relatively* direct we would say today, recognizing the theory-laden nature of all information acquired from the world), and terms constructed indirectly from these, the so-called *theoretical terms*. Let us consider in turn these two classes of things that need to be symbolized.

We have for some time had artificial systems, EPAM (Feigenbaum & Simon, 1984) being perhaps the most venerable, that are capable of learning to discriminate among different kinds of perceivable objects, of acquiring symbols to denote these different kinds (P-symbols), and of storing in memory, in association with the P-symbols, information about the objects (I-symbols). EPAM does this by constructing a large discrimination net, the different leaf nodes of which correspond to the different P-symbols, and by storing descriptive schemas, the I-symbols, at these nodes. At the nonterminal nodes of the net are tests of features of the stimulus that direct the signal down one or another branch to the next node. Thus, EPAM is a general-purpose system for recognizing stimuli.

EPAM learns by sorting a stimulus through the net, then comparing its features with the I-symbol associated with the leaf node that is reached, and creating a new test node and branches if the two do not agree. More detailed descriptions of how this is done can be found in Feigenbaum and Simon (1984) and Richman and Simon (1989). (The latter paper also contains a comparison between a serial way of performing the task, typified by EPAM, and a connectionist Parallel Distributed Processing [PDP] way.) Like the PDP simulations, EPAM does not deal with the raw sensory stimulus, but takes up the task after features have already been extracted from it.

EPAM-like mechanisms provide models for the recognition of sensory stimuli by the human brain, but they do not show what processes could extend meaning to philosophical abstractions like truth or beauty, or scientific concepts like inertial mass or specific heat, which do not correspond to directly observable phenomena. Recent progress in modeling processes of scientific discovery shows that such terms can be introduced and symbolized.

BACON is a computer program, realized as a production system, that takes bodies of data as inputs and seeks to discover scientific laws that describe the data (Langley, Simon, Bradshaw, & Zytkow, 1987). BACON can deal not only with numerical data but also with data involving distinct objects, labeled only by name. For example, it can be given data from an experiment on electrical circuits, using different batteries, designated only as A, B, C, and so on.

Having discovered Ohm's law by varying the length of the resistance wire in a circuit, using one of these batteries, and having observed the current for each level of resistance, it then discovers that the same law connecting current with resistance holds when the other batteries are substituted in the circuit, but with a different value of one of the constants that occurs in the law. Thus, $I = V/R$, where I and R are the measured currents and resistances, respectively, and V is a constant that takes on different values for circuits with different batteries.

BACON will now introduce a new property of batteries and assign as its value for each battery the value of the constant, V. We recognize these values as corresponding to the voltages of the batteries. Thus, BACON discovers and introduces into the theory a new theoretical concept, voltage, and constructs an appropriate semantics for it by devising a procedure for measuring its values.

In addition to voltage, in other experiments BACON has (re)discovered inertial mass, specific heat, refractive index, and other important physical concepts. A similar ability is possessed by other discovery systems, such as Weimin Shen's LIVE and Zytkow's GEL-MANN. The former rediscovered Mendel's laws, introducing the notions of dominant and recessive genes, in contradistinction to the observable phenotypes; the latter rediscovered quarks as components of elementary particles.

How general is the class of theoretical concepts that can be introduced into symbol systems in this way? As I am not aware of any general characterization of the different classes of theoretical concepts, the question must remain open. From work on model-theoretic axiomatization of physical theories, however, there is reason to believe that the methods used by programs like these are quite general (Simon, 1985).

Going beyond the kinds of theoretical concepts that appear in scientific theories, let me venture a few remarks about yet more abstract, and perhaps even nebulous, concepts. I will take truth as an example. Suppose we have a symbol system, and on its retina a pattern denoting some object that is visible to it at that particular time, and that we present the system with a spoken sentence: "The visible object is a cat." Now the system can determine whether the sentence is true by applying to the pattern on the retina the test that determines whether or not this pattern denotes a cat. If it does, the system declares the sentence to be true; if not, it declares it to be false. The phrase "truth-determining process" denotes the process just described. Here the denotation of the concept is not an external object but a process within the system itself.

A similar procedure can be used to define a concept like beauty, assuming that the system possesses a test that it applies to judge the pleasingness of objects visible to it. This is not fanciful, for the computer drawing program Aaron constructed by the artist Harold Cohen makes a continual series of decisions as to what lines it should add to a partially completed drawing and when it should declare the drawing complete. Of course, if we accept a definition of beauty of this sort, then we must accept the adage that beauty lies in the eyes of the beholder, and that consensus on what constitutes beauty is not intrinsic, but is created by a social process. But this is a conclusion with which many will agree.

Moreover, a drawing system that has the built-in equivalent of an autonomic nervous system, and hence has drives and preferences, can have nonsocial aesthetic criteria. For example it might prefer patterns that possess certain symmetries or other subpatterns that are detectable but not too easily detectable. Presence of unobvious detectable pattern has often been proposed as a (nonsocial) criterion of beauty. Notice that the detectability of a pattern will, in general, depend on prior experience and learning. What was initially confusing (no pattern was visible) later becomes pleasing, and finally boring (all of the extractable pattern has been perceived).

These brief comments suggest how it is possible to introduce very abstract terms, belonging to epistemology or esthetics, into a physical symbol system.

REPRESENTATION AND ITS USES

Information in memory (e.g., in human long-term memory) is not only retrievable—to answer questions, say—but is also usable for drawing inferences that are not explicit in the information itself. Thus, the information in my memory allows me to name the President of the United States in 1831 (Andrew Jackson), and the President in 1828 (John Quincy Adams). On the basis of these two pieces of information and knowledge that the term of a President is 4 years, I can infer that Jackson was probably the immediate successor of Adams. The inference is not quite rigorous, as Presidents do sometimes die while in office. The example, although trivial, illustrates that we can go beyond the information given—can make inferences.

The most common models of inference-making are logic and mathematics, both of which operate with information encoded in language: natural language or formally defined languages. It is quite natural, therefore, to think of reasoning and logic as almost synonymous, but however natural, the supposition is incorrect.

It is incorrect for two reasons. First, formal logic is a set of procedures for testing the correctness of conclusions drawn from premises and not a set of procedures for arriving at these conclusions in the first place: It does not discover them. Logic can be viewed as a nondeterministic algorithm. Its inference rules define what steps are legitimate as the next steps in a proof, but they do not indicate which of the permissible steps will lead to the desired goal (the theorem to be proved).

Second, procedures other than logic—procedures that do not use natural or formal language to represent information—can be used in many circumstances to make inferences. Thus, we may represent information in drawings or diagrams, and draw inferences that are implicit but not explicit in the information depicted.

Let us take a simple example of reasoning in economics. Suppose (see Fig. 11.2) we have a graph on which we have entered a supply curve and a demand curve. The supply curve shows, for each price, the quantity of a commodity that suppliers will offer on the market at that price. The demand curve shows, for each price, the quantity of the commodity that buyers will be willing to purchase at that price. We notice that the supply and demand curves intersect at a particular price coordinate, p, and quan-

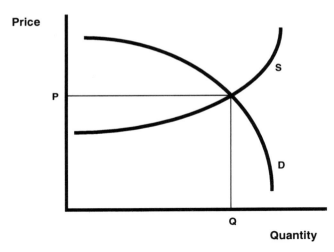

FIG. 11.2. Supply (S) and demand (D) curves in economics, with equilibrium quantity (Q) and price (P).

tity coordinate, *q*. We infer that the market will settle at price, *p*, and that the quantity, *q*, will be exchanged.

The reasoning here is not carried out by means of a syllogism or by solving two simultaneous equations (although we could use either of these devices to reach the same conclusion); it is accomplished by noticing the intersection of the supply with the demand curve, and knowing, from previous learning, that this intersection corresponds to the market equilibrium price and quantity (Tabachneck, 1992). Moreover, reaching the conclusion by noticing the intersection of the two lines on the diagram is not computationally equivalent to using the syllogism or solving two equations; the time required for each of these procedures may be different from that required for the others.

There are several interesting things about reasoning from a diagram. In logic, we are accustomed to distinguish between axioms, which may either be purely "logical" ("P implies P") or may incorporate empirical knowledge ("Socrates is a man"), and rules of inference, which are generally tautological—hold in all possible worlds. In our reasoning from the diagram, on the other hand, we do not limit ourselves to analytic inference rules; we commonly also use inference rules that incorporate empirical knowledge.

In the economics example, for instance, in equating equilibrium with the intersection of the two lines, we made the empirical assumption that the market would in fact settle at that point of intersection. If asked "Why?," we would have to do further reasoning (in some representation), but once we have satisfied ourselves that the inference rule is correct (that the intersection always gives the equilibrium price and quantity), we can simply store this rule and apply it in future situations without repeating its derivation.

A large part of the utility of graphs and diagrams derives from this possibility of building domain-specific inference rules that can be applied to the diagramatic representation of problems at low computational cost. The eyes can perform on diagrams a variety of rapid processes that notice features from which inferences can be drawn in a particular domain. They can notice intersections of lines, follow arrows from one point to another, notice the adjacency of two objects or the order of objects in a sequence, notice symmetries in figures, and so on. If these features can be provided with semantic interpretations in a domain, then they can be the basis for domain-specific inference rules (Larkin & Simon, 1987).

The notion of mental models also involves reasoning that is independent of natural or formal languages. Consider a problem space for the Tower of Hanoi problem in which the pegs, A, B, and C are contained in a list. Each of the pegs has an attribute: its list of disks (1, 2, 3, etc.). We call such structures *schemas*. At the outset of the problem all of the disks are assigned to A's list, and the goal is to change the situation to one in which they are assigned to C's.

An operator is defined (legal move operator) that transfers a disk from one list to another, subject to certain constraints (it must be the smallest disk on the source and goal pegs). Now the system can "reason" about the problem solution by searching (perhaps with the aid of some selective heuristics) for a sequence of moves that will transform the initial situation into the goal situation.

Of course, as Pylyshyn and others have pointed out, the information in schemas can be recoded into propositional form in some natural or artificial language, and then reasoned about. But even if the propositional and schematic representations are informationally equivalent, we have seen that they need not be computationally equivalent, or even approximately so. It may be much easier to make certain inferences in the one representation than in the other (Larkin & Simon, 1987).

The chapters in this volume by Johnson-Laird and Polk (chapter 10 and its discussion) illustrate very well the computational consequences of moving from one representation to another—in that case a linguistic representation, and a mixed linguistic-cum-mental-model representation that differ only in rather subtle ways.

There is much evidence that people use mental models of several sorts to solve many kinds of problems—perhaps most problems. As in the economics example, the inference rules (in the present case, the move operator) are not rules of logic but rules that incorporate some or all of the conditions that describe the task—they do not apply in all possible worlds, but specifically in the world that the task rules define. The power of symbolic structures, including graphs, diagrams, and schemas of a wide variety of kinds, to effect inferences goes far beyond the capabilities of language. Language, natural or formal, is just one of several means for reasoning symbolically, and the particular sorts of symbols that are used in language occupy no privileged position in reasoning.

People are not born with a fixed set of available representations to which they are bound. Most representations, and especially the task-dependent inference operators associated with them, are learned. A student who has studied the calculus approaches physics problems with a very different set of representations than one who has not. Hence, the study of symbol systems must include not only analysis of the computational differences among alternative representations for problems, but also the processes for learning representations and the operators used to draw inferences from them.

In sum, even if two representations of a problem situation contain the same knowledge (are informationally equivalent), it may be very much easier to solve the problem when it is stated in the one representation than when it is stated in the other (the representations are not computationally equivalent). Differences in task performance may reflect differences in strategies that employ distinct representations.

An important (and not yet extensively developed) research task in artificial intelligence is to understand what determines the computational efficiency of particular representations for particular classes of problems, and how problems, presented initially in an awkward representation, can be converted to one that is computationally efficient.

A DIGRESSION ON THE KNOWLEDGE LEVEL

I may add, parenthetically, that the prominent and ubiquitous role of representations and strategies in problem solving creates some difficulty for me in interpreting what Allen Newell meant by the *knowledge level.* Again this topic was on our active agenda for discussion, but the discussion had just begun when his life ended.

At the knowledge level, we are to predict behavior from the problem solver's task and what he or she knows. But "knows" is a highly ambiguous term. What people know depends not only on the information stored in their minds or presented directly to their senses but also on what part of their stored knowledge they draw upon, how they represent it, and what implicit knowledge they can make explicit, using the inference processes that are available to them in the representation they are using.

In the boundedly rational world in which I place my actors, I can seldom separate their knowledge from their problem spaces and strategies—that is to say, I cannot separate the knowledge level clearly from the symbolic level that lies beneath or the objective task domain, unknowable to them, that lies above. Perhaps an exception can be made for cases where the situation is so transparent that it is obvious what the actor knows—that is, is actually aware of or can calculate. If I give a dollar bill for an 89-cent purchase, perhaps I can assume that the clerk will simply "know" that I should receive 11 cents in change; but even in such simple situations, the computational processes of the actor cannot always be taken for granted. Fallible, strategy-dependent inference generally interposes between "knowledge" and behavior, even when the rational solution is "obvious." In most instances the obviousness of what the actor knows, when one can speak of such obviousness, must be a social phenomenon, based on our ability to empathize with other actors, placing ourselves in their problem spaces and using their strategies, and knowing their computational limits.

I have many reasons to wish that my discussions with Allen Newell were not ended, and this is perhaps the least of them. But we do need to set ourselves the task of clarifying the meaning of the knowledge level and its role in a theory of cognition. As formulating a problem at the knowledge level involves social consensus as to what people "know" in typical task situations, I have a hunch that our inquiry will lead us into the realm of social cognition; but I wish that I could try that hunch out on Allen—most likely finding, as so often in the past, how many new ideas could emerge from the chemistry of our old ones.

CONCLUSION

In this chapter I have reexamined the physical symbol system hypothesis with the aim of clarifying the nature of symbols, the roles that symbols play in a symbol system, and the categories of symbols that are involved in human and machine cognition. We have seen that all sorts of patterns (including patterns that are not localized) can and do serve as symbols in both serial and parallel (connectionist) symbol systems. Any pattern that denotes is also a symbol. It may simply serve as a pointer (P-symbol) to information stored elsewhere, or it may itself contain more or less extensive information about the thing it denotes (I-symbol).

Language is a symbol system that has special importance in interpersonal communication (including learning), but it is only one among many kinds of symbolic subsystems that are involved in human thinking and reasoning. Transformation from one symbolic representation to another, in order to find one that is computationally efficient in dealing with a particular class of problems, is an essential, and little understood, process in much problem solving.

Our analysis shows conclusively that physical symbol systems need not be linguistic in nature, nor need they be serial and localized (or parallel and distributed). The true nature of the symbol system that is used in human thinking cannot, therefore, be determined by philosophical analysis or argument, but only by looking at behavioral evidence on how it operates and physiological evidence on how it is put together.

Computer science in general, and artificial intelligence as a part of it, is an empirical science whose questions cannot be answered by mere theorizing. Mind will be understood by actually building and using intelligent systems, and by comparing them with human systems. We must conceive those systems daringly, incorporating a wide range of human mental functions in them and exercising them in a wide range of tasks.

This is the experimental strategy on which Allen Newell insisted, and that he practiced through his whole research career. If we continue to pursue it vigorously, we will draw nearer to the unified theory he had begun to explore.

ACKNOWLEDGMENTS

This research was supported by the National Science Foundation, under grant DBS-912 1027, and by the Defense Advanced Research Projects Agency, Department of Defense, ARPA Order 3597, monitored by the Air Force Avionics Laboratory under contract F33615-81-K-1539. Reproduction in whole or in part is permitted for any purpose of the U.S. Government.

REFERENCES

Feigenbaum, E. A., & Simon, H. A. (1984). EPAM-like models of recognition and learning. *Cognitive Science, 8*, 305–336.

Gibson, J. J. (1950). *The perception of the visual world.* Boston: Houghton Mifflin.

Langley, P., Simon, H. A., Bradshaw, G. L., & Zytkow, J. M. (1987). *Scientific discovery: Computational explorations of the creative processes.* Cambridge, MA: MIT Press.

Larkin, J. H., & Simon, H. A. (1987). Why a diagram is (sometimes) worth 10,000 words. *Cognitive Science, 11*, 65–100.

Newell, A. (1980). Physical symbol systems. *Cognitive Science, 4*, 135–183. Also available as CMU CSD Technical Report, March 1980, and in D. Norman (Ed.), (1981), *Perspectives in cognitive science.* Norwood, NJ: Ablex.

Newell, A. (1990). *Unified theories of cognition.* Cambridge, MA: Harvard University Press.

Newell, A., Shaw, J. C., & Simon, H. A. (1957, February). Empirical explorations of the Logic Theory Machine: A case study in heuristics. *Proceedings of the 1957 Western Joint Computer Conference* (pp. 218–239), Los Angeles, CA.

Newell, A., & Simon, H. A. (1976). Computer science as empirical inquiry: Symbols and search. *Communications of the ACM, 19*(3), 113–126. (ACM 1975 Turing Award Lecture.)

Richman, H. B., & Simon, H. A. (1989). Context effects in letter perception: Comparison of two theories. *Psychological Review, 96*, 417–432.

Simon, H. A. (1985). Quantification of theoretical terms and the falsifiability of theories. *British Journal for the Philosophy of Science, 36*, 291–298.

Simon, H. A. (1991). Black ravens and a white shoe. *British Journal for the Philosophy of Science, 42*, 339–342.

Tabachneck, H. (1992). *Effect of mode of data presentation on reasoning about economic markets.* Unpublished doctoral dissertation, Department of Psychology, Carnegie Mellon University, Pittsburgh.

Vera, A., & Simon, H. A. (1993). Situated action: Symbolic interpretation. *Cognitive Science, 17,* 7–48.

About the Authors

Gordon Bell is a computer industry consultant. He spent 23 years at Digital Equipment Corporation (DEC) as Vice President of Research and Development, where he was responsible for DEC's products. He was the architect of various minicomputers and time-sharing computers and led the development of DEC's VAX. Bell has been involved in the design of about 50 computers, 12 of which were multiprocessors, and many products at a score of different companies. From 1966 to 1972, Bell was Professor of Computer Science and Electrical Engineering at Carnegie Mellon University. He worked with Allen Newell on research that led to the classic books *Computer Structures: Readings and Examples* (Bell & Newell, 1971) and *Computer Structures: Principles and Examples* (Siewiorek, Bell, & Newell, 1982). His awards include the Mellon Institute Medal, IEEE's McDowell and Eckert-Mauchly Awards, the Van Neumann Medal, and the 1995 MCI-Smithsonian Award for Innovation. President Bush awarded Bell the National Medal of Technology in 1991.

Stuart K. Card is a research Fellow and Manager of User Interface Research at the Xerox Palo Alto Research Center. He received his AB in physics from Oberlin College in 1966 and came to Carnegie Mellon University where he pursued an interdisciplinary program in psychology and computer science with Allen Newell as his thesis advisor, resulting in a PhD in psychology in 1978. He has been an adjunct faculty member at Stanford University and an affiliate at CMU. With their former advisor, Card and Thomas Moran founded the applied Information Processing Psychology Project at Xerox PARC to work on developing psychological models that could be used as a basis for engineering practical systems. One result was the book with Newell and Moran, *The Psychology of Human-Computer Interaction*. Currently, his research is concerned with the design and analysis of interactive three-dimensional user interfaces for information access systems.

Darold Hemphill is a member of the technical staff performing usability engineering at Bell Communications Research (Bellcore) in Piscataway, NJ. He received his MS in cognitive science (1988) and his PhD in experimental psychology (1990) from Memphis State University. From 1990 to 1992 Hemphill held a postdoctoral position at Carnegie Mellon University. While at CMU, Hemphill worked with Patricia Carpenter and Marcel Just on modeling working memory capacity during problem solving.

Bonnie E. John is an assistant professor in Carnegie Mellon University's Computer Science Department, Psychology Department, and Human–Computer Interaction Institute. Formerly a mechanical engineer (BEng, 1977, Cooper Union; MS, 1978, Stanford University), she worked at Bell Laboratories specifying voice- and data-communications systems (1977–1983). Interested in designing systems that would be easy for people to learn and use, she earned a PhD in cognitive psychology at Carnegie Mellon University (1988). Her research develops "engineering models" of computer users and applies them to the evaluation and design of computer systems. These computational models produce a priori, quantitative predictions of human performance. They allow analysis at different levels of approximation and are straightforward enough for computer designers to use without extensive training in psychology. Because they are within a single theory of cognition (Soar), these models are integrated enough to cover total tasks.

Philip N. Johnson-Laird is Stuart Professor of Psychology at Princeton University. He received his BA in psychology from University College, London in 1964 and his PhD in psychology in 1967. He was Assistant Director of the MRC Applied Psychology Unit at Cambridge from 1982 to 1989. Prior to this appointment he was a member of the Laboratory of Experimental Psychology at the University of Sussex, as a reader (1973–1978), and then as a professor (1978–1982) and a lecturer at University College, London (1967–1973). He is the author of many papers and six books, including *Psychology of Reasoning* (with P. C. Wason), *Language and Perception* (with George A. Miller), *Mental Models,* and *The Computer and the Mind: An Introduction to Cognitive Science.*

Marcel Just and **Patricia Carpenter** received their PhDs in psychology in 1972 from Stanford University and then joined the faculty at Carnegie Mellon. Their work has taken several different approaches to uncovering the nature of the intelligence in language comprehension and visual thinking. In their experimental work, they have used various process-tracing techniques, such as tracking subjects' eye fixations as they scan a display, to determine the sequence and timing of mental events during comprehension and problem solving. In their research on intelligence, they have tried to account for the variation among individuals by determining which processes or resources distinguish one person from another. The resulting theories often take the form of a family of computational models whose differences in performance closely correspond to the differences among human subjects. The computational architecture that they have been recently exploring combines a symbolic, rule-based system with a connectionist underpinning, conjointly providing a form of graded symbolic processing.

David Klahr received his PhD from Carnegie Mellon's Graduate School of Industrial Administration (GSIA) in 1968. He held an assistant professorship at the University of Chicago from 1967 to 1969. In addition, he was a visiting research fellow at the University of Stirling, Scotland in the Fall of 1968 and a Fulbright lecturer at the London Graduate School of Business Studies in the spring of 1969. He returned to Carnegie Mellon with a joint appointment in GSIA and psychology in 1969, and became a professor of psychology in 1976. Since then, his efforts have focused largely on the application of information processing analysis to questions of cognitive development. From 1983 to 1993 he was Head of Carnegie Mellon's Department of Psychology. In collaboration with J. G. Wallace and with the enthusiastic counsel of Allen Newell, Klahr formulated the first production system model of children's performance on a variety of tasks. Klahr has published widely in developmental and cognitive journals and is author or editor of four books, including two in the Carnegie Cognition Symposium series: *Cognition and Construction* (1976), and *Complex Information Processing: The Impact of Herbert A. Simon* (1989).

John E. Laird is an associate professor of electrical engineering and computer science and Director of the Artificial Intelligence Laboratory at the University of Michigan. He received his BS from the University of Michigan in 1975 and his PhD in computer science from Carnegie Mellon University in 1983. His research has been driven by a desire to understand the fundamental structures underlying intelligent behavior, focused for the last 15 years on the development and continued evolution of Soar. A central part of this work is the construction and analysis of intelligent systems that interact and learn from complex dynamic environments. Laird is a fellow of the American Association for Artificial Intelligence.

Jill Fain Lehman is a research computer scientist in Carnegie Mellon University's School of Computer Science and the current principal investigator of the Soar project at CMU. She received a BS in computer science from Yale in 1981 followed by her MS and PhD in computer science from Carnegie Mellon in 1987 and 1989, respectively. Her research interests span all areas of natural language processing. Although Lehman pursued some nonlanguage research with Allen Newell in her early years as a graduate student, she joined the Soar project as a postdoctoral researcher, working with Allen and Rick Lewis on NL-Soar, the theory of natural language comprehension in Soar. She continues to work on NL-Soar with the grand scheme of unifying the current comprehension theory with theories of generation and acquisition.

Richard L. Lewis received his PhD in computer science from Carnegie Mellon University in December 1993. He attended the University of Central Florida in his hometown of Orlando, graduating with a BS in computer science in 1987. With the encouragement of his professors at UCF, he then entered the doctoral program at CMU, where Allen Newell undertook his education in cognitive science for the next 5 years. Lewis' research interests are in developing computational theories of human cognitive processes, particularly language comprehension, building on the comprehension work he began with Allen Newell and Jill Fain Lehman at CMU. He is currently a McDonnell research fellow at Princeton University in the Cognitive Science Laboratory and Psychology Department. His professional affiliations include the American Psychological Society, the Association for Computing Machinery, and the Cognitive Science Society.

George A. Miller is James S. McDonnell Distinguished University Professor of Psychology Emeritus and Senior Research Psychologist at Princeton University, where he has been since 1979. Miller received a BA from the University of Alabama in 1940 and a PhD is psychology from Harvard University in 1946. He is the author of seven books; the most recent, *The Science of Words*, was published in 1991. In that year he was also awarded the National Medal of Science. Miller is presently directing the WordNet project at Princeton University's Cognitive Science Laboratory. WordNet is an online database for English organized by semantic relations.

Tom M. Mitchell is Professor of Computer Science and Robotics at Carnegie Mellon University, and a member of the Human-Computer Interaction Institute. He received his BS in 1973 from MIT and his PhD in 1979 from Stanford University, both in electrical engineering. He taught in the Computer Science Department at Rutgers University from 1979 to 1986. In 1983 he received the IJCAI Computers and Thought award for his research in machine learning, and in 1984 he received a National Science Foundation Presidential Young Investigator award. In 1990 he was named a Fellow of the American Association for Artificial Intelligence. In 1986, Mitchell visited Carnegie Mellon for a year, during which he cotaught a course with Allen Newell and Geoff Hinton on integrated intelligent architectures. The following year he moved permanently to Carnegie Mellon, where his current research focuses on machine learning, artificial intelligence, robotics, and design.

Thad Polk graduated from Carnegie Mellon University with an interdisciplinary PhD in computer science and psychology under Allen Newell. His dissertation proposed a verbal reasoning theory of human deduction. He also developed a set of computational tools for the analysis of models with symbolic parameters (the ASPM system). Inspired by Newell's interest in cognitive architecture, Polk is currently working on a postdoctoral fellowship in cognitive neuropsychology with Martha Farah at the University of Pennsylvania. He is studying how environmental factors (specifically, co-occurrence of environmental stimuli) interact with correlation-based learning in the brain to influence the cognitive architecture in adulthood. Polk has been the recipient of a Kodak fellowship for graduate study, a Krasnow Outreach postdoctoral fellowship, and a grant-in-aid for postdoctoral training from the McDonnell-Pew Program in Cognitive Neuroscience.

Zenon W. Pylyshyn was a professor of psychology and computer science at the University of Western Ontario in London from 1966 to 1994 as well as Honorary Professor of Philosophy and Electrical Engineering. In 1994, he moved to Rutgers University as Board of Governors Professor of Cognitive Science and Director of the Rutgers Center for Cognitive Science. Pylyshyn is recipient of the Canadian Psychological Association's Donald O. Hebb Award and a Fellow of the Canadian Psychological Association and the American Association for Artificial Intelligence. He is also a past president of both the Cognitive Science Society and the Society for Philosophy and Psychology and was Director of the Canadian Institute for Advanced Research program in Artificial Intelligence and Robotics from 1985 until

1994. He has published over 60 scientific articles and book chapters and is author of *Computation and Cognition: Toward a Foundation for Cognitive Science* (1994), in which he first introduced some of the ideas presented in his chapter of this book.

Paul S. Rosenbloom received his BS in mathematical sciences from Stanford University in 1976, and his MS and PhD in computer science from Carnegie-Mellon University in 1978 and 1983, respectively. Since then he has been pursuing a range of research on intelligent behavior—and in particular, on the Soar architecture—first at Carnegie Mellon (1983–1984), then at Stanford University (1984–1987), and later at the University of Southern California (1987–), where he is an associate professor of computer science and Acting Deputy Director of the Intelligent Systems Division of the Information Sciences Institute. Rosenbloom is a fellow and councillor of the American Association for Artificial Intelligence. He has been chair of the Special Interest Group on Artificial Intelligence of the Association for Computing Machinery, an editor of the journal *Machine Learning*, and program cochair of the Tenth National Conference on Artificial Intelligence.

Mary Shaw is the Alan J. Perlis Professor of Computer Science and Associate Dean for the Professional Programs at Carnegie Mellon University, where she has been on the faculty since 1971. From 1984 to 1987 she served as Chief Scientist of CMU's Software Engineering Institute. She received her BA (cum laude) in mathematics from Rice University in 1965 and her PhD in computer science from Carnegie Mellon University in 1972. In 1993 Shaw received the Warner prize for contributions to software engineering. She is a Fellow of the IEEE, the Association for Computing Machinery, and the American Association for the Advancement of Science. She is a member of the IEEE Computer Society, the New York Academy of Sciences, and Sigma Xi.

Herbert A. Simon is Richard King Mellon University Professor of Computer Science and Psychology at Carnegie Mellon University, having joined the university in 1949 with the founding of the Graduate School of Industrial Administration. He is a recipient of the Nobel Prize in Economics, the Distinguished Scientific Contributions Award of the American Psychological Association, the Turing Award (with Allen Newell) of the Association for Computing Machinery, the Gold Medal for Research of the American Psychological Foundation, and the National Medal of Science. For 40 years, Simon was a frequent and close collaborator with Allen Newell, beginning with studies of information processing in air defense operations, and continuing with their early explorations (from 1955) in artificial intelligence that led to the Logic Theorist, GPS, and their book, *Human Problem Solving* (1972). Severally and separately, they have advanced the claim of physical symbol systems to be the natural habitats of human and computer intelligence.

Tony Simon is an assistant professor in the School of Psychology and a member of the Cognitive Science Program at the Georgia Institute of Technology. He has been on the faculty of the London School of Economics and Lancashire Polytechnic Departments of Psychology. He has also held research positions at the MRC Applied Psychology Unit in Cambridge, England, and Carnegie Mellon University. Simon's research focuses on the construction of conceptual knowledge, especially in the area of number and enumeration. Current projects involve Q-Soar, a computational model of early numerical skills, empirical investigations and numerical modeling of subitizing in young adults and aging populations, and numerical competencies of infants.

David Steier is a research scientist with the Price Waterhouse Technology Centre in Menlo Park, CA. Previously he was with the Engineering Design Research Center and the School of Computer Science at Carnegie Mellon University. He received his BS from Purdue University, West Lafayette, IN in 1982, his MS from Carnegie Mellon in 1985, and his PhD from Carnegie Mellon in 1989, all in computer science. His doctoral thesis was entitled "Automating Algorithm Design within a General Architecture for Intelligence." He is coauthor (with P. Anderson) of the monograph *Algorithm Synthesis: A Comparative Study*. He has held summer research positions at Schlumberger-Doll Research, Texas Instruments, and Evanston Hospital. His current research interests center on the application of artificial intelligence techniques, especially integrated problem-solving and learning architectures, to problems in intelligent data integration.

Milind Tambe is a research computer scientist at the Information Sciences Institute, University of Southern California (USC), and a research assistant professor with the Computer Science Department at USC. He completed his undergraduate education in computer science from the Birla Institute of Technology and Science, Pilani, India, in 1986. He received his PhD in 1991 from the School of Computer Science at Carnegie Mellon University. His interests are in the areas of integrated intelligent agents, agent modeling, and efficiency, parallelism, and scalability of artificial intelligence programs, especially rule-based systems.

Sebastian Thrun has been a student all his life. He received his bachelor's degree from the University of Hildesheim in 1988, and his master's degree from the University of Bonn in 1992, both in Germany. Currently he is enrolled in the PhD program at the University of Bonn. Thrun's main scientific interests are artificial intelligence, machine learning, and computers on wheels.

Richard M. Young studied engineering and artificial intelligence before earning his PhD in psychology from Carnegie Mellon University in 1973. From 1973 to 1978 he was a research fellow in the Department of Artificial Intelligence at Edinburgh University. Since 1978 he has been on the scientific staff of the United Kingdom Medical Research Council's Applied Psychology Unit in Cambridge. He is a former Chairman of Society for the Study of Artificial Intelligence and Simulation of Behaviour (AISB). His research interests lie in human–computer interaction and the use of artificial intelligence for the computer simulation of human thinking, problem solving, and cognitive skills. For the last few years he has been working with Soar, mainly to serve as the basis for models of the computer user. He first met Allen Newell when he worked as a research programmer for him in 1966–1967. (In those days, it was possible to learn what there was to learn about artificial intelligence in a single semester!) Allen Newell served as his PhD supervisor from 1968 to 1973.

Author Index

Numbers in *italics* denote complete bibliographic entries.

445

Subject Index

knowledge influence on reasoning, 391–392
reasoning with single quantifiers, 372, 373
syllogistic reasoning, 373
  atmosphere hypothesis, 374
  dispelling atmosphere hypothesis, 387–391
  mental model theory, 378, 380–382, 384
  difficulties, 384, 386–387
Condition–action contingencies, capacity-constrained production systems, 144
Condition ordering, evolution of Soar architecture, 29
Conditionals
  deductions with propositional connectives, 370
  mental model theory, 378–380, 383
Cone-tree visualization, hierarchical information, 303, 304
Conflict, Soar 2, 23
Conjunction, semantics and deductions with propositional connectives, 369
Connectionism
  study of cognitive architecture, 52
  symbolism, 419
Connectives, *see* Propositional connectives
Connectivity, systems integration, 220–221
Constraints
  mental imagery, 56–58
  self-generated in BT microworld experiment, 341
  symbolic system hypothesis, 418
  window environments, 297
Content
  human–computer interaction, 269
  language comprehension by NL-Soar, 134, 136, 138
  syntactic processing effects, 76
  -specific skills and working-memory capacity, 164
  word interchangeability and meaning, 124
Contextual representation
  computers, 126–128
  word sense associations, 124, 125
Contextual template
  language comprehension by NL-Soar, 136
  sense resolution, 128–129
Continuous-load secondary task, working-memory constraints, 153–155

Control element, repository architecture, 229–230, *see also* Database management
Control knowledge
  bounded-space representation in explanation-based neural network-Soar, 106
  evolution of Soar architecture, 17, 23, 29
Control structure
  mind models, 60
  problem solving, 5–6
  syntactic processing by NL-Soar, 81
Conversions boxes, integration of software environments, 238
Cooperation, scientific discovery, 351
Coreference, sense resolution, 122, *see also* Sense resolution
Cost, chip density, 199
Cost structure, information, 302
Counter hypotheses
  BigTrak experiment, 334, 335
  BT microworld experiment, 337, 338–340, 341
Counterexamples, verbal reasoning program, 405
Coupling, integration of software environments, 238
CPU, *see* Central processing unit
Credible value, model human processor, 263
Cube assembly task, age-related decrements in working-memory, 168
Cups, explanation-based neural network learning, 91–94
Current context, evolution of Soar architecture, 12, 13, 24
Current state
  evolution of Soar cognitive architecture, 33
  modular vs. interactive behavior of NL-Soar, 80
Cycle of activity, human–computer interaction tasks, 314–315

D

Data
  anomalous, psychological reactions, 344, 345
  global and Soar/IDBE system, 244, 245
  individual and Polk model of syllogistic reasoning, 182

Finger muscles, bandwidth and pointing, 289, *see also* Model-assisted design

Finst index theory, 67–71

Fitt's law, model-assisted design, 284–285, 286, 288–289
  Crossman and Goodleve derivation, 291–294

Floating-point operations, computer structure, 195, 200

Flowcharts, language processing, 119–120

FOCL, analytical/inductive learning, 90, *see also* Learning

Forgetting, capacity-constrained production systems, 145, 157–158, 159

Formal rules system, using propositional connectives, 367–370, *see also* Deduction

Frequency, polysemy correlation, 127, 137

Frontiers, scientific discovery, 349–352

Functional constraints, resource constraints comparison in Soar, 179–180

Functionality, Polk model of syllogistic reasoning, 181, 182

Functions, evolution of Soar architecture, 10

G

GEL-MANN program, scientific discovery, 424

General knowledge, syllogistic reasoning difficulties, 384

General problem solving (GPS)
  basic weaknesses, 9
  innovations and Soar cognitive architecture, 5–8
  subgoaling, 18

Generality design principle, computer structure, 190, 191, 208–209

Generalizations
  analytical learning, 86–88, 89, 102
  inductive learning, 88–89

Generate frame, *see also* Scientific discovery
  scientific reasoning experiment, 335, 343
  SDDS framework, 327, 328, 348

Generation
  basic functions in Soar 1, 10, 12, 13
  basic functions in Soar 2, 18, 21

Generational factors, problem solving, 167, *see also* Problem solving

Global data, role in Soar/IDBE system, 244–245, *see also* Data

Goal hierarchies, expert behavior, 319–321

Goal-recursion strategy, *see* Goals

Goal state, SDDS framework, 329

Goal tree, Tower of Hanoi puzzle, 150, 151, *see also* Problem solving

Goals, *see also* Subgoals; Supergoals
  achievement and use-centered design, 282
  capacity-constrained production system simulation model, 158
  GOMS model, 318
  Soar evolution, 8, 13–15, 21
  system development, 277
  Tower of Hanoi puzzle problem solving, 146, 147
    pupillometric responses, 155–156
    working-memory constraints, 149–155

GOMS model
  human–computer interaction, 265–267
  Soar, 318–322

Good instrumentation, assessment in BT microworld experiment, 340–341

Good vs. bad subjects, Polk model of syllogistic reasoning, 182

Governor, Information Visualizer, 303

GPS, *see* General problem solving

Grain size
  capacity-constrained production systems, 145–146
  Polk model of syllogistic reasoning, 183

Grammatical origin hypothesis, syllogistic reasoning difficulties, 386

Graphical interface user, food chain of ideas, 275, 276

Growth effect, chucking-Soar, 106

Guessing rate, Tower of Hanoi puzzle, 153, *see also* Problem solving

H

Hand-coded associations
  language comprehension by NL-Soar, 139
  sense resolution, 129, 136

Hard pointing tasks, using head mice, 287–288, *see also* Model-assisted design

R

RAMAC, information storage capacity, 201, *see also* Computers, structure

Rationality, principle and behavior of intelligent agents, 2–3

Raven Progressive Matrices Test
correlations studies with performance on Tower of Hanoi puzzle, 164–165
unitary vs. many pools of capacity, 171
working-memory constraints and problem solving, 147, 151–152

Reactive level, Soar 5, 40

Reading comprehension, resource demands, 155, *see also* Comprehension; Language comprehension

Reading Span task
unitary working-memory, 170
working-memory constraints with age, 167, 168

Real-world
context and SDDS framework, 329
semantics and computers, 416, *see also* Patterned matter
task performance and GOMS rules, 265

Reasoning, *see also* Deduction; Induction
imagery-based and cognitive architecture, 56–58
knowledge influence, 391–393
logic comparison, 425–426
single quantifiers, 371
symbolic structures, 427–428
tasks
intercorrelation among complex, 162
working-memory constraints with age, 165, 167
unlikelihood as purely verbal process, 393–397

Recall, relevant documents, 301, *see also* Human–computer systems

Recognition, symbolic systems, 413, 414, *see also* Patterned matter
invariant features, 411

Recognitional comprehension, NL-Soar, 78, 79, 81, 135–137, 139–140

Recognize–act cycle
cognitive architecture, 68
executing tasks, 213, 216
model human processor, 262, 263

Reconsider, evolution of Soar architecture, 39

Recovery productions, capacity-constrained production system simulation vs. human subjects, 159, 160

Reduced instruction set computer (RISC), availability, 195, *see also* Computers, structure

Redundancy
P-symbols, 413
recognition paths in EPAM systems, 421
replicatability in computer structure, 203

Reference models, derivation, 281, *see also* Human–computer systems

Refine, domain theory network, 93–94

Reflective level, evolution of Soar architecture, 40–41

Registers, computer structure, 201, 202, 209, 210

Regularities, finding through inductive learning, 89, *see also* Learning

Reinforcement, predictions in explanation-based neural network, 116

Relevant documents, retrieval, 301, *see also* Human–computer systems

Repair mechanisms, language comprehension by NL-Soar, 138

Replication design principles, computer structure, 190, 191, 202–206

Reporting cycles, interactive database management, 227, 230

Repository architecture
database management
simple, 227–230, 234
virtual, 230–233, 234
integration of software environments, 236–239
variations and shared information systems, 247–249

Representation(s)
cognitive architecture, 53–54
exhaustive and mental model theory, 378, 380–382
explicit in mind models, 61–62
shared and integration of software development environments, 238–239
symbolic, 4
three-dimensional model, 68
uses of, 425–428
verbal reasoning program, 405

Representation space, scientific discovery, 350

Representational states, modeling, 54–58